Big Ideas in Macroeconomics

Big Ideas in Macroeconomics

A Nontechnical View

Kartik B. Athreya

The MIT Press
Cambridge, Massachusetts
London, England

MIT Press books may be purchased at special quantity discounts for business or sales promotional use. For information, please email special_sales@mitpress.mit.edu or write to Special Sales Department, The MIT Press, 55 Hayward Street, Cambridge, MA 02142.

This book was set in Palatino by Toppan Best-set Premedia Limited, Hong Kong. Printed and bound in the United States of America.

Library of Congress Cataloging-in-Publication Data

Athreya, Kartik B., 1971–
Big ideas in macroeconomics : a nontechnical view / Kartik B. Athreya.
  pages cm
Includes bibliographical references and index.
ISBN 978-0-262-01973-6 (hardcover : alk. paper) 1. Macroeconomics. I. Title.
HB172.5.A789 2013
339—dc23
2013011175

10 9 8 7 6 5 4 3 2 1

For my grandparents, P. S. and Kamala Mani

Contents

Acknowledgments

My goal is to describe in nontechnical terms where modern macroeconomics gets its ideas and how it goes about its business. If I have succeeded at all, it is because of the efforts of many people, some directly and personally, and many via the journal articles and books they wrote. In college, I decided to major in economics when Professor Leigh Tesfatsion's Intermediate Macroeconomics course made a strong impression on me. I could see that people were thinking about hard problems in organized ways that I, at that time certainly, could not. So, I enrolled in the economics graduate program at the University of Iowa. At that time, I met Steve Williamson, Narayana Kocherlakota, and several others who gave me tools and homework problems that helped organize my thinking. My classmates, including Rebecca Saccaro, Ahmet Akyol, and Nicole Simpson, helped a lot too.

After graduating, I was hired by the Federal Reserve Bank of Richmond, where I was expected to do macroeconomic research and assist in the policymaking process. While here, my education has continued, through my colleagues, coauthors, and RAs. I thank two colleagues in particular for their help with the book: Felipe Schwartzman and Pierre Sarte. Speaking of where I work, if you should disagree with anything herein, remember one thing: the views in this book are mine alone, and do not necessarily reflect those of the Federal Reserve Bank of Richmond or the Federal Reserve System.

I must acknowledge the equally important efforts of the authors of some great textbooks and papers. As an undergraduate, I loved Robert Frank's *Microeconomics and Behavior* and Steven Landsburg's *Price Theory*. I then benefited, as at least a generation has, from Hal Varian's *Microeconomic Analysis*, from David Kreps's deeply reflective text *A Course in Microeconomic Theory*, and from Philip Reny and Geoffrey

Jehle's *Advanced Microeconomic Theory*. Most recently, I have learned a great deal from the text and homework problems of Andreu Mas-Colell, Michael Whinston, and Jerry Green's now-canonical book *Microeconomic Theory*. Lastly, my favorite economics book happens to be an entirely nontechnical one: Arthur Okun's *Equality and Efficiency: The Big Tradeoff*.

With respect to the framing and resolution of questions with a macroeconomic scope, like so many others, I have been aided enormously by the academic work of Edward Prescott, Thomas Sargent, Robert E. Lucas Jr., David Cass, and Peter Diamond, among others. The book-length treatments of Thomas Cooley's *Frontiers of Business Cycle Research*; Nancy Stokey, Robert E. Lucas Jr., and Edward C. Prescott's *Recursive Methods in Economic Dynamics*; and Thomas Sargent and Lars Ljungqvist's *Recursive Macroeconomic Theory* each have helped my entire generation make sense by giving us tools that enforced coherence in our efforts. I also am happy to have learned about the ideas and models of Truman Bewley, Ed Green, Robert Townsend, Mark Satterthwaite, and Glenn Loury. If their stature in the pantheon of economists known to the public rises, even (or especially?) at the expense of others currently there, I'll be happy.

Herbert Gintis was an early key to this project; he encouraged this attempt, but clearly is not to blame for its shortcomings. In terms of the writing, I want to thank Jeanette Weinberg, who read the entire manuscript for clarity, and Jane Macdonald, Emily Taber, and Matthew Abbate at the MIT Press. Without implicating them, I thank Chris Auld, Alex Cunha, David Brat, Charles Upton, and Andrea Moro. Special thanks go to John Cochrane, Jeff Ely, Doug Davis, Don Katzner, John Roemer, and Klaus Ritzberger. Each kindly reviewed or helped me understand the messages of material further away from my areas of specialization. Thanks also go to six anonymous referees who read the drafts carefully and, in several cases, offered very extensive and precise comments. I have not been able to accommodate all of their suggestions, but I hope they each recognize their imprint nonetheless.

Lastly, I thank my family. First, my wife, Teri Athreya, has always been an important balancing force and a source of perspective. Throughout my career, and especially during the lengthy and sometimes stressful self-indulgence of book writing, I've looked to her as a model for professional and personal behavior. My parents and siblings each helped along the way, and my cousin Padma Chadrasekaran has been perceptive on how I might want to introduce ideas in the book. My father, Krishna Athreya, has always led by example in the communication of technical ideas to broad audiences. In the end, though, my children may have helped the most: their existence is a daily reminder that the world has an "overlapping generations" structure (wait till chapter 5). The mortality risk that makes this so has spurred me to get this project done sooner, rather than . . .

Introduction

Economics is no longer a fit conversation piece for ladies and gentlemen. It has become a technical subject. Like any technical subject it attracts some people who are more interested in the technique than the subject. That is too bad, but it may be inevitable. In any case, do not kid yourself: the technical core of economics is indispensable infrastructure for the political economy.

—Robert Solow, emeritus professor of economics, MIT, and Nobel laureate (quoted in *New York Times*, March 20, 1988)

There are two related problems. First, by and large, journalists and policymakers—and by extension the US public—think about macroeconomics using the basically abandoned frameworks of the 1960s and 1970s. *Macroeconomists have failed to communicate their new discoveries and understanding to policymakers or to the world.* [emphasis added]

—Narayana Kocherlakota, president, Federal Reserve Bank of Minneapolis[1]

I.1   Why Do Macroeconomists Think What They Think and Do What They Do?

I think what Solow and Kocherlakota each say is true. Therefore, unless one finds their assessment a satisfactory state of affairs, the central messages of the now almost entirely technical discipline of macroeconomics should be made accessible to thoughtful and curious readers who lack the narrow background needed to read either advanced textbooks or articles in academic economics journals.

At the time of this writing, macroeconomic theory and practice are both under attack.[2] Critics of macroeconomics usually describe us macroeconomists in one of two fairly unappealing ways. The first is that we are credulous savants who, through an unfortunate combination of overdeveloped aesthetic sensibilities and naiveté, became so enamored of mathematics that we "mistook beauty for truth."[3] The second description is even less charitable: it is that we are stooges who spend miserable careers vainly trying to burnish the reputation of "free markets" against all comers (perhaps under the threat of excommunication by priests living either in Chicago, Illinois, or Minneapolis, Minnesota). One can hopefully sympathize if I or my colleagues at large would rather not choose to be described as either. The goal of this book is to describe the workaday practice of macroeconomists, and thereby clearly link the policy advice we give to a quite specific theoretical approach that we take seriously. Hopefully, in so doing, I may also convince readers that neither of the preceding caricatures applies to us.

The approach taken in this book is to first describe the main approach to macroeconomic model construction and then describe the bedrock "Walrasian general-equilibrium" framework, the modern version of which is known as the Arrow-Debreu-McKenzie (ADM) model. This is chapter 1. A sense of the profound importance of this model can be gleaned from the fact that modern macroeconomics, which seeks to understand and interpret important real-world economic "aggregate" time series such as GDP, interest rates, inflation, and unemployment, and is the source of many of the most influential policy interventions into the economy, is overwhelmingly based on applications of models rooted in the basic ADM model.

In macroeconomic applications, many additional frictions and "bells and whistles" are added to allow models to make contact with empirical phenomena, but the point of departure is essentially always ADM; *in most macroeconomic models in use today, one can recover the pure ADM model as a special case.* And for reasons that will become clearer shortly, this model provides the primary benchmark against which economists judge the efficacy of any given system of resource allocation and, relatedly, measure the difficulties created by real-world impediments to the nonwasteful allocation of resources.

In chapters 2 and 3, I will describe the nature of the relationship between prices, efficiency, and equality, and the two main results—the so-called welfare theorems—that govern this relationship within the ADM model. Chapter 4 gives special focus to describing some of the *processes* and *tradeoffs* that have led to certain "consensus" views about both macroeconomic model building and macroeconomic model "output." Having set the stage, chapters 5 and 6 cover the main classes of specific macroeconomic models in use today that spring from the Walrasian tradition, and some specific models used to understand events during the financial crisis of 2007–2008. One payoff to describing our process is that along the way the reader will also be introduced, quite inevitably, to those areas where macroeconomists' knowledge is rather incomplete. To the extent that my efforts leave readers persuaded of our generally held worldview—certainly in terms of the coherence of our approach to the knotty issues of the day—so much the better. But even if they are not persuaded, at least the reader and critic will have a better sense of "how the sausage gets made." And on this point, readers may note that the description of macroeconomics and macroeconomic policy advice in this book comes from someone who actually *does* both every day.

In the end, I hope to persuade the reader (i) that the modern approach to macroeconomics is coherent, and (ii) that this way of thinking poses no inherent conflict with the goals of either its relatively egalitarian-minded critics (including those who suspect decentralized or "free-market" outcomes of being far from ideal for other reasons) or those who suspect that the outcomes of free and competitive trade might indeed have some special properties. Instead, modern Walrasian macroeconomics is most vitally a "scaffold" to help with the construction of internally consistent macroeconomic *narratives* that are disciplined systematically by both mathematics and data. Looking ahead to chapters 5 and 6, we have moved far beyond the "representative agent," all parts of the acronym "DGSE" have their place, and "rational expectations" aren't just for fools.

I.2   Whom Do I Want to Reach?

This book has six chapters, and is deliberately modular: *The more economics you know, the more immediately you can skip directly to chapters 4, 5, and 6.* In writing this book, I have three specific audiences I want to reach, who all likely differ in their backgrounds in economics and mathematics.

The first audience consists of advanced undergraduates majoring in economics, who seek an accessible description of the approach to, and waterfront of, macroeconomic analysis. I particularly want to reach those in this group who are considering graduate education in economics; this is the group for whom this book is most closely tuned.

Advanced undergraduates, by virtue of the coursework they have had, will know some of what I cover in each chapter of the book and should find most of it rather accessible. But even for those who have had undergraduate classes in economics, chapters 1 through 3 offer more interpretation of the so-called welfare theorems and more intuition on the foundations of Walrasian equilibrium than they are likely to see in any standard economics class or textbook (see the following section for the specifics). As such, I hope it will be a useful complement to—though not a substitute for—formal class material.

However, this audience will almost certainly not know much of what is covered in chapters 4, 5, and 6. The latter are the heart of this book: they are where the approach to, and standard battery of, macroeconomic models and their implications are described.

The second audience is those who have recently begun graduate studies in economics, finance, public policy, and business-related fields, and who seek a companion reader that gives some "big picture" perspective on macroeconomics. In particular, the first-year graduate courses in macroeconomics are typically almost entirely about specific models and the technical methods needed to analyze them. In general, students are shown many, many "trees" but rarely, if ever, the (Walrasian-Arrow-Debreu-McKenzie) forest that most of the trees belong to. The emphasis on "tools"—and often severe abstraction—over perspective, while understandable and probably sensible, is so apparent in graduate training that I suspect that some students almost certainly become disenchanted with macroeconomics before they see any of its power. I hope this bunch finds chapters 1, 4, 5, and 6 especially useful. However, I sense that the median student in this group may also benefit from reading chapters 2 and 3. In a nutshell: I've tried to write the book that I wish someone had given me before I enrolled.

Nonetheless, I share the view of one anonymous referee that graduate students should want even more detail on many technical aspects that I have presented—and so the book is best taken in doses with standard texts, such as Kreps (1990) and Stokey, Lucas, with Prescott (1989), close to hand.

The third audience is those with a serious interest in or involvement with macroeconomics, but who never had the time or opportunity to acquire formal training in economics or mathematics. Most of all, I want to reach economic writers and noneconomist policymakers who work in central banking and fiscal policy arenas. Abstract technical ideas drive practical economic recommendations, so if one wants to understand macroeconomic policy advice at any level at all, one has to understand, at some level, the process by which we abstract (i.e., how we make macroeconomic models) and the abstractions (i.e., the models) themselves. This book aims to describe *why* we "do what we do and think what we think."

Given that the potential audiences for this book are unlikely to overlap, a tension I faced was the manner in which to introduce this last audience to certain ideas that are typically taught in undergraduate economics courses without slowing down the first two audiences. The latter will see that I have erred on the side of inclusiveness, and I am relying on those who know more to simply read past any material that is elementary for them.[4]

Yet, even though this book deliberately leaves out all technical machinery in an attempt to be accessible, especially to the third audience I listed, there is no doubt that it will still be hard for those with no exposure to economics. It presumes familiarity with ideas that I inevitably won't always flesh out fully, while in other places, the limits of English in conveying ideas precisely became overwhelming. In the end, I am not fully satisfied with the way I have handled some of these areas with respect to this audience. But I hope it's a start: ignoring noneconomists, especially economic writers and columnists, while it is largely the response of the field so far, seems unlikely to be productive, especially in the face of the many recent accounts of our sins of omission and commission.[5]

I.3 Some Key Features

On a more specific note, this book aims to address a set of topics that I view as inadequately covered in any such treatment of economics (macro- or micro-) I have seen. These are as follows.

1. *A detailed account of the standard recipe for macroeconomic model construction* This is not something that appears in any book I know of. However, it is vital to communicate these "rules of engagement" between macroeconomists, and then explain the reasons why we think these rules are indeed worth having. If successful, this part of the book (located in chapter 1 and again in chapter 6) will, I hope, clarify some of the tradeoffs involved that lead to macroeconomists' use of models and assumptions that many, including other economists, find patently silly.

2. *Macroeconomic equilibrium: what it is, and what it is not* Closely related to the preceding is what I regard as the most important aspect of macroeconomic model building: how macroeconomists make

predictions for the outcomes of the interaction of parties. Our notions of "equilibrium" are what perform this task. When successful, they winnow outcomes down to (hopefully) a small, or ideally, unique constellation of permissible actions for all parties that do not run afoul of limitations on resources, and do not (routinely) contradict the expectations of participants. To my taste, this is the heart of the matter: if you understand the notion of equilibrium being employed in a particular model, you understand the model; otherwise, you don't. Period. I am optimistic that sufficient attention to this topic alone will help any curious reader better understand how we do business.

3. *Detailed nontechnical presentation and discussion of the ADM model, the welfare theorems, and the main equilibrium existence theorem* These are chapters 1 through 3 of the book. Together, they give a detailed presentation of the ADM model and the so-called welfare theorems. While all good graduate textbooks on economic theory (and the occasional undergraduate text) will describe the Walrasian approach, the ADM model, and the three main theorems of Walrasian economics (the two welfare theorems and the theorem guaranteeing the *existence* of Walrasian equilibrium), this is the only detailed nontechnical presentation I have seen. The ADM is the bedrock model in macroeconomics, with the plurality of other models being special instances of it. Given the importance of this model for the work of macroeconomists, particularly in their evaluations of real-world phenomena, it is vital that the results and the reasoning behind them be made accessible to the many others who are interested in economic issues, rather than remaining cloistered in mathematics.

4. *Foundations for Walrasian equilibrium* Why should Walrasian equilibria command economists' attention as a likely outcome of "free trade"? To understand macroeconomists' preoccupation with "equilibrium analysis," the plausibility of Walrasian equilibria is critical. This book is the only nontechnical treatment I'm aware of that covers the body of work that addresses how "likely" trade in a given setting is to produce Walrasian equilibria. This is the work on the so-called foundations of Walrasian equilibria. I discuss four specific topics in this line of research: the core, market games, experimental economics, and local uniqueness. Each of these helps determine the extent to which one accepts the *relevance* of the existence and welfare theorems. In particular, the presumptions of economists that Walrasian outcomes are likely to happen in the "real world" are driven by, and predicated on, the findings of this body of work being supportive of such a view. This

part of the book will, I think, show clearly how apparently abstract notions give coherence to ideas that capture the imaginations of even the most "practical-minded."

5. *Don't deify decentralization*   A related, and more general, theme that runs through the whole book is that one should not deify decentralized outcomes, especially when it comes to promoting price-mediated trade (i.e., markets). Instead, I will argue that it is useful to treat a huge variety of institutional arrangements for the production and allocation of goods and services as a priori equal, and analyze each one in terms of the incentives it provides for doing "socially beneficial" things. In addition to the standard limitations on the efficacy of price-mediated trade, even when it is "competitive," I include a detailed nontechnical description of some of the research program known as mechanism design. (Again, this book is, as far as I have been able to determine, the first to provide a nontechnical description of this program.) En route, I will describe both the Gibbard-Satterthwaite and Myerson-Satterthwaite theorems. The former delineates limits on what is possible for a society that must provide incentives to elicit information, and the latter is arguably the most fundamental result economists have on the extent to which purely voluntary trading procedures can generate nonwasteful outcomes. In a nutshell, the welfare theorems and the Myerson-Satterthwaite theorem are two "bookends" on the extent to which self-interest, trade, and efficiency can coexist.

6. *Walras, modern models, and policymaking*   With the background of the welfare theorems, the existence theorem, and "foundations for Walrasian equilibrium" digested, the reader will be ready to see how the Walrasian approach shapes and unifies so much of modern macroeconomics. This is the heart of the book, and is the subject of chapters 4 and 5. The models I describe and explain in this section are the ones that fall directly into my own area of expertise. These models should make clear the influence of the ADM model, even though individual models typically depart in important ways from the basic ADM setting.

In chapter 6, I lay out the tensions that confront any economist seeking to build a clear narrative for a given set of facts. This leads naturally to a description of how to decide what to leave in and what to leave out. The choices that we make are properly regarded as compromises; but without a sense of what is gained and lost from the admission or deletion of any given feature of reality when trying to address a particular question, one cannot know if they are sensible compromises. In turn, there is no possibility of meaningful criticism of these decisions without first acquiring intimate knowledge of the costs and benefits. To this end, I focus on the roles played by the compromises that go by the names of "aggregation" and "rational expectations." I will also talk about the role of mathematics in modern macroeconomics. These are all areas that have exercised critics.

In chapters 5 and 6, I detail important models currently in use in macroeconomics. These include (i) the so-called neoclassical growth model, the parent of nearly all modern macroeconomics; (ii) the stochastic growth model, variants of which form the foundation for almost all research into business cycles; (iii) the so-called standard incomplete-markets model (SIM); (iv) the overlapping-generations model (OG); and (v) the standard search model. Variants of the SIM and OG models are more recent and are largely unknown outside academia and central bank research departments, but form the foundation of almost all research into the long-run effects of fiscal policy, education policy, insurance market policy, and financial market reform. Search models, too, are little known outside the profession, and yet organize nearly all macroeconomic analyses of labor markets and labor market policies at influential policymaking entities such as the CEA, the Fed, and elsewhere.

One narrow topic I tackle is the gap between the Walrasian approach and the old-style "Keynesian" one. This gap is an important source of public dissonance in which economists, the public, and too often policymakers at best talk past each other, and at worst argue acrimoniously.[6] On this point, readers should know that there has actually been near-complete convergence in methodology within macroeconomics. In particular, all modern macroeconomic models play squarely by the Walrasian rules of explicitly specifying the motivations and constraints of all decision makers, and ensuring that outcomes are feasible and always respect the behavioral motivations of households and firms.

One symptom of the total dominance of both the Walrasian approach and the ADM model is the centrality of the much-maligned "real business cycle" (RBC) model in essentially all modern work that pursues the ideas of the twentieth-century economist John Maynard Keynes. This dominance is striking because the RBC model is an archetypal ADM model, and so was initially seen as hostile to all things Keynesian. The "new Keynesian" models that are now employed are settings in which the basic RBC scaffold is retained, but where additional impediments to market function are incorporated. In such settings, economic policy can sometimes improve economic outcomes relative to laissez-faire, unlike in the pure RBC case.

As I describe models throughout, I will discuss criticisms of the Walrasian approach. To the extent that macroeconomics is the field where so much economic theory meets reality, it is useful to describe the problems facing the models lurking behind a huge share of modern economists' recommendations to policymakers.

7. *The crisis, the great recession, and macroeconomics*   Chapter 6 is concerned with what I view as a proper framing of the questions that macroeconomists and the general concerned public should be asking about the recent financial crisis and subsequent recession. It is rather early to offer last-word assessments of "what went wrong" and how to stop "it" from happening again, though. Therefore, I will spend my time instead detailing some specific models that macroeconomists have found useful in organizing their thinking so far.

I. 4   Pictures, Talk, and Homework

A book like this will probably reflect the idiosyncrasies and viewpoints of the author much more than is usual. It conveys beliefs that I hold at mid-career. It therefore incorporates all kinds of evidence: some of it formal, but a good deal of it informal, coming from my life experiences, my job, and especially my interactions with colleagues.

As a result, ideas I emphasize will not always overlap perfectly with what others find most critical. For example, the emphasis that I place on the "foundations for Walrasian equilibrium" mentioned above was born of what I think was my greater-than-the-average-macroeconomist discomfort level with the use of this notion of equilibrium in interpreting real-world outcomes. Similarly, I will promote a view of the value of various assumptions and the usefulness of certain models that, while widely shared among macroeconomists, leaves room for others to disagree. And my views on "macroeconomic priorities" and the relevance of technological progress in them are colored inevitably by the large amount of my life that I've spent in India. In each case, I leave those who disagree to write their own book.

The reader should always remember that the goal of this book is to provide a heuristic discussion of the models that we use to organize our thinking and how they push our policy stances in certain, sometimes opposing, directions. This goal requires, of course, that the book remain nontechnical and informal. I will therefore avoid all explicit mathematical and statistical constructions, and seek instead to complement what standard macroeconomics textbooks already do very capably. But this means that those who are curious after reading this book will need to seek formal expositions. The latter is where the details and the devil both reside. For macroeconomists to "know" something means knowing the statements and proofs of the key results, knowing how to pose the relevant optimization problems and to solve them. Usually, this also means knowing how to simulate them on a computer. To paraphrase the macroeconomist Robert E. Lucas Jr., "All else is just pictures and talk." Well, this book is *all* pictures and talk— and hopefully enough of it to whet one's appetite for the homework.

1   The Modern Macroeconomic Approach and the Arrow-Debreu-McKenzie Model

1.1 Introduction

Modern macroeconomics began about 140 years ago. The French economist Léon Walras, working in the late nineteenth century, provided in *Eléments d'économie politique pure* the first formal model of an economy in which private participants interacted through a system of interrelated markets. The advance made by Walras was to study a large-scale system in which all activity would be determined *simultaneously*, as it logically must be. Generally speaking, what happens in one part of any resource allocation system (market-based or otherwise) can both depend on and affect what occurs elsewhere.

Consider trade in cotton. Disturbances to weather, for example, could affect cotton prices, which then might have effects in the market for clothing or even the prices of things complementary to clothes, such as shoes. Conversely, a sudden change in fashion might depress the desire of households to wear certain kinds of clothes, and this in turn might alter the landscape in the cotton market. These "feedback effects" are what Walras's approach clarified, formalizing what economists and noneconomists had both surely long known: that it may be risky to talk about outcomes in an individual market without taking into consideration all the feedback effects that may be present.

A striking feature of modern macroeconomics is the extent to which it fundamentally mirrors Walras's conception. Most macroeconomic models in use today are roughly "Walrasian" in that they: (i) treat market participants as decision makers with well-defined objectives (such as profit maximization by firms); (ii) often (though not always) study outcomes that arise from market participants facing prices they cannot individually alter, but at which they find themselves able to buy and sell the amounts they wish to; and (iii) routinely and explicitly accommodate feedback effects across markets.

Modern-day versions of the Walrasian vision have a variety of names, such as the **Walrasian general-equilibrium model** and the **competitive-equilibrium model**. The benchmark competitive-equilibrium model is the so-called **Arrow-Debreu-McKenzie (ADM) model**. Before describing the ADM model in detail, however, it is useful to begin with a catalog of the ingredients essential to any modern macroeconomic model.

1.2   What Is a Macroeconomic Model?

A macroeconomic model is an *artificial* society that features mathematical representations of all participants. Participants come in three groups: **households** (or more generally **consumers**), **firms**, and sometimes a **government**. With the occasional exception of the government, model participants are assumed to always do what is best for themselves in an explicitly specified **trading arrangement** that spells out who knows what when, and how participants can transact with each other. The trading arrangement will tell us, for example, whether households and firms interact via a system of prices they have no control over, or whether they must compete in a particular kind of auction, or must search for each other (after which they will perhaps bargain according to a specific protocol), and so on. Lastly, a notion of **equilibrium** is used to make predictions for feasible outcomes arising from the interactions of all participants, all of whom are modeled as optimizing in their choices. These predictions will, ideally, take into account all feedback effects that are suspected a priori to be important.

It may help to recall the simplest "supply and demand" picture that some of you may have seen elsewhere, certainly in a *micro*economics class. That was a model in almost the same sense as I have in mind here. In particular, the supply and demand curves were both constructed by considering an artificial world in which all participants were asked the question: How much of a good or service would you choose to sell or buy if you faced a given price? As long as the participants responded truthfully, we could construct curves representing their answers on the chalkboard. We then could ask: At what price would these two curves cross?

In asking these questions, we already find ourselves in an "artificial" world. That is to say, while some markets do operate this way (e.g., some rice markets in Japan, according to McMillan 1994), this artificial world bears little resemblance to my own everyday experience, in which most items I buy have price stickers on them that I can take or leave.

We identified the price where the curves crossed with "equilibrium" because we thought that only such an outcome—given our assumed trading arrangement and, more specifically, *our assumption of price taking*—would have a chance of persisting long enough to make for a good prediction for price and quantities traded. After all, since households are assumed to be price takers, we must not give them any reason to *want* to change prices. And if the amount demanded did not equal supply, they would want to. For instance, if the price were such that demand exceeded supply, buyers would, unless somehow barred, take actions such as offering higher prices to sellers who will sell to them "first." The general message here is that one's notion of equilibrium must respect, if at all possible, the behavioral assumptions one has imposed on the decision makers in the model.

Modern macroeconomics often simply involves studying supply and demand in multiple markets at a time, rather than in a single one as microeconomists often do, but, importantly, where events in each market are routinely allowed to depend on what is happening, and is *expected* to happen, in many or even all others. Thus, it should be stressed that there are not different kinds of theories for macroeconomics and microeconomics. Any differences are fundamentally those of the *scope* of the questions being asked and, in turn, in the attendant level of detail in the models used to address them.

Since Walras's time, the family of macroeconomic models that now fit under the eponymous rubric has grown and is now too large to catalog in a way that a nonspecialist would find useful. This family now has members that differ very substantially from each other in the way they model aspects of the economy, and some of the models most used by policymakers allow for some features that are not classical Walrasian, particularly in allowing some model actors to have the power to unilaterally *set* prices, and thereby exert market power.

1.2.1   Macroeconomics as Hyperorganized Narrative with Hard-Nosed Data and Logic Checks

Let's now take a quick peek at the methodology of macroeconomics. My view is that a part of what we do is "organized storytelling," in which we use extremely systematic tools of data analysis and reasoning, sometimes along with more extra-economic means, to *persuade* others of the usefulness of our assumptions and, hence, of our conclusions. In this sense, I am in the camp of Dierdre McCloskey.[1] This is perhaps not how one might describe "hard sciences," and further below I'll describe two main reasons why economics and, I suspect, all social sciences differ from their physical cousins (I will not go into the sterile—and crashingly boring—discussion of whether economics is a science or not, since relabeling it would change neither the questions we asked nor how we approached them). But for now, let's talk about what we are trying to do.

Economics attempts to describe "causes" or "reasons" for what is observed in the real economic world. Specifically, economists are often searching for conditions under which real-world observations emerge as inevitable outcomes of the interaction of smart and self-interested participants. In this sense, models teach us about *assumptions*.[2] For example, let's say we observe that the young routinely earn less and save at lower rates than middle-aged households. An economist might ask to what extent households with stable preferences and a desire to maintain a stable lifestyle might account for this behavior. This explanation would be consistent with the behavior of both those antici-pating higher earnings in the future and saving less now as a result (the young), and those anticipating lower earnings in the future (the middle-aged).

If assumptions that imply a given set of observations are found, a next question is: Does one find them *persuasive*? In the previous example, can we really say that preferences for a stable lifestyle are the only pos-sible explanation for our observations? No. What if households simply valued consumption more when young and less when old? This type of preference might also account for the observations. To the extent that we cannot definitely rule out such preferences, we are left with ambigu-ity. Thus, what is vital is the extent to which the author's assumptions are the only possible ones that generate the observed data. This, unfor-tunately, will often fail: economics is replete with "observational equiv-alence" whereby two (or more) sets of assumptions match a given set of data equally well. The paucity of data rich enough and free enough of "selection biases" to decisively winnow the set of assumptions that lead to a given set of observations is a huge problem.

One important difference between economics and physical sciences is that we economists have a far harder time verifying the closeness of our standard assumptions to reality. We cannot, for example, actually check in any definitive manner the level of "irrationality" in individual decision making when we assume that all participants are fully rational. Compare this to the ease with which a physicist could check the amount of friction that might be present in a given setting where they might want to assume that friction is zero. Economists also lack axioms that closely approximate conditions in the real world the way that, for example, Newtonian axioms for projectile motion seem to. Seen this way, it is actually the collection of such assumptions that we "like most" which constitutes our understanding of the world.

There is a second, even more substantial difference from the physical sciences, especially for macroeconomists: for most important macroeconomic questions, *macroeconomists cannot conduct controlled experiments*. I could not, for example, be given control of a society, split it up as I wanted, and run parts under various tax codes, legal and regulatory regimes, and so on just for the sake of my research. Thus, the classic route to learning about causal relationships in medicines, pesticides, high-yielding crops, and so many other things is simply closed to us.

If that weren't enough, economists' presumption that those data we do observe reflect *purposeful decision making* further limits the inferences for policy one might be able to make. For example, if working mothers choose how many hours to work by thinking about taxes and child-care costs, then *observed* variation in their working hours as taxes vary will reflect the decisions only of those who chose to work, *not* of all mothers. In turn, we must be careful about jumping to conclusions if, for example, we observe that those mothers who do work don't alter their hours of work much when taxes change. We may have failed to observe enough of the set of all mothers who, at current wage rates, chose to not work outside the home (engaging instead in home production such as child-rearing and household management). Some, or many, of these people might, for all we know, change their decisions and work substantial hours in the marketplace if only taxes were lower.

In addition, the set of feasible outcomes from a set of participants interacting with each other in a marketplace is often large: many things are indeed possible. However, as will become clearer below, not all feasible outcomes are equally plausible. As a result, economists of all stripes select outcomes that (i) are "sensible" or "plausible" given the presumed behavioral motivations of the participants in a model (such as profit-maximizing behavior by firms) and (ii) describe feasible outcomes—i.e., they select outcomes that are equilibria. As to the first point, we economists can never verify definitively what people are

actually thinking, and so can never be perfectly sure that they are optimizing in any clear way. Nor can we know that a firm has chosen
optimally to maximize profits.

Thus, equilibrium requires taking the behavioral assumptions one
imposes on the model very seriously.[3] But deciding which one of a
variety of notions of equilibrium to use is a judgment call, and so is a
second point at which a reader may part company with an author.
Precisely for this reason, I will devote time in chapter 2 to explaining
why the central equilibrium concept of "competitive" or "Walrasian"
equilibrium (to be defined further below) is a sensible one in many, but
not all, instances.

Returning to the idea that economists are unable to rule out various
assumptions that may lead to similar conclusions, the issue for us is
how to choose between two (or more) theories, *none* of whose premises
can be verified exactly as either holding or not, and none of which can
easily be disentangled via either observed data or a giant natural experiment. A traditional answer has been to pick the model (the set of
assumptions) with the most accurate predictions, by some measure.
But this will not resolve many discussions in macroeconomics: as noted
above, generating *well-controlled* predictions to isolate the role of axioms
and equilibrium concepts is nearly impossible in most cases. This is
why I think persuasion plays such an important role, especially in
policymaking—it is the only means we frequently have to decide on
the *relevance* of any particular model.

1.2.1.1   Ensuring Internal Consistency

The situation I just described is essentially tough luck for both macroeconomists and society at large. And, unless one seeks no interpretation
of aggregate economic data, or until we have a more mechanical apparatus to definitively order competing narratives by plausibility, we *need*
persuasion. But there are certain standards: macroeconomic accounts
should be forced to be internally consistent. I cannot stress this point
enough: the only permissible form of disagreement about any explanation for a given set of facts (data) among macroeconomists should be
disagreement on the *appropriateness* of premises, not conclusions given
these premises.

Where informality returns in a macroeconomic conversation is in the
"persuading" described above. The interpretations offered by a given
social scientist, both before (to motivate the assumptions being made
and the equilibrium concept being used) and after (to convince the

audience that the model "sensibly" accounts for phenomena) a model has been described, are very important. Clearly, then, macroeconomics needs a recipe and a language to force macroeconomists to be honest and transparent with the public about the role of premises in the views they espouse.

As I'll argue in more detail in chapter 4, mathematics is the best known language for keeping things clear and, in the process, helps us prevent any associated smooth talk from taking on a life of its own. Outside of the bounds imposed by mathematics, macroeconomists would routinely be able to seek shelter in ambiguity and obfuscation to such an extent that even their premises could remain unknown to each other for long periods of time (in chapter 5, you will see how this has held up progress in some areas). Is a tax-paying public asking too much when they demand clarity on the premises and analyses of macroeconomists, who are sometimes influential?[4] Modern economics makes it essentially impossible to persuade without providing the mathematics and the data. If this has left a stodgier and less-expansive class of economists, so much the better.

1.2.1.2 Informed Criticism

This book is about the central role that theoretical economics plays in the work of practical or "applied" macroeconomists like me. The producers of economic theory, "theorists," are those who spend the majority of their time deriving the logical consequences of axioms that, for various reasons, they find interesting. There are many such theorists, and a distinguished one is Ariel Rubinstein. As you read this book, I urge you to look at Rubinstein's related work, especially the following two papers. First, my account of the so-called welfare theorems will be standard, while his paper with Michele Piccione, "Equilibrium in the Jungle" (2007), offers additional perspective. Second, his paper "A Theorist's View of Experiments" (2001) provides important criticism of economics as a whole, some of which will serve as a useful counterpoint for any reader who feels that I overadvertise what economic theory can deliver for us.

1.3 How Do Macroeconomists Account for the Facts?

One riddle macroeconomists have grappled with is how to account for the observed relationship between returns on risky and riskless assets. A striking observation in the data over a long period was the premium that holders of stocks received relative to the holders of bonds. Specifically, the gap in average returns between the two was approximately 6%. Now, at this point we have no way of claiming whether this difference is "large" or "small," because we lack a model that we find initially persuasive that tells us which it is. So in 1985 Edward Prescott, then at the University of Minnesota, and Rajnish Mehra at the University of California, Santa Barbara, set out to see if "standard" models *predicted* this so-called equity premium.

The "equity premium puzzle," as it is now rather deliberately named, is an example that highlights all of the various traits economists look for in a macroeconomic argument, and also involves a class of models (so-called representative-agent models we'll encounter later) that is heavily lampooned by critics. Moreover, the puzzle is instructive because it is a simplified ADM model (something I will detail shortly). Lastly, it is a landmark in persuasion, as evaluated by the approximately 700 cita- tions it has received over the past 25 years: it launched an industry.[5]

By "predicted," Mehra and Prescott (1985) meant something very specific. Namely, they asked:

If one assigned actual numerical values to the so-called "parameters" of the model that "sensibly" represented the willingness of households to take gambles and trade off their consumption of goods and services in the present for more in the future, and allowed them to trade stocks and bonds whose variability in dividends matched those observed in U.S. data, would the *equi-librium* of a model in which all households felt they could buy and sell bonds and stocks at prices that they could themselves not influence yield an outcome such that average return on stocks was 6% higher than that for bonds, as in the data?

The answer was a resounding no. They showed that for essentially any numerical representation of the representative household's willingness to take risk (as evidenced, for example, by data on insurance pur-chases), the broad *class* of Walrasian models under consideration would all fail! Now, for someone skeptical of modern macroeconomics, this probably comes as no surprise at all. After all, the model Mehra and Prescott studied belonged to the much-criticized "representative-agent" class. What was worse, all households were assumed to live forever! How could such silliness be expected to match the data?

Mehra, Prescott, and most of the rest of us did not, however, see it this way at all. Instead, what we saw was a persuasive contribution. And the reason it persuaded as it did, as seen by the flood of papers on the topic over the next quarter-century, was that it put an existing theory to the test very explicitly, found it wanting in very specific ways, and documented carefully the likely reasons for why it failed. It is the latter that set the stage for others to productively pursue resolutions. Some explanations have since persuaded some, but, to date, no one explanation of the equity premium puzzle has persuaded all.

1.3.1 How Macroeconomists Argue with Each Other (or, How to Argue with a Macroeconomist, if You Must!)

Let's now take a look at the more general recipe followed by essentially every research paper and seminar presentation in macroeconomics (certainly all the ones I have encountered). If you're considering graduate school in economics, you'll find that the following is a near-literal description of how a presentation by a macroeconomist to fellow macroeconomists would actually go, in print or in person. The recipe is extremely general: it does not require knowledge of any specific model of the macroeconomy, but does help ensure that macroeconomic models are "precisely wrong," in the way Mehra and Prescott showed one class of models to be.[6]

1.3.1.1 Step 1: They Tell Each Other Who Is in Their Model Economy, and What Those Participants *Want* to Do: Household Preferences and Firm Profit Maximization

The first step in "modern" macroeconomics is to state clearly the behavioral motivations that one assumes about the set of participants in one's model. These entities routinely fall into one of the three major groups mentioned earlier: households, firms, and the government. Households are represented exactly as in standard *micro*economic theory: as beings with the ability to *rank-order* any two bundles of goods and services that they wish to. (I'll give more detail on household behavior in a bit.)

Firms are represented as entities (think of them as machines) that are technologically capable of transforming arrays of goods and services into other arrays of goods and services. A firm may be able, for example, to employ workers and some specialized equipment, and use these to make tennis balls and racquets. Lastly, the government is an entity that is usually modeled as one with the power to tax, to issue debt, and in some models, to issue fiat money.

Turning first to households, the standard first step is to posit that households choose among the objects that they have access to (such as various consumer goods and services, and savings in various investments), attempting to pick which is best given their preferences. It is here that a "rationality" assumption, to be described in detail further below, is usually, though not always, imposed.

As for the objectives of firms, macroeconomists typically assume that firms act as profit maximizers on behalf of their owners, subject to the limits imposed by the "technology" they operate. (The standard definition of a firm in macroeconomic models, and the profit maximization assumption, will both be detailed further below.) For a while now, economic, finance, and accounting theorists have, in fact, studied models in which this is not assumed. However, it is widespread enough in modern macroeconomics to be called a "standard" assumption.

Lastly, governments are modeled in a variety of ways, depending on the question being addressed. In the context of monetary policy, for example, the government is sometimes modeled as a simple rule-following automaton, while in other cases, it too is modeled as a "rational" being who actively tries to pick what is "best" for the households in the economy.

Let's look back at how step 1—the clear statement of one's assumptions about the behavioral motivations of study participants—was carried out in the equity premium puzzle of Mehra and Prescott. These authors made stark assumptions. They announced that they were studying an artificial economy with a large number of identical households that live forever, and that each started life with exactly equal ownership shares in the firms in the economy. To boot, each household had a particular type of rational preferences that did not allow people's willingness to postpone spending to be uncoupled from their desire to avoid risks. As a result, an asset that offered high average growth rates in dividends over time would be valuable only to households that also did not mind facing risk. Yet it is easy enough to think of households that are "patient" and willing to hold assets that will pay substantially only in the future (i.e., have high growth rates in their prices) but that also greatly fear fluctuations in the value of such assets.

1.3.1.2 Step 2: They Tell Each Other What Their Model's Participants *Have*: Endowments and Technology

Having listed the objectives of both households and firms, the next step for a macroeconomist is to spell out what capabilities the various actors in the economy have. This involves specifying the various goods and services—usually called **endowments**—that each household (or, in some models, each *member* of a household) has, and importantly, what access households have to firms that will allow them to transform arrays of goods and services (i.e., "inputs") into arrays of other goods and services (i.e., "outputs"). There is a standard mathematical machinery for doing this, and the reader should be aware of the fact that an enormous variety of technological possibilities can be assumed at the outset. As for step 2, Mehra and Prescott assumed that all households were endowed with equal ownership shares in the firms present in the economy. And Mehra and Prescott's model of firms was stark and perhaps special as well. They assumed that a world with a finite set of firms would face randomly fluctuating capacity to produce the single good that households cared about, and could do so at no cost!

1.3.1.3 Step 3: They Tell Each Other How Model Participants *Can* Interact: Trading Arrangements

Once the attributes and endowments of households and the technology of firms have been described, the next step in any research paper or seminar will be to state the nature of trading arrangements facing the main actors. This is the point at which most macroeconomic models will begin to differ from one another. Much of what happens in model building has to do with how participants are allowed to trade with each other, rather than with how rational or nonrational their behavior may be. This is important, even if only as a description of how the profession works. Later, I will try to explain the nature of the tradeoffs that have led macroeconomists to accept this way of working, even when many find certain aspects of the standard specification of preferences and expectation formation implausible.

What one can ultimately do in a society depends fundamentally on what others do (this is what makes economics interesting to begin with). It is the trading arrangement that provides the opportunities for trade, as well as the terms on which that trade is possible. The most familiar trading arrangement in economic models, and arguably in the real world, is that of price-mediated trade—objects have price tags, and people and firms decide what to do based on the prices they think they can get. As I describe further below, one such trading institution is known in the folklore of economics as the "Walrasian clearinghouse" (WCH). It sets prices in a way that depends on the actions of all market participants.

With respect to step 3, Mehra and Prescott modeled all households and firms as operating in a marketplace in which prices, which they felt they could not alter, were quoted. They also modeled households as having a precise prediction for the price at which assets could be bought and sold in various future economic conditions. They assumed, for example, that households had correct predictions or **rational expectations** for what the prices of stocks and bonds would be in a boom or in a recession. Moreover, their assumption meant that even though households accepted that booms and recession could not be perfectly foreseen, they nevertheless agreed on a common set of odds for next year's macroeconomic performance.

1.3.1.4 Step 4: They Tell Each Other How Participants *Will* Interact: Equilibrium as Prediction

As we've noted, equilibrium is how an economist goes from assumptions about the motivations and capabilities of all traders, and the trading arrangement they operate in, to *predictions* of outcomes. At its most general level, equilibrium requires that optimizing traders *not be surprised* by what happens. This does *not* mean that situations are always predictable, as I will discuss further below. Rather, traders must not be surprised by what happens to their trading opportunities *given* the realization of all inherently random (unpredictable) aspects of the economic system (such as the weather, war and peace elsewhere, etc.).

At the individual level, if households and firms take those prices as given, they will perceive a set of "budget-feasible" opportunities. They are then modeled as solving the optimization problem in step 3, *subject to the constraint on their budget created by the price located by the WCH*. This illustrates that macroeconomic models are clear about how what one can do is affected by what others do, and vice versa.

To bring things back to the concrete, Mehra and Prescott used rational-expectations equilibrium. Thus, no household or firm in their model is ever surprised by the prices commanded by stocks and bonds *given the realization of aggregate corporate profits*. This is so even though none of them were certain, at the time they purchased or sold the assets, about what corporate profits would turn out to be in the next trading session. The restrictions imposed on admissible outcomes by their use of this notion of equilibrium immediately allowed Mehra and Prescott to use aggregate US data to compute the rates of return that bonds and stocks would each generate.

Given the equilibrium model chosen, the final part of step 4 is, in many cases, to evaluate the change in well-being of households. In all models that follow steps 1–4, this is readily done. Both the author and the reader are clearly informed about the benefits or costs flowing to various participants in the model. With this information, one can arrive at a meaningful judgment of how to act vis-à-vis the policy.

I have now described the structure for arguments that is essentially mandated by my profession. Failure to follow these guidelines will result in the argument, no matter how worthy, falling on deaf ears. Here again, a reader may (quite rightly) think: "What a dogmatic bunch!" The main defense I will offer is that each of the places in which macroeconomists routinely draw lines in the sand is a place in which they often recognize an inability to utilize known technical machinery to derive answers. This is the state of affairs, and if following this process makes the reader see macroeconomists as slaves to tools or technique, then I can only offer as a response the consensus view: we usually believe that it is more important to be able to say something correctly than to say many things vaguely.[7] This is especially true for those engaged in the longer-run research program of improving economic tools, even when it limits their ability to make definitive statements on matters of shorter-run policy.

1.3.1.5 It Takes a Model to Beat a Model

Given the presumptions about households and firms, and the presence of a well-defined trading arrangement, each party is immediately faced with a "constrained optimization" problem. A vast machinery of mathematics has arisen to deal with this problem, reflecting a theme that will be emphasized repeatedly, especially in chapter 4: modeling choices are made with malice aforethought—economists think ahead to see if a given set of assumptions will lead to an optimization problem that is capable of being solved with currently known mathematical tools. This can, of course, be taken as a criticism, and a clear admission that we "look where the light is," not where the problems are. On the other hand, routinely posing problems that seem more "realistic" or "palatable," but that one cannot solve or analyze, is not very interesting either.

The tension between capturing salient features of the real world, such as the not-unbounded rationality of real-life consumers or the clumsiness of real-world firm behavior, for example, and having a model whose "solution" can be found, is pervasive in economics generally, and in macroeconomics especially. We routinely struggle with questions of what to include and what to leave out. The reader will see this theme echoed in chapter 4 and in the description of standard macroeconomic models in chapter 5. In fact, before proceeding further, let me digress briefly on the issue of economists and assumptions.

The fact that an assumption is a "bad" description of something we'd like to model (in this case, household or individual choice behavior) is not helpful for deciding whether it should be made or not—what matters is what alternatives one has available. Our willingness as macroeconomists to make silly-looking assumptions is emphatically not the same thing as saying that we have made bad choices in constructing models of the economy. Knowing that assumptions are "bad" means that conclusions should be tempered or qualified, and that the robustness of the model to these extreme assumptions should be checked. But for anyone to know this, they'd have to have wrestled with the same tradeoffs, and have built a model that is both more realistic and only somewhat less tractable to analyze.

In sum, if there's one rule we play by, it is this: it takes a model to beat a model. One measure of the difficulty of achieving this can be seen in the high payoff to succeeding; it is what essentially all of the profession's biggest names, such as Paul Krugman, Edward Prescott, and George Akerlof, each did at some point.

1.4 Macroeconomic "Equilibrium": What It Does and Does Not Imply

"Equilibrium" is a term that seems to cause great confusion, with many taking macroeconomists' focus on "equilibrium states" as a tacit admission that complicated and violent changes in outcomes are inherently inconsistent with any notion of equilibrium—or, worse yet, that private outcomes are somehow always for the best. Both views are incorrect. Later in the book, I will emphasize the yawning gap that may exist between an "equilibrium" outcome in a given model, on the one hand, and both an "ideal" outcome and a "stable" one, on the other. Moreover, as we'll see, equilibrium in macroeconomics is almost always a highly dynamic object where *some* gap exists between the equilibrium outcomes and the ideal.

Some of the discussion surrounding equilibrium is just semantics, but an important part is not. This has to do with the dynamics one can imagine occurring in ways that *do not* surprise traders. For example, in a given year, farmers and wholesale buyers are likely to have a sense of how prices for their produce depend on the amount of rain that will fall between planting and harvest. As a result, if each plans sensibly, then while outcomes may indeed be unpredictable (because rainfall itself is), what will not be unpredictable are the prices and quantities that will prevail *given* the amount of rain that ultimately did fall. This example illustrates a more general theme: in settings where traders face uncertainty, they will (as long as they are sensible) act as if they have formulated contingency plans that dictate a course of action come what may. In this sort of setting, equilibrium means studying outcomes in which each trader is not incorrect, given the realization of uncertainty and the actions of all others (who will each be using his or her own contingency plans).

So the questions one should always ask when deciding on the validity of an "equilibrium analysis" are: Are the participants in question routinely surprised by what occurs? and, if there is uncertainty in the situation being considered: Are the participants surprised *given* the realization of uncertainty that has occurred? If not, then equilibrium analysis seems reasonable.[8]

1.5   Payoffs from the Standard Macroeconomic Model-Building Recipe

The recipe I have described, and the technical apparatus we macroeconomists use, were adopted by us to improve the usefulness of macroeconomics as a purely *applied* tool for policymakers. Here are some specific ways in which this improvement occurs.

1.5.1   Making Logical Errors Easier to Spot

As already asserted, arguably the biggest payoff from a near-religious adherence to the recipe outlined above is that it increases economists' ability to ferret out internal inconsistency. This helps keep us honest, and while it surely limits the scope of our inquiries, it helps those inquiries we do undertake to avoid being nonsensical, for two main reasons. First, following steps 1–3 of the recipe forces a transparent specification of the objectives and constraints faced by all the actors. Second, step 4 forces a description of equilibrium, which allows observers to decide on the extent to which the feasible outcomes selected are "likely," "plausible," or both.

1.5.2   Disciplining Claims about Causal Relationships

A frequently heard claim is that stock market movements have a "wealth effect" on aggregate household consumption. This is the idea that the (strong or poor) performance of the stock market is directly responsible for the (strong or poor) level of household spending. The idea has attracted serious attention; many authors have written papers documenting the joint movement of a stock market index and the sum of household consumption expenditures. In general, consumption and assets prices do indeed move closely together (see, e.g., Ludvigson and Steindel 1999), and on the face of it, the line of reasoning seems natural: households, looking ahead to the future, see that their stock portfolio has increased in value. So, rather than waiting until old age to sell the stocks and spend the money, why not sell some of it and spend more now?

The problem with this view is that, while it is certainly sensible when talking about any *single* household, it may not make sense when looking at aggregate data. In other words, to interpret the aggregate consumption expenditures of households in an economy as being "caused" by changes in the total value of firms in that economy may not be proper. This is because it was the collective impact of *all* households' consumption and savings decisions that helped determine the value of firms' profits—and hence the value of the stock market in the first place! That is, the same decisions that lead to household consumption behavior lead, when aggregated, to the value of the stock market too. Thus, one does not cause the other; both are determined jointly and simultaneously.

In this context, what might be a setting under which we would agree that stock values are indeed "driving" or "causing" consumption? Here's one: imagine a world in which almost all the ownership of firms resides in a few hands. Thus, wealth (i.e., claims to future profits of firms) is extremely concentrated. However, imagine that the few rich people who do own almost everything also save at high rates, and so consume little relative to the rest of the population. Now, imagine that these rich households get good news about changes in the productivity of investment. Perhaps scientists discovered a new source of cheap electricity in the future. In this setting, the value of installed capital would go up, and millions of households would see their stock portfolios do well. As long as the portfolios themselves are large relative to the income of the average household, and thus have a strong impact on the household's wealth, households will in general respond by consuming more—just as the empiricists might argue they tend to. However, since most households' portfolios are tiny relative to the total value of all firms, the stock of aggregate capital doesn't change much as a result of this change in household consumption behavior.

Is this plausible? Maybe, maybe not. For one, it seems to require that consumption not be too big relative to the capital stock, lest such changes in household behavior significantly alter the value of firms. But it is a possibility—and notice that here too, the underlying change that "caused" the others was a change in the "fundamentals" of the economy; that is, the news about improvements in future electricity production. Thus, even in a case where the data make it appear as if one event caused another, things are not so obvious. For an example of a formal analysis of a model in which stock prices are not causing consumption or savings, but where both are indeed responding to a single exogenous (outside) factor, see Lantz and Sarte (2001).

The point of this section is not to say that the interpretation provided by some in this particular example is necessarily wrong. Quite the opposite: it is to sharpen the discussion to determine the conditions under which it may be right. In other words, a macroeconomist often wants to know *what it would take* for a theory or assertion (here, about stock market values and household spending) to make sense. We can then decide whether the premises so identified are ones we are comfortable with.[9]

1.5.3 Better Policy Analysis: Welfare Economics

Policymakers and the public often want to address normative questions: Are deficits always bad? If so, why? And if not, why not? Should we have low marginal tax rates? Should we abolish Medicaid? Should we have universal healthcare? As you are reading this, you may be answering these questions to yourself. But I would ask you: How do you know what you think you do? On what basis did you arrive at the magnitudes of costs and benefits you have in mind? Whose welfare are you valuing, and how? Would someone smart, listening to you, be able to make sense of what you say? The standard recipe ensures that one will be able to answer each of these questions. Modern macroeconomics takes seriously the view that the main role of a model is to frame questions first and (hopefully) settle them later.

As we've seen, in Walrasian models, decision makers are typically sensible (i.e., "rational"). It is this tendency that permits us to have a meaningful conversation about whether the implications of policies are "good" or "bad" and why they are as such. Such statements are, it turns out, nearly *impossible to make once one drops the assumption of rationality*. This is a point that is not widely acknowledged. In other words, in worlds populated by irrational decision makers, one rapidly loses the ability to judge whether an outcome is "better" or "worse" for participants. What if a policymaker's evaluation on, for example, the adequacy of retirement savings for a given individual differs from those of the participants in an economy or, for that matter, from those of another policymaker? On what basis would we choose one over the others?

As long as one is altering policy and private decisions, one must feel strongly that an outsider can do better than an individual in making decisions on behalf of a private agent. This may certainly be true in a variety of instances, but it requires meeting a burden of proof that an outsider can do better. By contrast, in settings populated with rational decision makers, outcomes can be judged to be unambiguously wasteful ("inefficient" in the jargon). In such cases, the next step is an investigation of problems in *trading arrangements*—something far more directly observable, and amenable to improvements through policy. And this is exactly what helps protect (though not always successfully) the public from economists happily willing to supply unwarranted certitudes.

1.5.4   Better Policy Analysis: The "Lucas Critique"

Another payoff is that the insistence on fidelity to the Walrasian approach opened the door to overcoming the single largest obstacle in economics: the inability to run anything remotely like a controlled experiment. As mentioned, one simply cannot study the effects of fiscal policy, for example, by subjecting a random sample to one tax regime and others to something else and then comparing outcomes. Such experiments are a luxury that macroeconomists almost certainly should not have, anyway! As a result, modern macroeconomists are left with data, some models, and no more. Most modern macroeconomic models are analyzed with the help of computers—similar to the Sim City games that some may be familiar with. The great advantage of these worlds is that all manner of controlled experiments can be run. Even more vitally, macroeconomists can accommodate the key feature that when policies changes, *so might the behavior of agents faced with them*. This was a problem pointed out by Robert Lucas in 1976, in

"Econometric Policy Evaluation: A Critique." Overcoming the **Lucas critique** is of utmost importance if one wants to understand the likely effects of a novel policy. The relevance of such an ability should be obvious in the current financial crisis, where both the monetary and fiscal authorities are routinely attempting never-before-attempted policies. Without the modern approach, one would be helpless to predict the effects of such policies, as no historical data, by definition, can really help predict the effect of anything truly novel.

Macroeconomic data are closest to an in-game statistical summary for a team sport. It will be obvious to anyone in sports that such data require interpretation, and do not by themselves tell a definitive story or provide the last word in guidance for future actions. Rather, it is clear to anyone who knows any sport that such a summary is a statement about the joint presence of various constellations of players, and expectations of *future* constellations, from each team, rather than a statement about any one player. For instance, when interpreting such a summary, one needs to think about who, exactly, was playing and when. But this is hardly random. For example, when choosing a lineup to place on the field, each side will consider the specific makeup of the lineup the other team will choose. This, in turn, will result in all sorts of selection biases. As an example, think of a case from the 1980s, when the Boston Celtics and the Los Angeles Lakers were often playing each other in the NBA finals. How much data would one have for championship games on Larry Bird's performance against the Lakers when Magic Johnson was benched? Perhaps not a lot. After all, too much was at stake to repeatedly run an experiment in which Magic sat out big games when Larry was in. The same problems arise in understanding Magic's capabilities. So how do we really know how great these two are, if their career statistics were, in part, nullified by each other? The answer is that we can look for coaches who run bold experiments in high-stakes settings, but more realistically, we'll likely turn to those with deep inside knowledge of the game to fill in the blanks and get us past the limitations of the statistics—which, to repeat, is a record only of what happened, not of what might have happened. Since macroeconomists cannot run bold experiments, we're left with models that we tune or "calibrate" (a term I will explain later) to match what was seen, which then allows us to understand what was not seen, and why it was not.

Given the Lucas critique, the confluence of the improvement of economists' ability to study decision problems that involve choices over time and under uncertainty, and the huge improvements in the power to simulate artificial models of such trading among *large numbers* of households and firms in numerous markets, has been a very important event. As a result of these methodological changes, modern macroeconomics now is able to simulate economies populated by households and firms that differ vastly from one another, and subject these artificial societies to essentially any kind of experiment, including standard ones involving tax policy or competition policy.

Consider a society in which taxes have never been placed on consumption goods in large amounts. Instead, this society has relied on taxes on other items in order to raise revenue for whatever it deems useful. In this setting, economists are called one day by some politicians to make an assessment of the likely effect of a switch away from all existing taxes, toward a consumption-based tax. What would a modern macroeconomist do if asked this question? Note first that, barring some ideal natural experiment conducted on a large enough scale, there would be no data to stare at in order to divine the likely outcome. Economists would not be warranted in simply looking at existing data on how revenue varied when other existing taxes (say, on labor income or capital income) were varied. After all, the move to a consumption tax was likely motivated by a view that it would encourage saving. So where does that leave them? As will be discussed in chapter 4, the macroeconomist takes three steps. First, she constructs a model according to the rules in steps 1–4. Then she assigns numerical values to the variables in the model that are not expected to change with the policy change under consideration. This is done in such a way that the equilibrium of the model thus parameterized matches current data when current tax policy is used. With these parameter values now gleaned from the existing data, the macroeconomist changes the policy for taxes, and then *solves anew* the decision problems of households and firms, locating a new equilibrium. This is how the prediction is obtained. Notice, importantly, this way of proceeding takes account of the fact that when taxes change, so might behavior, and as a result, so might the relationship between tax rates and revenue that used to be a feature of the data.[10]

1.5.4.1 *All* Models Are Susceptible to the Lucas Critique, but Some More Than Others

It is unwarranted to view any model as truly free from the Lucas critique. *All* economists' work, especially the work of macroeconomists, lies somewhere on the continuum between "totally ad hoc" and "totally primitive," with none at the latter end. For example, in our models of consumer decision making, we typically do not model the brain, and even if we do so, it is unlikely that it will be at the molecular level.[11] Nor, for example, do we usually take account, in studies of the likely effects of a previously untried tax policy (of which there are many), of the probability that the change in tax policy might radically change the political landscape in a way that leads to the wholesale replacement of our primarily market-based system with one preferred by a charismatic dictator who doesn't like people with eyeglasses. And so on.

In essence, the tradeoff is as follows. The more ad hoc or reduced-form a model is, the easier it will be to analyze. But such an approach will leave us less comfortable with normative implications and, along with the worry about the Lucas critique, will invalidate any analysis of a novel policy intervention we might use the model for. This tradeoff forces us to select models that have ad hoc elements that we suspect will allow the model to make reasonable predictions in a variety of settings, while not being too prone to making poor predictions when it is used for policy analysis.

In the example of consumer decision making, my willingness as a modeler to ignore brain chemistry means that I will probably be off in my predictions whenever a policy affects the molecular structure of the brain in a way I did not allow for. In terms of our tax example, the original model may simply not have allowed for the chance of widespread rioting and unrest in response to the tax changes, since the data may not have exhibited such features. As a result, the model might not offer good predictions if we changed tax policy radically. On the other hand, questions pertaining to the effects of smaller changes in policies may well be predicted accurately in such a model.

To the extent possible, therefore, macroeconomists want to work with models whose parameters are genuinely likely (on a priori "smell test" grounds) to not be crude proxies for an amalgam of forces that will change easily, either over time or under the changes in policy we want to investigate. However, inoculating one's model against the Lucas critique is, strictly speaking, impossible—the model would have to capture all possible kinds of eventualities, and this would make the model . . . not a model anymore, but rather a perfect, and perfectly unwieldy, mess.

Instead, macroeconomists read the Lucas critique as a persistent and nagging warning that what one is predicting via a model may be dependent on at least some behaviors (summarized by what we call "parameter values") that *will not remain fixed when the policy changes*. It has raised our collective awareness that this effect is always possible, and has helped place tighter limits on us, especially when we want to apply any given model to a question for which it was not initially constructed to shed light on.

1.5.5 Making the Tent Bigger

A last, but extremely important, benefit of the way economics has bound itself to rigid rules for model building (especially its stiff resistance to the admission of irrational behavior or ad hoc expectations) is that, far from making economics the preserve of mathematically well-prepared savants, it is exactly what has broadened participation.[12] Most of all, a strict set of rules allows one to think about *far fewer new things* simultaneously and to utilize knowledge built up from the study of similar models.

1.6 The Benchmark Macroeconomic Model: Arrow-Debreu-McKenzie

The recipe for macroeconomic model building (and to a lesser extent, persuasion) that I spelled out above was created by a long string of brilliant *micro*economists. Their efforts culminated in the 1950s in a series of papers (Arrow and Debreu 1954; Arrow 1951; McKenzie 1954, 1959) that together created the archetypal modern macroeconomic model, known as the ADM model. This model specifies an entire society interacting through a system of interrelated markets, and makes predictions for the entire set of prices associated with the goods and services available for trade, the amount of these that each household in the economy consumes, and the amount produced by all the firms present. Thus, while not a "theory of everything," it is a theory of a whole lot.

Arrow, Debreu, and McKenzie derived several fundamental properties of their model. Of these properties, the most crucial one was that of the existence of equilibrium itself. The creators showed that prices would be guaranteed to exist that equated demand and supply in all markets. This meant that Léon Walras's vision (and indeed Adam Smith's even earlier)—that individuals in a society that is not centrally directed might still be guided by a system of prices to an "orderly" end—was indeed a *logical possibility*, if not an inevitability. (They also proved two other vital properties of the model that I'll introduce a little later.)

In what follows, I will provide a heuristic description of the ADM model and its notion of equilibrium. For those looking for a precise treatment of the ADM model, the canonical graduate microeconomics textbook, that of Mas-Colell, Whinston, and Green (1995, especially ch. 16), is extremely clear. I also suspect readers will find Weintraub (1979) valuable for an innovative pedagogical approach that yields more general perspective.

1.6.1 Understanding the Basic ADM Structure Is a Must

Important reasons for the primacy of the ADM model in macroeconomics are that it provides us with a clear benchmark against which to measure the dysfunction of the real world, and that it unifies nearly all macroeconomic models. By "unifies," I mean that many of the macroeconomic models in use today, while constructed deliberately to understand the effect of *impediments* to trade missing in the ADM model, reduce to the ADM model when these same impediments to trade are removed. This is true even for those models that would seem to constitute significant departures from it, such as the so-called standard incomplete-markets model and the standard overlapping-generations model.

Therefore, whether you are a student, an economic writer, a journalist, a policymaker, or an interested citizen, if you want to understand modern macroeconomics, you have to have passing familiarity with the basic structure and properties of the ADM model and its close variant, the Radner model (to be described later). If you do not know how these models arrange trade and equilibrate competing interests, and do not know the reasons macroeconomists have for believing in the empirical relevance of their implications, you will not be able to follow the arguments of professional macroeconomists. Gaining a useful level of familiarity with all these models may seem demanding, but I do not think it is too difficult for anyone wanting to get it right and willing to exert some effort. Let's start with some jargon.

1.6.2 ADM Terminology

The ADM model features a **finite number** of households and firms, and of **goods** and **services** that are traded in **markets** where all parties face a set of **prices**. "Finite" means that the number of households and firms can each be expressed as a number—e.g., 10—for which *we can find a number bigger than it*—e.g., 11. Of course, finite can be very big; 1 trillion is finite, after all. So a model that describes an artificial world with a finite number of households, firms, and commodities would not seem to be limiting the scope of its applicability too much.[13]

Prices, in turn, are viewed in the ADM model as being set "by the market" and as beyond any individual's power to control.

1.6.2.1   Households: Preferences and Endowments

Each household in the ADM model is described by a **preference ordering** that spells out the rule they use to rank various bundles of goods and services according to their desirability. A preference ordering is said to be **rational** if it has two features: it is **transitive** and **complete**. Rationality in economics means nothing more and nothing less—but what do these terms mean?

An intuitive way of describing transitivity is as follows: if one likes apples more than bananas, and bananas more than pears, then transitivity supposes that one likes apples more than pears. To my taste, this by itself is innocuous. It is the second requirement of rationality that seems to ask a great deal of individuals. This is the assumption that the preference orderings of all consumers is complete. Completeness means that an individual is intellectually capable of comparing *any* two bundles of goods and services, no matter how remote they may be from one's current circumstances or personal experience. For example, "completeness" would require that I be able to tell you whether a bundle of "100 orbits around the earth in a private space vehicle, a séance, and 16 ounces of a traditional Viennese veal-lung stew served eleven years from now on a hot day" is better, worse, or just as good as a bundle of "eight tennis balls, heli-skiing in the Alps, and a guided tour of Hindu temples in North India eight years from now." Moreover, completeness rules out confounding people with complicated choices—as long as they know what's in the two baskets they're asked to compare, anyone assuming completeness is assuming that people will be able to make a ranking. Completeness, especially in a setting like this where a decision maker has to decide what to do over time in conditions of uncertainty, is thus extremely demanding. Simply enumerating all the possibilities, let alone being able to assign anything like odds to them, seems out of reach in many, many settings.

Despite this concern, in chapter 4 I will describe some extremely practical reasons for making the assumption of household rationality anyway. Indeed, in the vast majority of both microeconomic and macroeconomic applications, preferences are restricted not only to being transitive but also to being complete.[14]

In many cases, when using the ADM models, macroeconomists will assume that household preferences satisfy some additional properties beyond rationality: often those of **monotonicity, convexity**, and **local nonsatiation.** Monotonicity just imposes that households always prefer more to less, and as such, implies that they can never get satiated. Here, both the level of aggregation of the good and the time periods described by the model matter. On a given day, for example, I can easily imagine myself getting too full of pecan pie, but less so of food as a whole, and even less of pecan pie in a given year. Convexity asks only that households not prefer extremes—that is, households with convex preferences are creatures of moderation: they prefer to have a mix of commodities over simply consuming just one. As the standard example goes, I'd rather have meat and potatoes than just meat or potatoes. This assumption is more likely to be met in a model that studies broader aggregated categories of goods. With extremely finely differentiated products, it may not closely describe how households might choose.

In many applications, monotonicity for every good or service under consideration is a very strong assumption: surely more is not better when it comes to the garbage created by restaurant kitchens. So it would be nice if economists' main model didn't apply simply to settings where such goods were ruled out at the outset. This is where local nonsatiation comes in. It means almost exactly what its name suggests: irrespective of the particular bundle of commodities that one is evaluating (e.g., one rental house on the beach, ten bananas, and a bicycle), there is always an available alternative that the household likes better that is *arbitrarily close* (hence "local") to the bundle we started with. In other words, your preferences (and the set of items that we can consider) have the property that even if you give me a teeny tiny window to work with, I can always find something you'll like better. This assumption rules out bundles at which households reach nirvana—wanting nothing more or less of *anything*. Local nonsatiation is a very mild requirement to assume about the behavior of households. Its real importance is that it is *all* that one needs to prove the so-called First Welfare Theorem, one of two central results that will recur throughout the remainder of the book.

In the ADM model, each household enters the economy with a set of endowments that are the claims to ownership of various goods and stakes in some or all the firms that exist in the economy. For most of us, the only real endowments we have are our time, skills, and our work ethic. We do not typically enter the world holding rich arrays of products that we then take to the dry goods store in exchange for some other rich array of commodities that we consume. As a result, our working lives are a process that economists view as "renting" ourselves (or, more specifically, our time and "human" capital) out to firms at the market prices prevailing for our particular bundle of skills. We, of course, then use the "dollars" (or direct bank deposit, typically) that we get paid at stores where we buy what we need. Some of us do, however, enter life holding ownership claims to firms such as stocks.

1.6.2.2 Firms

In the ADM model, a firm is quite simply a "black box" (i.e., something modeled in an opaque and arguably superficial manner) that combines arrays of some goods (we call these **inputs**) into arrays of other goods (we call these **outputs**). Formally, a firm is literally described by a **production set**, which mathematically describes the set of feasible activities that the firm is capable of. In many, but not all, instances, each of the finite number of firms is described by a set that, like households, satisfies the condition of convexity

Think of an ADM firm as a cookbook: it spells out all the ways in which particular arrays of the goods and services in the economy can be combined to produce other arrays of goods and services. For example, one ADM firm might simply be a cookbook with two pages. On page 1 it tells us that we can combine x hours of labor effort and y units of CPU power to write a book or construct one bicycle, but not both. On page 2 it tells us that another feasible array of output is that we can make ten chicken eggs through a combination of two pounds of feed and a ton of aluminum siding (to house the chickens).

In specifying the initial endowments in an ADM model, one has to list the set of firms and who owns them. Think of things this way: at the initial pretrade time, the economy's households each own a portion of any profits that would arise from using the cookbook they jointly own to produce a profit-maximizing array of outputs given the prices of all goods and services that their book informs them how to use as inputs. It is important not to think of the ADM firm as having inputs of its own. Rather, it is simply an encapsulation of know-how for combining arrays of items (inputs) into other arrays (outputs).

The ADM conception of a firm as a blueprint leads to a broad interpretation of the kinds of firms that exist in the real world. In fact, all
of us own an ADM firm outright. This is the firm whose blueprints are
dictated by whatever knowledge each of us has personally on ways to
combine inputs into outputs. For instance, I have an ADM firm because
there is, in my head, a set of recipes for how to make various things.
This includes one recipe for French toast and one for housecleaning
services. It's no doubt a very bad firm for the production of many
goods and services (including French toast and housecleaning). Of
course, this is also why my personal firm, yours, and almost all others'
remain *inactive* in almost all markets almost all the time: it makes sense,
at the prices we observe, for us to usually not produce using our home-
grown recipes. Of course, at some prices, we do activate our firms:
we might all cook more meals at home if the price of restaurant meals
rise enough in the wake of commercial real estate rent increases,
for example.

Of course, many firms are more traditional than the solo operations
described above. In a traditional firm, the body of knowledge it
holds and the rights to any profits from using the recipes it is defined
by are owned by many households that each have fractional ownership. In these instances, the decision to activate the firm in the production of various items will be dictated in the ADM model by
whatever happens to be profit-maximizing at the prices faced by all
participants.

Clearly, then, the ADM model allows for firms to differ, or not to.
Once time and uncertainty are explicitly modeled, the ADM conception
allows for an almost arbitrarily rich "date- and state-contingent" listing
of what a firm can do. This can include the firm essentially not existing
for many dates, which would be captured by having the ADM firm be
defined such that all input arrays yielded zero for some dates and situations. We can also capture a firm experiencing technological progress,
whereby it could transform a given array of inputs into successively
higher levels of outputs as time passed. And so on. There is also nothing
in the model that precludes a world with a huge number of perfectly
identical firms. Indeed, most modern macroeconomic models have just
this structure. To sum up, each firm is simply a cookbook spelling out
what combinations of inputs and outputs are feasible at what dates
and in what circumstances, and which, if used to produce objects for
sale, will send any profits or losses back to its owners, however many
or few.

1.6.2.3   Profit Maximization

ADM firms are presumed to maximize profits on behalf of their owners.
Profit maximization is perhaps a poor approximation to what complex
organizations really do, even if they try. After all, for some questions
firms are best seen as *alternatives* to markets themselves, arising precisely to overcome various informational and cheating possibilities of
an anonymous price-mediated interface of ADM.[15] This view of firms
is most famously pursued by Oliver Williamson in his 1985 classic *The
Economic Institutions of Capitalism* on "transaction cost economics," and
in the vast literature on the "principal-agent problem" (which I'll say
more about later).

For example, think of the question of what role executive compensation plays in generating excessive risk taking at banks. An ADM model
with firms that faced no problems with financing, or banks modeled
in a limited manner, would provide no insight, because it would fail
to predict that managers would have the contracts we routinely observe
them as having. By contrast, a setting in which the costs of contracting
was in part what gave rise to the kinds of incentive plans for managers
we observe might be more helpful for answering the question.

Nonetheless, at the end of the day, production in most market economies does take place under the aegis of a firm of one sort or another,
and the focus of the ADM model is to incorporate this fact in as simple
a manner as possible. In other words, one can imagine many rich webs
of contracting relationships as the "true" description of a firm without
losing sight of the fact that such a network may still act "like" an ADM
firm well described by its ability to transform inputs into outputs.

For instance, if one were interested in predicting the effects of an
investment tax credit to firms, then as long as within-firm incentive
issues were not paramount for this question, the ADM model's more
spare representation of production and firms would allow the macroeconomist to construct a richer model of the physical investment
process at firms and obtain sensible predictions. In other words, the
ADM model simplifies firms and thus gains tractability, but loses the
ability to analyze any serious questions having to do with the nature
of incentives within organizations. This is a tradeoff, certainly. So, for
now, it is most useful to think of the ADM firm as a book of blueprints,
with each page giving us a specific recipe for one or more objects. I'll
elaborate more on this in chapter 4.

1.6.2.4   Markets and Prices

Let's next consider the actual goods and services in the ADM model that households have rational preferences over and that firms choose to use and produce. Goods and services are said to be **private** if they have the *physical property* that their consumption by one party precludes their consumption by any others, and **public** when one party's consumption does nothing to diminish the services received by another, and when one's consumption *cannot be prevented* from providing consumption to another, whether they want it or not. Tennis balls and haircuts are examples of private goods, while national defense is about as "public" as a commodity gets. In the baseline ADM model, all goods are private.

When every good that anyone is interested in is available for trade, the model exhibits what economists call **complete markets**.[16] In the baseline ADM model, markets are complete. This is a very strong assumption, and chapter 5 will show how a large amount of modern macroeconomics is engaged in understanding the effects of **market incompleteness**.

The nature of goods and services allowed for in the ADM model is exceedingly broad. In the model, *anything* that an individual deems to be relevant for differentiating between what might appear to an outsider to be the same "basic physical good or service" is what determines whether the item in question is indeed different. This means that a complete market is one in which goods and services must be distinguished by a complete description of the circumstances in which they are consumed or produced.

In what follows, I will sometimes refer to all goods and services as **commodities**, with the understanding that this can mean something much broader than what the term encompasses in daily parlance (i.e., a product that cannot be meaningfully distinguished by buyers, such as bales of a given grade of cotton fiber).

Prices in the ADM model are defined in terms of how much of one good must be given up in order to obtain another. Therefore, prices are inherently relative. This is a bit abstract, perhaps. Think of two situations, one in which you have $100 to spend, and in which tennis balls cost $10 a can and basketballs $20 per ball. Now consider another situation, this time in which you have $150 to spend, but where tennis balls cost $15 dollars a can, and basketballs cost $30. Are these two settings actually any different? The obvious answer is no—you can afford exactly the same combinations of basketballs and tennis balls in either world, and so you are no better or worse off in either one relative to the other. In daily experience, we see prices listed in "dollars" and we get paid for our work in "dollars" as well. What the ADM model presumes is that we can see through this situation to the actual rates at which we give up the ability to buy one good in the marketplace when we buy another one good instead. In the previous example, under either situation, what you give up when you buy a basketball is two cans of tennis balls. As a result, in any setting where buyers and sellers are not bamboozled by changes in the units used to measure things, we are free to name all prices in terms of dollars or, more conveniently, all prices relative to each other. When we describe the Walrasian clearinghouse in the next chapter, use whichever of these you find easier to think about.[17]

Prices for goods are said to be **linear** if they are set to a constant per-unit amount, irrespective of how much one chooses to buy or sell. Think of yourself in a grocery store. Although there may be some bulk discounts at times, usually no matter how many bags of potato chips or gallons of gas I buy, I pay the same (or nearly the same) price for the next bag or gallon I might buy. We will say that households and firms act as **price takers** when they inhabit an environment in which (i) there are trading institutions that allow for price-mediated trade, and (ii) households and firms either cannot or *do not act to manipulate* the formation of these prices. In the ADM model, all prices are linear, and all households and firms are price takers. It is Walrasian.

Intuitively, however, price taking in the "real world" is an *outcome*, not a deep feature of a household's or a firm's behavior. For example, do we really think that a single convenience store on the side of a West Texas highway is going to look to see what its counterpart in suburban Dallas is charging for gas, and then mimic this price? Probably not; the rural highway gas station can reasonably be thought to have some market power (Last Chance Gas!) relative to its counterpart in the suburbs. As such, they will think hard about how to set prices to strike a balance between fleecing those willing to pay and losing those who aren't. For the price-taking assumption to make sense, economists envision a setting for competition in which a price is essentially "forced" upon market participants, each of whom has then only to decide how much to sell (firms) or buy (households).[18]

Walrasian prices are a key element of the ADM model. They are defined to be the particular values of linear prices for the set of whatever goods or services are being traded that equate the desired purchases of self-interested, rational-preference-maximizing, price-taking households to the desired production levels of profit-maximizing, price-taking firms.

A **competitive market system** is one in which trading partners interact only *anonymously* via a system of Walrasian prices that are known and taken by all of them as *unchangeable*. The key aspect of this system is its decentralized nature: no participant is assumed to have *any* information about anyone or anything beyond prices and his or her own preferences or production capabilities, and the *only* decision for each consumer and producer is how much of each good or service to purchase or produce, respectively, given the existing prices. The ADM model is just such a system.

A **Walrasian allocation** is a complete description of how much of each good is produced by price-taking firms that maximize their profits at Walrasian prices and is consumed by price-taking households choosing the affordable combination of goods and services they deem best, at these same Walrasian prices. The shorthand term of **Walrasian equilibrium** (WE) (or "competitive" or "price-taking" equilibrium) is then used to describe the pair of Walrasian prices and Walrasian allocations.

1.6.2.5   Pareto Efficiency and the Core

Economists' most central criterion for judging an allocation as being wasteful or not is named after the Italian economist who invented it, Vilfredo Pareto, more than a century ago. It is known as **Pareto efficiency (or Pareto optimality)**. A Pareto-efficient allocation is a complete description of the goods and services consumed by each household and produced by each firm, with the property that there is no conceivable and feasible alternative distribution of goods, services, and production responsibilities in which all households could be made better off. Notice that, starting at a Pareto-optimal allocation, the only way to improve the well-being of one household is at the expense of at least one other one. Thus, if goods were allocated across households in a Pareto-optimal way, no trades would take place between any two households even if they had full freedom to do so: Pareto-optimal allocations "exhaust all gains from trade."

The final piece of terminology is that of the **core** of an economy. In a situation where all individuals have the freedom to decline to trade and are not fooled by the transactions they enter into, no one can end up worse off after trading. If, in addition, communication and the ability to commit to deals with one another were perfect, what would be a "stable" outcome of "free trade"? To answer this, let's first define an allocation of goods and services across people to be in the core of an economy if there is no subgroup that can take its endowments and make all its members better off than they would be by remaining in the proposed allocation. Notice that core allocations are guaranteed to be Pareto-optimal: if they weren't, the entire group could do better! However, not all Pareto-optimal outcomes are in the core; to be in the core is therefore a more demanding requirement. Core allocations are also stable, in the sense that no subgroup, however large or small, could gain by taking its resources, defecting, and making its own members better off.

1.6.2.6   Don't Misunderstand Pareto Efficiency

The historically unfortunate use of the term "efficiency" as part of the phrase "Pareto efficiency" may mislead the reader into viewing the economists' preoccupation with Pareto efficiency as a preoccupation with material wealth or income maximization. Nothing of the kind is true.[19] Pareto efficiency in no way refers to a "mechanistic" property of outcomes. It does not inherently require, prescribe, or elevate outcomes that feature the maximization of wealth, income, output, or work hours over ones that prize equality or leisure. Rather, for an outcome to be Pareto-optimal, it must be feasible, and it must respect the *preferences* of the individual consumers present in the economy. Therefore, *all* aspects of individuals' attitudes, such as their attitudes toward risk, work, present and future rewards, and *each other* (such as envy), are relevant for determining the extent to which outcomes are Pareto-optimal or Pareto-efficient.

Pareto efficiency simply asks: In the current state of affairs, are there any trades between any members of a society that would leave some better off, *as seen through the (possibility extremely idiosyncratic) lens of each trader's own personal preferences,* and leave no one worse off? If so, we have a found an outcome that **Pareto-dominates** the one we're at, and so we are *not* at a Pareto-efficient outcome. On the other hand, if no reshuffling of goods or services, or commitments to future provisions of the same can improve the lot of some (where, again, "improve" is exactly as defined by each person present in the economy) without hurting others, society has found a Pareto-efficient outcome. So if it helps, think of a Pareto-efficient outcome as one from which there exists no Pareto-dominant move.

Two final points are worth emphasizing. First, Pareto efficiency is a property of allocations. Its definition depends in no way on any particular trading system. Second, Pareto optimality does not imply equitable outcomes. In fact, profoundly unequal outcomes can meet the standard for Pareto optimality. For example, in a world where all people like "more better than less," giving everything to one person (and nothing to anyone else) leads to an outcome that is Pareto-optimal! Nonetheless, the standard of Pareto efficiency is not so weak, especially when, as in real life, society has many people and many goods and services, and where people differ in both their preferences and endowments of these items. That is, in many settings most outcomes will *not* satisfy Pareto efficiency, and so it is a standard that, in many practical cases, meaningfully restricts outcomes. Lastly, even if one asks that outcomes satisfy additional standards beyond Pareto optimality, such as a minimal level of equality, asking for less is hard to justify: if all can be made better off, why not do so?

Chapters 3 and 5 will cover some of what is known about the nature of the conflict between equity and efficiency. In chapter 3, we will see that both under ideal conditions and sometimes under realistic ones, the goals of efficiency and equity are not perpetually in conflict. In fact, they are sometimes even complementary. As a result, the study of the approximation of Pareto-optimal outcomes remains of fundamental importance, even for those interested primarily in ensuring equitable outcomes. And in chapter 5, I will showcase modern models, called "standard incomplete-market models," that allow macroeconomists to make more precise statements about the extent to which inequality is not efficient and the effects that various public policies might have on inequality and its evolution.

1.6.3   The ADM Model: An Example and a Picture

To illustrate a macroeconomic model from soup to nuts, let's now study an economy using a graphical tool called an **Edgeworth box**. As the leading economic theory textbook of the day, that of Mas-Colell, Whinston, and Green (1995), emphasizes, "there are virtually no phenomena or properties of 'general-equilibrium exchange economies' that cannot be depicted in it." As will be clear by the end of this book, "general-equilibrium economies" are indeed the backbone of macroeconomics, and the "exchange" variety consist of a simpler version that nonetheless is useful in organizing one's thinking.[20]

Noneconomists: persevere here, and work through this example. It will help you understand what we macroeconomists do for a living better than almost all the writing I am doing now. Think of a society that is very simple: there are just two goods, corn and wheat, and just two people, Josef and Jaco, who are farmers. Let's visit these two farmers just after they've each harvested the year's crop, and let's assume for simplicity that it's the last year in which they'll exist (an asteroid is en route), so that we needn't worry about any interaction between these two after this year. Both have grown wheat and corn, and both desire both corn and wheat because they both like tortillas and pancakes, and nothing else. Thus, a complete set of markets requires that two markets be open: one for corn and one for wheat. In any given year, there may be room for them to swap one product for the other with each other—for example, if one of them grew a lot of corn and not a lot of wheat, and the other the reverse.

To figure out what is feasible for the final outcome of trading, we simply add up the total amount of corn that each produces, and the total amount of wheat. If, for example, Josef grew nine bushels of corn and four bushels of wheat, while Jaco grew five bushels of corn and seven bushels of wheat, we could draw a box that was eleven bushels of wheat "long," and fourteen bushels of corn "tall." We see a general picture in figure 1.1. Now, let's represent each farmer's willingness to swap corn for wheat (or vice versa). Point E in the figure is the endowment point, to signify that the parties start with these resources. Notice how our box lets us describe how much each farmer has of each good with just a single point; just measure, starting from the origin, to see what Jaco gets and from the northeast corner to see what Josef gets.

We can now ask about all the other combinations of corn and wheat each would like just as much as any given bundle. If we collect all these points, we get a curved line for each, called an **indifference curve**. Jaco's indifference curve is a dashed line and Josef's is dotted. They're curved this way because each farmer is a normal sort of guy: the more of something he has, the more he'd give of that item to get some more of the other item. Now look over at the straight line that separates the two indifference curves that touch at point A, and goes right through E. This is a line that would tell each farmer the set of bundles he could get if he could sell or buy corn at a price of P_c. The slope of the line tells each farmer how many bushels of wheat it costs to get a bushel of

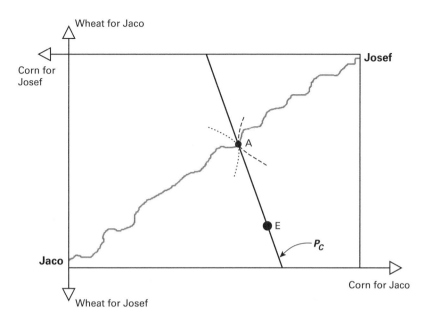

Figure 1.1
The Edgeworth box and Walrasian equilibrium.

corn, and so is given by $-P_c$. Notice that the price of corn is expressed in terms of how much wheat you have to give up in order to get it. We could name both corn and wheat prices in "dollars," as long as we recognized that what these farmers ought to care about is only the rate at which one good can be swapped for another. In other words, these farmers wouldn't see any difference between a world in which corn was $10 per bushel and wheat $5 per bushel, or if corn was $2 and wheat $1.

Let's now assume that the marketplace determines the relative price of corn in terms of wheat, denoted by P_c, that both farmers take as given (i.e., as beyond their control). What will happen? Both Josef and Jaco will choose point A. A is what we mean by Walrasian equilibrium. Why? First, because both parties are optimizing taking prices as given; A is the best bundle they can each afford, starting from what they brought in. Any bundle to the northeast is unaffordable to Jaco, and since more is better, any bundle that didn't lie on the line could be improved on for Jaco by a bundle to the northeast that was still affordable. Ditto for Josef, with the word "southwest" replacing "northeast." Second, A represents Walrasian equilibrium because point A is certainly something feasible since it's inside the box. And that's all we require.

Keep in mind that this example only had two people—so they probably would each try to manipulate the price that came out. But it's better to think of the box as representing many identical farmers of each type. As long as there are many and real-world markets work *as if* there's a WCH, we'll locate Walrasian outcomes. With many people, and many different types, we'd have a hard time drawing the box: it would be a cube with three farmers, and a hypercube with more. But the point would remain the same.

So we've taken information about all the members of a society (as represented by these two farmers) and used that information to predict the prices of all the commodities in the society, and to predict just how much of each commodity each household ends up with (yes, there were only two, but still). While I abstracted from the production process here, mainly because it clutters the picture, it too can be accommodated with conceptual ease. The ADM Walrasian model is thus hugely ambitious: it is a theory of just about everything that really matters in economics, and offers predictions in exactly the same sense for *any* society, no matter how rich or diverse.

1.7   Concluding Remarks

In chapter 1, I have spelled out the way in which macroeconomists structure discussions with each other in order to arrive at conclusions. I have described the key ingredients of the benchmark macroeconomic model—that of Arrow, Debreu, and McKenzie (ADM)—and have worked an example. I now turn to the insights that the ADM model offers on the relationship between Walrasian equilibria and the measures of the desirability and stability, respectively, of Pareto efficiency and the core.

2   Prices, Efficiency, and Macroeconomics

2.1   Introduction

In the course of this chapter, I'll describe two of the three most influential findings economics has yet provided. The first is known as the First Fundamental Theorem of Welfare Economics, or the "invisible-hand" theorem. According to this theorem, in an economy where all goods and services are available at Walrasian prices, the choices of preference-maximizing consumers and profit-maximizing firms, taking these prices as given, will generate outcomes that are Pareto-optimal and in the core. Importantly, the result holds even if consumers are entirely self-interested, caring only about the bundle of goods and services they consume. The second result is that Walrasian prices exist very generally. I will then describe the relevance and limitations of these two results for interpreting "real-world" macroeconomic outcomes, especially as informed by theoretical and experimental work that does not simply presume that Walrasian prices will be available to all participants, or that they will be taken as given.

In chapter 1, I laid out the rules of the game for macroeconomic model building, and then described the benchmark Arrow-Debreu-McKenzie (ADM) model. I'll now describe how this model informs macroeconomists trying to interpret observed outcomes, especially through the central role it gives to Walrasian prices. It is important to recognize that the ADM model *presumes* the presence of Walrasian prices, but it does not spell out how such prices are arrived at. This was done once already, in the example of Jaco and Josef facing a price of corn in the last chapter that the "market" somehow confronted these two with. So let's start by being very literal-minded and consider one hypothetical procedure through which society might actually establish a set of Walrasian prices.

2.2   A Fanciful Macroeconomic Trading Institution: The Walrasian Clearinghouse

Consider a society in which all households and firms are as in the ADM model, and assume that all buyers and sellers are anonymous. That is, no household knows anything about other households' preferences and endowments, nor about any firm's capabilities other than the ones in which they have an ownership stake. Similarly, no firm knows any household's preferences, nor do its managers necessarily know any other firm's capabilities.[1] Now consider the following institutional arrangement for trade, which we'll call the Walrasian clearinghouse, or WCH.

1. All households and firms are in a setting in which the *only* way for them to trade with each other is through a single "clearinghouse." Think of this clearinghouse as a giant department store in the city center. Its task will be to purchase goods and services from sellers, stick a price tag on them, and then open its doors to buyers. For concreteness, think of firms as selling directly to the clearinghouse.

2. The goal of the clearinghouse is to locate Walrasian prices: this giant department store wants to find prices such that, if households and firms took them as given, the total amount that households wanted to buy would equal the total amount that firms wanted to supply. It will set prices for *every* good or service that even just one household cares about. Thus, the WCH features complete markets, and is a clearly *macroeconomic* trading institution in its scope.

3. The clearinghouse has no access to outside resources. It therefore cannot sell more to buyers than the firms collectively want to sell. Assume next that it faces prohibitive storage costs, so it will not offer to buy more from firms than buyers collectively want to buy.

4. To find Walrasian prices, the clearinghouse asks all firms to report the amount of each good and service they would like to produce in the hypothetical event that they were allowed to sell *any* level of output they wished at a given set of linear prices—call it P—and to do so for *all* possible linear prices. Analogously, the clearinghouse asks all households to report the amount of each good and service they would like to purchase or sell in the hypothetical event that they could do so at a given set of linear prices P, and to do so for *all* possible linear prices.[2] Think of the simplest demand-supply model you may have seen, as

this step just allows us to construct the demand and supply curves that we typically draw. Here, however, it is the demand and supply for *all* goods and services.

5. Assume that individual buyers and sellers *believe* that their actions do not matter for the eventual prices set by the clearinghouse—households and firms act as "price takers." Thus, the WCH is a competitive market system where all participants will truthfully report their desired demands and supplies (and in particular will certainly do so if they expect all others to).[3]

6. The clearinghouse then uses households' and firms' truthfully reported demand and supply behavior to locate a set of prices, one for each good, such that the demand for each good by all households is equal to (or no more than) the supply of that good by all firms. If it can locate such a set of prices, these are, by definition, Walrasian prices for the economy. Call these prices P^*. The clearinghouse then announces to all households and firms that it stands ready to sell and buy at P^*.

7. **Production:** Households then go to work, and rent out any capital equipment (e.g., machines) they own to the firms at the P^*, and sell any other items they wish (at the prices announced) to the clearinghouse.[4] Firms then use the labor and equipment they've hired to produce an array of commodities.

If it helps, think of it this way: The clearinghouse gives anyone or any firm who sells it something credits (think of these as just like dollar bills) determined by the prices it announces. For example, in a world with only apples and oranges, if the clearinghouse had located Walrasian prices for apples at $10 a bushel and oranges at $8 a bushel, and firms grew 100 bushels of each, the clearinghouse would pay out $1,800 in credits to firms, which would then pay their workers and shareholders in the form of credits with the clearinghouse.

8. **Spending:** The clearinghouse then stocks its shelves full of the products they just acquired from households and firms, and sticks the Walrasian price tags on each item it has acquired. Households go shopping and choose what they like best, given their budget. Since all trade took place at Walrasian prices, all households and firms will find themselves able to buy or sell the bundle that they find optimal at the announced prices, and will do so.

9. Everyone goes home.

2.3 Why Is This Trading Process Interesting?

Why is a WCH of any interest at all? After all, for all we know so far, it is simply one recipe for locating Walrasian prices, and a weird one at that. It clearly does not much resemble markets most of us have contact with. In particular, unlike daily life, it is hypercentralized, in that all conceivable goods and services are considered, prices constructed, and all markets are cleared *simultaneously*. What a wild department store: it would sell haircuts, soap, guns, furniture, appliances, cars, industrial equipment, gold, wheat, oil, chemicals, and anything else you might think of.[5]

The apparent lack of information flows between participants should also lead one to worry about the ability of this institution, or any competitive market system for that matter, to help all parties locate and consummate even a minority of all mutually beneficial buying and selling opportunities. This concern should be especially heightened in the arena in which we used the WCH—that of an economy in which traders are both anonymous and *so numerous* that they all take prices as beyond their ability to manipulate. After all, in any large society there will likely be vast differences across members in preferences, endowments, and, especially, knowledge of production methods for various goods and services. As such, just leaving traders alone to do what's privately best for them, in a system where the only thing they see are themselves and Walrasian prices that they take as given, would seem a poor candidate for a scheme to allocate resources well.

And yet it should be acknowledged that the WCH does capture *some* features of real-world trade, especially in modern advanced economies, but even elsewhere. Most importantly, it makes explicit use of linear prices that market participants feel they have no power to change, facilitates trade without much (or any!) direct communication between buyers and sellers, and, if it was used daily, would yield an outcome in which prolonged gluts or shortages would not be seen. So I hope we agree that locating Walrasian prices would be a big deal, simply from the perspective that they allow for "workable" outcomes in large and complex societies.

But is there any *more* that we can say about Walrasian outcomes than this? That is, if I saw a society in which meaningful linear prices prevailed for all the goods and services anyone cared about, and I thought that households were sensible (rational) in their choices, that firms were greedy (profit maximizers), and that members of each group made decisions solely on the basis of prices and without any knowledge of anyone else's preferences or capabilities, could I conclude anything in addition to noting how orderly outcomes were? The answer is yes.

2.3.1   The First Welfare Theorem

In what may be the most remarkable finding economics has yet provided, the **First Welfare Theorem** (also known as the "invisible-hand" theorem) tells us that if a society were composed of rational price-taking households and price-taking, profit-maximizing firms, then *competitive market systems with complete markets—such as the WCH above—generate Pareto-optimal outcomes that, furthermore, lie in the core.* Thus, despite their individual ignorance or even complete disregard for the well-being of all others, households and firms are led collectively by Walrasian price signals to an outcome in which not a single forgone opportunity for making *everyone* better off remains: any additional improvements for one member will have to come at the expense of another.

The fact that Walrasian outcomes are in the core is an important indicator of their stability, and a key strengthening of the more limited stability that comes with a Pareto-optimal allocation that is not in the core. Recall that outcomes in the core are ones where no subgroup, however large or small, can take only their endowments and make their members better off. The punch line: if households and firms have enough information to arrange the coalitions imagined by the core, then once we located a Walrasian outcome, no subgroup, however large or small, would be willing to remove itself from the rest of society, taking only their endowments with them.[6]

Remarkably, the coordinating power of Walrasian prices that are taken as given will prevail irrespective of how many participants there are, or how different they are in their preferences for, or in their ability to produce, goods and services. In the proof of the First Welfare Theorem, one sees (rigorously) that a central part of the argument is that all parties face a common set of Walrasian prices which they take as given. The proof is straightforward and, beyond complete markets and optimizing behavior, depends only on the local nonsatiation of consumers, and not at all on the behavior of producers. The assumption needed is that consumers' preferences are such that one can always make them better off no matter how small a distance from the status quo bundle one is forced to search—i.e., there is no "local satiation."

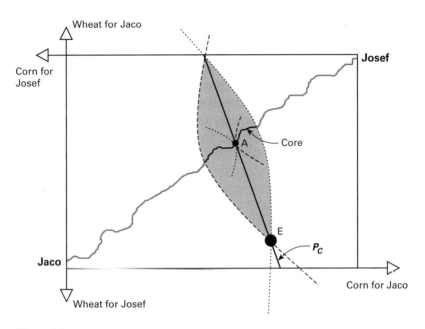

Figure 2.1
The First Welfare Theorem.

Given this condition, we can be assured that consumers will trade to a Pareto-optimal allocation that, furthermore, lies in the core.

Let's revisit Farmer Josef and Farmer Jaco from chapter 1, and look at a slightly modified version of figure 1.1, shown in figure 2.1. First, notice the thin gray line, which represents all Pareto-optimal allocations that exist for the world of these two farmers. The thin gray line, however, contains only Pareto optima that are not in the shaded area. They are Pareto optima that could not arise from these two farmers meeting to trade, because one of them would always be better off by staying home. Why? Because the indifference curves that go through those points will represent bundles that are worse than the one that goes through the initial endowment for at least one of them. One segment of this line is black: it represents all the Pareto optima that also leave *both* farmers better off than how they started—and neither could achieve this point by themselves with their endowments alone. The black segment is therefore the core.

With this in mind, consider point A: it was the Walrasian outcome we looked at before. Since the indifference curves touch at this point, there is no shaded area defined by point A, which immediately means that A is a Pareto-optimal point. However, because it is a Pareto-optimal outcome that also lies inside the shaded area defined by the farmers' indifference curves through point E, it is in the core. And with that, we've illustrated the First Welfare Theorem: complete-market Walrasian equilibria are Pareto optima that lie in the core.

2.3.2 Why Are Walrasian Outcomes So "Coordinated"? Some Intuitions

We know *by definition* that in any Walrasian outcome, the amount demanded by households will be no greater than the amount supplied by firms. Thus, it is ensured that the diverse plans of the myriad households and firms involved in this market will be collectively "workable." Next, each household, if it purchases a good at all, will (under some mild conditions) purchase an amount such that the value of an *additional* unit is just equal to the price, no more and no less. If the household did not do this, it could improve its well-being by altering its purchases. Since all households face the same prices, the preceding logic tells us that they will *all place identical value on an additional unit of each and every good*. This means immediately that there is no way a well-meaning planner could reassign any collection of goods from one household to another and improve everyone's welfare—*even* if the planner knew everyone's preferences, which of course is completely impractical. This is the sense in which the distribution of whatever is produced occurs as if guided by a benevolent "invisible hand."

As for producers, profit-maximizing behavior will (again under mild conditions) lead all firms that produce at all to choose to produce a quantity at which the cost of an additional unit of output (so-called marginal cost) is equal to the benefit from producing one more unit—which is given simply by the price that output will fetch. Since all firms face the same price for their outputs, competitive industries will be ones (as long as output can be adjusted smoothly) in which *all firms' marginal costs will be the same*. But what is so special about situations where marginal costs across firms are identical? Just as with marginal benefits for consumers, such a situation is one in which it would be impossible for even an all-knowing and benevolent "social planner" to reassign production responsibilities in a manner that would generate the same level of output using less resources. This is the sense in which the production of goods and services occurs as if guided by an "invisible hand" even when no firm is assumed to know or even consider the capabilities of any other.

Let's bring the preceding facts together in the context of any single good, say kerosene. In a Walrasian equilibrium, all buyers and sellers will face the same price, call it P_k. After choosing optimally, there will be no household in the economy that values an additional ounce of kerosene at more than P_k, and no firm in the economy that faces a cost of producing an additional ounce of kerosene of less than P_k. As a result, there are no mutual gains from further production and trade: there is no firm willing to produce an additional unit of the kerosene at a price that any consumer is willing to pay for one more unit of it. And this is true for *every* good! As a result, we can say that the "right" (in the Pareto sense) levels or "mix" of the myriad goods and services valued by consumers and producers has been produced as well.

On the production side, three additional points are worth noting. First, in the short run, the firms active in an industry may differ significantly from each other in their ability to produce. However, when all firms face the same price for the products they make and maximize profits, firms that are relatively more productive will generally find that the production level at which marginal cost reaches the price at which they can sell output is *larger* than that of their less productive counterparts. As a result, price-taking profit maximizers ensure, entirely inadvertently, that inputs flow very naturally into the hands of the most productive. Slightly more formally, the logic is this. Under plausible conditions, profit maximization by any single firm implies a technologically efficient production choice for it. This means that no firm that maximizes profits can find a way to produce at least as much of every good, and more of some, *without using more* of at least one other good.

Second, in the longer run, some firms may choose to exit and others may choose to enter any given industry. When entry is free, it can be shown fairly easily that the only sustainable long-run outcome is for all firms to produce a quantity that minimizes the long-run average cost of the *most* efficient of all firms. Thus, in the long run, as long as there are "enough" firms with access to efficient production methods, output is produced in the cheapest possible way, and consumers pay no more than this cost because producers cannot extract pure profits for themselves.

Third, under weak conditions, it will also be true that the profits generated by adding up the profits of all the firms in an industry, acting independently (i.e., with no communication whatsoever between them), will be exactly *as if* someone had access to all firms' production capabilities, and deliberately chose a production to maximize aggregate profits from the outset. In other words, an industry of price-taking, profit-maximizing firms will *look* as if it had set out to solve the profit maximization of a fictitious single firm that embodies the entire economy's production capabilities. Of course, no one *is* doing any such thing! Immediately, then, by the earlier logic, we know that the industry has chosen something technologically efficient *for the economy as a whole*.

2.3.3 The Incentival Role of Prices

One often hears the expression that "economics is all about *incentives*." What, then, are the incentive-related properties of the ADM model? The answer lies in the fact that in any Walrasian setting, participants take prices as given, and indirectly, in the fact that the ADM model makes the behavioral assumption that firms act to maximize profits. As for the first reason, price taking means buyers and sellers work under the presumption that the marketplace has the commitment to pay for, and charge for, *only* what was produced, no more or less. Firms in the ADM model, for example, won't get paid if they decide today to produce no goods or services, and this clearly incentivizes them to consider producing if they wish to maximize profits. Moreover, items or services will be paid for according to buyers' valuation of their characteristics. In the ADM model, a car with square wheels cannot generally be sold for as much as one with round wheels. Therefore, if they both cost the same amount to make, then production of the square-wheeled car would not be as profitable as production of the round-wheeled car would be. As a result, ADM firms, like their real-world counterparts in well-functioning modern economies, do not wish to make items that no one wants. Correspondingly, ADM presumes that firms can and will charge consumers for any resources they use: there is no question, for example, of running your air-conditioner all day, and then not paying for the electricity when the bill arrives.

Similarly, in standard microeconomic examples, one often notes that protracted supply disruptions are rare in market economies, due to prices. Say a storm has damaged a city's water filtration plant. Upon seeing something fundamental like this occur, buyers and sellers form expectations of future prices for relevant goods and services such as, say, bottled water, and then act on the basis of these forecasts. In the short run, it can be sensible for all sides to expect even *perfectly competitive* prices to be high: it may take unusual time and effort to deliver water, with nearby bottlers facing constraints on production: think of fallen trees destroying a local bottling plant. Moreover, the population might be uniformly desperate for water. But these forecasts imply immediate *incentives* for both sides of the market that put downward pressure on *longer-run* prices. Why? Because expectations of high prices incentivize buyers to conserve and sellers to produce.

As a result, barring impediments to raising bottled water production at the level of the economy as a whole, longer-run forecasts of high prices for bottled water would not be so sensible: the incentives such a forecast would create would lead to outcomes that rendered the forecast incorrect. To be pedantic, think of the incentives of producers and consumers in a world where prices of bottled water were expected to remain extremely high for a very long time. Under price-taking behavior, firms all over the local, regional, national, or even international economy, would perceive a profit opportunity from producing more bottled water and sending it to the affected town. As a result, the availability and prices of bottled water would return to pre-storm levels "quickly" even if the local bottler remains closed indefinitely—making this forecast wrong. In a world where the uncertain elements in the environment were themselves "stable"—in the sense that storms were frequent occurrences, and so gave suppliers experience with prices in their wake—we would not expect post-storm price forecasts by water producers to routinely be far off. And when they are forecasted correctly, prices ensure that resources do not either fail to be allocated where valuable or get allocated where they are already plentiful.

In this sense, prices that are forced upon buyers and sellers provide very sharp incentives for them to use resources mindfully.[7] A price that is taken as given is a commitment to reward a supplier and a commitment to extract payment from a buyer. By contrast, notice that many real-life institutions do not have the market's commitment to reward or withhold payment for poor performance: think of a family's unwillingness to excommunicate a member for bad behavior, or even a manager who has a tough time firing nonperforming employees.[8] In the ADM model, by contrast, it is simply *presumed* that owners can implement profit-maximizing production plans using just the linear prices in the marketplace. But this is clearly often different from practice: paying the manager per hour might yield poor results relative to a scheme that paid him such compensation as a "wage plus bonus" contract, or some other more complex arrangement. Keep this in mind for later.

An important complication that real-world decision makers face, and one that can be shown to be consistent with the more complex kinds of contractual arrangements one sees, is the presence of **asymmetric information**. For example, in many settings, real-world firm owners must motivate managers and workers to work when they cannot freely observe the actions of these other groups. This is the famous "principal-agent problem," which I will discuss later when we talk about mechanism design, which is part of the general study of incentive provision under asymmetric information.[9]

To sum up, note that while the ADM model says nothing explicitly about the key buzzword of "incentives," they are there: price taking and the presumption that firms act to maximize profits yield an environment of "pay only for performance" and "performance only for pay." Incentives in the ADM model thus hide in plain sight.

2.3.4   The Informational Role of Prices

Macroeconomists are frequently asked by our employers whether prices (especially asset prices) are "right." (In chapter 6, this issue will surface in the context of "bubble detection.") Aside from the direct incentives they provide, prices are viewed by economists as being important for two additional reasons: first, because prices may be thought of as aggregating or *coordinating* the use of an enormous amount of information that is initially very dispersed; and second, because they may *transmit* this information across participants.

2.3.4.1   Prices as *Aggregators* of Information

Consider the production and allocation of a standard type of good, say, a plain-vanilla barstool used in many airport bars. Now think of a WCH (or just an auction, as is often held in the real world) being operated to allow trade in these barstools. Imagine that there are many active and potentially active furniture makers, and that the industry as a whole uses only a small fraction of the world's supply of steel and wood. As a result, these producers take all prices (for the barstools they'll make, and for all the inputs they'll use) as beyond their ability to manipulate.

To start, notice there are likely to be many types of laborers involved in the production of barstools, such as carpenters, lathe operators, forklift drivers, etc. There are also many possible input materials, and many different possible production processes. Importantly, the myriad ways in which various inputs can be *substituted* for each other in barstool production is knowledge that can only be acquired through experience in the field.[10]

In our WCH, each furniture maker will, at various prices, carefully consider all the ways in which inputs can be substituted for each other. If, for example, walnut is particularly expensive relative to oak, and oak can easily be substituted for walnut because it won't also necessitate the use of harder-tipped and more expensive saw blades, for instance, the oak will be used. In this way, the experience and almost-inevitably accumulated wisdom of those who have *specialized* in the production of any given product are brought to bear fully in the industry's use of inputs even though no firms are assumed to communicate with any others within the industry.[11] The net effect of production choices by price-taking profit maximizers is that given the fundamentals of an economy (the preferences, endowments, and varying technological knowledge of the firms present), the *entire industry* acts exactly like a single firm that knows the efficient constellation of inputs for any level of production.[12] That this occurs despite the firms' being uninterested in each other's well-being gives a clear sense in which a system of Walrasian prices leads to the exploitation of much of society's vast repository of *initially* privately held information, in this case on barstool production.

All of the preceding discussion can be applied analogously to consumers. Consumers also have deep knowledge of the possibilities for substitution among the various goods and services dictated by their preferences. In turn, market prices will reflect the aggregation of such knowledge. In our example, the consumer is the owners of airport bars. As long as they seek to make themselves better off while taking prices as given, they will consider carefully all the ways in which furniture at various prices can be substituted for the huge variety of other goods and services they could potentially buy instead in their pursuit of profits. For example, a firm that owns bars in several concourses of a busy airport may decide to have more chairs in some places than others, and to replace them more frequently, and will have a keen sense of how keeping customers standing will hurt their business. As a result, their collective market demands at various prices will reflect choices that, in turn, reflect such knowledge.

Moreover, notice that when *input* prices are taken as given, even a pure monopolist is nudged toward nonwasteful production methods. Think of a world in which all barstools are made by one firm alone, and where this firm is protected from competition by a patent on barstools. This entity will, just like any competitive firm, seek to use those inputs efficiently in ways that reflect any knowledge it has on how inputs may be conserved. After all, all else being equal, this behavior will earn it even more profits.[13] In this sense, to the extent that many raw materials in modern economies are "commodities" in the marketing sense of the term (i.e., are utterly homogenous goods for which buyers do not care who the seller or producer is), the "production side" of the economy can be viewed as a machine dedicated to (production-side-, which does not imply Pareto-) efficiency.

Prices and the Size of Messages

Recall that a narrow view of the First Welfare Theorem is that it is simply a mathematical fact about Walrasian prices that are taken as given. As such, it need not have any connections to "markets"—after all, for all we know, the prices could come from a centralized (e.g., government) entity. In this view, holding entirely aside the question of how exactly one constructs the Walrasian prices themselves, what is remarkable is just how little each member of the society would have to know to take actions that, collectively, yield a Pareto optimum.

Can we do better than using Walrasian prices? The answer turns out, in substantial generality, to be no. In a series of papers, Leonid Hurwicz (later a Nobel Prize winner), Kenneth Mount, Stanley Reiter, and others worked to answer this question. They asked, roughly: What is the minimal "amount" of the *information* needed to ensure a Pareto-optimal outcome occurs? The seminal papers of Hurwicz (1960) and Mount and Reiter (1974), among others, established in related settings that in a very precise sense, Walrasian prices required the least informational "storage" requirements of any scheme to lead participants to a Pareto-optimal outcome.[14] This is another sense in which an economist can claim that she is impressed by the power of Walrasian prices to coordinate.

Before moving on, it is worth keeping in mind that the First Welfare Theorem allows society, in principle, a way to attain efficient outcomes *anonymously*; that is, with no governmental authority needed to track or disburse goods and services. This seems useful.

The preceding line of work, like Hayek's, focused exclusively on the *informational* aspects of prices; it set aside all problems having to do with individuals' *incentives* to misrepresent information in a given institutional arrangement for allocating resources. In this sense, this literature can be interpreted as either working with pathologically truth-telling participants or working in settings where incentives to misrepresent are essentially zero—or both. Recall how I assumed earlier in the description of the ADM WCH that there were so many people and firms that one was left with little to no incentive to lie about one's demand and supply in order to manipulate the prices that the WCH ultimately agreed to trade at. This incentive-related problem would later become the central focus of the mechanism design approach.

2.3.4.2   Prices as *Conveyers* of Information

In the preceding, while prices and optimizing behavior led to the use of a vast amount of initially widely dispersed information, let me emphasize again that, at least in spot markets, no one was *learning* anything about anyone else or anything. As the WCH disbanded, and buyers and sellers got into their cars to go home, no one learned the identities of anyone else, their preferences or production capabilities, or anything else at all! So, in this context, we simply cannot meaningfully assert that Walrasian prices have conveyed information across participants.

So what of the excited descriptions one sometimes hears of prices as vital *carriers* of information, of signals? These ideas become particularly relevant in the in the context of financial markets. First, notice that markets exist both for goods and services to be immediately consumed and for claims to future consumption. The former are often called "spot" markets, while the latter are known as "financial" markets. A first point to recognize is that, in the Walrasian model, prices do *not* generally convey any information between spot market participants. In the markets for goods and services, no one learns anything about anyone else's preferences or production capabilities, and yet efficiency can obtain even when all of these remain unknown to all others. Walrasian spot prices, *if* they are taken as given, simply *constrain* all households and lead all firms to choose to consume and produce in a way that results in a Pareto optimum. And yet there is still a sense in which they aggregate information.

The key feature of financial assets is that they cannot themselves be used to produce goods, and cannot be consumed directly: they must be *sold* first in return for the goods the consumer or producer ultimately desires. This immediately means that the value placed by each trader on financial assets depends on how he believes *others* will value them in the future. Moreover, in a setting where all traders may have privately held information that is relevant for the valuation of a good (say, each knows something in advance about the future weather in a market for an agricultural futures contract), each will try to guess all others' information.

One useful formalization of the idea of prices as "transmitters" of information would be to show that the market price of financial assets is (usually) *as if* all traders had all others' information. If this were true, we could assert precisely that prices "aggregate" or "reflect" initially privately held, and widely dispersed, information. To show this, though, it turns out that one needs to be very specific about the way in which people trade.

In the WCH construct used at the outset, we allowed for trade in all goods at the same time. We therefore had no need to speak of financial assets, which are (only) useful because one cannot contract ahead of time for all the goods that one might desire throughout the relevant horizon. Sanford Grossman, Joseph Stiglitz, and others in the 1970s and 1980s developed models that helped us better understand the extent to which financial markets could (or could not) be "informationally efficient" in the sense that prices inevitably reflected initially dispersed information. Among the key ideas was that of "fully revealing prices" (see Grossman 1989). Roughly, Grossman showed that there could be a range of circumstances in which trades occurring through certain market institutions (so-called **limit order** markets, such as those used by major stock exchanges to set opening prices each day) would yield prices that would be the same ones that would emerge from a world in which all agents knew all others' information! The notion of equilibrium in these models is known in the parlance as "rational-expectations equilibrium." For now, the point is that one can construct a clear demonstration of the power of prices to convey information.

Having said this, let me emphasize that for prices to convey information, *the rules for trade matter*. In the real world, then, the question is whether the rules for trade are hospitable to information revelation.

The interested reader should read the review by Kreps, in Kreps (1990). In particular, he notes (in the context of a celebration of Sanford Grossman's work) that "real questions remain" for the extent to which observed trading institutions can implement rational-expectations equilibria. More recently, a growing number of macroeconomists have been studying the *decision* of market participants to become informed about various aspects of their environments, especially when those choices are costly. The interested reader who has some prior knowledge of probability theory and statistics (as well as economics) is referred to Veldkamp (2011), and the references therein. This body of work is further sharpening our views on the way in which information is produced and transmitted, and the way in which we think the rules of trade play a role.

Information, and problems with it, lie at the heart of economists' concerns with market performance. As we'll see in chapters 5 and 6, such problems may well play a dominant role in insurance- and financial-market dysfunction.

2.4   Walrasian Prices Will Exist

While Walrasian prices seem incredibly useful to have, will they ever exist? Economic theorists and mathematicians have, over the past half-century, proved that the answer is that they will,with great generality. Starting in the 1950s, with the work of Arrow, Debreu, and McKenzie, economists began to prove their existence in many different settings. At first, we had the proof that they'd exist in the familiar "commodity space" of n-dimensional Euclidean space. This is a setting where one has a finite list of households, firms, and goods and services. As before, keep in mind that finite doesn't mean "small"; ten trillion is perfectly finite. Since then, economic theorists have proved existence in cases where commodity spaces are allowed to be general enough to much more fully accommodate the open-ended (i.e., infinite) nature of time and the potentially arbitrary (again, infinite) richness of product variety that the basic ADM is capable of approximating.[15]

2.4.1   Time and Uncertainty
It was crucial to extend existence results for the case where outcomes are uncertain and information about the future is slowly revealed over time. This case clearly describes the world we live in. Moreover, for the central variant of the ADM model that is the basis for the practicing

macroeconomist—the "Radner model"—having such a result is downright essential. Radner's trading arrangement is the basic adaptation of the ADM model to allow for repeated trading in response to time and the resolution of uncertainty. In chapter 5, I will discuss at some length a natural way of using markets to allow for the kinds of trades households and firms living in such settings would want to have (these are markets in the so-called Arrow-Debreu contingent commodities). The good news: when such markets are available, the existence theorem and First Welfare Theorem (and Second Welfare Theorem too, as we'll see in chapter 3) carry over *automatically and fully*.

This is a big deal; without saying a single word about the real world, the moral of the "existence of Walrasian equilibria" in these cases might be this: it is remarkable, I think, that something as conceptually simple as a complete set of linear Walrasian prices (that are taken as given by self-interested optimizers) are a device that, in principle, can efficiently reconcile competing interests in a stable manner and in an exceedingly broad array of settings, including those that differ profoundly in their physical, temporal, or stochastic structure—all in the absence of *any* communication between market participants.[16]

The ability, at least in principle, of prices to render orderly outcomes under uncertainty is particularly important for the most traditional parts of macroeconomics that are concerned with booms and recessions. Here, the ADM model suggests that prices can allow the smoothest possible response of the macroeconomy to *changes* in the underlying fundamentals of an economy. It teaches us that when faced with non-manipulable Walrasian prices in the wake of a possibly abrupt and negative change (say, a war or natural disaster), society immediately and inadvertently harnesses (or "aggregates") vast amounts of dispersed and otherwise hard-to-elicit information on substitution possibilities in the service of efficient reorganization of input use by sellers and efficient distribution across buyers. For instance, in the discussion of barstools, think about a tree mold that destroys the main wood used for barstools. At this point, does the knowledge of substitution possibilities again get employed, this time to think about alternative types of wood that might serve well in barstool production?[17] These are things no outsider could have much of an idea about.[18]

2.4.2 Convexity and Existence

A somewhat technical point (and one I'll revisit in chapters 4 and 5) is that in the ADM model, in order to show that Walrasian equilibria exist, it helps that certain objects, such as the production capabilities of firms in the economy or the set of bundles of goods and services that all would prefer to a given outcome, satisfy the property of convexity. We briefly encountered convexity in our discussion in chapter 1 of preferences. Convexity assumptions force, more or less, economists to restrict attention to only those production and preference structures in which everything "intermediate" is possible (for firms) and everything intermediate is preferred (by households). For example, if a firm could feasibly make 100 motorcycles each day, or could make 10 in a given day, then convexity forced the macroeconomist to assume that the firm could also produce any number in between. But the equipment and production process needed for making 100 motorcycles may well differ substantially from those needed to produce only 10, with in-between levels of production being simply infeasible. Or notice that we can't easily obtain a refrigerator that is fully custom-built to the cubic inch. Why is this? For starters, firms may well face increasing returns to scale over some ranges of production because, for example, their workers "learn by doing." As a result, refrigerator makers may well be unwilling to invest in the equipment to make made-to-order refrigerators at a price that is simply a scaled up (or down) version of whatever existing fridges are currently being mass produced. Similarly, households that like either eggs or oatmeal for breakfast probably do not want an egg cracked into their bowl of oatmeal. Thus, convexity seems restrictive. It essentially limits the granularity of the objects being studied to those aggregates for which the assumption of convexity makes sense (e.g., maybe you do prefer mixing eggs and oatmeal: the latter on weekends and the former on school days).

So convexity of firms' production capabilities and households' preferences helps us establish the existence of Walrasian equilibria. However, entirely intuitive or natural ways of describing the motivations and capabilities of households and firms can thus lead, equally naturally, to the inability to produce a given Pareto-optimal outcome via the use of a complete set of Walrasian prices. Contrast this with the extremely easy-to-satisfy requirements on household preferences (local nonsatiation), and the complete absence of requirements on firms' production sets, needed to make the First Welfare Theorem hold. Convexity therefore would appear to limit the value of the Walrasian model as a description of a real world that often seems filled with nonconvexities, even if we wanted to take it only as a narrow assertion about the theoretical reach of Walrasian outcomes (i.e., even if we did not care about any notion of the "real-world" applicability of the result).[19]

It is fortunate, then, that the convexity assumption is actually not very demanding in the places in which price taking would be likely to occur: economies with large numbers of participants. A key fact is that the Second Welfare Theorem asks for the convexity of sets that are themselves the *sum (or average) of other sets*—such as the set describing what is collectively feasible for all individual firms. And, usually, the number of sets being added together (or "averaged") depends directly on the number of households and firms present in one's model of the economy. This is where a result from mathematics comes to our rescue: the **Shapley-Folkmann theorem** tells us that the sums or average of sets, even if they are entirely individually nonconvex, will be approximately convex and will get "more" convex as the number of sets being added or averaged grows.

Note that economies with large numbers of households are the only places, intuitively, where price taking will likely be a sensible strategy for a household or firm. But the Shapley-Folkmann theorem then gives us the convexity we need to invoke (if we could set up complete markets, of course) in order to obtain any efficient allocation. In sum, in essentially any setting in which the price taking already presumed in the ADM model is plausible, we are virtually guaranteed the existence of linear Walrasian prices which, if taken as given, would deliver us a given efficient outcome.

2.5   Decentralized Outcomes and the First Welfare Theorem

Existence does not mean inevitability; the fact that Walrasian prices *can* coordinate trade doesn't mean that they do so in the real world. So far, I've left unanswered something that should strike you as a (the?) key question: Will the real world act like one big WCH? As we'll see further below, there are both good informal and formal reasons to think it will, up to some market incompleteness.

To start, though, let's acknowledge that Pareto-optimal outcomes will generally be hard to find in any direct manner. Most obviously, to the extent that any modern macroeconomy features millions of people who only rarely know anyone else's preferences well, and similar numbers of firms whose technological capabilities for the production of millions of goods and services are known only to (some of) their

owners, the attainment of approximately core Pareto-optimal allocations alone would seem completely out of reach under *either* a planner
or free trade. In fact, the set of Pareto-optimal outcomes is so small
relative to the set of all possible outcomes that if one picked outcomes
at random, one would *never* locate even one.[20]

Thus, in general, a well-meaning planner whose only goal was to
produce and distribute private goods and services according to a point
in the core (and hence to a Pareto-optimal location) faces a seemingly
intractable optimization problem. After all, it would seem impossible
to be able to achieve such an outcome without having detailed knowledge of the statistical *distribution* of the attributes of all consumers
and producers in the population. Moreover, being wrong in even a
few instances could mean disastrous misallocation—think of any case
where the victims placed great value on an item they were not assigned,
while others were assigned these same items but placed little value
on them.

Of course, instead of employing a planner, we could allow individuals to trade "freely," in the sense of not placing restrictions on the ways
in which they may transact. This is unlikely to make them worse off,
and as a result, free trade will probably push us in the direction of
Pareto optimality. Consider an extreme example where a warehouse
full of different goods is initially *randomly* allocated to a population. In
all likelihood, there will now be opportunities for mutually beneficial
trades because some people will have been handed items that they
place little value on, but that others value greatly. Therefore, if allowed,
trade will occur and surely make participants better off.

So the question now is: Will the preceding generate core outcomes?
With even a few goods and many people, it would seem impossible to
find such an outcome, especially in cases where people cannot easily
communicate with each other. What's worse, when trading partners
are few, some will have the ability to drive hard bargains with others.
Think of a single person who owns most of the water in a large but
isolated town. Might this situation prevent efficient outcomes from
happening?

As a general matter, the answer is yes: bargaining under incomplete information about one's trading partners will *not* yield efficient
outcomes. This is the key result of economic theory known as the
Myerson-Satterthwaite theorem, in Myerson and Satterthwaite (1983),
and which we'll see more of later on. For now, note that this result

tells us that whenever any two people trade, if both have privately held information about their valuation of a given item, and can decline to trade altogether, it is actually *impossible* to attain Pareto-efficient outcomes through voluntary trade. Note that this result holds in all settings where buyers and sellers feel they actually have bargaining power.

Nonetheless, one might imagine that as the number of buyers and sellers grows, i.e., as markets get "thick," the inefficiencies associated with bargaining might give way to settings in which most, if not all, participants are "forced" into accepting terms of trade that are set by them collectively, i.e., by the "market." This, as we'll see, is a largely correct intuition, especially for any private (i.e., nonpublic) good. As a result, in large economies, *so long as prices are constructed*, one might expect them to look roughly "Walrasian," and in turn, one might even start to expect decentralized outcomes in large economies to be coordinated and orderly.

So where does this leave us? As Jehle and Reny (2001, p. 187) stress, a fundamental message might be as follows:

Points in the core seem very far indeed from becoming reality in a real-world economy. After all, most of us have little or no direct contact with the vast majority of other consumers. Consequently, one would be quite surprised were there not substantial gains from trade left unrealized, regardless of how the economy were organized—centrally planned, market-based, or otherwise.

Until, that is, one looks at trade organized through a competitive market system in which markets are complete. Moreover, the price taking required for complete-market competitive market systems to deliver core outcomes becomes most plausible in economies with large numbers of households and firms.

As we'll see now, economic theory, as well as experimental evidence, gives us reason to believe that in any thick market, especially any involving purely private goods and services, outcomes *will* be well described as Walrasian. This is remarkable, and its truth should not be obvious to you. Best of all, perhaps, when prices are used explicitly, as they routinely are in our big and complex world, price taking of Walrasian prices can be expected. This gives society a chance to obtain approximately efficient and stable outcomes "for free" exactly when no other method would seem equal to the task—a happy coincidence.

2.5.1　Decentralized Trade Seems to Generate "Workable" Outcomes

A long line of thinkers have commented on the pervasive orderliness of the world in the absence of any central coordinator. The architect of much of twentieth-century economics, Kenneth Arrow, in his Nobel Memorial Lecture (1972), has, for example, described how the "experience of balance [of demand and supply] is so widespread that it raises no intellectual disquiet among laymen; they take it so much for granted that they are not disposed to understand the mechanism by which it occurs," and that while many objections may be raised against free markets, *"sheer unworkability is not one of them"* (emphasis added).[21]

Generations of past economists had conjectured that the fundamental force ensuring order was the pervasive system of meaningful prices they observed in the real world that, moreover, most traders found themselves unable to modify. Prices therefore seemed to be interpretable, without undue strain, as approximately Walrasian (though that moniker would have to wait). With the existence results above, economists validated the logical possibility that prices *alone* could equilibrate all competing interests.

Recall now the extension of the reach of the First Welfare Theorem to cases in which people want to know what others initially know only privately. This illustrates again the aggregating power of linear prices that are taken as given. But, perhaps more importantly, it also shows that in many settings (such as modern-day auction houses and stock exchanges), the construction of trading rules may reflect very deliberate efforts to facilitate the exhaustion of gains from trade and to *limit* the use of privately held information and monopoly power to the advantage of individual traders. Again in the context of mechanism design, economists have begun to evaluate the extent to which a higher level of competition in "trading platforms" (see, e.g., McMillan 1994) among those who facilitate transactions between producers and consumers (often called "market makers") may be an important part of why decentralized trade appears to be so effective.

2.5.2　Decentralized Trade Seems to Centralize (and Locate Ownership) Sensibly

Firms are places where prices are *not* used and where, instead, outcomes are largely planned. So why doesn't this lead to the huge waste and relatively poor performance that it did in places where central planning was widely used? Economists suspect that decentralized competition within societies also does better than any alternatives at centralizing via firms when that is the sensible thing to do. We rarely see restaurants where every waiter's instructions are spelled out to the last iota of precision, with the owner paying a price for each of these actions (number of time increments talking per customer, smiles per customer interaction, etc., etc.). Instead, we find a hierarchical relationship where one party "hires" the right to direct the other in a broad range of actions that will be flexibly defined. Importantly, though, linear prices still are germane: the overall *bundle* of jobs that constitute the job of "waiter services" *is* generally priced linearly. Part of the reason is that labor services are generally seen as being priced competitively—few restaurant owners can dictate the average hourly wage of the time they rent from workers. Competition thus works to constrain the ambit of price-based trade away from areas where it would be foolish (while of course still sometimes failing to prevail in all those places in which it would be useful).

Most of all, perhaps, competitive pressure helps locate "ownership" where it should. Ownership refers to "residual-claimant" status: the owner is the last person to get paid, for worse and for better. When information and commitment to contracts are perfect, ownership is irrelevant; it does not affect how the assets used by the firm are deployed. In financial economics, this point is referred to as the **Modigliani-Miller theorem**, which tells us that in well-functioning settings, the way a firm finances itself is entirely irrelevant to its production decisions. The theorem, along with the fact that capital structure hardly seems irrelevant in the real world, tells us to look for where information, and/or commitments to act as promised, are imperfect. In chapter 6, we'll see how this allows us to account for the pervasive use of "debt," a contractual form that now is in the news as an "amplifier" of financial crises.

This is connected to the "principal-agent problem" mentioned above. Think of how well you might clean your yard, compared to the pressure you might have to place on hired help to get the same result. You're the owner, so if the yard is dirty, it's your problem. Why can't you incentivize a yard worker? You can, but if there is luck involved in the outcome (the wind might blow trash into your yard) that the worker cannot control, then harsh punishments will require higher average pay to get him to accept your offer over those of competitors. This creates a tension between the goals of providing incentives and the need to compensate employees for risk. With perfect information, this tension would be a nonissue. You might now see why asymmetric information can hinder the appearance and function of what would otherwise be competitive markets.[22]

2.5.3 "ADM Minus Some Markets" Seems Like a Useful Description of the Real World

For purely private goods that are not "intertemporal" in nature (i.e., do not involve obligations that stretch out over time), markets look awfully complete and brutally competitive.[23] The proximate source of constraints on consumers and rewards to producers certainly appear to be a mostly linear price system that most regard as beyond their control. If we think of how the bulk of our consumer transactions go, such as our purchase of groceries and other everyday consumer products, and of the pressure felt by employees of firms that must compete in their pricing and services to survive, it is clear that prices and competition are features of the environment.

In addition to this pure impressionism, there is a large body of formal work that, taken as a whole, deepens our confidence that decentralized processes will often lead to Walrasian outcomes. Specifically, this work gives macroeconomists three concrete reasons to suspect that, for goods and services which do not feature the usual difficulties associated with intertemporal trade especially, decentralized trading with any more than a handful of buyers and sellers will be approximately as predicted by the ADM model.

First, a body of pure theory clarifies that Walrasian outcomes are indeed very likely as outcomes of trading between large numbers of traders, almost no matter how they might interact with each other. Second, there is the now-large corpus of experimental results that, interestingly, shows that Walrasian theory works even *better* than our a priori theorizing tells us it should. Third, the overall conclusion one gets from the vast literature on industrial organization is that, with two exceptions, pervasive and important degrees of monopoly or oligopoly power do not play a dominant role in most modern economies most of the time. The exceptions have to do with the select role market power may be playing in the rate of innovation that we think governs long-run growth in living standards, and in the way large or complex financial entities leave taxpayers cornered in crises.

The latter arises from the ability of financial "intermediaries" such as banks, insurance companies, and hedge funds, among others, to become considered "too big to fail" (TBTF). In this case, a very poisonous dynamic arises not just from the size of the entity concerned, but also from the presence of a *benevolent* policymaker unwilling to tolerate collateral damage from the firm's demise. Worst of all, knowing this, firms have incentives to grow big for no reason other than to become TBTF. Preventing TBTF and the corrosive effects on behavior that it generates are big pieces of unfinished business from even the narrow vantage of efficiency, as chapter 6 will describe.

Even if we ignore problems arising from market power, though, there are two other spheres where important dysfunction can arise. These are in the arenas of public goods and insurance or credit markets. Between the technological difficulty of constructing competitive markets for the former (since one cannot exclude nonpayers) and the ability of privately held information to inhibit *insurers and financial markets* from offering coverage or funds for many of the eventualities covered in the ADM model, market completeness is not a good description of the world around us.

As for missing competitive markets, I view the risk to newborns of beginning life in a disadvantaged family as a very big one, and one that is poorly dealt with in most societies. Relatedly, I see incompleteness in the set of financial and insurance commodities compromising households' ability to weather shocks during working life and retirement and where, again, substitute arrangements are not easily available. For instance, a reasonable reading of the now-vast literature on consumption is that while household choices look fairly rational most of the time, they smell of market incompleteness, especially against labor income risk. That is, models of rational decision makers operating in uncertain environments and facing a limited set of markets for intertemporal trade (i.e., limited insurance and credit markets) are able to account for a large proportion of observed behavior on consumption, labor supply, and asset market behavior (see, e.g., the review of Attanasio and Weber 2010). In chapter 5, we'll see that arguably the most prevalent deviation from the ADM model in macroeconomic models of the past two decades has been the allowance for incompleteness in markets for intertemporal trade, such as insurance and credit, rather than any great allowance for irrationality, serious market power, or incompleteness for "spot" market trade.

To sum up: mainstream macroeconomists are justifiably confident in letting *competitive* trade run unconstrained for private goods and services that do not have a significant intertemporal component to them, do not view the world as pervasively monopolized, and do not worry much about consumer and producer irrationality as a source of

aggregate instability. What they do worry a lot about is (i) *"competitive-*
yet-dysfunctional" and *"might-be-competitive-but-can't-exist"* markets
for public goods, insurance, and credit, and (ii) financial entities
growing too big to fail.

2.5.3.1   Externalities as Missing Markets

Missing markets are also connected to a classical source of inefficiency:
externalities. This term refers to outcomes in which some agents end
up "directly" affecting what others consume or produce. Of course, the
only way that agents can't "directly" affect others is if (i) there are a
finite numbers of agents and the trading arrangement somehow *prevents* them from acting "strategically" (i.e., where traders take into
account how their actions map via the institution to constraints on, or
allocations for, others—for example, lying about one's preferences to
manipulate the prices set by the WCH), or (ii) their individual actions
are literally too small to affect anyone else.[24] Otherwise, agents always
affect each other, but in a way that just reflects their power, and not in
a way that we might call "externalities." So with all this in mind, we
can amend a *non-institution-specific* definition of externalities to remove
what we might call "power" to say:

There are externalities when the trading arrangement is such that, even in
the absence of any attempts by agents to take into account how institutions
translate their individual actions to allocations for others (or an inability to
affect how institutions do so), parts or all of some agents' allocations depend
solely on some other agents' choices.

This definition is useful because it covers even cases where agents
individually have no meaningful ability to affect what others end up
with. Now, it turns out that this definition fits very neatly into the idea
that every externality is just a symptom of one or more missing competitive markets. Why? Because the First Welfare Theorem tells us so:
if complete competitive markets yield efficiency, then inefficiency must
imply the absence of these kinds of markets.[25]

**2.6   *Should* the Real World Look Like One in Which Most Trading
Is Run via a WCH, and If So, Why? Theoretical Foundations for
Walrasian Equilibria**

Having described the casual empiricism that motivated so much of
what is now Hall-of-Fame economic theory, let's raise the bar further.

Can economists give us more airtight reasons for connecting large economies to Walrasian ones, especially when we do not want to simply *presume* completeness of markets and the presence of Walrasian prices? As I mentioned earlier, the answer is that they can. Let's start with what should be the elephant in the room. *Where do Walrasian prices come from?*

For a theory of price-based trade, the lack of any explicit treatment of price formation seems ridiculous. Worse yet, in the ADM model, everyone takes prices as given, so who *could* set them anyway? Usually, reference is made to a mythical "Walrasian auctioneer" who runs the WCH. Since there is no such entity, it is important to know whether models that are more explicit about the trading process yield, or approximate, Walrasian outcomes. Moreover, it is important to learn more precisely which features of these environments are most crucial in ensuring, or approximating, Walrasian outcomes. If a wide range of trading processes do so in a wide range of empirically relevant circumstances, we can be confident in using Walrasian equilibrium to make predictions for outcomes, and otherwise, we cannot. In sum, the key question to answer is: Should the real world look like one in which most trading is run via a WCH, and if so, why?

As for the main ingredient, prices, there are many price-forming institutions that operate in the real world. This is especially true in markets for so-called commodities, i.e., goods that are hard to differentiate in a meaningful way. In particular, for agricultural produce, crude oil, metals, and other commodities (and financial assets too), the primary means of price formation and allocation are large auctions, which are likely a proximate source of the prices seen in many sectors in the US and world economy. That is, once prices are formed in these markets, most downstream producers (users of these inputs) have prices they can use, and even if they are not always the perfect price takers imagined by a textbook, these producers are usually viewed as setting their prices in a roughly competitive manner.

As a result, in markets with many buyers and sellers, given their guess about the price that their competitors will charge, firms produce (under mild conditions) such that the marginal cost for their output is usually close to this expected price. And most of the time, most downstream buyers are probably not surprised by the market clearing prices set by the commodity auctions (conditional on the economy's current aggregate state variables), nor are the eventual buyers.

Even though we might not be able to verify perfectly whether a given "real-world" outcome is Walrasian, or nearly so, pure economic theory offers a way out by telling us what the equilibrium outcomes of various trading settings "ought to be." I have suggested that the most essential idea in any notion of equilibrium in economics is that the interactions among individual actors be such that none are persistently surprised by the actions of others or by the evolution of those objects that impinge on their ability to pursue goals.[26] Somewhat more precisely, an equilibrium is a situation in which no one wants to change their behavior, given what they expect others to do, and where these expectations are *proved correct* after the fact. Given this, we can see that Walrasian outcomes are genuine equilibria because they meet this criterion, so long as we make the *assumption* that agents act as price takers.

Recall our earlier definition of price taking as the situation where market participants do not act to manipulate the trading process by which market-clearing prices are formed. In the WCH construct, each household and firm knew that it and all others were reporting truthfully simply because each participant's perceived negligibility ensured that the WCH would locate and allow trade only at the prices which cleared markets. Analogously, in any setting where all decision makers in an economy act as price takers, they believe that they can execute any trade that is within the budget determined by the prices they expect to prevail in the market. Moreover, because each buyer believes that she can always buy from someone at a given price P^*, she would never agree to pay more; and given that each seller believes that she can always sell an item to someone at P^*, she would never accept less than P^*. If the prices are, in turn, Walrasian, then everyone *will* get what she planned on. We thus have a true "equilibrium": given their beliefs, all participants are optimizing, taking as given the actions of all others, and no one's beliefs are disconfirmed by outcomes.

Research on the topic of foundations for Walrasian equilibrium can be divided broadly into three strands: (i) the axiomatic or "cooperative" approach, (ii) the strategic or "noncooperative" approach, and (iii) the experimental approach. Each approach has been important in generating insights, and each has its strengths and weaknesses, which I will touch on briefly further below.

The preceding work generates two conclusions. First, in theoretical settings, "large" and "anonymous" trading institutions generally yield approximately Walrasian outcomes, whether or not prices are explicitly used to mediate transactions. Second, in contrast to the first two approaches, the (now vast) experimental literature suggests strongly that in price-mediated trading arenas, Walrasian outcomes occur in far more than just settings with large numbers of anonymous traders. These two points should provide some comfort to anyone uneasy with the plausibility of Walrasian outcomes as a prediction for allocations, and with when prices are explicitly used for them as well.

2.6.1 The Axiomatic or "Cooperative Game Theory" Approach

Axiomatic approaches are those in which a modeler lays out only a list of conditions that he would consider satisfactory in defining the "stable" outcome of some strategic interaction. For example, the core said nothing at all about how people interact. Instead, it simply asked about what would be left if one looked only at outcomes immune to group defections. The usefulness of this approach is that one doesn't always know what the nature of competition looks like, but one might ask that outcomes, however determined, satisfy conditions that we think would reflect "competitive" interaction. Much of the reasoning of economists, especially when casual, is done in the spirit of the axiomatic approach. For example, we often argue that asset prices should have certain relationships with each other, lest they violate the quality of being "arbitrage-free." In turn, when assets are priced using "no-arbitrage" restrictions, the economist is not modeling or thinking clearly about the nature of competitive interaction within asset markets, but instead is asserting that any "sensible" competitive outcome should be arbitrage-free. This can be a very powerful approach: in the early 1970s, it gave us the famous Black-Scholes option pricing formula.

Returning now to the core, in small economies this fails to rule out many outcomes (i.e., the core is "large"). Nonetheless, we know that Walrasian outcomes are always in the core. Remarkably, in very large economies the converse is approximately true! Specifically, as the number of traders grows, the number of core allocations shrinks, and so "nearly" all core allocations in an economy with many participants will be "close" to a Walrasian equilibrium.[27] The celebrated theorems on core equivalence (Debreu and Scarf 1963, Aumann 1964, Anderson 1978) show that in economies with "many" participants, all core outcomes are approximately *as if* all households optimized with respect to Walrasian prices that they each regarded as beyond their control. The "as if" part is important, and I will explain why in the following section on how one might rightly regard the role played by prices.

2.6.1.1 The Equivalence Principle

Interestingly, other "axiomatic" or "cooperative" solution concepts have also been shown to be equivalent to Walrasian equilibria *in "large" economies*. These include the Shapley value (Aumann 1975); the bargaining set, kernel, and nucleolus, and the Mas-Colell set (Mas-Colell 1989); and the set of fair net trades (Schmeidler and Vind 1972). The Nobel-winning game theorist, economist, and mathematician Robert Aumann (1987) has called the preceding the **equivalence principle** between what he calls "price equilibria" (Walrasian equilibria) and the solutions to more explicitly modeled strategic interaction:

> Perhaps the most remarkable single phenomenon in game and economic theory is the relationship between the price equilibria of a competitive market economy, and all but one of the major solution concepts for the corresponding game. Intuitively, the equivalence principle says that *the institution of market prices arises naturally from the basic forces at work in a market, (almost) no matter what we assume about the way in which these forces work* [emphasis added].

Allocations that are in the core or in the "bargaining set" or that attain the Shapley value of a trading environment with "large" numbers of participants are all *competitive* outcomes in the sense that (i) each agent's resources are "small" relative to the total resources of the economy, (ii) all agents are assumed to be very well informed about each other, and (iii) all agents are able to enter into any binding agreements they find mutually advantageous. Remarkably, therefore, the equivalence principle tells us that the outcomes of trading in settings that we would all agree on as being highly "competitive" *look unavoidably Walrasian*.

2.6.2 The Noncooperative Approach

The equivalence principle teaches us that Walrasian equilibria should give us good predictions for allocations for a variety of underlying competitive trading processes. However, the settings used in cooperative approaches are nearly always ones in which agents are extremely well informed about each other, and furthermore, can bind themselves to agreements effortlessly. What about when most people and firms do *not* know much about each other, and/or cannot stick to agreements so easily? Can we still expect Walrasian prices and outcomes to emerge? After all, widespread anonymity seems to be the empirically relevant case anyway; each of us knows very little about other consumers' preferences, and we know almost nothing about the producers from whom we buy things each day. It turns out that Walrasian equilibrium gives us good predictions for competitive outcomes when market participants make *explicit use of prices* and know very little about each other, too. This idea is formalized in the so-called noncooperative approach to providing foundations for Walrasian equilibria. In a nutshell, it is a research program that explores the extent to which the Nash equilibria—which are the relevant kind in settings where parties have and recognize bargaining power (and which I'll define more fully momentarily)—of a given situation are "similar" to Walrasian equilibria. This is vital in part because the Nash concept is always rational, unlike price taking, and learning when these two concepts approximately coincide is precisely how economists learn what sorts of circumstances are ones where Walrasian outcomes are likely to emerge. So just what is Nash equilibrium?[28]

2.6.2.1 Nash Equilibrium: The Most Important Kind of Equilibrium in Social Science

We have seen Walrasian equilibrium already; it involved all participants taking prices as out of their control, and then simply choosing what would be to them the ideal amount to either purchase (if a consumer) or produce for sale (if a firm). As long as the prices were Walrasian, all parties would be successful in executing their plans, and we'd have a perfectly well-defined equilibrium. Clearly, this is a notion of equilibrium that has no "strategic" elements. The price is the only thing anyone pays attention to, and it is an object that the market *imposes* on an individual decision maker.

By contrast, in some settings each participant may experience having the decisions of *individual* "others" directly impose a constraint on what he can do. Nash equilibrium is the concept that economists use to describe an equilibrium situation where such influence is present. In one sense, it is the "opposite" of Walrasian equilibrium: it asks each participant to be acutely aware of what *every single other* participant is planning to do. An example is a case where there are two identical firms deciding how much to produce *simultaneously* (i.e., without knowledge of the other's choice), where each knows that the total production will be auctioned off at a marketplace. The key aspect of the auction is that it is a trading forum that will establish a single price at which each firm can unload its output, and this price clearly depends on the *sum* of the production decisions of both. In such an environment, there is no doubt that the relative size of each is too large to be ignored—the price that emerges from the auction will surely reflect the actions of each individual firm. Contrast this with the WCH we discussed at the outset, where individual firms were assumed to be too minuscule for their decisions to even be noticed by the "market."

In this setting, then, each firm, seeking only to maximize its own profits, surely has to take into account the level of production that its competitor will choose. We can see right away that each firm could easily have many conjectures about what its competitor will do. But in most of these cases, if the two parties were to actually produce, take their output to the auction, and then learn the price that obtained, they would be incorrect in what they expected their rival to do.

What about the cases where they were each *correct* about what the other firm was going to produce? This is what is called a **Nash equilibrium**. It is a pair of *correct* guesses, one for each firm, about the actions of the other that lead each firm to find the optimal choice of its own production levels to be just what was guessed by its competitors. More precisely, a Nash equilibrium is a "strategy profile" (in this case, a [tacit] "agreement" to a collection of strategies) or, if you will, a *prescription* for behavior, one for each participant, where a *unilateral* departure from the agreement is undesirable for each party (i.e., as long as you think others will stick to the deal, you do best by sticking to it yourself). We can call this an equilibrium in that it is an equilibrium of "expectations" and "strategies" because in such a case, the conjectures of each do not lead to optimal behaviors that contradict them.

In our example, let's say it turns out that *if* each firm *expected* the other to make 100 tennis balls, the profit-maximizing output for each one given this expectation was 100 tennis balls. Then, as long as each expected the other to make 100 tennis balls, both would find that they were proved right in their forecast for the price (which emerged from auctioning off a total quantity of 200 tennis balls). In this case, we'd say that the outcome "Firm A makes 100 tennis balls, Firm B makes 100 tennis balls" is a Nash equilibrium. Note clearly that a Nash equilibrium involves *spelling out a list of strategies, one for each participant*. Note also that it, just like a Walrasian equilibrium, is a "correct-expectations" equilibrium.

If it helps, here are some additional ways to think about Nash equilibrium. First, think of a case with the two firms above. Imagine that they get together in a smoke-filled room and shake hands over a promise to each produce 100 tennis balls. Now, only promises that were part of a list of Nash strategies would have a chance of actually being followed through on. Otherwise, one side or both would be proposing something that, given the other's promise, would *not* be best for themselves. In a Nash outcome, once the CEOs of the two firms left the room, *as long as they expected the other side to stick to the bargain*, they would then do best for themselves by sticking to the bargain. Second, we can think of Nash outcomes as ones where, after everyone has chosen her action, if we asked each player if *she alone* could now change her own action having seen what the others have done, each would say no.

2.6.2.2   Why Look at "Nash" Outcomes? Because "*Not* Nash" Means "Not Likely"

When macroeconomists study situations where parties recognize their interdependence (and so would not, in price-mediated trade, for example, take prices as given), they almost always employ Nash equilibrium as the filter to isolate the outcomes that they will study. If you write about economics, this is important to remember. But keep in mind that I have said nothing about the *plausibility* of Nash equilibrium. In other words, one needs to ask: When should outcomes look like Nash equilibria? And moreover, if there were more than one Nash equilibrium in a given setting, as often will be true, and even if we insist that each player will play according to *one* of the Nash equilibrium prescriptions, why should participants agree on *which one* the others will play according to? A large body of literature has investigated this question, and the evidence is mixed. Nash equilibrium involves substantial coordination in many cases, particularly when a game features more than one Nash equilibrium. As a result, it is a generally less robust and hence more suspect notion of equilibrium than Walrasian equilibrium. Unfortunately, Walrasian equilibrium is likely a terrible notion in cases where participants do see that they might have the ability to influence the terms at which they can trade with each other, so *some* alternative is certainly needed.

Nash equilibrium has at least two other things going for it as well. The first is one that I've noted before: in many instances, the question of how to make predictions for the outcomes of the interactions boils down to the economist specifying that particular conjectures are held by each of the model's participants (say, each group of firms) concerning the behavior of the other participants. By studying only these conjectures that will be proved correct in actual play, Nash equilibrium removes the economist's discretion over the conjectures of participants in their model. The second advantage is also a practical one: Nash is a *necessary* condition for an "obvious way to play a game." *Any* setting in which strategically interacting parties "seem to know how the others will play" is a Nash situation. This is by definition— "seeming to know" means being right in one's expectation, and if all parties are proved right, and all parties are doing what's best for them based on their expectations for others' behavior, we must be describing a Nash outcome.[29]

We can now say more about the lack of enthusiasm macroeconomists exhibit with respect to stories that feature widespread market power. An implication of the necessity of Nash behavior, especially for anything we routinely observe as the outcome of interactions in which parties recognize their interdependence, is that behaviors that are *not* Nash are not likely to persist. And economists have shown that in a large variety of settings, genuinely collusive outcomes are not Nash. To see why, let's say I proposed a model in which, for example, the sensible prediction was that two firms would agree to "act as one," produce limited quantities of a product, and thereby reap the profits that would be available to a monopolist. What you'd want to do next is to check the incentives of each party to stick to this deal. And what you'd nearly always find is that as long as each firm thought that the other one would stick to the limitation on output to which they'd agreed, they themselves would want to renege on their end of the deal. Why? In this case, because as long as each thought that the other producer would hold back from flooding the market, prices would indeed be relatively high, thereby creating an opportunity for the other firm or firms to sell large amounts at a price higher than they'd otherwise get. At the other end, consider firms in an industry that is competitive enough that it acts as if it has a well-functioning WCH. In this case, each firm's actions in a Walrasian outcome are again (trivially) Nash—everyone is "best responding" to what everyone else will do simply by choosing what's best for them given the price. And the price is what summarizes to each what everyone else wants to do. Thus, it is simply implausible that "non-Nash" outcomes should generally obtain a large claim on macroeconomists' attention.

2.6.2.3   What If Interactions Are Repeated and Not Anonymous?

I just asserted that most collusive arrangements ask that participants do things that are not Nash. There is an exception to this: when interactions are *repeated*. Intuitively, if you and I knew that we'd keep interacting into the indefinite horizon, we could potentially start to impose punishments on each other for reneging on any collusive deal we'd arranged for up front. As a result, this freedom to punish might allow one to sustain all manner of collusive outcomes *as Nash ones*. This logic, as stated, is very powerful—so powerful that it is known as the **folk theorem for infinitely repeated games**. It tells us that almost any outcome can be a Nash outcome if the players involved are *"sufficiently" patient*. In one way, the folk theorem is clearly not good news for those wishing to use Nash equilibrium, since the latter might simply fail to narrow anything down. But there is another way in which it is not limiting. First, let me define "patience."

In the context of firms that want to strike deals with each other to, say, raise prices, "patience" refers to the discounting that the managers and shareholders of the firm apply to profits that accrue in the future. An obvious yardstick to apply is the rate they perceive to be available from other routinely traded assets like government T-bills, as this may be the rate that the owners of the firm would be able to obtain for sure if they received the profits now instead of in the future. If the profits are seen as very risky, then a higher discount rate may be applicable—profits in the distant future are worth even less now because many things could happen in the interim, including those that the firm's owners are averse to, such as bankruptcy. In either case, the idea is that the lower the discount the parties apply to future profits, the more "future-oriented" they each are, and hence the more bite is carried by any future sanctions that each threatens to impose in light of any violation.

Lastly, there is another a priori reason not to succumb to the idea that observed real-world outcomes reflect pervasive collusion even when parties interact repeatedly. It can be formally demonstrated that as the number of participants grows, the "patience" needed for sustaining collusive outcomes via the promise of retaliation also grows and, typically, will become fairly rapidly unattainable.[30]

2.6.2.4   When Should Households and Firms Take Prices as Given?

As emphasized above, Walrasian economics *defines* competition as *price-taking* behavior at Walrasian prices. And while the cooperative approach suggests that the cores of large economies will look "as if" all participants faced Walrasian prices that they took as given, these models do not make explicit mention of prices, and remain very inexplicit about the nature of trade. Since "noncooperative" games allow us to specify trading rules that make explicit use of prices, they can provide us some more easily interpreted answers (relative to cooperative concepts) to the question of when the Walrasian model is applicable.

To start, even though it is patently silly, let us solve for a Walrasian equilibrium in a setting with just **two** firms by insisting (i) that firms make price forecasts that they *perceive* as invariant to their own actions, (ii) the firms then each make output decisions based on their solutions to the price taker's optimization problems relevant under their forecasts of prices, and (iii) the realized market price—which does indeed depend on the output of both firms—*coincides with the forecasts of the firms*. Specifically, let each of the two firms believe that its own actions have no effect on the price at which it can sell output, so that what remains is the price it thinks its output will fetch at the market. Assume that each makes the forecast that it can sell whatever it chooses to produce (q_1 and q_2, for firm 1 and 2, respectively) at \$10.

Now, let the output of each firm be brought to an auction in which the price is determined in a way that depends on aggregate production as follows: price at auction $= 50 - (q_1 + q_2)$. Assume that neither firm knows this—because otherwise they'd know right away that their actions *do* influence prices. Now, let's say that each firm, after figuring out the output level that maximizes their profits, decides to produce 20 units. What will the resulting price be? It will be \$10. That is, each firm is able to sell its output for \$10, just as they believed they could. Since neither firm's beliefs about prices and their influence on aggregates was disconfirmed, their expectations for prices can be said to be rational. We then have a Walrasian or competitive **rational-expectations equilibrium** (sometimes abbreviated as REE). It is important to recognize that both Walrasian equilibrium and Nash equilibrium are simply special cases of economists' current favorite notion of equilibrium: that of rational-expectations equilibria. These are, at their most general, situations in which the beliefs of market participants lead to actions that do not lead to contradictions of beliefs.

In this example, each firm is assumed to think that its actions have no effect on prices, and, when acting on this premise, the firms are not contradicted by forecasting that they will be able to sell all they produce at $10 per unit. But each firm accounts for 50% of all production, and so is clearly affecting prices via its own individual output decisions. Firms in such a setting would probably figure out that there are big gains to be had from trying to exploit market power. Therefore, a carefully modeled game in which each party chose actions knowing that they directly affected the others would likely deliver much more sensible predictions for prices and quantities.

It is critical to recognize that it was the fact that both firms took Walrasian prices as given and then optimized which led to a Walrasian, and hence a Pareto-optimal, outcome. This is precisely what others in the past, such as the "market socialists," *correctly* understood to be the critical lesson of Walrasian theory: i.e., "If we can just get *a complete set of Walrasian prices that all traders take as given*, we'll end up consuming and producing efficiently!" But in a society in which a firm is free to do as it pleases, one can show that the "best response" by one firm, if it expects the other to act as a price taker facing Walrasian prices, is *not* to act as a price taker! Instead, a smart firm would exploit this passive behavior by its rivals, perhaps by producing less in order to drive prices up. Thus, in a market with just two firms, when prices are taken as given, neither is behaving as a "competitor" in any way. Rather, it is precisely the fact that firms *ignore* each other's existence that ensures a Pareto-optimal outcome.

One lesson of the preceding is this: "competition" or "rivalry" between self-interested parties per se cannot be deemed necessary to attain efficiency, and with small numbers, may even be ruinous to efficiency. Instead, what suffices (as long as participants optimize and cannot be forced to trade) is that the trading institution in which they participate (i) form Walrasian prices and (ii) render Walrasian price taking the *best* strategy for each firm and household. If these requirements are not met, one should not be sanguine in advocating unfettered decentralized trade. In the context of price-mediated trade, the real question is therefore the following: *Will the active rivalry present in a given instance lead to approximate price-taking and optimizing behavior?* As we now know, active rivalry, when coupled with Walrasian prices and the inability of individual traders to move them, leads to the tremendous coordination that describes Pareto-optimal outcomes in societies of anonymous traders. As far as price taking goes, in a mass market, it essentially must happen—traders begin to lose the ability to influence prices via their actions—making the price taker's problem the only relevant one for them. To be clear, what happens when a trader becomes "negligible" in a market is that at the same time he is locked into a severe competition with many others, he needs to pay less and less attention to the actions of any single competitor and instead must pay attention to prices that he has no real ability to manipulate in his favor. For these finite-agent settings, a large body of microeconomic theory is more explicit about the nature of trade and price formation than is the "bare-bones" Walrasian model, and attempts to locate when and where Walrasian outcomes are likely. Before concluding this section, let me note that in the case of what mathematicians call an "uncountably infinite" number of participants—to which they give the name "continuum"—price taking is the exactly correct thing to do. In the real world, which is the "large-but-most-certainly-finite" case we all live with, it may still be the best thing to do. We'll see such economies again later, starting in chapter 4.

2.6.2.5   Market Games

In the noncooperative approach to understanding Walrasian equilibria, one provides an explicit description of competition by first specifying clearly the "game" in which firms find themselves playing against each other. Critically, in this approach, the decisions between firms are required to emerge in a way that *respects the desires of individuals to collude and cooperate*. If there are cases in which these decisions, even after allowing for such cooperation, begin to resemble those that would obtain if all firms were confronted with Walrasian prices and took them as given, we could say that we better understood what Walrasian outcomes represented. We could then study the mechanisms of this model further to locate when such interactions will lead to participants (i) literally facing Walrasian prices that they take as given, or (ii) acting as if they do.

A requirement of the game theory approach is that the only "strategy profiles" (i.e., a list giving each of the players' proposed strategies in the game) that players can contemplate are those that these yield a feasible outcome. This raises a problem for the "price-taker" assumption of Walrasian macroeconomics whenever one studies an economy in which there is a finite number of participants. The problem is as follows: in an economy with a finite number of households and firms, price taking is an equilibrium (in the Nash sense—each person, expecting the others to play their part in the set of strategies under contemplation, will do best by also sticking to his part) only because the modeler is allowing for strategies that yield infeasible outcomes. To see this, think of a setting in which there is a single Walrasian equilibrium. Now, think of the predicament facing a household that must choose an optimal response when all other households have chosen the Walrasian bundle. That is, all other households have chosen the bundle best for them when they face Walrasian prices. Now think of what is feasible for our household. Can it actually select a non-Walrasian bundle, which is what is presumed? The answer is no: any non-Walrasian bundle would not be feasible for the household to actually consider, because as one of a finite number of participants in the market, this household matters for the aggregate outcome: it is not negligible. So what is a household that considers asking for such a bundle supposed to think about how such a demand would be accommodated? The game-theoretic approach would never allow for this ambiguity—it always insists that whatever participants select collectively must remain feasible. In chapter 4, we'll take this up again, in the context of why macroeconomists employ the mathematical construction of the so-called continuum in their analysis of price-taking behavior. For now, the interested reader is directed to Gale (2000) for further elaboration of the problem just described, and more generally, readers are directed to the body of work on "market microstructure," in which economists studying financial markets have analyzed detailed and specific trading rules. The survey of Biais, Glosten, and Spatt (2005), and the classic text of O'Hara (1995), are good places to dig deeper.

Cournotian, Bertrandian, and Bargaining Foundations
The seminal papers of Novshek and Sonnenschein (1978) and Mas-Colell (1982) consider *single*-market settings in which prices are used to mediate transactions, trading partners are anonymous, price taking is assumed among *buyers* of a good, and sellers act strategically. These papers formalize the intuitively appealing idea that when such markets are "large" relative to the "capacity" of individual firms, strategic competition between firms (in particular, the Nash equilibrium of Cournot quantity competition) approximates the perfectly competitive outcome. Thus, the perfectly competitive model can be viewed as a good and

tractable way of modeling what might be more involved interactions among competing firms. It should be noted, however, that in these settings, participants—and in particular sellers—are assumed to have knowledge of a "demand curve" that tells them what amount will be demanded by customers who face any given price. Buyers, for their part, are assumed to take the prices as given (an assumption that can be motivated by positing that they are too numerous to be able to credibly drive a hard bargain with the sellers).

In related work, Kreps and Scheinkman (1983) have shown that a fairly natural way of interacting, whereby profit-maximizing firms first simultaneously announce and commit to a level for their production capabilities, i.e., where they choose "capacity," after which they simultaneously announce a price, leads to Cournot outcomes. As a result, here again, with large numbers of firms, we get approximately Walrasian allocations. Similarly, in partial equilibrium settings with free entry and many potential entrants, the only Nash equilibria not involving "noncredible threats" (known as "subgame perfect" Nash equilibria) of a two-stage entry game converges to one where price is equal to the minimum of the long-run average cost, which is the long-run "perfectly competitive" outcome. Such outcomes occur inexorably with large numbers of small players. Similarly, in many auction settings, the Nash equilibria of a variety of modes of interactions lead to the Walrasian outcomes when there are many players, each of bounded size.

One point that should be noted is that the assumption that sellers know a demand curve is a potentially very demanding one. This is because it presumes that all participants know what the implications of different prices will be, *after taking into account the many feedback effects* between the prices in the market under study and all other markets. Therefore, even though the *limit*—as firms become very numerous—of these interactions is the Walrasian one in which all participants need to know only prices, for any finite number of firms, each participant is assumed to know a much more complicated object (see Arrow 1986 for a useful discussion of this). Note, however, that even in these settings the following is still true: while (it can be shown that) for any finite number of firms, the result is an output level that is lower than the Walrasian level, consumers are still assigned whatever level is produced in a way that leaves no further gains from trade between them. This occurs because they all face the same price per unit from sellers. In this sense, price-based trading still achieves enormous coordination between strangers.

In the multimarket, or general-equilibrium, settings of so-called **market games** (begun by Shapley and Shubik 1977), researchers have shown that the Nash equilibria of trading games in which there is centralized price setting as a function of the aggregate market actions of agents converge to Walrasian outcomes. Such a setting likely provides a useful approximation to price formation in the many large auctions held daily to price commodities such as agricultural produce, oil, and metals. A thoughtful recent summary of the research program is given by Giraud (2003), who supplies the reader with a list of the landmarks of this literature.

Market games are particularly instructive because, although they presume a fairly centralized structure for trade and price formation, they fully acknowledge the feedback effects between markets and do *not* presume price taking. The latter is important to note: we mentioned earlier the importance of the price-taking assumption in making Walrasian outcomes genuine "equilibria" (i.e., situations in which no one wants to unilaterally change her behavior, given that she expects everyone else to play according to the proposed equilibrium). Of course, such an assumption may not even approximate the behavior of traders in circumstances where they have, and know they have, the ability to manipulate the terms of trade in their favor. In market games, all participants are always doing what is best for themselves, given the exogenously imposed institutional arrangements for trade and price formation. In particular, market games are always explicit about how the actions of each individual influence and constrain the options available to all others.

In contrast to the centralized nature of markets and price formation modeled in the market games literature, there is a literature on "search and bargaining," which explicitly models the interaction of traders who must first find and then engage in bargaining with others, knowing that there are others with whom they may bargain. In these settings, researchers have established conditions under which the resulting outcomes are as if all agents perceived and took Walrasian prices as given.[31] One lesson of this work for macroeconomists is that the "large numbers" of traders usually present in our models may not always be enough to ensure price-taking behavior. Instead, what may be vital is the extent to which traders remain *anonymous*, because once trading partners can become known to others, the outcomes from repeated bargaining can encompass a much wider range of outcomes, many not overlapping with Walrasian outcomes. This is important for the insight it gives into the range of applicability of Walrasian approaches for predicting outcomes.[32]

No Surplus!

Lastly, the important contributions of Makowski and Ostroy through a series of papers (discussed in Mas-Colell, Whinston, and Green 1995, and Makowski and Ostroy 1992) show that in economies with a large number of participants, Walrasian allocations are the *only* ones with the property that each individual trader obtains as a reward precisely the marginal value of his contribution to social welfare (see Mas-Colell, Whinston, and Green 1995, ch. 18, for an accessible statement and proof of this idea). This idea is valuable because it demonstrates, yet again, why Walrasian equilibria should have a definitive claim on macro-economists' attention. In essence, Walrasian outcomes are the only truly "competitive" ones, if we take "competitive" to mean that no one collects more, or less, than the value of their marginal contribution. This result also tells us that as long as households enter the economy with similar endowments, Walrasian outcomes have a serious claim to being the only "fair" or "just" outcome. Of course, households might not enter with similar endowments, a point we'll return to later.

2.6.2.6   Summary of the Noncooperative Approach

The lesson of the preceding section might be that large numbers and Walrasian outcomes go tightly together, with the latter being most relevant under conditions of anonymity at the individual level. Just as was the case with the cooperative approaches, nearly *any* specification of interactions between *individually negligible* market participants leads almost inevitably to Walrasian outcomes, and barring restrictions on trade that lead to market incompleteness, these outcomes will also be Pareto-optimal. The reader will likely find the nontechnical review provided in Mas-Colell (1984) very useful. The author refers to the need for large numbers as the **negligibility hypothesis**, and describes how the three seemingly disparate solution concepts—Walrasian equilibrium, core, and no surplus—all coincide under "negligibility."

In settings of negligibility, it would seem that vast unexploited gains from trade in the absence of serious informational problems in discerning product quality (a case that describes many products we consume daily) are not likely. For example, almost any model with many firms would conclude that any firm that believed all its competitors would leave a market unserved would react by serving that market. Relatedly, any competitor that felt that all its rivals were charging prices in excess of marginal costs would enter the market (absent barriers) and charge a lower price. As a result, Walrasian outcomes emerge naturally from underlying settings in which they are *not always an inevitability* (e.g., even if, for example, the number of potential producers was small).

The great value of this research program, which seeks to provide the "foundations of Walrasian equilibrium," is that it teaches us what is required for Walrasian analysis to be reasonably justified. Moreover, both the cooperative and noncooperative approaches teach us that it is essential to have *active rivalry* between market participants in ensuring all three premises of Walrasian economics of price taking, profit maximization, and market completeness.[33]

2.6.3   The Experimental Approach

We have presented evidence that from a *purely theoretical* perspective, in "large" economies, allocations will be approximately *as if* all actors faced Walrasian prices which they took to be out of their control, almost irrespective of the way in which trade is operationalized. However, the theoretical approach to understanding when interactions between not inherently price-taking traders will lead to Walrasian outcomes assumes that all participants are exceedingly smart. Specifically, in any setting where they are modeled as playing a game (such as the noncooperative approach), economists assume heroically that all players understand and forecast perfectly the strategies of all other players. As a result, this may not convince us that such theories are robust enough to generate sensible predictions for real-world markets exhibiting the rough-and-tumble of trade arising from (i) small numbers of agents, (ii) each of whom may be a quite imperfect decision maker.

Moreover, even when most trade in a real-world market occurs at a single price, the normative implications of the theory are not guaranteed, because we cannot so easily observe household preferences, firm technologies, or whether either households or firms optimize in the way assumed in the theory. For example, maybe Walrasian outcomes obtain, but do so in a way that routinely surprises or befuddles real-world traders. As a result, even though the terms at which one good can be exchanged for another under free trade seem to be out of the control of households and firms, and also seem to result in the absence of serious shortages or surpluses, the allocations may not be what are ideal for market participants. It is therefore important to investigate further whether decentralized trade can generate Walrasian *allocations*, not just Walrasian prices.

The field of **experimental economics,** pioneered by Edward Chamberlain and dramatically extended by Vernon Smith and others, is a branch of economics in which actual human subjects are placed into highly controlled trading environments. This allows us to understand behavior, and is now a very important area of economics overall. For the purposes of this book, the question at hand is whether households and firms are actually able to "find" Walrasian equilibrium in such controlled settings. If not, macroeconomists may well be employing a notion of equilibrium with little to no descriptive content or empirical relevance.

In the experiments aimed at understanding the relevance of the Walrasian equilibrium concept, the most important control imposed by the experimenter is to *induce* preference orderings and a production "function" for the participating individuals who play the roles of consumers and producers, respectively, and also to control the number of firms (sellers) active in the market. Trade between these groups is then allowed to occur, and the outcomes are evaluated.

To be concrete, consider an experiment with five people designated as "sellers," and eight as "buyers." The designation of "seller" means that these subjects are each given a table that specifies how much it will cost them to produce any given number of units of a single good. The designation of "buyer" is operationalized by giving these subjects a list that details the maximal value that one would place on each successive unit of the item they purchased. Next, sellers are told that they may keep the profits they generate. That is, whatever difference between the amount for which they are able to sell a unit and the cost they incurred in producing it is theirs to keep. Then think of the buyers as "personal shoppers" who work on behalf of the experimenter, with a deal that allows them to keep any difference between the valuation that they were given for each unit and the price they paid for it. This setup now gives both buyers and sellers incentives to get good deals. What is not assumed is that anyone knows anyone else. In fact, these experiments almost assume the opposite: preferences and costs are purely privately held information.

Next, trading rules are specified. Two popular types of rules are those that define the "single-price sealed-bid" auction and the "double auction." I will focus on the former, because it is essentially a WCH:

buyers and sellers each specify how much they'd be willing to pay for any given number of items. These individual reports are essentially buyer- and seller-specific demand and supply curves, spelling out how much they'd buy or produce at various prices. The experimenter then adds up these curves to obtain market demand and supply curves and then announces that he stands ready to buy and sell at the Walrasian prices so computed—just as the WCH was described as doing in chapter 1.

Now, you may recall that in chapter 1 I hinted that the WCH with a small numbers of participants would, because of the procedure it employed to locate Walrasian prices, seem ripe for manipulation. In particular, buyers and sellers, if few in numbers, should realize that falsifying their reported demand and supply curves would allow them to influence the price that the experimenter will eventually compute and allow trade at. Thus, the experimental setup I have described here seems real in some important ways: parties are ignorant of each other, and parties are not presumed to passively tell the truth. All manner of lies are perfectly permissible.

Given these features, the key attribute is that the experimenter is able to "see" the things market participants rarely will: the preferences, technology, and endowments of *all* market participants, and even the "level of competitiveness." As a result, we have some hope of learning about the relevance of Walrasian equilibrium as a prediction for market function.

2.6.3.1 Markets as Calculators

A vital point to recognize is that if a market appears to be in Walrasian equilibrium, then even in a single-market context, the "market" is acting as if it has solved a system of nonlinear equations with as many equations and unknowns as there are consumers and producers (as well as one more equation for prices). It may help here to recall the Edgeworth Box examples given earlier. As Plott (2000) makes clear, these equations arise from the optimization problems of consumers and producers who take prices as given but know *nothing* about any more than prices and the equations describing what is optimal for them alone! The reader should keep this firmly in mind, as it is at the crux of the power many economists attribute to competitive trading.

The stunning punch line is that experiments with real human subjects have shown repeatedly that it takes only a few agents to get essentially Walrasian outcomes. Plott (2000) gives a very accessible overview. See also the valuable collection of papers (and review essay by the editors) in Friedman and Rust (1993) on experiments and theory pertaining to the double-auction market. In the context most relevant to this book, Plott (2000) reports that multimarket settings with "double-auction" (DA) or "single-price sealed-bid" exchange processes generate outcomes that look essentially Walrasian, *even with relatively few participants, and even under uncertainty* (i.e., even in the sequential trading version of the ADM model). Vernon Smith (quoted in Friedman and Rust 1993) refers to the overwhelming success of Walrasian equilibrium theory in predicting the outcomes of the DA trading institution as a "scientific mystery": we are simply not sure *how this comes about*. Smith in particular considers this finding as evidence that Walrasian equilibrium is an *"emergent"* phenomenon in which the collective is able to solve problems well beyond the ability of any subset of participants. Relatedly, there is reason for some optimism that societies tend toward organically efficient institutions via essentially "natural selection" mechanisms. A thoughtful exposition of this "evolutionary" perspective can be found in the Nobel Prize lecture of Vernon Smith (2002), and in his book *Rationality in Economics* (2010).[34]

To see the "mystery" described by Smith more explicitly, a Walrasian equilibrium is something that students in economics routinely solve for in their homework. But to allow this, students are given *all* the actors' information: the student who is solving the problem knows every household's preferences and endowments, everyone's ownership share of every firm, and every firm's production capabilities. Yet, as I have emphasized ad nauseam, what makes the First Welfare Theorem an interesting finding about the power of linear prices is the very fact that the individual participants modeled in the Walrasian scenario are assumed to know *nothing* beyond prices and their own capabilities or endowments. How interesting would it be if I told you, "Hey, I know everything about everyone, and I can locate a Pareto-optimal outcome"? The ignorance being presumed is of the sort that we are probably comfortable with as a description of many real-world market scenarios. And, after all, the amazing part of the First Welfare Theorem is that it tells us that there is a way to locate (stable!) Pareto optima that requires rational individuals and firms to know almost nothing . . . we "just" need a complete set of Walrasian prices that participants take as given.

Bad News for Economic Theory: The Right Answers for the Wrong Reasons

The fact that market participants *lacking a WCH* are able to trade as if there were one is thus amazing and, interestingly, not such good news for modern economics. As Robert Wilson notes in Friedman and Rust (1993), formalizing the game that is entailed in even a standard experimental DA is extremely involved. It certainly requires tremendous sophistication on the part of market participants, and what is worse, it requires an incredible amount of knowledge (at least statistical, if not individual-level, knowledge) of one's competitors. Lastly, it also requires parties to have a keen sense of the rationality of the decision-making processes of opponents (so-called common knowledge). As a result, theoretically based support (or doubt) of the likely outcome of a given set of rules is not necessarily a great source for good explanations of *why* outcomes look "competitive." This is especially true whenever market participants lack information about each other and lack a central aggregator such as a WCH. So, if Walrasian equilibrium works well to predict outcomes in the lab, we may have the right answer, but for the wrong reasons.

Notice that when running an experiment in which participants interact, the real-world experimental subjects involved surely realize that they may have some ability to influence prices. After all, they are, in many of the experiments, very few in number. And on top of this, in any modern game-theoretic representation, it is true that a great deal of information is assumed in a Nash equilibrium, because it is the case in which everyone's strategy is best for them and is based on their correctly having guessed *everyone else's* strategy! This is implausible in any real market setting, where anonymity is the rule. On this, I direct the reader again to Smith (2010). But one clear takeaway is this: macroeconomists using Walrasian models can take comfort in the ability of at least certain types of trading rules to force Walrasian outcomes in a wide array of settings that much more closely resemble the rough-and-tumble of the outcomes of deal making between buyers and sellers of bounded (humanlike) rationality who, furthermore, suffer from general ignorance of the nature of their competitors.

So how does the "single-price sealed-bid" auction, among others, so reliably produce Walrasian outcomes with just a few participants, none of whom even knows anyone else's preferences or costs? The lack of clarity on the manner by which experimental markets so routinely generate highly efficient outcomes has led to work, notably by Satter-thwaite and Williams (1989) and Rustichini, Satterthwaite, and Williams (1994), studying (in a manner that perhaps invites some of the cautions we have seen from Wilson and Smith) the "symmetric" (whereby all identical players do identical things) Nash equilibria of a trading game in which consumers and producers have privately known valuations and production costs. Very roughly, they show that bidding behavior converges quickly to the truthful reporting by all participants of their values/costs, often in settings with fewer than ten players! The market is similar in structure to the Walrasian clearinghouse discussed at the outset, though limited in scope to only arranging trade in one good. Truth telling is the essence of price taking: agents (nearly) give up on bidding and on inflating/deflating their reports in order to influence prices, and do best by instead accepting the price that emerges from their collective (near) truth telling.

As noted, the preceding game-theoretic analyses depend on *very* sophisticated reasoning by agents. Interestingly, it turns out that simple learning heuristics like those in Gjerstad and Dickhaut (1998) and Gintis (2006) can also lead to convergence to Walrasian equilibrium— even when agents know only their own preferences and endowments. Both of these papers illustrate how explicit descriptions of what people actually do can allow a society to solve a complex mathematical problem when information on preferences, technology, and endowments is "dispersed" a la Hayek.[35] Perhaps most striking of all are the findings of Gode and Sunder (1991), who show that so-called zero-intelligence traders, who are simply restricted to not making any money-losing bids or offers, still end up rapidly trading only at the prices and quantities predicted by Walrasian equilibrium theory. Gode and Sunder's work is important because it suggests that the rules of trade themselves may be a good *substitute* for the information possessed by, and rationality of, individual traders. It further suggests that in the feedback between outcomes and the design of institutions, an *evolutionary* process has delivered trading rules that are extremely good at ensuring that gains from trade get realized.

Lastly, let me note that DA markets are not always successful and again offer macroeconomists some not-so-tasty food for thought.[36] Markets for trading financial assets using DA rules are notoriously susceptible to speculative pricing bubbles (see e.g., Smith, Suchanek, and Williams 1988).[37] The role of "margin" requirements that place limits on the ability of some to borrow to finance the purchase of assets that they suspect to be underpriced does seem to help, see, e.g., Smith (1998). By contrast, other rules, such as those that limit trading in the event of a large price decline within a trading session, do not seem to help. In the latter, Smith conjectures that the problem could be that trading under such a rule might lead people to correctly conjecture that losses will be limited, and in turn, lead them to take greater risks. In light of recent events, the profession has to keep in mind that bubbles can certainly form, but that their regulation is fraught with potentially perverse outcomes. More generally, trading rules can significantly affect outcomes. Yet, even here, the news is not all bad. Crockett and Duffy (2010) find in recent work that outcomes routinely avoid the pricing bubbles that have been persistently observed in other DA contexts.

2.6.3.2 Experiments, the Invention of New Trading Institutions, and Mechanism Design

Experimental work thus suggests that in some instances, the very specific rules embodied in different trading institutions affect outcomes. It is important to recognize, however, that this result is not entirely negative. In fact, it is an area in which economists have most famously contributed to improving practice. The well-publicized successes of FCC "spectrum" auctions (see, e.g., McMillan 1994), among others, show that economists have been able to create markets where trading was previously not possible. Specifically, economists have been able to design institutions such as markets where computers aggregate information or assemble prices for component units in a way that allows efficient exchange. These are clearly efficiency-enhancing mechanisms, as they allow market forces to allocate goods that were *previously only allocable by administrative fiat* (particularly a variety of "composite" goods such as landing slots at airports and spectrum space). A review of these developments is Roth (2002).

   The fact that rules can matter is, at one level, hardly surprising. Chess is not checkers, and the rules are why. Nonetheless, even though in a wide range of cases, the rules fundamentally "made" the game, we noted that this was not always true. The theme encapsulated in the equivalence principle made almost the opposite point. It emphasized that once the number of participants in a trading arrangement gets "large," outcomes start to look almost inevitably Walrasian. In settings with smaller numbers of participants, though, the rules matter.

Mechanism is the jargon for the complete specification of a group of buyers and sellers, their options, and the manner in which their choices affect and are affected by (potentially) the actions of all others. The reader may have noticed that I have already inserted this term into the text with minimal fanfare by repeatedly speaking of the WCH as a "mechanism." The WCH, the variety of experiments, and the practical experience with the "design" of mechanisms for adjudicating competition between buyers and sellers are all examples of a much bigger, and currently central, research program in the theoretical economics of mechanism design. I will return to mechanism design later in the book.

Mechanisms are relevant for macroeconomists because we are perpetually predicating our assessments of market function and dysfunction on the extent to which economic theory suggests that a given trading arrangement lacks the preconditions to generate the efficient production and exchange of goods and services. Theory tells us where to look for problems. However, the findings presented here make clear that through a battery of experiments, we often know *what* will happen, but we may know less than we might have earlier imagined about *why*.[38]

2.7   The ADM Model Does Not Require "Perfect Information" to Deliver Pareto-Optimal Outcomes; It Requires a Complete Set of Walrasian Prices

The First Welfare Theorem is a "theorem": it is true anytime its preconditions are met. Therefore, it is important to note clearly that many of the preconditions sometimes alleged to be required for its "truth" are not in fact required. In particular, the theorem requires people to understand the quality of the goods they are buying, know prices, and act *as if* they have no influence on them. The theorem does not require "perfect information" about anything beyond the knowledge of one's own preferences, the quality of the good being traded (more on this later), and the set of relevant prices. Nor does the theorem require "large" numbers of agents. Settings with large numbers of traders and good information flows about quality are simply ones where the *assumed* behavior has a good chance of making sense. Macroeconomists, being the main end users of the model, should be clear on this, as well as on the distinction between the requirements of the theory itself and the requirements for its *relevance*.

Even in the textbook treatment of the Walrasian model, especially the ADM model, there is simply no requirement anywhere that households and firms have "perfect information." Quite the opposite: the standard consumer's and producer's problem in the ADM model makes perfectly clear that market participants are assumed to know exactly *nothing* beyond their own preferences or capabilities, the quality of good or service they are trying to buy or sell, and the Walrasian prices for these goods and services. Vernon Smith is clear on this point:

> The alleged requirement of complete, common, and perfect information is vacuous: I know of no predictive theorem stating that when agents have such information, their behavior produces a CE [competitive equilibrium, a synonym for Walrasian equilibrium], and that *in the absence of such information, their behavior fails to produce a CE*. (Smith 1998, p. 62; italics added)

What about the need for perfect information to make the theory empirically relevant? First, one must acknowledge that it matters vitally that participants be able to discern the quality of the good or service they are buying. As I will discuss further in chapter 4, one generally cannot hope to set up a market structure that yields efficient outcomes otherwise. Relatedly, a second place where one must concede that information may help (though it still may not be necessary) is in ensuring the *formation* of Walrasian prices that are *taken as given* by buyers and sellers. Such prices and behavior are important for the relevance of Walrasian equilibrium as an equilibrium concept. For example, it may help a market organizer such as a WCH to know all this information, so that they can directly *compute* Walrasian prices and confront market participants with them, or avoid being cheated by scheming bidders who might try to influence prices in other ways. In fact, information may well matter when credit is involved, as it may help to know facts about one's counterparties—so clearly information *can* matter (more on this in chapter 4). But in any market for "spot" trade, it simply cannot be asserted that "information must be perfect" (beyond that on prices and the quality of the good or service in question).

In the market for any single good, for example, one can imagine a sealed-bid auction being used to form prices and allocate items. In this case, with a large number of bidders, one can show that outcomes become closer and closer to Walrasian, but at no point is information "perfect" in terms of anyone knowing anyone else's preferences of endowments with certainty.

Lastly, as a practical matter, we saw that the experimental evidence suggests that effective Walrasian price formation and outcomes can, and routinely do, occur with far fewer buyers and sellers—all of whom are unknown to each other—than standard noncooperative theory suggests they should. So again, one simply cannot claim that perfect information is critical even for the *empirical relevance* of Walrasian theory. So much for "large numbers" being vital, too.

In the end, the preceding arguments cut down both the authoritativeness of the claims of modern theoretical work purporting to explain efficient market function, as well as the claims of those who argue that the failure of certain (imagined) preconditions renders the results of the theory inapplicable. Walrasian theory works, but, as Smith (1998) puts it very well, it "works better than we have any right to expect."

2.7.1 The Interpretation of Prices: What's at Stake?

I described at the outset the view of prices as effective "coordinators" whereby traders could, by paying attention to nothing more than prices and knowing nothing about anyone else, reach a Pareto-optimal outcome. This is *the* classic view of the role played by prices, and is mirrored in the writings of a long line of authors, including Adam Smith, Hayek, and others. It is very much the view that I have emphasized thus far. It is not the only view, however. A rather opposite viewpoint is that prices are really not used as coordinators by most, but simply *reflect* competitive processes in which far more information, *with little or none of it price-related*, is used to arrive at outcomes. This argument is made most forcefully by Makowski and Ostroy (reviewed in a 2001 paper), who construct explicit models of trading in which prices are actually merely *byproducts* of competition, as opposed to existing "first" and then coordinating the behavior of traders. As Roemer (1995) notes: "Indeed, in their theory prices do not play a coordination function at all: as they write, prices are what appear after the dust of competitive brawl lifts." Notice that Makowski and Ostroy's view of prices is exactly akin to the message embedded in the fact that, in "large" economies, all core outcomes are Walrasian. In the latter case, one could say, "after the dust of 'core' brawl settles, it will look *as if* everyone faced, took as given, and optimized with respect to a complete set of Walrasian prices." In the competition envisioned by the core (at least as described by its inventor, F. Y. Edgeworth), *no one actually uses prices* at all, so they are clearly not doing any of the coordinating.

A huge amount is at stake in one's interpretation of prices. Specifically, what is at issue is the extent to which one can view prices, by themselves, as sufficient information for traders to base decisions on to achieve a Pareto-optimal allocation. Recalling Stiglitz (1994), the "coordination" view of prices is precisely what gave hope to egalitarians who wanted to attain efficient or near-efficient outcomes while retaining centralized production and ownership without requiring any trader to know anything about anyone else. On the other hand, if we view prices as simply reflecting a "competitive brawl," then we have to tone down any claims about the extent to which prices themselves "lead" market participants to good outcomes in the presence of ignorance of others' preferences and technological capabilities. Indeed, if prices reflect complex competitive interaction instead of coordinating all competitors, it is perhaps the case that all traders are working extremely hard, using and desirous of all manner of information, prominently highly idiosyncratic *non-price* information, in order to extract concessions from others. Residential housing prices seem to have some of this flavor, in fact. And in this case, we can identify with the idea that the decision problem of traders is vastly more complex than the relatively simple one faced by participants in a WCH, or other explicitly price-forming trading institution. As a result, in such a world, one cannot speak persuasively of the coordinating function of prices—and in turn, one has to acknowledge that a primary argument for using the First Welfare Theorem as a reason for fostering decentralized trade is substantially weakened.

Most important, in my view, is that if we think that traders in general do not have perfect knowledge of everything relevant about their trading partners, then we must also be skeptical that the hurly-burly of "free" trade will have *any* chance of exhausting the gains from trade. The Myerson-Satterthwaite theorem tells us this already. And we cannot so easily appeal to the core to make predictions for outcomes, either. After all, why should one presume that each trader knows as much as is presumed by a solution concept such as the core? It seems quite implausible that in large settings, which are frequently the germane ones, traders would ever know even close to enough about the characteristics of others (i.e., their preferences for various goods, and their capabilities for production) to assemble coalitions to defect from noncore outcomes.

As I noted much earlier, the view of prices as pure byproducts, and their exclusion as coordinators, seems extreme to me (see again Roemer

1995). For instance, in line with the reasoning in the previous paragraph, the presence of institutions whose task is precisely to *generate* explicit prices at which participants can trade is clear evidence of the use of prices as coordinators: commodity markets are the leading example. In these settings, individual traders are left with the decision of what to consume and produce upon finding themselves able to trade at only one price. Moreover, in any market that was repeated frequently in a relatively stable aggregate economy, traders would presumably learn to "expect" a price, and then, as long as their desired trades remain small relative to the totality of market participants', they will make decisions based on treating this price as a parameter that they could not change. In such a setting, prices are once again undeniably acting as *coordinators*. Casual empiricism suggests that in daily life many (or most) consumers, and even most producers, take most (though of course, not all) prices as given when making decisions. For any of these groups, therefore, prices act as coordinators.

Thus, it is my sense that if prices are byproducts of competition at all, then they are likely so only for a rather special subset of economic agents, namely, *producers with significant market power*.[39] In other words, the extent to which prices reflect a "competitive brawl" seems directly related to the extent to which traders are either trying to exploit, or limit, *market power* of various sorts. And unless one sees such power as pervasive, a position for which there is little empirical support, one can reasonably view prices as coordinators.

In many settings, especially those where price taking makes sense, there is not such a pressing need to provide incentives. Put another way, traders in competitive societies do not appear to be forced to carefully engineer incentives in as many instances as does a planner working with more "monopolistic" agents (e.g., state-run firms) that do not compete with many others. In many cases, *the "threat" of competition creates incentives for them*. For example, even in a world where producers needed to borrow resources to finance the purchase or rental of capital equipment, they could not simply promise to pay an amount that would leave them with a higher profit level than other potential users of the same equipment. Similarly, in a double auction with thousands of buyers and sellers, traders quite literally can't do much to alter terms of trade by, say, falsifying reports of their preferences or technology. By contrast, a large monopoly, especially one with government backing, might be able to survive while being wasteful. As a more general matter, even when incentives do need to be provided under decentralized competition, it does appear that ownership and control arrangements frequently appear well designed to deal with incentive problems (e.g., in a world where a principal had to deliver a "competitive" rate of return to investors, he might set up a contract that just "sells" the project to the agent). Again, the need to sensibly structure incentives is driven by the fact that if one firm does not do so, another may, and then will garner relatively more funding.

In each of these cases, what is then left for "price-mediated trade" to solve is the coordination problem. And at least casually, it certainly seems that prices perform this function. As noted earlier, consumers, for their part, are routinely confronted with a vast array of prices that they regard as immutable. Similarly, even many large firms must accept prices for their products as essentially "market-determined" and so beyond their direct control (as mentioned earlier, even airlines seem to take the price of jet fuel as out of their control). Moreover, even given market power, prices may still coordinate; a monopolist restricted to linear pricing and facing price-taking buyers, for example, is certainly solving a coordination problem for society by (unintentionally) ensuring that the marginal willingness to pay of all anonymous buyers is equated, one with the other. This coordination occurs even though the monopolist ultimately produces "too little" output. And if instead of being a monopolist, he's an oligopolist with even a modest number of firms, he'll not only allocate production efficiently across buyers, but will produce more nearly the right amount, too. Similarly, even if an entire price-taking industry faces input prices that are set by a party with market power, it will inadvertently organize production among its firms efficiently, even though no producer knows anything about any other. Thus, in all these instances, prices, again, clearly coordinate activity rather than being mere byproducts of a more complex trading procedure.

2.8   Some Real-World Complications

I've argued that in the real world, missing public-good and intertemporal markets (particularly those that deal with credit markets and insurance), and not irrationality or market power, are the main barriers preventing decentralized trade from yielding efficiency. Here are a few additional caveats.

2.8.1 Walrasian Prices Are Sufficient, but Not Necessary

It's important to be very clear on one point: There is *no* result in economic theory that one could invoke to assert that the explicit construction and use of a full set of Walrasian prices, or "free markets," is
necessary for the attainment of a Pareto-efficient outcome. We have
already seen an instance of this in the fact that core outcomes, which
certainly do not involve explicit prices, are guaranteed to be Pareto-
optimal. We also see instances of this in our daily lives: in our marriages
(if they are working well), in our interactions with our neighbors and
friends, and in the variety of other institutions through which we interact with others. For instance, being served a bowl of ice cream late at
night in your own bed in return, perhaps, for the prompt unloading of
the dishwasher the next time around, is a transaction that likely occurs
daily in the US. It is one of many trades that are routinely handled
inside the institution of the household, with little or no market interface. Of course, market provision of many often-home-produced goods
and services does exist, but the point is that they often are *not* delivered
via an impersonal market at Walrasian prices. And yet one doubts
whether there are many mutually beneficial changes now failing to take
place within the family that would take place were they to be moved
into the Walrasian forum.[40]

Other examples involve those of public goods, or market incompleteness more generally. Such features might well thwart the attainment of efficient outcomes. But they do not always *have* to. In the case
of public goods, many human institutions, such as clubs, exist, charge
members fees to defray the costs, and then restrict their usage to
members only. Similarly, community groups may provide all kinds of
insurance to the members of a society, even when a macroeconomist
would not be able to point to an overt insurance market in which
households bought policies at linear prices—as imagined by a WCH.
Just think of neighbors pitching in to help each other after a fire hits
one person's home. As these examples show, diagnosing market incompleteness is difficult, and doing it correctly requires knowing about the
actual consumption of goods and services of households as well as the
extent to which this consumption is insulated—by the entire array of
market and nonmarket institutions available to a household—from
life's vicissitudes. Chapter 5 will take this idea up in more detail.

The lesson here is that one cannot so easily detect whether outcomes
in the world are inefficient simply by "looking" and seeing that the real
world does not have an obviously *visible* complete set of competitive

markets with linear Walrasian prices that are taken as given. We'll see later some ways that macroeconomists have attempted to glean whether "markets are noncompetitive or incomplete," and if so, by how much. Just as a preview, that line of research generally checks whether the outcomes are consistent with the *observable* implications of the Pareto-optimal allocation of goods, services, and income risk and, to the extent that they are not, describes the outcomes as being consistent with "market power, or market incompleteness." This way of thinking underscores that it is useful to judge resource-allocating institutions against a standard like Pareto optimality that has no dependence on any institutional arrangements for trade, but rather, is simply a condition of *outcomes*, however they come to be.

2.8.2   Costless Enforcement

For markets to be complete, property rights must be well defined. In the ADM model, the enforcement needed to ensure this is assumed to be perfect and costless. A silent assumption of the ADM model is that property rights are *so* well defined that on a day-to-day basis, society needs to spend literally *no* resources at all punishing those who use the property of others without paying them for it. It is implicit in the ADM that property rights and law enforcement are so very pervasive and credible that literally everything that anyone cares about is owned by someone, and no even *thinks* about breaking the law. In the ADM model, there are no police, there is no army, and there are no private security guards for rock stars. Instead, there is an unmodeled "eye in the sky" that all participants feel will catch any transgression *with certainty*: the ADM God is always watching, and just as importantly, credibly committed to meting out punishments vicious enough that households and firms *never* find it useful to consider breaking the rules.

But this is not quite how things work in any decentralized economy. As of this writing, more than 1% of all American adult males are incarcerated, and people do routinely get robbed, shot, and embezzled each day. This suggests clearly that people do try their luck, and while some get caught, we know by virtue of their attempting a crime that they may not have viewed being apprehended and punished as a certainty. The real-world costs of contract enforcement, or the inability to enforce property rights, the overhead costs of running an insurance firm, etc., all more or less preclude the formation of the kind of markets envisioned by the ADM model.

Modern economics has spent a lot of effort in delineating the importance of the fact that it almost always takes resources to credibly enforce contracts. Among the noteworthy early efforts here is that of Bowles and Gintis (1993), who develop a theory of "contested exchange." More recently, a large research program has emerged in which this part of the ADM model is relaxed, and parties are modeled as being unable to credibly promise to deliver on all their promises. This inability matters for the ability of markets to deliver efficient outcomes. This research program on "limited commitment" is now a central part of macroeconomics, and informs economic analyses of credit markets and fiscal policy, among other areas. Predictably, the inability to commit to delivering as promised makes the operation of markets difficult, if not impossible—which returns us to market incompleteness as an ultimate casualty of the absence of costless enforcement.

All this work fits into the larger body of work of the subfield of mechanism design, since contractual performance is itself modeled as being susceptible to incentives, and not simply mandated by an unmodeled enforcement apparatus. The focus on bringing enforcement into the discussion seems perfectly natural: in many instances when one can view markets as malfunctioning, parties either have difficulty verifying the behavior of others on whom they depend (a boss and employee, a contractor and homeowner, etc.) or have difficulty meting out punishments for nonperformance, or both. In sum, costless enforcement is important because it is related to both market incompleteness and to some fundamental tensions in policymaking.

2.8.3 Market Power

As I've implied already, macroeconomics is fixated on *competitive* models with incomplete markets, not on models with complete but monopolized markets. Business cycles, investment, consumption, and asset pricing are all typically studied in (near-) Walrasian settings. This is just another way, of course, in which one sees the primacy of the Walrasian approach. And as I already argued, aside from TBTF, searching for and destroying market power is unlikely to be a central barrier to efficiency.[41]

There are important exceptions to this, however. First, labor in the real world is nearly always allocated through a messy process of "search and matching," in which market power can sometimes exist in the sense that bargaining and price-*setting* behavior may be relevant. The importance of the labor market to household well-being is undeniable, making this market's deviation from the Walrasian benchmark potentially very important to understand. More generally, the causes and consequences of "non-Walrasian" labor markets now occupy much of the attention of macroeconomists, as we'll see in chapter 5. By contrast, the study of widespread and sizeable market power in, say, product markets (tennis balls, shoes, etc.), looms less prominently in macroeconomics.[42]

Second, in recent work on the financial crisis, noncompetitive behavior (look for the term "fire sales") figures importantly as well. In more mundane commodity markets, an (in)famous example is that of lysine price fixing orchestrated in part by the large agribusiness Archer-Daniels-Midland. In addition, firms and consumers (or coalitions of them) may work to influence the political system (think of the various powerful lobbies active in the American landscape, such those representing the interests of the GSEs Fannie Mae and Freddie Mac). More extremely, in places where property rights are more fluid than in most developed countries, some may resort to outright theft or coercion.

Why is this bad? The answer is the one we noted in passing above: the Myerson-Satterthwaite theorem tells us that most decentralized interactions between parties will yield *in*efficient outcomes, especially when parties do not face prices that they take as given.[43]

2.8.4   Imperfect Monitoring

Thus far, the premise has been that parties can detect any deviation from the initially agreed-upon promises. This is what really gives the folk theorem so much force. However, it is implausible that individual parties have substantially detailed and timely information about the preferences (in the case of households) or technological capabilities (in the case of firms) of other parties. It is from precisely this vantage point that a complete set of Walrasian prices indeed has remarkable coordinating power. *With* detailed information held by most about most others, it would not be so surprising that society might be able to attain efficient outcomes.

So, in cases where monitoring the actions of others is not so easy, what might occur? Very interesting findings here include those of Green and Porter (1984), and that of Green (1980), who show that competition may be *aided* by the inability of parties to monitor each other, for the natural reason that cheating on any collusive agreement (which is almost always beneficial—if you can get away with it) becomes harder to detect.

For macroeconomists, this branch of research has proved very useful, particularly for those interested in policymaking. The seminal work of Abreu, Pearce, and Stacchetti (1990) is especially important. These authors came up with a computationally tractable way to pore over the set of (the many) Nash outcomes of repeated games with imperfect monitoring. For obvious reasons, such a technical feat is of great practical value: macroeconomists now have begun to consider many problems involving policymakers who must interact repeatedly with others (particularly with those whom they regulate), and yet lack the ability to perfectly monitor each other's actions. While this work is far too technical to detail here, it showcases how a seemingly technical research program has aided exceedingly practical sorts of inquiry, just as does the next idea, the famous Myerson-Satterthwaite theorem.

2.8.4.1   The Myerson-Satterthwaite Theorem

With the idea of Nash equilibrium available to us, we can return to the topic of how market power causes problems. We usually posit that market participants are not aware of each other's needs and capabilities. Yet we know that as long as there are enough of them to make truthful reporting of each one's demand and supply, the WCH could locate Walrasian prices and still obtain a Pareto-optimal outcome.

Recall that when I set up the WCH, I finessed matters by insisting that it was the *only* way for people to trade with each other. But this is clearly restrictive in many cases: think of your favorite department store. What it really is is a "market with posted 'take-it-or-leave-it prices'" via which sellers (the people and firms who made the stuff on the shelves) sell to the buyers. And there are many such stores. We will therefore require that whatever trading arrangement the sellers and buyers employ, it will have to yield them an expectation of enough gains that they will actually *choose to participate* in it.

The seminal contribution of Roger Myerson and Mark Satterthwaite, in "Efficient Mechanisms for Bilateral Trading" (1983), was to show that this setting makes efficiency impossible![44] These authors set up a very general sort of problem in which there are two parties with some potential gains from trade. The situation holds some uncertainty, however: the valuation that the seller has for the item depends on the realization of a random event for each party. For example, a woman has a piece of art in her apartment that won't fit into the new house that her controlling fiancé has chosen for them. Worse, from the buyer's point of view, whether the seller's spouse-to-be likes the artwork or not will determine the couple's willingness to unload it at a low price. The potential buyer, for his part, may face a shock to his income, which of course will matter for his willingness to pay for the art. Each party does know, however, the relative likelihoods of the other party's valuation of the artwork.

Bayesian-Nash Equilibrium: A Quick Detour
Myerson and Satterthwaite are thinking of a "game" between these parties in which each player is *uncertain* about a relevant aspect of the other's "*type.*" Such games are called "games of incomplete information." In these games, economists typically employ a version of Nash equilibrium that incorporates a role for the *beliefs* of each party about the likely type of their opponent(s). This is an entirely natural thing to do, of course and, in the jargon, leads to a modified version of Nash called **Bayesian-Nash equilibrium** (BNE). The modifier "Bayesian" refers to the statistical notion of how one should use observed information (such as what a player does) to sensibly "update" one's assessment of the type they are. For example, if the bargaining protocol between the parties allowed a number of back-and-forth offers and counter-offers, each participant might well change their view on the type they were actually dealing with based on what they observed the other party doing.

Bayesian-Nash equilibrium requires each party to choose his strategy (here, what to offer for the artwork) in a way that is optimal given his beliefs, and furthermore, that the beliefs that each party holds are *derived from a correct prediction of the strategies* his opponents will use. If this sounds demanding, it absolutely is.

But, as usual, once unobservables such as beliefs, expectations, or preferences enter the picture—as they must in many settings—economists need a way to avoid the pell-mell of specifying such objects in any which way they choose. In this instance, the tradeoff is between a rather demanding notion of equilibrium that takes discretion away from the economist modeling the situation and less demanding notions that allow economists a lot of freedom in essentially selecting the outcomes they find plausible.

Something Weaker than Nash: "Rationalizable" Strategies
One prominent notion of equilibrium for the outcome of interactions between parties is that of **rationalizability**. This concept, due to

Bernheim (1984) and Pearce (1984), rather than requiring that each participant be correct about what the others *end up* doing, requires "only" that each player can justify her chosen action as something that survives the successive elimination of strategies that are "never a best response." One does this by first looking at the payoffs to each player, as a function of what all other players do, and then eliminating any choices for each person that simply cannot be a best response to *anything* that one's opponents might do. Once this is done, we stare at the game to see if we can eliminate any more choices. When we cannot, we are done. While rationalizability weakens the requirements on individuals relative to the Nash notion, it is not free. This is because there are typically outcomes that are rationalizable that are not Nash (all Nash are of course rationalizable—by definition). And this is why economists view rationalizability as "weaker": it kills off fewer outcomes. As a result, a macroeconomist using Nash will be able to weed out outcomes and have a model that makes "sharper" predictions than if they insisted only on rationalizability. This is the tension.

2.8.4.2 The Revelation Principle

Using the Myerson-Satterthwaite example, we can now ask: If we had to design a bargaining scheme via which these two parties interacted, and where the expected gains to each from participating had to be enough to get them to interact (i.e., I can't force them to bargain), what's the *absolute best* scheme we could come up with? To answer this question, you might think that you'd have to search over an essentially infinite set of different bargaining protocols, something that seems totally impractical.

But it isn't. Here's why. Let's say we're going to restrict attention to the BNE of any bargaining protocol we might consider. So fix a particular bargaining protocol—decide who gets to make an offer first, how the other can respond, etc., and let's call it "P-star" ("P" for protocol). Next, locate the BNE of this protocol. This means "find the pair of beliefs and strategies that if each expects the other to stick to their part, each does best by sticking to theirs, and each is correct." Call these strategies "S-star" for the seller and "B-star" for the buyer.

Now, what would happen if you and I entered the room and made an offer to the two parties, telling each participant that we'll do the bargaining for them, and we'll do it *by playing the BNE strategy* of each player for the valuation that *they tell us they have*. Would they want to lie? The answer is no.

To see this, let's take some steps. First, if the seller placed a value of just $100 on the painting (her fiancé hates it, so she'd sell for any offer greater than a $100), then let's say her BNE strategy under the protocol we're currently considering is to offer to sell for $140. Similarly, let's say her BNE strategy under the same protocol, P-star, would have been $180, had her fiancé hated the painting a bit less. Now, in the event that he actually hates the painting, would she tell us to make the offer as if he *didn't*? In other words, would she lie? From the fact that $140 was her best strategy when her fiancé really hated the painting, against the BNE strategy of her opponent, we know it was a best response to the buyer's expected offer. This immediately means that she will not lie. And neither will the buyer, when faced with the question of how he valued the painting.

In short, therefore, the promise of a third party to always institute play of the BNE strategies of each player against the others *for the types they say they are* means that we have located a way to reproduce the BNE outcome of the bargaining protocol P-star via a **direct-revelation mechanism** (it is so called because it is a direct procedure in which each side is simply asked their valuation, and we assign outcomes according to the *Nash strategies given these announcements*). Since we can do this for any bargaining protocol we can cook up, we have found a much easier way to find the best protocol: just search among the set of direct-revelation mechanisms in which truth telling and participation are what the participants want to do.

The idea that we just used is known as the **revelation principle**. It is tremendously handy because it allows us to look at a single kind of problem to locate the properties of the best of *all* possible bargaining protocols between these two. And I mean *all*. Together with the notion of Nash equilibrium, it is a clear example of an apparently abstract theoretical notion serving the most practical sort of goal. It is a result that has had widespread use in macroeconomics, especially in the literature in which macroeconomists have sought to locate ideal schemes for insuring at-risk populations without destroying their incentives to work. The need for incentives arises because in these models, work effort is not easily visible to policymakers. Even more famously, it is *the* tool that has facilitated a great deal of analysis of auction procedures, and has contributed significantly to the design of governmental auctions of various publicly held items, such as wireless spectrum bandwidth.[45]

And now, Myerson and Satterthwaite's result can be cleanly expressed. Using the revelation principle, these authors show something striking and disappointing: when there is a possibility that are no gains from trade, there is *no* protocol for bargaining that will always allow the parties to realize gains from trade for all the possible "valuations" they may, as the result of the shocks each faces, wind up having. Ely (2010b) states this in a nice way:

> The problem is one of information. If B is going to be induced to sell to A, the price must be high enough to make B willing to part with the good. And the more B values the good, the higher the price it must be. That principle, which is required for market efficiency, creates an incentive problem which makes efficiency impossible. Because now B has an incentive to hold out for a higher price by *acting as if* he is unwilling to part with the good. And *sometimes* that price is more than A is willing to pay. [italics added]

Notice that in some instances, the combination of bargaining protocol chosen by the type of spouse the potential seller had and the type of shock the potential buyer received will result in the efficient thing happening—i.e., the art being exchanged for payment when both gain from such an exchange. What the theorem tells us is that it simply cannot be efficient for all the possible realizations of these shocks. In sum, the privately held information that each has thwarts what, in a Walrasian setting, would of course allow for all gains from trade to be realized for certain. It is precisely in this sense that market power yields inefficient outcomes and renders relevant a form of privately held information that, *under Walrasian conditions, would be no hurdle to efficiency.*

Why do macroeconomists care about all this, and why should you, if for example, you're an economic writer thinking about macroeconomic questions? After all, the work I have referred to has, overwhelmingly, been conducted by microeconomic theorists, with far fewer notable contributions from macroeconomists on questions of a more macroeconomic scope. But it is this work that gives us a more sophisticated view of when one should be concerned about whether competition is sufficient or not. Moreover, in those models in which macroeconomists impose forms of market power, such as standard models used in monetary policy analysis, it is the preceding work that helps provide discipline and expose incoherence. For example, in so-called new Keynesian models of monetary policy, a vital input is a measure of the "stickiness" of prices, which in part determines the extent of market power a firm has. Here, macroeconomists routinely appeal to microeconomists' work to appropriately parameterize the size of such stickiness. But in the same class of models, microeconomic theorists have noted a host of problems related to the assumptions made about the "commitment" of firms to produce in situations where macroeconomists' models merely assume they would. Microeconomists have been an important part of the macroeconomic enterprise by directly helping macroeconomists "assign numbers" to our models (we'll encounter this again in chapter 5, when we discuss "calibration" procedures), and by holding our feet to the fire when aspects of the behavior assumed by macroeconomists do not seem to make much sense.

2.8.4.3   Further Reading

The interested reader looking for a more general and exhaustive nontechnical treatment of the limitations of the First and Second Welfare Theorems and the ADM model will find useful the work of Nobel Laureate Joseph Stiglitz in *Whither Socialism?* (1994). Stiglitz's book is a must-read for anyone interested in a critical view of the ADM model as a tool for interpreting the real world, even whatever is *good* about decentralized market systems, and comes from the consummate insider. He covers a huge list of aspects of reality, some of them quite subtle, that call into question the relevance of the First and Second Welfare Theorems as sufficient rationales for using decentralized resource allocation mechanisms.[46]

2.9   The Observational Implications of the ADM Model

The basic ADM model is so general that it has no direct implications for what one should observe in the data. In a sense, this should not shock us. We simply see that a model that allows nearly unlimited richness and variation among its constituent parts also implies few sharp observable implications. With no further restrictions on the attributes of households and firms, we ought not to expect any more definitive implications from the ADM model.

This is, in one way, an excellent state of affairs: macroeconomists have some key results that are not sensitive to many conditions that are unobservable. Specifically, we won't usually know who is risk-averse, or to what extent, nor who risk-loving, nor their patience level, nor what firms can do, etc. And yet, if we have a complete set of competitive markets, we're guaranteed both that we'll have a set of Walrasian prices (i.e., we have "existence") and that the welfare theorems apply to outcomes.

The unobservability of many aspects of the ADM construction is not all good, of course. Most obviously, it causes us real problems in assessing the relevance of the ADM model in describing what we see around us. For example, we cannot check directly the extent to which Arrow-Debreu presumptions are approximated.[47] Nor can we check whether "markets clear" in any direct manner: one cannot definitively see if an inventory pile-up is really unplanned, nor if households are "surprised" by the outcomes they ended up with in trade, and so on. What one can at best observe is how much each household earns (and maybe what they spend it on), and what each firm produces.

In fact, with no further restrictions than local nonsatiation of household preferences, we ought not to expect any more definitive implications from the ADM model, such as outcomes (equilibria) that match even *qualitative* features of the data. One example of a qualitative feature of aggregate US data is that consumption is smoother than output, and output is smoother than investment. The basic ADM model has no predictions for this ordering. For example, by not insisting for its three results (existence and two welfare theorems) that households be risk-averse, the ADM equilibrium can easily be coaxed into being one where consumption is the least smooth, output next, and investment after that. If households actually liked risk a lot, this is indeed what one might expect. But this ordering of "which data fluctuate more" is suggestive of risk-averse behavior. As a result, only an ADM model further restricted in terms of the characteristics of market participants' risk attitude is likely to have any chance of matching these data.

More generally, the preceding implies that to generate predictions for actual observable data, we need to add more structure by restricting preferences and technological features of firms' production sets in ways that allow the ADM (or Radner) equilibria to match salient data. If we are successful, we can logically assert that it is possible to interpret what we see as the unfolding of a (perhaps incomplete-market) Radner equilibrium. As we'll see in chapter 5, this means we have to starting assigning *magnitudes* to things like how risk-averse (or not) households are, or what kind of production plans are feasible for the firms present.

2.9.1 Sonnenschein-Mantel-Debreu . . .

In the early 1970s, a series of papers were written in which it was shown that the number of Walrasian equilibria that were possible even in the presence of only very "nicely behaved" households and firms (each optimizing given prices) was very high, potentially infinite, in fact. One particular problem was that two Walrasian outcomes might be very "far" away from each other (measured, say, in terms of the utility levels obtained by consumers in each), even though their "data"—i.e., households' preferences or firms' technological capabilities—were extremely close to each other. The sequence of mathematical statements that gave such precision to this potential hypersensitivity of outcomes to initial conditions was due to three important economists: Hugo Sonnenschein, Rolf Mantel, and Gerard Debreu. Thus, the result is known by the last names of each, Sonnenschein-Mantel-Debreu, or SMD for short (see Mas-Colell, Whinston, and Green 1995, ch. 17, for a clear discussion).

From a modeling perspective, an implication of SMD is that if an outside observer was told by a macroeconomist that a given model economy had many Walrasian equilibria, that observer could not with any confidence infer that the multiplicity of equilibria was due to some quirky way of modeling household preferences or firm production capabilities.

Why must the SMD result be true? The details are both essential and technical, but the crux of the problem can be conveyed fairly easily. Think of a household that goes to a market to buy a bundle of goods and services. If prices for some goods are a bit higher today than yesterday, how does it change an individual's behavior? First off, when some goods are more expensive than before, households may opt to buy less of those goods. This effect is called the "substitution effect," and it always moves the consumer away from more expensive goods. Second, the increase in prices makes the individual poorer overall; he simply cannot afford exactly the same things he could afford yesterday. This effect further depresses the consumer's demand for all goods—not just the ones whose prices went up. This latter effect is called the "income effect." The size of these forces and the direction in which they move a consumer's purchases both matter for determining the ultimate effect of the price change. And here is where problems arise: without knowing more about how a given consumer's preferences for goods and services look, usually well beyond knowing that they are rational, we cannot know if the income effect will be positive or negative. Moreover, the size of these effects will depend, in general, on the incomes of households, and possibly on the distribution of income across households. As a result, the effect on the aggregate amounts of goods consumers as a whole would choose to purchase at different prices may vary, possibly wildly, with prices. It is precisely this fact that gives rise to the possibility that many different constellations of prices can be Walrasian.

2.9.2 . . . and Boldrin-Montrucchio

A result that is closely related to the SMD theorem is that due to Michele Boldrin and Luigi Montrucchio in "On the Indeterminacy of Capital Accumulation Paths" (1986). The emphasis in macroeconomics on models in which decisions were made through time led in the 1970s and 1980s to questions that were similar in flavor to the ones that preceded SMD. In particular, economists became interested in learning about what kinds of outcomes were possible for the more special case in which household-level decisions took explicit advantage of the special structure of "intertemporal" decision making. For example, households in such cases are usually modeled as maximizing "additively separable" representations of their underlying preferences, and are almost always modeled as discounting payoffs that will arrive in the future at a constant rate (known as "exponential" discounting).

In the mid 1980s, Boldrin and Montrucchio proved a striking result for the case of models in which households made decisions through time. These authors showed that in general, a very wide class of paths over time for an economy's fundamentals (output, investment, etc.) could be perfectly optimal for an economy populated by "reasonable"-looking decision makers, i.e., who conformed to the standard assumptions just mentioned. Boldrin and Montrucchio's theorem applied to the solution of any problem of optimal decision making through time, whether the optimal policy for decisions was for an individual household or firm, or for an entire economy. Now, we know from a result of Constantinides (1982) that any complete-markets Walrasian outcome looks as if it were the solution to a single, *optimizing*, representative agent. But by Boldrin and

Montrucchio (BM), we know that even if that outcome involved "wild" trajectories for income, consumption, output (or all three!), it could still be an optimal path for a society full of "reasonably behaved" individual decision makers.

There are two reasons to emphasize this result. First, it should put to bed the idea that macroeconomists only study settings in which things can't get too crazy. Second, that optimality, at least in the Pareto sense, does not mean "stable-looking" behavior. As a consequence, without a reason to suspect otherwise (and there may be reasons—I am not prejudging matters—wait till chapter 6), wild paths may not be so obviously improved on.

SMD and BM are simply facts about the nature of Walrasian outcomes and the restrictions created (or not) by individual- and firm-level optimization. To the extent that we think that the institutional arrangement for trade in most goods and services is indeed one in which consumers choose how much to purchase taking prices as given, the fact that income and substitution effects might be confounding is "just the way it is."

2.9.2.1 Does It Mean That "Anything *Will* Happen"? No

Now, think of a case where one is working with a model in which there are multiple Walrasian equilibria. Some commentators have taken this case to mean that "free-market outcomes are doomed to displaying wild oscillations." *This is incorrect.* What does such a setting, if it is indeed the routine one, tell us about how "wild" the fluctuations displayed by such an economy will be? The answer is: nothing. The key to understanding this point is that the theorem tells us that an economy with "nicely behaved" households and firms may still be one in which there are many Walrasian equilibria, and that's all.

As a technical matter, SMD is a statement about the properties of the so-called **excess demand function (EDF)**. Think back to the idea of the WCH. For any given prices, we could ask: How much more would households wish to buy above what firms wanted to sell? If the answer came out to be a positive number, we'd say that there was "excess demand" at these prices, and if not, we'd say there was "excess supply." If prices were such that there was neither excess demand nor excess supply, we'd have found a Walrasian outcome. What SMD established was that the "shape" of the EDF could be such that there could be many sets of prices at which excess demand was zero.

Now, it is crucial to understand that the preceding is not simply a statement about what any one of those equilibrium outcomes looks like. That is, the fact that there are many equilibria in a given economy does not tell you what is happening in any one of them. This means, for example, that some of an economy's equilibria may indeed be ones in which there is a lot of fluctuation over time, while others feature outcomes in which all important variables like consumption or output remain stock-still. Alternatively, all of an economy's Walrasian equilibria might display vicious fluctuations. The point is simply that the characteristics of outcomes in a given equilibrium are in no obvious manner linked to the number of equilibria that a given specification of preferences and technology might allow for.

All this is a highly rarefied part of economic theory that is far away from the direct expertise of applied users like macroeconomists (present company included). In chapter 5, I'll show that SMD or BM have mattered for the construction of modern macroeconomic models because they force macroeconomists to place quantitative restrictions on the values of model "parameters." We'll discuss the quantification of the ADM model, in the guise of so-called dynamic stochastic general equilibrium (DSGE) models, and we'll see that the SMD and BM theorems are dealt with by studying narrower classes of economies in which the preferences, endowments, and technologies are quantitatively restricted to match data and, as a result, tend not to allow for wild fluctuations at all. In the case of SMD, income effects tend to be too muted to allow for many outcomes as equilibria; and in the case of BM, the levels of impatience needed to sustain very wild paths imply, under reasonable conditions, counterfactually high interest rates. This is a general type of response by economists to models that, without further restriction, permit multiple equilibria. Multiplicity is a symptom of an incomplete model. After all, something will occur, and the fact that your model says many things can happen just means you haven't adequately restricted the parameters or equilibrium concept of your model. Lastly, to the extent that wild oscillations arise in an ADM model, both welfare theorems hold—which immediately implies that one cannot simply point to observed fluctuations as evidence of inefficiency.

Having said all this, there are actually some tight implications of preference- and profit-maximizing behavior under price taking at the individual level. Roughly speaking, these results establish that under just these two behavioral premises, price taking implies a version of the law of demand for households and a law of supply for households. The former says that at the level of the *individual* household or firm, prices and quantities demanded by households move in opposite directions, and the latter, that prices and the supply of goods and services move in the same direction. These findings go in the literature under the terms "weak and strong axioms of revealed preference" (WARP and SARP), and "weak axiom of profit maximization" (WAPM)—simply consult any microeconomics text.

This suggests, then, that the key to establishing such "traditional" behavior (i.e., "demand curves slope down and supply curves slope up") at the level of a single market with many households and firms, or in a system with many interrelated markets, is to place restrictions on the kinds of heterogeneity that participants display, especially on the consumer's side. As we'll encounter later, this is the path taken by the literature.

And in fact, all economists essentially take as given that markets exhibit sufficient regularity that laws of demand and supply apply to market demand and supply. Starkly put, when instructors draw the "usual" picture of a competitive market, they are *assuming away the perversions of SMD*. As a quantitative matter, this isn't so bad! After all, we teach it to all introductory students. And it is what leads us to many "home truths" that we hector noneconomists about all the time: that when you tax something, less of it will be produced and consumed, and when you subsidize something, more will be. These seem plausible implications at many levels, but SMD tells you that no such thing need be true—market demand curves could be upward sloping. So the strength of criticisms of macroeconomics for failing to come to terms with aggregation applies with equal force to the work of microeconomists, or any other economist, for that matter. To somehow view any branch of economics that deals with price-taking participants, macro- or otherwise, as inherently (theoretically) immune to SMD is senseless: whether SMD perverts both single-market or aggregate behavior is fundamentally a solely quantitative question. We'll describe how quantitative discipline is brought to bear on macroeconomic models subject, in principle, to SMD and/or BM, in chapter 5.

2.10 A Macro-Hippocratic Moment

Even though macroeconomists will generally concede that markets won't always work well for many public goods or for executing a variety of intertemporal trades, the substitution for, or repair of, these institutions is a tricky business and hence not always advisable. This is because the forces that create market dysfunction, especially those coming from some parties behaving counter to a given agreement because they know more about their actions than others do (so-called moral hazard), or from the inability of some to commit to honoring promises, will frequently hinder policymakers and governments just as they hinder markets.

All this is why macroeconomists in policymaking positions will typically ask proponents of any ostensibly efficiency-improving policy (e.g., alternative energy, national defense) to spell out which ADM presumptions are violated, and then why a more "centralized" policy intervention will be able to overcome the forces leading to these violations. And all this is why we are also generally slow to endorse many forms of regulation, especially taxes and quantity restrictions (such as any that accompany price controls), since they can interfere with the formation of many Walrasian prices all at once. In sum, the ADM model, the supporting evidence for its relevance, and the difficulty of overcoming the barriers faced by private-market participants, together lead modern macroeconomists to usually urge policymakers to leave the competitive market largely intact, and focus instead on case-by-case repair or substitution of any market suspected of malfunction, with careful attention to what precisely the public sector can do to overcome whatever hobbled the private sector.

2.11   Concluding Remarks

When (i) markets are complete, (ii) all buyers and sellers are rational optimizers of their preferences and profits respectively, and (iii) all face Walrasian prices and take them as given, core outcomes result. This is a version of the "invisible-hand" theorem, conjectured by Adam Smith. Thus, Walrasian prices, if taken as given, will generate astonishing coordination among purely self-interested parties who know nothing about the rest of the world beyond prices and their narrow interests. In cases where all goods are private, practical (informal), theoretical, and experimental research all suggest that competitive free trade in economies with "many" households and firms should be viewed as a reliable "machine" for producing Walrasian prices, price-taking behavior for all parties, and hence, Walrasian outcomes for a wide, *though emphatically not complete*, range of goods and services.

I also discussed the importance of the assumption of "nonstrategic" (i.e., price-taking) behavior both for the adequate performance of institutions which formed Walrasian prices (such as the WCH) in which price-taking behavior was critical, and for any narrative in which prices themselves were claimed to be responsible for the vast coordination implied by Walrasian outcomes. In particular, I noted that if one viewed prices as primarily the observed *outcomes* of a deeper and vastly more complex "competitive brawl," then one could not meaningfully point to prices themselves as "doing" any coordinating. The religious language of the "magic of the price system" would have to be thrown out. I then argued that, while some prices clearly were byproducts of such a "brawl," a view of all prices as such was too extreme, and that, indeed, prices are likely coordinating a good deal of daily economic activity.

We have so far taken the initial endowments of goods and skills of households *as given*, and have asked about how Walrasian resource allocation schemes might do relative to the standard of the core (or Pareto efficiency more generally). But what if these initial endowments are grossly unequal? After all, we did note at the outset that the satisfaction of the core or Pareto standards does not impose any real restrictions on inequality. The reader may say, "Who cares about efficiency?" or alternatively, "If the only efficient outcomes free markets can attain are extremely unequal, then I simply don't care about attaining efficiency; I will take an *inefficient but equal* society instead." These are perfectly sensible reactions, and addressing what is known about the tradeoff between equity and efficiency leads us first to chapter 3, and eventually, to chapter 5, where I will detail some aspects of what we can claim to know as a *quantitative* matter.

3   Macroeconomists, Efficiency, and Inequality

3.1   Economists, Efficiency, and Inequality

The business of "positive" economics can keep macroeconomists busy for a long time. The daily work of research macroeconomists is typically aimed at measuring (by unearthing empirical regularities arising from the messy and decidedly nonexperimental data that real life provides) and understanding (by providing quantitatively and qualitatively plausible accounts of observed phenomena as equilibrium outcomes from the decentralized trade that characterizes most economic activity). Examples include the research programs in business cycles, labor market activity, and consumption (and, as I noted, the not yet fully successful attempts to explain the equity premium).

One dimension of macroeconomic practice is the positive assessment of policy proposals. How do capital income taxes alter long-run wage rates? By how much did extension of unemployment insurance benefits lengthen unemployment spells? If there is a big shock to oil prices, what will happen to outcomes under different fiscal or monetary policy responses? How will major financial regulatory reform affect growth? And so on.

A great many of these policies, in turn, came into being from attempts to equalize well-being and shield people from market outcomes. Efforts at redistribution financed via taxes on capital income, the presence of social insurance schemes like the US unemployment insurance system and Medicaid program, restrictions on prices such as minimum wage and rent control laws, and financial regulation are all clearly about altering outcomes arising in the "marketplace." These often disparate policies are thus persistent reminders of a fundamental—and widely shared—unwillingness to tolerate unfettered market outcomes, even in a country so apparently "pro-market" as the United States.

But macroeconomists working in government or in central banks often do more than measure or predict "how much" a policy will matter for outcomes. They routinely *recommend* to policymakers that policies be adopted or rejected. On what basis are these judgments made, and what do macroeconomists really have to offer to the discussion on the extent to which market outcomes *ought to be* altered? In this chapter and the next, I will detail how the ADM model directs our thinking on the modification of market outcomes. With this material in hand, readers will find it easy to follow the discussion in chapter 5, where we will encounter some of the most important kinds of models currently in use to answer questions related to the costs and benefits of "public" interference in economic activity.

As we go along, though, I hope the reader will keep one fact in mind: the views of macroeconomists, dentists, sheet metal workers, lawyers, and everyone else all have equal claim to being evaluated when it comes to deciding what is "just" or "fair" or "right." The only expertise that the macroeconomist brings to bear, though it is not minor, is a toolbox for thinking about and, especially, measuring, the tradeoffs that may be associated with different policies.[1]

3.1.1 Decentralized Trading and Inequality

The great criticism of all decentralized trading systems, such as primarily private-ownership (i.e., "capitalist") systems like those increasingly in place worldwide, is that they generate inequality or, worse yet, *require* it in order to function.[2] How does the ADM model—which, after all, is our main benchmark model of an economy as a whole—influence our view of these criticisms? The first point when thinking about markets and inequality is this: the ADM model tells us that inequality in outcomes will generally reflect the resources with which market participants *arrive* at the marketplace. This is not surprising: if I have only a handful of green beans and eight tennis balls to my name, it is unlikely that the prices of these items will be sufficiently high that I can swap them for a house, car, and nice meals at my favorite restaurant.

More seriously, imagine the plight of high school dropouts in the United States. Under current and foreseeable future circumstances, there is little chance that their skills will command many dollars per hour. Thus, even if these individuals were lucky enough to live in a society with a smoothly functioning WCH, they would only be assured that in the end there would not be any mutually beneficial trading opportunities left over; no missed opportunities for them to sell their labor time to someone at a rate that both would find agreeable. Yet they would not be assured in any way that their lives would be materially comfortable; indeed, they probably will not be. Thus, while asking that outcomes be efficient may rule out many outcomes, there will almost always be horrifically unequal and yet fully efficient outcomes that remain. Pareto efficiency may seem, then, a rather weak standard by which to judge outcomes.

But notice that the fact that inequitable outcomes can be fully efficient tells us that one cannot take observed inequality as a foolproof indicator of a "malfunctioning" economic system, at least through the narrow lens of Pareto efficiency. That is, trading arrangements may be doing as well as they can—in the sense of leaving no opportunities to make *all* better off—*given* the initial inequality present in the capabilities and resources of market participants.[3] Thus, some concerns that markets perpetuate inequality miss the point: markets are simply human contrivances for allowing mutually beneficial gains from trade to take place. They are *not* institutions engineered to make people more equal. As such, it is a non sequitur to tether markets to observed inequality. In fact, it seems intuitive that if people entered markets with more equal capabilities, they'd leave more equal too. This is a correct intuition and will be discussed further below.

3.1.2 Economists' Preoccupation with "Efficiency"

Throughout this book, I have emphasized the notion of Pareto efficiency. When it comes to policy, the related notion of **Pareto improvement** is of central relevance. This term means what it sounds like: a change that *all* households prefer. These changes are hard to come by: almost any policy will create winners and losers, and absent any compensation of losers by winners, will not yield Pareto improvements. Still, economists are usually more interested than policymakers in the extent to which a policy would yield even a *potential* Pareto improvement, where losers from a policy change *could* be compensated in principle, even if they are not, to make them better off. In fact, we seem, at least superficially, ready to promote even those policies that would appear to increase inequality, so long as they appear to be potential Pareto improvements. Examples include economists' frequent advocacy for policies that allow market processes to work unimpeded—such as letting the prices of essentials spike in disaster areas, eliminating minimum-wage laws, or in macroeconomic cases, urging the removal or alteration of policies like taxes on capital income or luxury goods—policies that society explicitly created to achieve distributional aims.

So is it that economists do not share the same distributional goals as the average (or median) voter? Surely some do not, but there are several other reasons for the high priority most economists give to the pursuit of Pareto efficiency, and each of these is informed by our ADM-based perspective. First, the most important reason: once (macro) economists start lobbying for non-Pareto improvements, they are making judgment calls about the distribution of well-being across members of a society. On this issue, they should have no greater claim to anyone's attention than anyone else. However, our tools *are* suited for a more prosaic task: they can analyze a trading arrangement, or a policy, or a combination of the two, and determine the extent to which it is wasteful or productive for various classes of an (model) economy's participants.[4] This type of work, which is the bread and butter of macroeconomic policy analysis, can assist in locating the least wasteful way to achieve whatever distributional goals society elects to pursue.[5]

A second reason for economists' focus on efficiency is that policy, if it is trying hard, ought to look for Pareto-optimal outcomes. To do otherwise is to admit that in the end, outcomes under the policy will be ones where everyone can be made further off! But locating a Pareto-optimal allocation to target is very hard: policymakers would need to know essentially everything about consumers and producers that we have argued is impractical for them to know. Moreover, it would almost surely be undesirable for them to have the requisite amount of information, barring an (unrealistic) ironclad guarantee that policymakers would not use the information to manipulate or blackmail the citizenry. Thus, our ability to choose a Pareto-efficient outcome is exceedingly limited. Unless we are able to generate, via policy, the preconditions for the First Welfare theorem: In this case, letting decentralized trade occur and deliver a Walrasian outcome would yield us a Pareto-optimal outcome. But this would only be so for whatever the initial endowments were, and thus might be grotesquely unequal.

In general, unless they simply are lucky, policymakers will almost certainly select outcomes that while perhaps more equitable than the status quo, will leave at least some mutually beneficial exchanges unrealized. And here is where this informational hurdle creates a serious problem for redistribution in particular, and for policy in general: unless we know that the costs of inefficiency will not be borne substantially by the relatively poor, the distributional consequences of policies may be perverse (I will describe some textbook examples, those of rent control and "luxury" taxes, further below). As a result, economists always fear, at least a little, interventions lacking solid upside for potential Pareto improvement, or ones that do not represent a move toward meeting the preconditions of the First Welfare Theorem.

A third reason for economists' general perspective on inequality is that in some, though emphatically not all, instances in which inequality arises *from* market dysfunction, policy authorities may not be able to do much. For example, take a case where households face individual-level labor market risk that they cannot fully insure against. Think of trying to buy a contract from an insurance company to be used in the event that you get laid off. If you cannot obtain such protection, you may have to save money for a rainy day. But this means that as time goes by, those who avoid a layoff will likely have larger bank balances those who did get laid off. As a result, workers' own personal histories of employment outcomes will affect how unequal their wealth is at any given moment.

Now consider the case where the lack of comprehensive privately provided income insurance occurs because an insurer cannot observe how much *effort* an insured worker exerts if and when she is laid off. This is known as **moral hazard**. As a result, if the insurer were to offer a contract that fully replaced earnings losses upon layoff, it might not be able to do it at prices the worker would find attractive. In this instance, any well-meaning publicly funded government unemployment insurance program will indeed help the recipients, and, by eliminating the need to accumulate "precautionary" savings, the program could make society even more equal in its wealth and consumption. However, society at large will see a lowering of work incentives that may well lower total societal income and indirectly hurt many. Of course, this is a tradeoff that most might find well worth it, and the widespread existence of publicly funded safety nets worldwide suggests that most do. However, it is very unlikely to be without negative implications. In the presence of such insurance, the overall economic pie is likely to be smaller than it otherwise would be.

Or think of a situation where the average person cannot obtain credit at low interest rates because lenders do not trust him to repay debts. The government can certainly help this group as well, and by equalizing credit access, can help equalize household standards of living. However, such help, especially if it comes in the form of subsidies that effectively allow lenders to relax credit standards, will lead to credit

flowing away from other, more productive uses, and will almost necessarily lead to an increase in loan default rates and generate the negative
side effects such events seem to carry.

The examples above capture what economists believe to be the two
main sources of market dysfunction: *privately held information* and/or
a *limited ability to commit* to acting as initially promised. Unless we think
policymakers are particularly privileged with information or particularly able to commit to punishing a breach of contract severely, they
may not be able to improve on the organic mechanisms that private
trade has evolved to deal with such problems (sometimes with only
partial success).

Thus, in all realistic settings, there is almost certainly an **equity-
efficiency tradeoff**.[6] Chapter 5 will discuss some models used by macroeconomists to *quantify* this tradeoff, and will show how active this
area of research is. For now, though, we simply note that the mere
existence of this tradeoff will lower the extent to which most people,
including economists, value redistribution.

I've now given several reasons for the concern that equality may
come at the price of efficiency and therefore might be costly to all
members of a society. The goal of reaching a Pareto-efficient outcome—
or at the very least, chasing after Pareto improvements—then seems to
gain ground relative to the promotion of policies aimed more directly
at altering inequality. So it is fortunate for those worried that a great
deal may be lost by pursuing efficiency alone that improving efficiency
actually sometimes *helps* to equalize. In these cases, equity considerations are best dealt with *via* the pursuit of efficiency. As we'll see in
chapter 5, a good deal of recent work suggests that much observed
inequality can be interpreted plausibly as a *symptom*, or consequence,
of missing markets, especially those offering protection or insurance
against certain risks. These include the absence of easily available
private insurance against unemployment (especially disability), impediments in the market for unsecured consumer credit, and the risk of
having poor, or sometimes, simply incompetent, parents. From the
perspective of a new entrant into society, this last risk is arguably by
far the most important.

There are also clear instances in which the absence of some markets
may allow other markets to *perpetuate* inequality. For example, a lack
of an insurance market for some risks may leave relatively rich agents
more willing to take on certain higher-risk–higher-return projects that
their poorer counterparts would not (such as incurring debt to send

even their less well-prepared children to college in hopes that they will complete a degree and attain the high earnings that seem to go with it, a risk that poorer parents might not be able to tolerate). In the longer run, the former may then get relatively (and absolutely) richer, all else being equal. In fact, as will be discussed in chapter 5, it is an extremely general point that once certain markets are missing, Walrasian outcomes will not be efficient even given the limited capabilities of the remaining markets! This is called "constrained inefficiency" and offers a negative view of laissez-faire that is more sophisticated than the usual arguments.

In instances where we know that trading is hindered not by moral hazard, as in the earlier unemployment example, but rather by the ability of some to not participate in the market, public policy *can* help. For instance, if most people knew their own risk of unemployment in a way that an insurer did not, the ones with little risk might not purchase any unemployment insurance, and so might leave the pool seeking insurance relatively riskier. This would necessitate higher premiums for private insurers to break even, which would further lower the incentives of the remaining relatively low-risk persons to stay in the pool, and so on. In such instances of so-called **adverse selection**, policy can assist efficiency by simply making participation in some insurance schemes *mandatory*. This is the basic idea behind the mandates one sees in auto insurance (and now in health insurance as well). Similarly, if we know that limited commitment to honoring contractual obligations is what prevents some mutually beneficial exchanges in a given market, we might be able to help with policy. For example, to the extent that uncollateralized credit is expensive for poor households, public policy might be able to help efficiency. A direct route would be to credibly commit poor households to repayment by making loan default more legally onerous. These interventions will be case-specific, of course.[7] It is interesting to notice that in both of these examples, while the policy responses were aimed at enhancing efficiency and not deliberately at alleviating inequality per se, they both can potentially help households remain more equal to each other than they otherwise would be.

In the two examples above, people would become unequal simply because of the presence of uninsurable risks and their resulting attempts to "self-insure" through wealth accumulation or credit use. The inequality in wealth or indebtedness that would follow from the different labor market experiences of different households is surely something we might all view as reflective of an inefficient system of markets.

This view of inequality as indicating the inefficient function of a given trading system is a powerful one, as I will emphasize in chapter 5. It is to my mind a real and coherent way to reconcile certain kinds of policy that, while superficially appearing merely redistributive, might be best viewed as implementing insurance arrangements that *all* would agree on, and therefore as Pareto improvements. And while purely redistributive transfers may reflect either corrupt political processes or potentially quite arbitrary judgments on the importance of different citizens' well-being, the "before the fact" perspective offers a different view. A reader may detect the ideas of the philosopher John Rawls (1971) in the preceding, and they would be partially correct. In Rawls's **maximin** prescription, well-being cannot rise under a policy change unless the well-being of society's worst-off member rises. The version I will give is due to John Harsanyi (1975), and while it nests Rawls's preferred recipe as one rather extreme case, it does not commit one to it.

The reasoning above, when taken as a whole, means we must think carefully before advocating large-scale redistribution that is not motivated by efficiency-related concerns. It leads macroeconomists, in the main, to focus on remedying market dysfunction wherever possible, and to be less likely than many others in society to support aiming directly at inequality. Moreover, in the cases where macroeconomists support explicitly redistributive goals, they will usually look for ways to equalize primarily through policies which affect not market prices but rather the "initial" endowments that people bring into the markets in which they trade. The feasibility of the latter strategy is suggested by the so-called Second Fundamental Theorem of Welfare Economics, to be introduced further below. First, though, it's useful to provide intuition about what is wrong with any tax that alters the prices faced by buyers and sellers in any single market.

3.1.3   Deadweight Loss from Taxation
A fundamental idea in economics is that any tax that varies in size with decisions that people or firms take will lead to something known as **deadweight loss**. An example of such a tax is a sales tax applied to meals eaten at a restaurant. Typically, this tax is a percentage of the total value of the meal you just ate. The more you spend, the larger in absolute terms your tax bill is. The key idea from the theory of "public finance" is that the economic damage (when expressed in dollar terms) caused to participants from whom a given amount of revenue is

extracted will, in such settings, almost always be *greater than the revenues that are raised by the tax.* In other words, you can rarely, if ever, hope for the pure transferring aspects of a lump-sum tax. The difference is called the deadweight loss.[8]

For macroeconomists, who routinely weigh in on issues of how to tax, what to tax, and whom to tax, deadweight loss is extremely important, especially when there are potential spillovers created by a given taxation policy. For instance, if a macroeconomist is consulted on the usefulness of moving to a "flat" tax regime that applies to the income households spend on all the goods and services they value, she will construct a model in which part of the model's output will supply information on the deadweight loss that is created in the entire market system as a whole. The deadweight loss is therefore a measure of the "collateral" damage caused by a tax, here used in the narrow sense that the market participant facing the tax would rather simply pay the tax in a lump sum than have his choices distorted. This certainly sounds like a compelling reason to use lump-sum taxes to raise whatever revenue a government wants to, right? Well, not quite, as we'll see shortly. But before we call such taxes into question, let's look at a case where they're just what is needed.

3.2   The Second Welfare Theorem

Given that equality, in addition to efficiency, will likely be a concern for most citizens, a natural first question to ask is: Which Pareto-optimal allocations would be accessible to a society that used "free markets" (or a well-functioning WCH!) to facilitate trade? The answer, if you have complete competitive markets, is in general: *all* of them! The result known as the **Second Welfare Theorem** formalizes this.

Here's what it says: under some "reasonable" conditions, every Pareto-efficient allocation "looks as if" it was generated by self-interested households and firms operating in complete competitive markets that entered with a particular set of initial endowments and ownership shares and then faced prices that were Walrasian for these initial conditions. Therefore, if we knew the preferences of households, and the technological capabilities of firms, and if we could somehow assign initial endowments prior to any trade at all, and if free trade acts like a complete-markets WCH, then we could ensure ourselves efficient allocations for *any* level of inequality we are comfortable with as a society.[9]

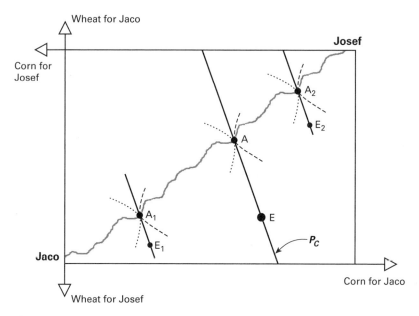

Figure 3.1
The Second Welfare Theorem.

To illustrate the theorem, let's go back to our two farmers from chapters 1 and 2, and return again to the Edgeworth box in figure 3.1. Now, though, let's say that, for whatever reason, a benevolent policy-maker wanted an efficient but less egalitarian outcome such as point A_1 or A_2. Can she achieve both aims? The Second Welfare Theorem assures that if the policymaker has access to person-specific lump-sum taxes before trade occurs, she can indeed. "All" she has to do is move the pretrade allocation to *any* point on the line connecting the endowment point and the desired Pareto-efficient outcome. So, for example, a move of initial (pretrade) endowment to point E_1 will, if the economy acts as if it has a WCH, take the outcome after trade to the Walrasian equilibrium at A_1, as desired. Or to obtain the Pareto-efficient outcome A_2 as a Walrasian outcome, the government can take the line implied by the tangency of the farmers' indifference curves at A_2, and place endowments at any point on it, such as E_2. Since all that is required is to move endowments, we can transfer the good that is most easily transferred or pick the set of transfers that in some metric is easiest. For example, we needn't move pretrade endowments directly to the Pareto optimum we are trying to implement. And we can do this for any Pareto optima—no matter how equal or unequal.

The punch line of the Second Welfare Theorem is, then, at least twofold. First, it tells us that, under its premises, *insisting that outcomes be efficient doesn't put any allocation beyond the reach of Walrasian prices.* One needn't resort to inefficiency-inducing measures to attain distributional goals. Put another way, under the premises of the theorem there is *no equity-efficiency tradeoff.* You can have any efficient outcome no matter how far it is from the (efficient) pure laissez-faire outcome. Simply levy the "right" lump-sum taxes and transfers to ensure that the initial (i.e., post-lump-sum-tax) endowments are such that when households trade from them, the resulting Walrasian outcome with the desired distributional characteristics is attained.

Knowledge of the Second Welfare Theorem is thus a source of consternation to macroeconomists whenever they view complex or bureaucratic procedures aimed at achieving distributional goals. Think of the complex US tax code, the very existence of a corporate tax, the newly enacted healthcare legislation, and so on.[10] Under the premises of the theorem, such policies guarantee that any hope of Pareto efficiency is lost. In other words, messy, non-lump-sum approaches guarantee that we'll suffer social waste. Of course, one's distributional preferences might lead one to support some or all of the policies mentioned above, and, as I've stressed, that is perfectly legitimate, but one must acknowledge the near-certainty that pure social waste will follow—and the Second Welfare Theorem tells us why this must be true.

An implication is that the government, if it is involved at the outset, can achieve society's distributional goals by sticking to a narrow role as a "check-writing operation" and needn't play any role in the actual production and distribution of anything. Nor need it impose taxes of the kind guaranteed to induce deadweight loss, such as any that create a gap between the price paid by buyers and that received by sellers. In the main, most of us draw a bright line between the financing of an activity and its production, and generally prefer to employ government as fundamentally a "personal shopper" that makes its purchases in existing competitive markets, but stays far away from the actual production of goods and services. The Second Welfare Theorem reminds us that the government's central advantage may lie in its ability to tax and transfer.

Along these lines, the theorem also has an implication at the level of the individual: if you care not a whit for the tasks and conditions of your work, then to do good, it would be best to locate the highest bidder for your time (or acquire the skills to be valuable), work incessantly, and make lump-sum transfers to others. Would-be conscientious citizens who are eager to assist others should be concerned, in general, that their career choices—if not substantially remunerative—may well be primarily self-indulgent, and only secondarily philanthropic.

A second broad lesson of the Second Welfare Theorem is that it tells us that even if prices are not used explicitly in a trading system, linear "efficiency prices" lurk beneath any Pareto-efficient distribution of households' consumption and firms' production efforts. We've seen this idea in another context: recall that if an economy was "large" and its participants have (very) good information on each other's activities, they might achieve core, and hence Pareto-efficient, and hence Walrasian, outcomes without any explicit mention of markets or prices. In sum, this theorem, in conjunction with its Siamese twin, the First Welfare Theorem, connects efficiency to Walrasian outcomes in a tight way.[11]

In fact, as for distributional justice, it may be that *only* Walrasian outcomes are even potentially "just" or "fair" in ways other than being "no-surplus" outcomes. An interesting set of results, due disproportionately to economists Hal Varian and William Thomson (see, e.g., Thomson and Varian 1985), is the rather uncanny emergence of a particular kind of Walrasian outcome, known as an income-fair Walrasian equilibrium (IFWE), as the *only* one that satisfies a variety of desiderata for what one might consider "fair" or "just." It thus certainly seems useful to achieve one's distributional goals via Walrasian outcomes. And if we view the real world as a decent approximation to a WCH, then this again leads us to focus on efficient means of redistributing purchasing power, as opposed to any number of other perhaps more informationally demanding schemes for redistribution.

To be clear, there are many caveats, as we will see.

3.2.1   The Welfare Theorems Inspire a Form of Central Planning!
Notice that the First Welfare Theorem establishes only that a complete set of Walrasian prices and cost-minimizing producer behavior is sufficient for "efficiency." The Second Welfare Theorem returns prices (at least "efficiency prices") to a more vaunted role. These ideas help explain the reaction of market socialists to Walrasian theory, as expressed in the seminal works of Barone (1908a) and, later, Lange (1936). The leaders of this movement believed—for precisely the reasons behind the welfare theorems—that it was indeed vital, for

efficiency's sake, to confront consumers and producers with Walrasian prices that were both taken as given and optimized with respect to, but that purchasing power could be equitably distributed if firms were owned by the state and people were entitled to an equitable share of any profits.

In particular, market socialists felt that one might be able to obtain even better outcomes with state-owned capital equipment (and producers, perhaps) than with private capital markets for three reasons. First and foremost, they felt they could achieve efficient outcomes that were also equitable. Second, they felt that state-owned production could be set up to circumvent the problems of monopoly power that would lead market societies to inefficient outcomes. Third, they were deeply concerned about the "boom/bust" cycles in investment that they felt plagued free-market societies. They viewed the state as being less prone to "speculative" manias in which investment rose rapidly, only to fall and take financial institutions and real production in its wake. The last idea may sound familiar to us in light of the Great Recession that has followed the housing investment bust.

Importantly, however, market socialists correctly saw Walrasian economics as completely mute on how one might ensure the *construction* of Walrasian prices. Mechanically, market socialists envisioned a structure where an actual WCH type of institution would be operated regularly to compute Walrasian prices for a large variety of goods and services. Then, based on the prices, the state-run firms would be instructed to produce the amounts that maximized profit. Households would supply labor based on these prices and their preferences, and then given their labor income, place their desired orders for the output. Markets would clear, as long as the prices were computed correctly. Most, if not all, production units (firms) and physical capital (e.g., plants and equipment) would be collectively owned, and private ownership—and hence trade in ownership claims (equity stock)—would be ruled out. The government would also be the lone (or predominant) employer of labor. Any profits that it collected would be used as general revenues either to be redistributed to the public or to be reinvested in firms. Any losses it sustained (if, for example, it failed to sell what it produced) would have to have come out of the pockets of consumers, through either lower payments to workers or higher prices. Thus, market socialists' proposals fully exploited the power of prices as devices that would allow society to attain efficient outcomes through entirely *decentralized economic decision making*.[12]

Nonetheless, market socialism, where it was tried (mainly eastern Europe), was not a great success. So what went wrong? Here, it's efficient to follow the arguments of Joseph Stiglitz, as laid out in *Whither Socialism?* (1994). Roughly, Stiglitz's argument is that given the preceding caveats, a state-run WCH that vainly formed linear prices and exhorted firms to use profit-maximizing behavior would have been trying to make prices do "too much" relative to what they are "asked" to do in real market economies. Here, "too much" includes asking them to provide incentives under private information while lacking commitment to allow failure (state-run firms had constituencies interested in keeping them alive, much as large firms do in modern market economies). By contrast, in actual market economies, a portion of these problems is solved by team production (firms) in the face of shareholders who will find their shares devalued if the firm wastes funds, and in the face of creditors who will force a bankruptcy if the firm becomes insolvent. Indeed, private ownership, i.e., "capitalism," without competition, is capitalism without a commitment to allowing failure, which in turn is capitalism bereft of Walrasian incentives. This, in the end, is then capitalism that is almost guaranteed to be inefficient and, worse, unequal.

It thus appears that well-defined property rights and "good old-fashioned competition with failure as a real possibility" are essential to making the environment a passable approximation to the premises of the ADM model, especially market completeness and profit-maximizing behavior by firms.

Stiglitz also notes that the ability of decentralized arrangements to provide (i) meaningful competition, (ii) a commitment to allow failure (among firms), and (iii) innovative contracts to deal with incentives problems and innovation itself, all are central to their success. On the latter, a particularly famous body of work is that due to Nobel laureate Elinor Ostrom, who documented a variety of instances in which even in the absence of markets for "commons," outcomes were hardly tragic.

Lastly, Stiglitz makes another interesting argument: he contends that if primarily decentralized approaches are superior to other alternatives such as market socialism, as they do appear to be, the ADM model is not helpful for telling us why. In particular, he argues that in the real world, prices (and certainly linear, Walrasian ones) are not central to outcomes, especially because a great deal of central planning happens in ostensibly "market" economies within firms; but, as I've noted, the boundaries of these centralized activities have a "rationality" to them.

In sum, experience across countries and across time shows unequivocally that primarily decentralized trade is unparalleled and, really, unique, in its ability to provide meaningful competition. It is workable, and from the relative performances of it and centralized alternatives to it over the twentieth century, we can assert that it alone is workable. Its deepest weaknesses—and they are serious—lie in the areas of insurance and credit provision (something, as I will repeatedly emphasize, that includes the dissolution of long-term relationships we coin "employment"). Unfortunately, these are weaknesses not trivial to remedy, least of all not through centrally sponsored behemoths with no accountability to consumers, and with access to state coffers. As a result, even in the current ferment in which wholesale alternatives to "capitalism" are being discussed with more seriousness than usual, none has much promise when compared to incremental repair or substitution for narrow classes of those markets that are poorly performing, combined with measures preventing pro-business policies from subverting pro-market goals. The latter has been argued to be a real risk by many, most recently Zingales (2012).

3.2.2   A General Lesson of the Second Welfare Theorem: Taxes Can Hurt

Since the Second Welfare Theorem teaches us that "things that are efficient always look like Walrasian outcomes," it offers us some clarity on just why *any* tax that is not lump-sum carries some baggage. We've already noted above that taxes create deadweight loss. However, that fact is routinely demonstrated in contexts that are narrow in two ways. First, as I noted, it is a fact that is almost always taught in the context of a single market. Second, it is a fact that is demonstrated in settings where relatively strong assumptions are made on the "smoothness" of households' responses to changes in the prices they face, whether tax-induced changes or otherwise. But what if we didn't want to make any such assumptions? What if all we were willing to assume was that households were locally insatiable, as we did when describing the First Welfare Theorem? Is it still true that non-lump-sum taxes invariably create efficiency loss? The Second Welfare Theorem tells us that the answer is yes. The reason is this: the contrapositive of the Second Welfare Theorem is: "not 'as if' Walrasian implies not efficient." But this immediately means that unless we have a setting where *all* parties—households and firms—choose outcomes "as if" they faced (or literally did face) the same Walrasian prices, we cannot be describing an efficient outcome. And non-lump-sum taxes, by definition, rule out the possibility that all parties face the same prices.

3.2.3 Caveat 1: What's an "Initial" Endowment, Anyway?

At this point, especially given what I've said, the Second Welfare Theorem might thus strike you as an endorsement for imposing what economists call "lump sum" taxes on the assets held by households as the best way to raise revenue. That is, shouldn't we look right now to impose tax liabilities on people in ways that they cannot alter through their actions? Not quite. As already noted, the Second Welfare Theorem imagines a reshuffling of endowments and purchasing power *prior to any trade whatsoever* and, equally importantly, where the measure of welfare ignores the "true" initial distribution (the distribution prior to the policymaker reshuffling endowments and ownership shares). Viewed this way, it says something much more limited. Namely, if I measure the well-being arising from the consumption of goods and services made financially feasible once I have reshuffled initial endowments, and define Pareto efficiency with respect to this post-reshuffling measure of well-being, I can achieve any Pareto-efficient outcome via a WCH.

So this theorem seems a theoretical curiosity, to be sure: we are already in the "middle" of time, and the "initial" endowments (e.g., the houses, stocks and bonds, and cars that people own) will matter for people's well-being: we cannot blithely pretend that reshuffling right now will not leave anyone worse off! To the extent, for example, that current trading arrangements can be expected to lead to efficient outcomes (say, the economy functions like a well-oiled complete-markets WCH), but where outcomes are more unequal than some like, we really cannot reshuffle endowments and ownership shares without making some worse off. All this having been said, let's circle back to a message that one can take from the result: the Second Welfare Theorem teaches us that Pareto-efficient outcomes have a fundamental connection to Walrasian prices—and anything that makes outcomes non-Walrasian opens the door to their being inefficient as well.

3.2.4 Caveat 2: Knowledge and the Limits to Lump-Sum Redistribution

Leaving entirely aside the question of what constitutes "initial" in the real world, let's now simplify matters and give you the keys to a brand-new society that has, in its central square, a perfectly working WCH. You have some preferences for equality that you'd like to impose, but you also want efficient outcomes. So you consult your friendly neighborhood macroeconomist, asking her: "What should I do?" She hands you a statement of the Second Welfare Theorem. "Aha!" you say, "I just need to make some transfers of initial endowments across people." And in this case, because the society hasn't started up yet (and hence no one has been assigned an initial bundle of endowments and ownership shares yet), all you need to do is just *start people off with the right endowments*. You can then sit back and watch, content to know that an efficient outcome that meets your criterion for equality is unfolding before your eyes.

This sounds good enough, right? Well, yes, except that there is an obvious problem. Barring omniscience, neither household preferences and their abilities nor the technological capabilities of existing firms are directly known to any government or other redistributive authority. If they were, we wouldn't need markets. So anyone wishing to use the theorem must *elicit* this information. However, if policymakers have to rely on the reports of those it questions, such information will potentially be misrepresented whenever participants find it in their interest to do so. Moreover, to the extent that factors such as intelligence and other personality characteristics matter crucially in a modern economy, genuine redistribution of these "endowments" may well be infeasible. As a result, the only feasible redistribution will involve efforts to redistribute the proceeds of individuals' labor efforts and capital income. However, once the proceeds of actions are taxed, unless "effort" and ability are directly observable, such schemes will necessarily alter the incentives of households to work, consume, and save. In turn, the "lump sum" or "pretrade" transfers under which the Second Welfare Theorem can be invoked are not available to society. Therefore, unless society at large is content with the distributional outcomes that arise from zero interference in the economic system, there is a problem.

In fact, it can be shown that the only fully efficient outcome that can be attained via a competitive market system is the pure laissez-faire outcome.[13] And for obvious reasons, such an outcome may not be a preferred one for many. A consequence is that, in reality, there is almost certainly a tradeoff between equity and efficiency.

Pursuant to this, the entire area of economics known as public finance seeks to measure and understand the tradeoffs necessarily associated with redistributing the fruits of individuals' efforts in instances where household preferences and actions are not observable without cost. In other words, public finance is the study of what happens when one does *not* have available the information or ability needed to employ the Second Welfare Theorem.[14] Aside, perhaps, from understanding how innovation occurs, it is difficult to see an area of economics that is more important.

A part of public finance uses what is known as **implementation theory** (see Jackson 2001, especially sec. 7, or Mas-Colell, Whinston, and Green 1995, ch. 23). Roughly, the modern perspective on how a society can deal with privately held information that will typically block the attainment of Pareto-optimal outcomes (because, very generally, individuals can use this information "against" society to better themselves) stresses the need to construct games or mechanisms in which the rules mitigate the incentives to act in ways that impede efficiency. I'll return to this later, but for now, think of the different types of auctions or protocols for organ donation/assignment that one sees in use. Each of these schemes creates incentives, and the systematic analysis of just what incentives they do create is an area of extremely active research. In fact, the 2011 Nobel Prize in economics was given to two economists, Alvin Roth and Lloyd Shapley, for work in exactly this area.

3.2.5   Caveat 3: Lump-Sum Redistribution Might Require Surprising People

Many items that we see around us, especially durable equipment (cars, factories, roads, etc.), resulted from decisions that people made in the past. Critically, they are the result of decisions people made in the past based on their assessment of how they would derive benefits from these items in the future. This assessment of benefits includes the vital question of how the benefits would be treated by policymakers later. So it would appear that the only kind of reshuffling that will not alter decisions at any time in the economy's existence (and hence the only decisions that look even superficially like the ones imagined by the Second Welfare Theorem) are ones that come as a total surprise to current cohorts of households, and apply to the durable assets that exist in the economy at any given point in time.

For example, what if we surprised everyone by suddenly announcing that the government would reshuffle the ownership of houses, stocks, bonds, and cars, in an attempt to "level the playing field," and then never *again* tax at all? On the one hand, this looks as if it does not distort the society: the houses and cars are already in place, and the stocks and bonds have already helped finance the factories that made them. And the promise to never again tax, if credible, will not change anyone's decisions from here forward. So we could, then, attain relatively equitable outcomes from today onward without creating any deadweight loss, right?

Maybe not. Think about what being able to do such a reshuffling requires. It requires that the institutional limits on policymakers be such that we empower them to undertake a confiscation that can surprise people completely, and yet that people will believe the policymakers when they say it will never happen again.

So in the current "real world," the only reshufflings that look like the ones imagined by the Second Welfare Theorem (if we agree to ignore the plight of those who lose under the confiscation) are true surprises: changes that no one placed any probability on occurring. It should be acknowledged, I think, that such opportunities for surprises are not only rare, but we probably want them to be so! Moreover, even if they were surprises, if we are in an economy that yields efficient outcomes starting from any "initial" distribution of ownership shares and endowments, then, to invoke the Second Welfare Theorem, we have to ignore the well-being of the people from whom we took resources!

3.2.6   The Second Welfare Theorem Does *Not* Require More Assumptions than the First Welfare Theorem

Let's wrap up our discussion of the Second Welfare Theorem on a technical note. When is it true? If you elect to study the ideas in this book formally, you will see that in typical proofs of the Second Welfare Theorem (e.g., Mas-Colell, Whinston, and Green 1995; Kreps 1990), convexity is assumed for firms' production sets and households' preferences. These are strong assumptions, much stronger than the single condition of local nonsatiation needed for the truth of the First Welfare Theorem. But convexity assumptions are simply not needed for the substantive aspect of the theorem. Maskin and Roberts (2008) give a short and clear proof showing that *if* a Walrasian equilibrium exists from an initial endowment assignment that is itself Pareto-efficient, then the prices in that Walrasian equilibrium will be such that the initial endowments themselves constitute a Walrasian allocation. The proof requires only local nonsatiation, no more than the First Welfare

Theorem.[15] The punch line: "convexity" is needed, if at all (recall chapter 2), only for existence, but *granting existence* is absolutely not needed for the Second Welfare Theorem.

The substantive importance of this apparently technical arcana arises because, as I noted in chapter 2, existence of complete-market Walrasian equilibria in large economies is a robust phenomenon, primarily because the helpful feature of convexity is aided by the size of the economy. Thus, existence is generally assured in any settings in which the Walrasian model has relevance: large societies in which strangers compete actively.

3.3   What's Right with *Non*-Lump-Sum Taxes? Or, Sometimes Lump-Sum Taxes Are Bad for "Insurance"

Lump-sum taxes are, by and large, politically infeasible now, and have been infeasible historically as well.[16] This should make macroeconomists who advise policymakers nervous. Are we missing something important? The key reason for opposition to lump-sum taxes is that in most cases, such taxes are described by opponents as "unfair" because both rich and poor must pay the same amount, which strikes many as not quite right. Here's a way to give more teeth to this unease: many of us view the economic situation of a given individual as only partially governed by his or her own efforts, with the rest coming from purely random factors—*uninsurable* risk. If one views uninsurable risk, or luck, as important in describing the situation confronting someone at a given time and place, then lump-sum taxes will have poor "insurance" properties. Put another way: if you didn't know whether you'd end up rich or poor, would *you* want a tax system that asked for the same amount from you no matter what? If you said no, you are likely risk-averse. And the facts that most of us buy at least some insurance, that risky assets generally pay higher rates of return (recall Mehra and Prescott 1985, discussed in chapter 1), and that we are often willing to pay a lot for an airbag that we may never need suggests you are not alone.

More generally, consider the opportunity to purchase a comprehensive insurance contract at the beginning of your career. This contract will pay you in the event of all manner of misfortune, covering job loss, divorce, sickness, etc. But if you couldn't buy such insurance without a deductible (which, by its very existence, makes one at least partially bear misfortune oneself), then your future circumstances will indeed depend on the realization of various kinds of luck, good and bad. Now think of yourself in the society described here, where you lack full insurance but where there is an additional wrinkle: you and all other citizens fear invasion from the outside. All agree that your society needs a defense system, and you collectively must now decide how to pay for it.

Let's say that the society narrows its choices down to two possible schemes: a lump-sum tax in which all households pay a constant amount, or a tax that extracts a higher share of income when households are doing well relative to the median household and a lower share in the opposite case. Given the lack of insurance against the various shocks they face, citizens may well balk at the first alternative. The second one, though, might have promise: it doesn't ask that one transfer resources to the state even when those resources are worth a great deal to households (i.e., in the wake of misfortune). Thus, from the perspective of the polity, the progressive tax may seem preferable to *all* voters! All this sounds good if you like the idea of progressive taxation. But does incomplete insurance give proponents of progressive taxes carte blanche? No. To see why, let's first bring in some useful jargon.

3.3.1 Jargon Digression: "Ex-Ante" and "Ex-Post" Pareto Efficiency

When choices involve accepting uncertainty as a reality, which is essentially any setting macroeconomists consider (and every setting policymakers think about), there is a "before" and an "after." The first refers to the time at which a choice or policy is put into place, and the second is after uncertainty resolves (blessing some, cursing others). The jargon in economics is "**ex-ante**" for "before the fact" and "**ex-post**" for "after the fact."

Pareto efficiency can be defined in both ex-ante and ex-post terms. **Ex-ante Pareto-efficient** outcomes are those that are Pareto-efficient when viewed by households prior to the resolution of uncertainty. **Ex-post Pareto-efficient** outcomes are those that are Pareto-efficient when viewed by households after relevant uncertainty has resolved itself. And so, going back to a previous section: what's wrong with any tax that is not lump-sum is that it will create *ex-post* inefficiency.

What is the relationship between these two kinds of efficiency? First, ex-ante efficient outcomes are always ex-post efficient. Second, the converse is not true: ex-post efficiency does not imply ex-ante efficiency. Third, ex-ante inefficient outcomes may sometimes be improvable through policies that allow for, or even require, actions that ensure ex-post *in*efficiency. Let's examine these points in turn.

First: ex-ante efficient outcomes are always ex-post efficient. Take an example where two farmers, Athreya and Bewley, have fields that, on average, produce identical yields, but where each one faces the risk of crop failure. However, matters are not so grim: they live far away from each other, and the risk of crop failure is such that the total harvest between them is constant. If one has a bad year, the other has a good year, and the total output is always 100 bushels of corn. If they are risk-averse, we can imagine them agreeing to split the harvest evenly, which guarantees each of them the average yield, which is a constant.

Now, each year, after the harvest, one of them must drive the promised amount of corn over to the other's home. Let's say each owns a tractor, but Farmer Athreya's tractor is unreliable, and in a typical trip, will go so slowly that ten bushels will rot en route. Farmer Bewley has a new machine that is extremely fast and so generates no such loss; furthermore, it runs on free solar power.

The ex-post efficient outcome is to use Farmer Bewley's tractor every time the crop has to be transported. That is, once the harvest is determined, the smart thing to do is to get Farmer Bewley's tractor to the field that yielded a good harvest, and move produce to the other's place. Now consider an arrangement where that was not true: Athreya and Bewley would sometimes both do the hauling. It is clear that matters could be improved relative to this arrangement from the perspective of *both* parties even prior to the uncertainty resolving. They should just agree never to use Farmer Athreya's tractor to transport corn. This immediately tells us that the arrangement in which Athreya was to transport corn was ex-ante inefficient. In other words, we've shown that "Not ex-post efficient implies not ex-ante efficient," which is the same thing as saying: "Ex-ante efficient implies ex-post efficient."

The second and third points are related. They assert that a commitment to ex-post efficiency may cause problems for ex-ante efficiency, and that we can sometimes increase ex-ante welfare by committing ourselves to, and then executing, actions that are ex-post *in*efficient. These are both natural ideas. Imagine a society that decided not to care at all about property rights, and refused to impose any penalties for theft. In this setting, to the extent that anyone worked, they might find their produce stolen promptly. What's true, though, is that given the theft, the society would waste no *further* resources in the wake of a theft by spending money locking the thief up and feeding him for years on end. As absurd as this example is, it should clarify that the ex-post standard can include some really silly-looking policies. What exactly is silly about this, though? The answer is that if you view it as silly, it's likely because you view things through an ex-ante lens. The ex-ante perspective says it is silly: in this society, people, anticipating theft, would be much less likely to work as hard and accumulate the instruments of production that would make them and their descendants rich, as they would otherwise. Punch line: ex-post efficiency does not imply ex-ante efficiency.

Now think about a society that lacks a perfect law-enforcement system. With no guarantee that every criminal act will be detected with certainty, some will try their luck in this society, and so crimes will be committed. This society might opt for a system in which those convicted of crimes are punished in ways that, ex-post, hurt all parties involved (e.g., taxpayer-funded jail time for offenders, who in turn are unproductive). Can this be efficient? If we use the ex-post standard, the answer is no.

But what would ex-ante efficiency suggest we do with criminals? One can imagine that an alternative policy that credibly committed society to harsh sanctions for crimes might go far in ensuring good outcomes from the ex-ante perspective. And, critically, this could be true even though, ex-post, society might well routinely spend (i.e., ex-post "waste") substantial resources incarcerating people. Punch line: policies that allow ex-post inefficient outcomes—or, indeed, that prescribe them—can help support outcomes that from the ex-ante standpoint can sometimes be better for everyone than when ex-post efficiency is always adhered to.

Since we've acquired the jargon we needed, we can now return to the issue of the value of alternatives to lump-sum taxation that the ex-post efficiency standard would prescribe. Here, a relevant question is how much the incompleteness of market-based, or decentralized, insurance arrangements opens the door for ex-post inefficiency-inducing tax and transfer schemes to be ex-ante welfare-improving. I will argue that the answer hinges on the view one holds of the ability of the economy's participants to modify outcomes through their actions. If one's view is that they can't do much, many policies that ensure ex-post efficient outcomes are indeed ones that yield ex-ante efficiency (think of a world where people were consumed, no more than once in their lives, by the uncontrollable urge to punch a close friend). It would make no sense to send the offenders, if caught, to costly jails. Conversely, if criminal acts came from hard-boiled calculations that all citizens considered each day, many ex-post efficient outcomes could be quite bad ex-ante. In the example here, we'd want to be careful about forgiveness, lest it get many of us a broken nose.

There is another complication, however. If we are in a setting where, in principle, the imposition of an ex-post inefficient sanction or punishment might improve ex-ante well-being, we need to calibrate these actions suitably. In other words, the problem is squarely quantitative, since competing forces are being traded off against each other. There is no "basic principle" on which we can fall back to guide us. For instance, from the ex-ante perspective, it seems essential that we levy some penalties for criminal acts. But to the extent that this means spending resources jailing people, we need to think about how many we'd likely be jailing, how often we'd jail an innocent person because of judicial system imperfections, and so on. This is often a complicated problem, but is exactly the stuff of modern macroeconomics, as you'll see in chapters 5 and 6.[17]

3.3.2 Back to Lump-Sum Taxes Being Bad for Insurance . . .
Let's go back to our example in which households face risks that would resolve only later in life, and against which they had no insurance. Once everyone's life prospects were ascertained, some of us would be poor, others rich. If ex-post efficiency were our criterion, then we'd certainly not want to beggar ourselves by imposing non-lump-sum taxes. But what about ex-ante efficiency? In the example, I suggested that in the absence of insurance against the risk faced by the members of that society, all of them might prefer the presence of a non-lump-sum tax, or even a progressive tax to fund their defense. In the case where literally everyone did prefer a non-lump-sum tax, we can sensibly say that it "Pareto-dominates" the lump-sum option. In other words, ex-ante efficiency points to choosing a non-lump-sum tax over the lump-sum alternative.

Or does it? What if progressive taxes diminished work effort and made many items more expensive than they'd otherwise be (say, by making wages high for the few hours that anyone does work, and making goods and services expensive)? Now the situation is not so clear, even by the ex-ante measure. What to do? The answer is not obvious. One first needs a way to measure the extent of uninsurable risks prevailing in households' lives, the distribution of risk aversion across members of the public, and the tastes of households for work effort in the face of taxes. Given this, one then must weigh the impact of these risks against the inevitable (and ex-post) deadweight loss that any non-lump-sum tax entails. Chapter 5 will showcase some findings of researchers on these topics. But the message here is that it is complicated, it is quantitative, and that the nature of available markets can turn a naive misapplication of theoretical results that hold perfectly logically under a set of premises into something that might be damaging.

Thus, for macroeconomists, good analysis of public policy often requires reconciling, to the extent possible, doctrines aimed at minimizing ex-post inefficiency (such as the classical public-finance view of taxation and deadweight loss), with the results sometimes reversing these conclusions under an ex-ante view, especially when markets are incomplete (think of the lack of an insurance market above). As a result, macroeconomists must do some hard thinking each time they are consulted about the desirability of any policy. In particular, they will want to know the extent to which the policy in question can help improve outcomes in the face of private markets that are missing, and the extent to which, even ex-ante, the pie will shrink. The job of a macroeconomist consulted on such matters is to assess the applicability of the *premises* under which various results hold and, when necessary, to provide a quantitative assessment of the tradeoffs that sometimes present themselves.

My own view is mainstream: the ex-ante standard is the one to use. In particular, I am a "Rawlsian-with-CRRA-parameter-of-somewhere-between-two-and-four-and-try-to-remember-Pareto-efficiency alloca-tionist." (The jargon will get clearer as we go along. For now, just think of it as using a risk-averse, but not too risk-averse, utility function to evaluate uncertain outcomes.) This is a resolutely consequentialist position and so does not line up cleanly with others "isms" or "ists." It values some forms of state intervention, especially to ensure that competition prevails, to protect new entrants to the economy from poor childhood environments, to insure the unlucky in cases where private insurance appears incomplete, and to provide only pure public goods (defense and our global climate, e.g.). It worries about clumsy distortionary forms of intervention, regulation, and redistribution; is skeptical about the need for regulation in competitive settings at all; and is pessimistic about the ability to regulate without inducing waste, corruption, or both.

Such a criterion never elevates anything to an inviolate "principle" or "commandment" in order to sidestep the language of tradeoffs. As a result, it often accepts compromises. It places my views in line, I'd guess, with many in the silent majority who do not see the world in a black-and-white or Manichean manner. This stance keeps adherents from arguing in overwrought, and often conspiracy-theoretic, terms about the great ongoing struggle against either rapacious corporate forces or leviathan. Instead, it leaves one in a place that simultaneously holds various positions from the right and the left, and where one is generally dismayed by the choices made available through the political process.

3.3.3   Why *Shouldn't* I Trade Ex-Ante Efficiency for Equity?
I argued above that because, sometimes, inequality might well be seen as ex-ante inefficiency, the pursuit of equality becomes entirely consistent with the objective of efficiency. Such a view puts a friendlier face on redistribution, and gives credence to the idea that the tradeoff between equity and ex-ante efficiency is not so stark after all.

But what if there *was* a stark tradeoff? Would it really be so bad to *give up* ex-ante efficiency to get equity? In other words, a first question regarding the desirability of Pareto-optimal outcomes might be: Why even care about Pareto optimality? After all, we've noted that even some grotesquely unequal outcomes can be Pareto-optimal.

The answer is that inefficient outcomes are bad for at least two reasons which I noted in passing at the outset. First, they are by definition unambiguously wasteful; two or more parties could be made better off without hurting anyone else. Second, even for those concerned with equality, it is critical to recognize that the consequences of inefficiency are not likely to be borne only those for whom the consequences are mild. In other words, the oft-heard refrain that "to get greater equality, one needs to give up (a little?) on efficiency," while almost certainly correct, hides a serious problem: many policy actions which create, or simply allow, ex-ante inefficiencies also themselves *induce* inequality. Think of developing countries' barriers to trade that clearly hinder ex-post efficiency, and in turn likely hinder ex-ante efficiency as well: people in LDCs are unlikely to opt en masse for such restrictions. These are policies that, studies show (see e.g., Parente and Prescott 2002; Restuccia and Rogerson 2008), impoverish the inhabitants of these places relative to those in richer countries, and so create world-level inequality.[18]

3.3.3.1 Why Efficiency Is Important

I have talked a lot about the efficiency arising from a Walrasian price system that is taken as given. I described the coordination that such an environment fosters. The visible manifestations of such coordination are everywhere, from the almost-universal availability of Denver omelets late at night to the incredible productivity of American farms. In other words, the coordination I described very much governs our standard of living. What we are learning, from the work above, is that inefficiency, with respect to any given technological state of the art, kills. That is, absent the efficient use of inputs, life in developed countries would resemble life in the less developed world.

The almost incomprehensible suffering of the world's poor, of which there are more than 2 billion, is occurring on our watch. It is taking place contemporaneously with the greatest per-person consumption levels ever seen: American poets drive cars while their Sri Lankan counterparts are lucky to have a bicycle. But this has essentially nothing to do with a lack of innovation, and everything to do with the lack of efficient application of technology that a Walrasian outcome would feature. Unless one thinks that something mysterious happens when you cross an artificial demarcation of a national boundary, the evidence is strong that cross-country variation in income arises from the inefficient use of inputs given the current state of technology.

As a result, even though economists are fond of saying that innovation is everything (and I will say something similar later in the book), it is critical to recognize the *scope* of that point of view. It simply is not correct to say that lack of innovation is a lynchpin in currently seen disparities. In fact, to say so represents a loss of perspective. Innovation is everything for the species as a whole, certainly in the long run. But, from what we have learned, it is the lack of application of currently available technology—a lack of attention to Pareto efficiency—that is the proximate cause of the overwhelming mass of suffering we see in the world around us.

3.4   A General Approach to Thinking about Allocations and Trading Institutions: Mechanism Design

Given the focus of this part of the book on the theoretical roots of the tradeoff between efficiency and equality, let us note that this tradeoff is essentially *created* by the absence of information. Recall the Second Welfare Theorem: its practical inapplicability stemmed completely from the inability to impose lump-sum taxes in the "right amounts" on the "right people." We simply do not know the capabilities and preferences of individuals and the production sets of the firms they own to the extent needed to set lump-sum taxes the right way. Instead, what society typically has done has been to opt (perhaps quite knowingly) for systems of taxation that ask *all* households to pay amounts that depend on the value of their endowments and on the extent to which they sell certain endowments, especially their labor time. But of course, such taxes are avoidable through the agency of the entity facing them: a tax on labor income, for example, can be avoided by simply working less. More corrosively, it may lead many people to not even acquire skills, as the returns to such activity are lowered by taxes on labor income. Given the "public good" nature of general skills, the social cost of such reductions will be, all else equal, relatively substantial. Very generally, the attendant changes in behavior under a regime of non-lump-sum taxes would no longer lead inputs and outputs to flow in a manner consistent with Pareto-optimal outcomes. So what to do?

Since the seminal work of Hurwicz (1972), economists, especially modern macroeconomists, have become sensitive to the idea that informational- and commitment-related constraints may be impediments in much the same way as physical resource limitations in the pursuit of efficient outcomes. This idea has given rise to an entire subfield, called **mechanism design** (MD), that seeks to precisely lay out the limitations created by privately held information on the ability of a society to achieve efficient allocations. We were already introduced to this in chapter 2; the goal there was to show that market powers matter (via the Myerson-Satterthwaite theorem).

The grandfather of the MD approach was Leonid Hurwicz. He, along with many others—including, most notably, Stanley Reiter, Mark

Satterthwaite, David Schmeidler, Hugo Sonnenschein, Roger Myerson, and Eric Maskin—developed a large body of work that has deepened economists' insight into the nature of constraints created by informational problems.

As its name suggests, mechanism design is the branch of economics that seeks to understand the manner in which information and the rules for trading both matter for outcomes. A hallmark of the MD approach is that it is not utopian: it seeks to always respect the limitations on information possessed by well-meaning policymakers, and the informational advantage possessed by (typically) self-interested participants in the "mechanism."

The approach of MD turns the traditional focus of macroeconomics (especially) on its head. At least a generation of microeconomists asked, and macroeconomists still do ask: What can we say about outcomes that arise when the participants do, and do not, face a set of Walrasian prices that they view as unalterable for all the goods and services they care about? The MD approach instead asks: How might one best set up the "rules of the game" via which potential trading partners interact? Notice that when phrased this way, the narrowness of the traditional approach becomes fairly obvious. MD reflects the idea that a scientific economics is one that systematically examines the properties of resource allocation schemes without prejudging them. In this view, markets with prices, Walrasian or otherwise, are just one of potentially many ways of allocating goods and services.

MD also highlights that there are really two kinds of "policy." I cannot do better than to quote Kenneth Mount and Stanley Reiter (1974):

> Problems of economic policy may be grouped in two broad classes which may be loosely described as those involving choice of the value of a "parameter" within a given system of economic institutions and those involving *choice among institutions* [italics added].

An example of the former might be a question about how a change in, say, a flat-tax rate on restaurant meals, affects the prices restaurants charge for meals and the number of active restaurants that operate. By contrast, an economist working in the MD tradition might, for example, ask: What is the best way to raise a given amount of revenue, out of the *entire spectrum* of ways available, especially when I do not have any clear idea of the technological capabilities and abilities of a given would-be restaurateur?

For modern economists, much recent work has gone into understanding how one might facilitate trade effectively in the presence of both privately held information and self-interested strategic behavior. It is one area in which economists have actually contributed to the practice of the better "design" of markets. In areas as diverse as the auctioning of federally owned spectrum rights for information transmission, to electricity markets, and even kidney exchange, economists have been useful in improving actual market performance.[19]

Now, one can ask: What happened to all the enthusiasm for decentralized trade that I have tried to express? Why should we presume that economists (or anyone else) could meaningfully improve market function? The answer is that my enthusiasm was principally for the ability of decentralized trade to *generate* Walrasian prices that are taken as given in any instance where work on the "foundations of Walrasian equilibrium" told us to expect them. However, in a variety of instances, the preconditions prevailing among people or firms with something to trade should not be expected to yield such an outcome. As seen in the discussion of the Myerson-Satterthwaite theorem, there are many natural instances where the total number of participants is very small, as might be the case when an item (such as spectrum space) is valuable only to the handful of firms that already have very specific know-how and infrastructure, or when one party has no way to commit to behaving in a particular manner in the future, or when one party comes into the trade knowing something that would alter the other side's willingness to pay for it. Any reliance on unfettered trade is then justifiable mainly if we think we can't rearrange rules to yield better outcomes, or that the trading parties themselves can't come up with something that yields efficient outcomes. Certainly, under the premises of the Myerson-Satterthwaite theorem, we know that no mechanism can fully rid us of the problem.

3.4.1 Limits on Mechanisms

We have actually already broached the topic of setting up a game and giving incentives for people, and the firms they run, to "play" with each other in a manner than generates an efficient outcome: this was the WCH we have returned to now and again. It has been our explicit mechanism to implement efficient allocation via Walrasian prices that are taken as given. I've cheated a bit, though: as I have repeated many times already, I assumed at the outset that all participants acted as price takers, and in so doing, we simply swept all incentive-related problems under the rug. Specifically, I noted briefly in chapters 1 and 2 that unless participants knew they simply could not influence the prices set by the WCH in response to the reports it received from households, they would have incentives to lie about their demands (as consumers) or production capabilities (as firms), just to manipulate price formation. In the jargon of MD, we would say "the 'direct' mechanism that solicits reports from households about their preferences and the technologies of the firms they own is not, in general, '**incentive-compatible**.'" That is, knowing how their reports are translated into societal outcomes (here, a set of Walrasian prices at which all must trade), participants might *not* have the incentive to truthfully provide the information being asked of them. Think back to the public-good example of national defense described earlier.

The preceding problem is very general: a central aspect of the findings of the literature on MD is that limits on information place some rather severe limits on the sorts of outcomes that can be "engineered" by setting up the "rules of the game" in a particular manner. On a more positive note, however, in general, large numbers of interacting households ameliorate the incentive problems that will generally plague a given mechanism. In the jargon, "thick" markets are almost inevitably competitive. This is, of course, just repeating the message of Aumann's equivalence principle, which we saw in chapter 2 (though his remarks there were not directly in the context of a setting where agents could manipulate a resource-allocating institution).

3.4.1.1   Implementing Social Outcomes: Gibbard-Satterthwaite and the Importance of the "Solution Concept"

An MD approach proceeds by constructing a game and asking participants to play it (potentially giving them incentives to do so—if participation cannot be compelled), and then assigns an allocation according to the entire set of actions taken by all participants. The hope is that MD can help policymakers obtain efficient outcomes despite lacking information on household preferences and firm technologies, simply by providing clever incentives—including pitting individuals "against" each other by connecting the payoffs to each person to the actions of all.

To be concrete, consider a mechanism aimed at providing a nation with an army of efficient size, in the sense that the collective benefits conferred by a further increase are fully offset by the additional cost. One mechanism might be to ask each citizen to report how much he or she would value an army of a given size, and then ask each to pay an amount proportional to this value. However, this approach will not work because in any game, each player will consider how the others will play in choosing what to do. The presence of this interdependence thwarts efficiency. Intuitively: if I think someone else in society will pay for the army, I will not be willing to. On the other hand, in a society large enough to render any individual contribution irrelevant, if I think no one will pay for it, there is no point in my paying for it: my contribution would be too small to matter.

Thus, the Nash equilibrium in terms of "pure" strategies over how much to report as one's own valuation for an army of efficient size will lead everyone to report a valuation of zero, irrespective of what the others will do. In the jargon, each player in this setting has a **dominant strategy**, where the payoffs to each participant leave each with a strategy that yields him or her the highest payoffs, *regardless of what anyone else does*. Essentially, it is as if there are no others in the game at all: their choices have no bearing on the payoffs to each player. In such instances, there is little for each participant to consider. In the context of our example, this would be a case in which we designed a game in which, no matter what one believed the others planned to report as their valuation of an efficiently sized standing army, one had incentives to tell the truth.

Now, returning to the perspective of MD, we would like to construct a game in which payoffs to participants are such that truthful behavior is a dominant strategy. This is a practically motivated desideratum: as a general matter, the more complicated the notion of interdependence is, the less plausible it is that real-world households and firms will play as predicted by the theory of rational decision making that game theory employs. In the pantheon of equilibrium, or "solution" concepts, the Holy Grail is being able to implement a given rule for making collective choices under any realization of preferences as a **dominant strategy equilibrium**.

Sadly, this is not to be; at least not with dominant strategy equilibrium. This is the message of the **Gibbard-Satterthwaite (GS) theorem**. Three pieces of jargon are in order before we move on to define it. First, a **social choice function** (SCF) is a rule that describes the way a society's members might agree to translate the characteristics of all members (say, their preferences and endowments) into an outcome (say, a Walrasian allocation) for each one. Suspending our disbelief for a moment: if the economy, when left alone, acts as if it has a WCH, then a society that opts for "free markets" has chosen the particular SCF that takes reported household characteristics for all reported demand and supply behavior and computes the Walrasian prices implied by the *reported* behavior and forces all trade at those prices. Second, an SCF is called **Paretian** if for any collection of household types (in terms of how households prefer various objects to others), the SCF picks an outcome that is Pareto-efficient. Lastly, an SCF is called **nondictatorial** if there are no participants whose individual preferences always dictate the outcome irrespective of the characteristics of the rest of the participants.

The GS theorem says that there is no hope of locating a rule for making collective decisions that one can implement in dominant strategies for all possible realizations of the preferences of the subjects in a mechanism. The GS theorem thus quashes the idea that by being clever about rewards, society can fully overcome informational problems—whether there are relatively few participants or, sometimes, as in the classic problem of public goods provision, even when there are many.

Three less negative messages can be delivered, though. First, for private goods (i.e., those that can be consumed by more than one individual), the presence of large numbers ameliorates problems. As a result, in "thick" (densely populated) markets for private goods and services, the imperative for clever mechanism design is far lower—because "the market does the work." Second, the GS theorem applies only to dominant strategies. There are many other equilibrium concepts, such as Nash equilibrium more generally, in which the range of outcomes that can be "implemented" via careful construction of the game is substantially expanded. This was the subject of intense research in the late 1980s and early 1990s. See Repullo and Moore (1988) for a review of this branch of economic theory, known as **implementation**. Third, as noted above, experimental economics suggests that outcomes frequently look both more and less Walrasian than the received theory might lead one to expect, leaving open the possibility that some efficient outcomes may be feasible to implement even when strict economic *theory* suggests that participants would cheat "too much."

3.4.1.2   Why Do Macroeconomists Care about Mechanism Design, and Why *Should* Policymakers?

The preceding section covered some of the "purest" sorts of economic theory. It described a part of economics that investigates only the theoretical limitations created by informational constraints. But with only a little imagination, one should be able to see why such theory ought to matter rather centrally for a macroeconomic policymaker. Any scheme one might imagine for the provision of public goods (national defense or the stock of national parks, for example), insurance against poor circumstances at birth (such as welfare transfers to expectant women), the regulation of banks, or income redistribution more generally (for example, fiscal policy) can be informed by MD. In each case, a policymaker must discern the valuations and capabilities of participants for consuming and producing various goods and services in order to decide the optimal levels of provision. At the same time, policymakers must confront the limits on information facing them and think of ways to elicit the information. In keeping with the GS theorem, this will, as a general matter, force a compromise, where those with privately held information are given incentives to reveal it. But this almost inevitably means that the price of information is not zero, and hence, neither is the price of public goods provision or redistribution. Thus, it is MD theory that helps macroeconomists both to better understand the nature of the equity-efficiency tradeoff awaiting any redistributive efforts we embark upon, and to locate the most efficient way to proxy for markets that would otherwise remain missing (including some for insurance and, especially, those for public goods). MD helps bring alive the welfare theorems. Unsurprisingly, as already referenced in chapter 2, the entire subfield of macroeconomics known as new dynamic public finance seeks ways to deliver levels of social insurance (unemployment, disability, etc.) and public goods that are efficient in the face of informational limitations.[20]

Absent this knowledge, there would be little efficiency-based justification available to macroeconomists and the policymakers they advise for either intervening or not intervening in decentralized outcomes. For now, let me simply note that the GS theorem, along with the literature on implementation, certainly suggests that policymakers face some daunting limitations on their power to help a society attain outcomes that are efficient and equitable. This itself is important to explaining or understanding why, even when outcomes appear "bad," one might sensibly not intervene as a policymaker. MD tells us that "doing no harm" is not easy.

3.5   Concluding Remarks

In this chapter we have covered some issues related to how economists think about inequality, the role of markets in its creation, and how to deal efficiently with it. The actual types of models that study the equity-efficiency tradeoff will be the subject of chapter 5. To describe the structure of those models, though, it is first useful to lay out the nature of another set of tradeoffs: those involving the construction of macro-economic models. This is the topic of chapter 4.

4 Macroeconomic Shortcuts

4.1 Introduction

In chapters 1 and 2, I described how Walrasian models are constructed, and the way in which Walrasian theory connects macroeconomic outcomes arising from decentralized competitive (price-taking) trade to efficient outcomes. Chapter 3 then looked at the ideas that are most likely to be influential in macroeconomists' views of the connections between decentralized outcomes, efficiency, and inequality. Those three chapters were intended to give readers a sense of the benchmark model most macroeconomists use when starting to frame questions, and against which most macroeconomists judge the outcomes from messier models where the welfare theorems do not hold.

In this chapter, we'll address some methodology important to ensure a clear layman's understanding of how macroeconomics is done. These ideas are infrequently discussed in existing work for nonprofessional economists.

To start, let's note the intensity of the dissatisfaction with modern macroeconomics among economists themselves. Two recent and well-publicized complaints are those of Hamermesh (2011) and Colander et al. (2010). For its bile alone, it is worth quoting Hamermesh in detail. He states:

Macroeconomics is in disrepute. The micro stuff that people like myself and most of us do has contributed tremendously and continues to contribute. Our thoughts have had enormous influence. It just happens that macroeconomics, firstly, has been done terribly and, secondly, in terms of academic macroeconomics, these guys are absolutely useless, most of them. Ask your brother-in-law. I'm sure he thinks, as do 90% of us, that most of what the macro guys do in academia is just worthless rubbish. Worthless, useless, uninteresting rubbish, catering to a very few people in their own little cliques.

My own reaction to this is best captured by Ariel Rubinstein (2001):

To criticize something, you need to know it intimately; the best way to know it intimately is to do it yourself. Once you have done that, you do not want to criticize it yourself.

Are there reasons for using an overall approach to macroeconomics that seems to give easy ammunition to critics? Explaining macroeconomic method seems worthwhile, if only to communicate the difficulties that face anyone confronting macroeconomic questions. It is lack of appreciation for these difficulties, I think, that explains why we are taken to task for bad outcomes in ways that physicians, even when they can do nothing for patients, are not. Doctors are seen (perhaps rightly) as having a *method* that is better than any other. Macroeconomists certainly are not seen as holding any such "engine of discovery."

4.1.1   Our Four Sins: Aggregation, Rationality, Equilibrium, and Mathematics

While Hamermesh's reaction is overexcited, a more sedate reaction that, in the end, is essentially equally critical is that of Colander et al. (2010) in the so-called Dahlem report. The authors detail a lengthy case against business as usual in macroeconomics. It is useful, in light of these criticisms, to break the sins of macroeconomics into roughly four categories. These are the sin of "**aggregation**," the sin of studying primarily **rational decision makers**, the sin of studying "**equilibrium**" outcomes, and finally the sin of having adopted (a while ago now) **mathematics** as the main way to communicate. Of all the things that modern macroeconomists are lampooned for, our willingness to study rational behavior and employ something known within the profession as "aggregation" are both very high on the list.[1] Therefore, I tackle these two issues first, with some effort given to defining terms and describing what they buy us. The reason macroeconomists seem fixated on equilibrium states is next—and as I've already noted more than once in the book, "equilibrium" implies neither that outcomes are somehow for the best nor that outcomes are "stable" in some superficially obvious manner. The fourth area of emphasis—that of why we always couch arguments in terms of mathematics—is perhaps slightly broader. I will discuss these as general notions first, and then describe more specific instances of each topic within each of the models I detail. In the end, if I have been successful, the reader will have a clear sense of the overall strategy now used for deriving quantitative and qualitative predictions in a rich array of macroeconomic models. This is the other bookend, figuratively, to the discussion in chapter 1 on "How to argue with a macroeconomist, if you must."

I will also highlight limits on these models but, as the reader will notice, will generally not take these limits as an indictment of them. Instead, in each case, I will describe events through a narrative in which specific features arise somewhat naturally as a *compromise* (if an uneasy one) between expanding the "reach" of a model and retaining its internal consistency. This, to my mind, is *the* central tension in macroeconomic model construction. Most macroeconomists want to be immediately relevant, but most also want to be part of a more cumulative and long-run process of knowledge building. Being relevant requires combining "intuition" and experience to "fill in the holes" left by formal models so that one can discuss ongoing real-world issues and provide policy advice. Knowledge building requires being able to suspend disbelief, while at the same time perpetually "dotting i's" and "crossing t's," even if that means the models that do so end up being limited in the scope of phenomena they can speak to, sometimes severely.

An example of a pressing short-run question for which macroeconomists lack good models is the extent to which, in the recent financial crisis, severe recession, and sluggish recovery, certain types of financial contracts ought to be restricted. Such contracts include those facilitating the so-called maturity transformation activities of unregulated, non-bank entities such as hedge funds. Good formal models for the effects of regulating such contracts are not yet available, and especially not in a form that is amenable to answer the question of how much regulation is needed. So policymakers and economists have been forced to proceed on the basis of more informal analyses, including the collected experience of a vast array of public- and private-sector practitioners.

At the same time, formal models aimed at providing tightly constructed and internally consistent narratives of the crisis are a big research program in macroeconomics. These models are still, however, in their infancy, and one can understand why "intuition" and "experience" may well carry the day in a discussion of policy over a coherent but oversimplified model. But it should be acknowledged that having a clear gut instinct on what to do need not reflect or constitute meaningful understanding of the processes at work. For example, I know that having a Coke at 2 PM most Tuesdays makes me feel good and will perk me up, but I would have no idea why this happens without scientists having taught me that it was caffeine at work. Thus, even having a strong sense of "what must be done" should merely spur the study of *why* it works.

Lastly, it will not surprise any reader who has read this far that I will provide some endorsement for the study of equilibrium outcomes and so-called steady states. However, I urge readers not to prejudge how limited such outcomes of a model can be; they might be surprised. In fact, it might not be an exaggeration to suggest that formal admission of dynamic elements into economic models has revolutionized what the terms "equilibrium" and "steady state" mean. These terms now encompass outcomes that involve tremendous volatility and, not infrequently, quite unpleasant outcomes for market participants. One example, which will be developed further later on, is that of the equilibrium states of models in which people search to match their talents with job openings for various employers. In such "search models," equilibrium situations involve some groups of workers wishing to work but finding nothing, and others refusing offers that are poor deals for them. Critically, in such a model, there can be no presumption whatsoever of efficiency in the equilibrium states.

The reader will notice a change in the tone of the discussion here compared to that taken in chapters 1, 2, and 3. Those chapters consisted in large part of reporting key theoretical results, without relaying too much of my own views or emphasizing the *judgment calls* that working macroeconomists must make. The quotation from Rubinstein is perhaps apt here, and one can take it in (at least) two ways. In the first interpretation, once one actually has "bought in" to the field, one falls in love with it and becomes incapable of seeing its flaws. But the second interpretation is that, once one has done the work, one realizes that the existing structure is not arbitrary and naive, but rather reflects substantial accumulated wisdom vis-à-vis tradeoffs in modeling.

4.2 Macroeconomic Compromises

As I see it, our approach is shot through with ongoing *compromises* between internal coherence and tractability. Given all the criticisms, i.e., descriptions of the costs of our approach, the arguments that working macroeconomists need to put forward now are those that describe the *benefits* they see to these compromises.

4.2.1 Aggregation

Aggregation theory in economics is the body of knowledge that developed in response to the question: Under what conditions are differences between decision makers in an economy *not* important for the way in which certain aggregated quantities behave? Examples of specific questions are: Under what conditions does the *total* spending of households on food not depend on differences in their preferences, wealth, or income? When does an industry produce quantities, and respond to prices, as if it were just one large firm operated by a single centralized management?

As should be clear, making the assumptions that yield aggregation in a model involves the deliberate, not wanton, suppression of heterogeneity in an economic environment. What makes such an ejection of detail useful is that if done sensibly, what remains is something in which causes and effects are intelligible, and where the model itself is "manipulable." Of course, if it is too extreme, we lose usefulness. A map is a useful analogy to a macroeconomic model, as it shares some of the same features. Pick up a paper map of the state you live in—if you still own such a thing. Start with the map touching your nose. Some details will be visible, perhaps, but even these will remain out of focus and garbled. Now move the map away from your face, slowly. Objects such as small towns nearest your nose are now becoming discernible. Keep going. Large towns and lakes are now resolving in front of you. Moreover, the shape of the state itself is coming into relief. Now keep moving, the small towns are disappearing, and we once again start to lose important information. So it is with macroeconomic models. Too much detail means total incomprehensibility, and too little leads to uselessness.[2]

All economic model building is simply an exercise in judicious aggregation. There is no economic model that does not aggregate; the only issue is *how* one aggregates. Even the data that one tries to account for are often already heavily aggregated. Examples are objects like state- or national-level production, investment, and depreciation. Similarly, at the household level, macroeconomists are not asked about the behavior of individual US consumers. Instead, they are asked how a given change in policy, for example, will affect the sum of consumption decisions across all households in a state or nation.

Aggregation assumptions can be divided into those that apply (i) to each class of participants (firms, households, and sometimes the government), and (ii) the commodities being traded in a given macro-economic model. We will start with the aggregation of producers.

4.2.1.1 Aggregation of Producers

In the context of producers, the question that aggregation theory asks is: Is it true that a group of firms (or production units) will act in the same way as a single firm possessing the capabilities of the industry as a whole? If the model one is studying has the necessary attributes to make the answer to this question yes, the payoff is obvious. Take, for example, the case of a macroeconomist interested in how house-holds make consumption decisions (i.e., how much to spend for the various goods and services they prefer). Suppose also that the macro-economist wants to allow the households in the model to work to earn labor income—for instance, because for a household facing a layoff, picking up a second shift might be an important option to keep their spending on goods and services from changing much over time. Suppose next that the macroeconomist is interested in the behavior of households with a particular skill level (e.g., a high school education), and wants to study a setting competitive enough that these households have the choice of earning similar wages at a variety of firms.

As described above (and if she performs no further simplification), the problem in front of the macroeconomist is fairly involved. She must decide, notably, how many different types of firms she wishes to include, how the various households in the model choose to work at each one, and each firm's choices of production and hiring. In a setting satisfying the conditions under which production-side aggregation holds, she has a far simpler option because she can use the fact that the collective set of firms will act just like a single one. She therefore can work with a model with a single firm, worry about the labor supply of households just for this firm, and concentrate on the demand for inputs of this firm alone. Production aggregation results are, therefore, extraor-dinarily useful in constructing models.

So the real question is: Are the contexts in which production-side aggregation holds very restrictive? The answer is yes, and no. What is required for a given part of the economy to act as if it has a single firm is that the firms being considered for aggregation are (i) "competitive," in the sense of facing and taking prices for inputs and outputs as given, and (ii) not subject to pervasive and binding constraints on the ability to *finance* input purchases. Under these conditions, what is true (and this can be easily proved) is that the industry as a whole—even if composed of many firms, which may differ substantially from each other in their ability to produce goods and services—acts *exactly* as if it had one profit-maximizing manager operating all the economy's firms as if they were merely plants in his empire. This is what macroeconomists mean when they speak of a "representative firm."

The key to the applicability of this result is that in the standard Walrasian model, firms are not subject to what are known as "wealth effects." In particular, the presence of competition—whereby the effect of any firm's output choice or input use on the market price of these items is null—and the absence of borrowing constraints mean that in the benchmark ADM model, "firm wealth" is not a well-defined concept. Firms are owned by households, and it is only household wealth that is well defined. Recalling the discussion in chapter 1 on the objective of profit maximization, households, which ultimately own any firm, may or may not be wealthy, but under the premises of the ADM model they will still *unanimously* agree to ask the firm to choose a production plan that maximizes profits. And then one can invoke the preceding result: aggregate output, costs, and profits will be exactly as if there was a single profit-maximizing firm endowed with society's production capabilities.

Given that we have identified conditions under which production aggregation holds, and may be concerned that the conditions are strong—especially the part about firms not facing "borrowing constraints"—the next question is: How *misleading* is having a representative firm likely to be in a given context? After all, we may be willing to tolerate the approximation to reality provided by a model with a production side that aggregates, especially if it simplifies the model enough to allow us to incorporate other features we are focused on in a given project. The answer is suggested by the preconditions needed for the result. If, for example, one is studying the behavior of small businesses, each of which is suspected strongly of facing potentially binding constraints on its ability to borrow, then there is no reason to suspect that aggregation will hold. In this case, there is every reason to think that the wealth positions of each individual owner-operator matters a great deal for the choices being made. As a result, a single large firm, with access to deep and liquid capital markets, will likely make substantially different decisions than each individual small business and, more importantly for the macroeconomist modeling the situation, than the behavior of total output of all the small firms put together. A great deal could potentially be lost in glossing over such heterogeneity. The quality of answers to questions about tax policy applicable to small business will therefore likely be substantially altered—for the worse—if we simply forged ahead and aggregated them.

So, in the case of production-side aggregation, for the end user of macroeconomic research, the key questions to ask when evaluating the sensibility of a model that has presumed a representative firm are the following. First, are the firms being "represented" indeed (i) more or less incapable of altering prices significantly away from those of any competitors? And second, even if so, (ii) do they also have access to enough credit to execute any plan that might, at the prices they face, be profit-maximizing? On the other hand, if one's focus was on policy analysis of the effect of welfare-to-work programs on household labor supply, for example, one might not be led astray by ignoring the features that void production aggregation.

4.2.1.2   Aggregation of Consumers

The aggregation question on the consumer or household side is essentially identical to that on the production side of the economy. It asks: Under what conditions will there be a "representative" household whose actions always mirror the aggregate (or, more precisely, the average) behavior of a collection of households, each of which may differ substantially from one another? In other words, if all I saw as an outside observer were the total amounts demanded for goods and services at various prices by all the consumers—say one thousand of them—in a given marketplace, would those data make it appear that the market was populated by one thousand perfectly identical households, each with the average amount of income of the original bunch? If so, it would certainly make the modeling problem of an economist interested in the behavior of demand within a market far simpler.

Unfortunately, the answer to the question posed above is: only under stringent conditions. In fact, even granting that all households take prices as given, and none face borrowing constraints (just as with the requirements needed for the aggregation of firms), we need quite a bit more to happen before the consumer side of a market displays aggregation. On a slightly positive note, the price-taking assumption is more readily satisfied here relative to the production side of the economy. In a very large array of circumstances, households do indeed face prices that are linear (as we discussed earlier) and which they have little choice but to take as given. However, we need much more to go right for us in order to ensure aggregation.

Intuitively, what is needed is that household demand for goods and services, when they act as price takers, is such that if one took money from one household and gave it to another, then the first household's desired purchases of each good will fall by *exactly* the amount that the second household's demand rises. In this case, it is clear enough that the total demand of all households will simply no longer depend on the distribution of incomes across the households themselves. In turn, we, as macroeconomists modeling these consumers, could relax a bit and not worry about explicitly modeling all the different household types that might actually be present, and not worry about ensuring that our model captured the distribution of income across participants in the market under study.

Unfortunately, what is needed is something very, very, stringent. This is because households, in contrast even to firms lucky enough not to face borrowing constraints, will be susceptible in general to wealth effects. And wealth effects are precisely what lowers the possibility that one can locate a specification of "representative" preferences such that the level of purchases of a consumer with those preferences will coincide, given the aggregate wealth of all households, with the aggregate purchases of the original collection of consumers. In fact, in the 1950s it was proved that household preferences would have to be of a very particular type, known as **Gorman form**, for the wealth distribution to not matter for either market-level or economy-wide demand for goods and services. And what is worse, this presumes that there are no borrowing constraints and there is price taking. Consumer-side aggregation is indeed rarely in the cards in a given economic environment.

Let me now turn to a distinction between types of aggregation. What I have described so far, in the context of both firms and households, is what is known as **positive aggregation;** namely, we have asked when the aggregated data that one might observe (and one, in fact, will rarely observe more granular behavior than this) will "look like" it came from a single type of firm or household. If there are conditions under which one *can* find such a **positive representative consumer** or **positive representative firm,** it would make modeling easier, as long as the needed conditions do not turn out to be very extreme or poor descriptors of the relevant reality being modeled. The economist could proceed to analyze a given market or other trading arrangement, and be able to understand aggregate quantities and prices, if they are used in trade, by deriving the optimal behavior of just the one representative household.

Constantinides (1982) is precisely such a result. It is an assertion that the Walrasian outcome of any complete-market setting (i.e., a genuinely ADM setting) will look as if it was chosen by a large population of identical single "stand-in" households that each owned identical—and hence average—shares of the economy's wealth. Put another way, Constaninides's result tells us that "representative consumers always lurk in a complete-markets setting." This result is limited, however, in important ways. First, it asserts that a given Walrasian outcome, which of course depends on the *distribution of initial income or wealth*, will look as if it were chosen by a representative or "average" person. But if we change the distribution of these initial resources, the resulting new Walrasian outcomes will each look as if they were chosen by a representative household, but that this household may well differ from the one before the change. In other words, the economy is emphatically not one where the Gorman form is guaranteed to hold. Indeed, we already know that the Gorman form is *necessary*, not merely sufficient; and barring its being satisfied by the case under study, the stronger form of aggregation we described above fails to hold more generally.

The reader will likely have already thought of just what a limited result positive aggregation actually is. But it gets a bit worse. Why? Because positive aggregation can hold, and yet still tell us nothing useful about what we often want to know: What is the impact on household *well-being* coming from a change in market conditions? For example, if policymakers are considering whether or not to impose a tax on a good, or on capital income more generally, what can a macroeconomist offer by way of recommendation? The answer is: without some more structure on the preferences of households, not much. In particular, it should be clear that just because the consumer side displays positive aggregation, the preferences of the positive-representative consumer may not coincide with those of even a single household in the underlying economic environment. In the jargon, there may be no specification of preferences that precisely represents a meaningful **normative representative consumer** whose preferences represent a sensible or natural aggregation of the preferences of all households. And while it will take us too far afield to talk about the extent to which the data can be described by a normatively relevant representative household, we can note that the conditions for this type are indeed extremely stringent, i.e., limited. So why should we care about the implications for the well-being of a fictitious agent whose preferences, in a normative sense, represent absolutely no one? The answer is that we probably should not, but what's the alternative?

Arguments for Homogeneous Preferences

The prospects are thus dim for a market displaying enough aggregation, especially on the consumer side, and especially of the normative kind. And some of the most strident criticism of mainstream economists' willingness to gloss over patent differences between households has come from commentators who also have argued that the aggregated models of modern economics are predisposed to giving "markets" an unduly glowing place in the pantheon of societal institutions.

Yet, in practice, the road taken by macroeconomists has usually been to forge ahead—and often in a seemingly extreme manner. We assume that households in the main actually have perfectly *identical* preferences (or, in some cases, that households each belong to some large classes whose preferences are allowed to differ from each other; e.g., high-school-educated vs. college-educated households). Are we obtuse? Sure, perhaps some of us are. But that's not likely true of all of us who make use of such aggregation.

In large part, economists impose identical preferences because preferences are hard to observe directly. Economic data are often simply not detailed enough to decisively distinguish between macroeconomic models using populations whose members differ in their preferences. So if macroeconomists are given too much freedom in the no-man's land of heterogeneity, we will lead our audiences off cliffs: we'll be able to "account," rather trivially of course, for *just about anything*. Our inquiries would be made immediately vacuous. Thus, in large part, and just as with rationality and rational expectations, the suppression of the manifest but, crucially, unobservable heterogeneity in the real world protects the public from economists.

There is an even more powerful reason to nearly always proceed by assuming all households have the same preferences—*especially* over the broad aggregates of goods and services that macroeconomic models deal with (yes, we do know that some people most certainly like chicken wings more than others). In chapter 5, I will illustrate how market dysfunction, especially in the form of the absence of certain types of insurance and financial markets, can make people slaves to risks that they could otherwise pool with others. As a result, some inequality—in consumption, wealth, and earnings—will emerge purely in response to bad luck. Given this, allowing preference heterogeneity will nearly always make the case for unfettered competitive markets *stronger*: the more one allows households to vary along unobservable dimensions, the less one will be able to attribute to market pathology for driving outcomes that one dislikes. Of course, this will strike some as fine, but to the extent that one is uncomfortable with versions of laissez-faire, preference heterogeneity is not a friend, however realistic it may strike us.

To see the preceding point more concretely, consider the question of where wealth inequality comes from. The most routinely followed current approach (which I will show you in chapter 5) is one where a population of households with perfectly identical preferences is buffeted by shocks to their earnings, health, or productivity that they may only deal with by accumulating and spending their savings (or running up debts). In such a setting, if one instead allowed for preference heterogeneity, the most obvious result will be that some of the inequality that one initially attributed to market incompleteness under the standard approach would get "soaked up" into heterogeneity. For example, if we allowed households to vary in their future orientation (i.e., how "patient," or willing to delay gratification, they were), then we'd almost certainly attribute at least *some* of the heterogeneity as coming from differences in impatience. This would surface in the form of the poor being disproportionately composed of impatient people—grasshoppers in the fable of the ants and the grasshopper. Similarly, if we allowed households to vary in their *appetite for risk*, one would almost certainly be led to conclude, to a greater extent than one would otherwise, that the poor were poor because they simply lacked the courage to invest in high-risk, high-return investments—and by extension, those who did get rich were disproportionately society's path breakers and risk takers. The attendant interpretations of their relative positions would then be hard to employ for anyone interested in the reform of the existing institutional structure (market, legal, custom, and governmental).

An uncomfortable example would be to allow a social scientist to posit that some households of a given group, say South-Asian Americans (like me), have a deep "tendency" for hard work and are "future-oriented," in order to account for the disproportionately low poverty and incarceration rates of that group. Do we really want to go this route and risk missing the institutionalized advantages available to many first-generation South-Asian Americans (such as the favorable US immigration policy toward the parents of highly educated members of this ethnic group) that might well propel *any* one of them to success, no matter how impatient and impulsive? Preference heterogeneity thus has, for those of us uninterested in making economics "eugenics lite," little to recommend it. Barring crystal-clear measurable and unequivocal biochemical evidence of preference heterogeneity, something we almost (can) never have, it seems a risky and distracting route to take. And I think it should be viewed as risky precisely by those who worry that markets work poorly and wish to propose improvements via public policy: the more outcomes are innate, the less culpable in bad outcomes are a society's trading institutions.

None of this suggests that one should never allow for differences in preferences. But to the extent that they can significantly color one's interpretation of outcomes, all the while remaining unobservable, it seems a far less than ideal starting point for most (macro)economists. Of course, it is certainly possible that such differences are indeed the best proximate explanations one can devise, but they will routinely be ones that might substantially implicate individuals and their character "defects" in their own fates. Therefore, unless one wants to intervene to change preferences, one might wish to look harder at features of the institutional arrangements for trade that foster inequality before settling for an explanation rooted in preference heterogeneity. Thus, by weighting downward the contribution of market and institutional dysfunction, preference heterogeneity will unwittingly aid the case of anyone wanting to demonstrate the effectiveness of decentralized outcomes in reflecting, and so *respecting*, the underlying preferences of households.

What does all this mean for the workaday practice of macroeconomists? My own view is certainly traditional, and hence in line with the preceding: preference heterogeneity should be a last resort, with focus on other reasons for divergent behavior across households. These "other reasons" include: differing prices, differing income, differing family size, etc. In fact, from a preempirical perspective, macroeconomists (or economists at large, really) are resigned to the difficulties in consumer-side aggregation, and view their job as almost being *defined* by the extent to which they are able to account for using identical preferences.

Approximate Aggregation

In the early 1970s, some microeconomic theorists—especially the program spearheaded by Werner Hildenbrand—started to ask the optimistic question: Just *how much* heterogeneity in the preferences of households can a macroeconomist hell-bent on treating their collective behavior as coming from a single type of household brook? Hildenbrand (1994), in an authoritative treatment, laid down a variety of conditions on the *distribution* of wealth across consumers that if preserved by a given policy change, would still yield a positive representative consumer. The upshot of this work is that aggregates can indeed sometimes behave essentially as a single decision maker, and can do so in a wider array of settings than may have seemed possible. Yet remember that these results are always about positive representative consumers, and in no way imply that the well-being of this representation has any information on the well-being of those being aggregated: it is not work about the presence of a normative representative consumer.

An interesting finding, due first to Krusell and Smith (1998) (and to be clarified in chapter 5 in the context of the "standard incomplete-markets" model), is that in a fairly broad set of circumstances, outcomes in macroeconomic models that do not assume a representative agent (and hence allow for heterogeneity) display what has been termed "approximate aggregation." The nutshell description of this finding is that the implications for economic aggregates, such as total economy-wide consumption, investment, and output, can sometimes look "almost as if" there were a (positive) representative agent—*even* when the model under study simultaneously matches salient kinds of heterogeneity in each of these aggregates found in US data.

Approximate aggregation is an important finding because it allows us to segregate the models we use by the questions we ask. For example, if one's main concern was to have a model that spoke to economy-wide aggregates, such as aggregate investment, one can (more) safely study a representative-agent model, and get the associated simplification without compromising the quality of answers to the question. Of course, for questions where inequality is the central concern, a representative-agent model is a nonstarter.

Approximate aggregation is a feature of a wide-enough class of macroeconomic models displaying heterogeneity that it is very important to keep in mind when worrying about the apparent willingness of macroeconomists to gloss over the heterogeneity present in a given setting. Though infrequently, if ever, stated by macroeconomists, a compelling defense of the standard battery of representative-agent models aimed at describing causal mechanisms for economic aggregates over very short horizons (i.e., "business cycle" models) is precisely that within a rich class of nonrepresentative-agent models, we know that heterogeneity *just doesn't matter that much for the behavior of aggregates*. Of course, the preceding is a statement about the properties of macroeconomic models; the "real world" may fail to exhibit such a property, and hence, heterogeneity may indeed matter for even the behavior of aggregates. But this is all we can ever really say with authority; the rest would be pure speculation. Lastly, while it will probably remain cryptic, let me note that approximate aggregation occurs, rather ironically, *because* of the way in which wealth inequality occurs in most developed economies! To the extent that one views such inequality as itself a symptom of market malfunction (a view I describe further below), this is a funny situation: the same inequality that exercises critics of modern macro *abets* aggregation, and strengthens the case for a representative-agent view of positive aggregate outcomes!

4.2.1.3 Aggregation of Commodities

In most macroeconomic models you will encounter, it will be assumed that households choose "consumption," not a detailed list of oranges, cereal, wine, gasoline, etc. Many models will not even distinguish between durables and nondurables, despite their obvious dissimilarities. Such an approach is a particularly brutal form of aggregation, glossing over so many types of goods to arrive a single "composite" good. In fact, in most standard macroeconomic models, there will typically be just one good available at any point in time, which we call "the consumption good."

More recently, such aggregation across commodities at a given point in time is growing less common. The models most prominently used in studies of business cycles now have begun to routinely feature a set of commodities so rich that they are modeled as elements of the continuum! That is, in many of the models that go under the (co-opted) heading of dynamic stochastic general equilibrium (DSGE) models, the representative consumer has preferences over an uncountably infinite array of differentiated commodities that are sold to her by a parallel uncountably infinite group of monopolists.

Another form of aggregation concerns the treatment of a given commodity consumed at different moments in time—where the differences that are relevant are determined by whatever a household's preferences may be. In fact, when it comes to periods even as long as one year, macroeconomists routinely refuse to regard goods available at different moments in time as different. Instead, they will often treat a flow of consumption goods over the entire period as the relevant measure. This is called **time aggregation**. For example, even if people's consumption of strawberries, or the amount of them produced, varied substantially week to week, the macroeconomist might disregard these variations and count any two sequences of weekly strawberry consumption or production as identical, so long as their sum over say, one quarter, was the same.

Now, neither households nor firms choose their total expenditure over long periods at one time. If they did, there'd be no need to model time at all! But in any macroeconomic model, decisions are taken for the whole period, which, if long enough, will indeed represent poorly the actual flexibility firms and households have in real-world settings. So it is clear that something is lost by this approach. But other things are gained.

One such gain offered by time aggregation is that there are models in which decisions take place continuously; but in these models, households are usually not allowed the freedom to choose from a very large set of commodities. Moreover, modeling decision making at such fine time increments precludes the detailed accommodation of granular decisions that typically occur, in real life, *within* periods. In particular, the mathematical tools of *calculus* help make such a model tractable.

Smoothness and Convexity: A Sidebar

As some readers will know, the calculus is a tool for problem solving in "smooth" settings. And smoothness requirements place rigid constraints on the model—and rule out lots of types of questions (e.g., Should I take a job or not? Should I buy a washing machine or not?)—that we might want to model tractably. Moreover, once we drop the "smoothness" needed to invoke the calculus, do the welfare theorems still work? Are we guaranteed the existence of Walrasian equilibrium? If so, we must acknowledge that our theory isn't so general.

Going back to general-equilibrium theory, the practical concern highlighted by this example was that the calculus-based approaches to the existence of Walrasian prices and allocation were far too narrow to capture the possibly very nonsmooth preferences of households and production capabilities of firms. This is exactly what led to the "convexity"-based revolution of Arrow and Debreu, where smoothness was completely dropped as an assumption. The move to convexity-based analysis by economists in the 1950s is useful to keep in mind as an instance in which more-abstract tools decisively expanded the ability of economists to understand "practical" issues. Later on, though, I will describe how another highly abstract modeling device, the so-called nonatomic measure space formulation, allows economists to dispense with even the assumption of convexity! To my taste, this is just one more instance of severe eggheads once again helping us to understand the real world.

4.2.1.4 Aggregation and Modeling Tradeoffs

Having defined aggregation, let's now return to the criticism I reported at the beginning of this section. A first question is: Is what these writers are saying true: that aggregation is hardly ever "truly" justifiable? Maybe. After all, critics of economics are not all naive, and I suspect, understand the points above well enough. Moreover, the circumstantial evidence does look rather bad: it is certainly true that macroeconomists do spend time analyzing the behavior of entire economies populated by brilliant, well-informed, and perfectly identical agents—and worse yet, identical agents who live forever! As Angus Deaton (1991) has noted with characteristic flair: "Representative agents have two problems: They know too much, and they live too long."

What could possibly be gleaned from such silly settings about the real world, with its wildly differing people, each of whom certainly lives for less than 120 years? How could aggregate consumption and savings in our messy world ever appear as if they were the solution to the problem of maximizing the well-being of just one, infinitely lived being? More subtly, even if the quantities and prices of goods and services consumed and invested do look *as if* they were the solution to such a problem, why should we be persuaded that the well-being of such a mythical "(positive) representative agent" has any bearing on the well-being of the flesh-and-blood participants in our real-life economy who seemingly differ so substantially from each other? These are natural, and thorny, questions.

I've made no effort to persuade you that aggregation is without cost—it is not, and you hopefully know more now about why it's so hard to get it to obtain. Costs, by themselves, are not quite enough to make decisions, though. There are benefits to consider. And economists are, if nothing else, determined to never let the perfect be the enemy of the somewhat useful. The tradeoff is *never* between "aggregation short-cuts in a given economic model" and "no aggregation short-cuts in the *same* model." Instead, the tradeoff has always been between "aggregation in a model with more richness elsewhere in the model" and "no-aggregation short-cuts with less richness elsewhere in the model."[3] So if the issue is not just that one must aggregate, the question then is: Along what dimensions, and by how much? And here, only an insider who spends his days stating and solving models can have much to say about the relative value of different degrees of aggregation. Period.

A particularly stark illustration of how one can gain insight into some aspects of macroeconomic concern by simplifying through aggregation assumptions comes from macroeconomists' benchmark model of asset pricing, the Breeden-Lucas "fruit tree" model. As we will see, the approach allows us to locate prices "for free" because the equilibrium quantities are mandated by the structure of the model. Mehra and Prescott's equity premium puzzle, the vehicle I used in chapter 1 for illustrating macroeconomic argumentation, uses this convenient fact to aid the computation and analysis of the relative rates of return of assets.

4.2.1.5   An Example: The Breeden-Lucas "Fruit Tree"

In the mid 1970s, Douglas Breeden and Robert E. Lucas, working independently, introduced an approach to asset pricing that has since become the defining manner in which macroeconomists explain asset prices (see Lucas 1978 and Breeden 1979). Recall from our early example of Mehra and Prescott's work that the research program in asset-pricing theory asks the following question: How do the fundamental features of households and firms interact (usually in a competitive, i.e., price-taking, economy) to produce differences in the distribution of the rates of return across different types of assets?[4] For example, how do household traits like aversion to risk or willingness to delay consumption, and firm-related characteristics such as the costs involved in producing output, matter for the mean, the variance, or other "moments" of the distribution of returns?

Breeden and Lucas posed this question in the context of a highly simplified model that had a set of households and firms. On the household side, they imagined a simple world in which everyone was identical and preferred their consumption of goods to be "smooth," all else being equal, but everyone was also forward-looking (rational) and took the prices of assets as given. On the production side of the economy, things were also kept extremely simple.

For simplicity, we'll focus on details of Lucas's model. It is best described in the following parable. Imagine a world with a large number of fruit trees, which each produce a random amount of fruit at harvest. Next, imagine that every morning, there is a harvest that delivers a random amount of fruit. These fruit are then delivered to two classes of security holders. Those holding a piece of paper called a "bond" always get the same number of fruit, no matter how many fruit were produced in the harvest. The others hold a piece of paper that entitles them to a *share* of the fruit in the tree.

Lucas then asked, if all households were identical both in preferences and in their endowments of shares and bonds, what the relative returns on stocks and bond would have to be for the representative household to hold the asset and consume all dividends (the fruit). This is clearly the simplest case one could consider, and also in line with my discussion earlier about economists' default position against heterogeneity in preferences. Now, you may notice that people with identical preferences and endowments have no need for markets: there are no gains from trade. So what were these authors thinking? Note that when all participants are identical, they will want to do the same thing at all prices. As a result, the only Walrasian price for these assets has to be one that leads to no trade at all. What they wanted to know was: If one were to hold an auction for the bonds and shares in the fruit trees, what would prices have to be in order for households to agree *not* to want to trade away from their initial identical positions—i.e., to agree to retain ownership of the fruit trees in the economy? This question is relevant as it tells us about how the resulting prices are tied to the underlying fundamentals—even when there is no trade to speak of.

Why do macroeconomists like this model so much as a starting point? First, it connects the relative returns on assets to the underlying motivations of the households that buy them. Second, it clarifies the extent to which price movements are consistent with no one being routinely surprised by them, in particular showing when the classic "random walk" specification should hold and, maybe more importantly, when it does *not* hold. Third (although I will not discuss it here), the Lucas framework, when suitably adopted, will also allow one to predict the implications of policy changes on asset prices, such as taxes, as well. More than thirty years after its construction, the Lucas tree approach shapes the way macroeconomists think about asset pricing. It is the point of departure for much of the qualitative literature on asset pricing, as well as on the quantitative assessments of our models of asset prices. Its basic structure also guides the choices of additional features we add to reconcile our models with the data.

4.2.2   Rationality

Remember when I asserted that "Of all the things that modern macroeconomists are lampooned for, our willingness to 'aggregate' has got to be very high on the list"? I suspect that economists' use of rationality causes even more consternation and, ultimately, disbelief in the implications of our analyses. So let me describe what this assumption gets us.

4.2.2.1   No Rationality, No Utility Function

The careful reader will note that I have always characterized household behavior in terms of their "preferences." Namely, I have consistently spoken about the motivations of households by the way in which they *rank* bundles of goods and services against each other. However, in applied work, preferences are less tractable than a related object called the **utility function**. A utility function is a mathematical object that takes any given bundle of goods or services that one might consider, and *assigns a number* to that bundle. For example, I might use a utility function that assigns the number 53 to a bundle of "five bananas and a pair of shoes delivered to me at 5 PM tomorrow," and the number 18 to the same bundle to be delivered a day after that.

For a utility function to have any meaning, we need to assign numbers so that they *preserve* the way a household actually ranks, or "prefers," the goods and services under consideration. This leads to a natural conclusion: a utility is a meaningful representation of the underlying preferences of a household if (and only if) it assigns more preferred bundles a larger number than that assigned to less preferred bundles. In our example, then, our utility function sensibly represents a given household's preferences only as long it is the case that the household actually prefers five bananas and a pair shoes at 5 PM tomorrow over five bananas and a pair of shoes the day after. If not, we'd have to reassign numbers.

Remember that a utility function is just a representation of preferences: beyond telling you if a given set of objects is preferred over other sets of objects, the utility numbers have no relevance whatsoever. Any rule for assigning numbers to the various bundles under consideration by a household will lead the household to make the same choices as any other numbering scheme that has the same ordering. For example, if, instead of using the numbers 53 and 18 for the "bananas and shoes" combination tomorrow and the day after, I instead used the numbers 14 and 11, *nothing would change*. I would still be able to look at the numbers and decide which bundle the household liked best. In fact, if you can tolerate the departure from standard usage in economics, keep the term "preference representation function" in mind when someone talks about "utility function"; the former is more accurate and evocative.

At a really mundane level, the value of having a utility function available to represent preferences is that the entire mathematical apparatus of **optimization theory** can be brought to bear to analyze the behavior of a household. In particular, precisely because it does not matter how I pick the numbers that go with various bundles, except to make sure that I assign bigger numbers to the more preferred bundles, I have great freedom to choose among utility functions. This freedom is very important; by choosing cleverly the form of the utility function, I as an economist can bring a huge body of mathematical machinery to help me obtain solutions to the underlying household's problem of picking the (affordable) bundle that their preferences tell them they like best. One example is differential calculus, which is a particularly useful tool for solving optimization problems. Therefore, by working with utility functions that, in addition to representing preferences in the way I want them to, also have a property called "differentiability," I can use those tools to make the problem easier to solve—and best of all, increase the richness of my model elsewhere.

For example, if I am concerned with assessing the consequences of long-term risk for a household's well-being, I can first choose a tractable utility function to represent households' preferences among bundles of goods and services that, for instance, reflect an aversion to risk that I think is empirically plausible. Similarly, I can work to find a simple form to represent preferences for current consumption over future consumption. Given the tractability of my chosen utility function, I can accommodate the model, without fear of having the problem become insoluble, in the various long-term risks households face, such as getting sick, or becoming unemployed, or having sick children who require sustained time and care, etc.

If we could not work with a utility function, it is not clear that we could even build a model that we could analyze, especially given these other important risks we might wish to accommodate. In fact, it is difficult to see how any part of economics, *micro or macro,* that tries to provide numerical magnitudes for the behavior of prices and quantities and the effects of policies could proceed without the aid of utility functions.

Having (I hope) persuaded you that utility functions do indeed have enormous value, let me drop the hammer: the *only* preferences that even have a chance of being represented by a utility function *are rational ones.* This is sad but a fact. And it goes a long way in explaining the general reluctance to eject rationality from the list of descriptors of one's model: it would mean dropping utility functions too!

And in a sense, matters are even worse. One can also ask if rational preferences place sufficient structure on the choices people will make to guarantee that their behavior can be summarized by a utility function. The answer is no: only some rational preferences can be represented by a utility function.

4.2.2.2   Bounded Rationality

In the body of work aimed at relaxing the rationality requirements of the ADM approach, economists have pursued a varied set of paths, including attempts to create tractable but axiomatically founded alternatives, in which households experience difficulty understanding the economic environment within which they operate. For example, they may have difficulty assessing odds in uncertain situations or working out the implication of their decisions for outcomes in the distant future, and so on. Other economists have studied the implications of simply replacing rationality with alternatives such as **rational inattention,** a model in which households and firms "sensibly" ignore certain things because it is costly to pay attention to everything. In still other cases, economists have studied models in which they have more directly limited the computational abilities of model decision makers. It is no exaggeration to say that for a not-very-small group of economists, delivering a tractable model of bounded rationality has been a much-desired goal. It has, at various times, occupied a veritable Who's Who of modern economists, most notably the 2012 Nobel Prize winners, Thomas Sargent and Christopher Sims.

Among the models that have emerged are some that specify households' preferences to allow for features that go by monikers of "unawareness" or "ambiguity aversion," or in which households face what is known as "Knightian" uncertainty (after the economist Frank Knight, who asserted that there is a meaningful distinction between risk, which one could represent in terms of the "odds" or probabilities of various events, and uncertainty, which refers to cases in which even the odds of certain future events cannot be assessed). The work of Lars Hansen and Thomas Sargent has explored a related issue: in a world where one is never sure of the truthfulness of one's model, and where one suspects that the world may be well described by more than one model, how should one make decisions? This work is known, rather naturally, as the theory of **robust decision making**.

While far beyond the scope of this book, suffice it to say these models have the potential to lead to revisions of some of the conclusions mainstream economics has thus far reached on various topics. Of particular interest is the work on consumer finance, where these alternative models of decision making may lead to changes in the way economists view institutions aimed at ensuring that contracts remain simple, comprehensible, or otherwise restricted. The newly created Consumer Financial Protection Bureau (CFPB) has a mandate that is self-explanatory, and through the lens of robust decision making or rational inattention, may be easier (for us economists, anyway!) to understand as a welfare-improving entity. Lastly, as the Nobel award makes clear, the reader can see that these efforts are entirely within the mainstream of modern economic research.

It should also be made clear that *tractable* models of bounded rationality *are* already used in areas such as asset pricing and monetary policy, areas of great relevance for macroeconomic policy for nearly two decades thus far. Leading professionals (see Lettau and Uhlig 1999) have examined the implications of bounded rationality in well-received research. I have even used one such model in my own work.

A central point to keep in mind is that every one of these concessions to messy reality relies on innovations delivered uniformly by those with deep command of existing decision theory (usually *micro*economists) who understand the need to deliver tractability in addition to "realism." In particular, in models of dynamic decision making, such as those trying to explain consumption and saving through time, the most fruitful innovations in bounded rationality have been those which lend themselves to "recursive" formulations because they allow us to use the already-well-developed machinery of **sequential statistical decision theory** (the work that leads to the ubiquitous **Bellman equation**). Without such tractability, models incorporating "bounded" rationality would require much more cumbersome mathematical machinery, and in turn would inevitably lead to models that were *far more stylized (i.e., "unrealistic") along other dimensions.*

An Example of How Model Richness Is Not Free: Households with Habits
The last point is worth more emphasis: it is spectacularly optimistic to think that a model that captures vastly more of the foibles of individual decision makers will also remain tractable when one adds in other aspects of the lives of the same households. For example, let's say that I think consumers are creatures of "habit" of both the "internal" and "external" variety. By "internal habit," I mean the way one grows accustomed to a lifestyle given one's *own* past lifestyle. An "external habit," on the other hand, refers to the effect that we each experience when we see *others* around us consuming more (or less). Envy and empathy are, to some extent, manifestations of this sort of preference. Common syntax even suggests that such preferences may be relevant; Americans have coined the term "keeping up with the Joneses" to capture this notion.

Now, the problem facing a household that understands that they are creatures of habit, both internal and external, is substantially more complex. As a result, economists who have decided to incorporate these elements into their model now have to think about how such households will choose consumption and savings. In natural specifications of the problem, we would imagine that a household would enter more gingerly into a given spending decision, knowing that it might commit them to a path of higher spending in the future, if only to avoid the disruption created by becoming habituated to a given lifestyle. This approach immediately requires that any spending decision taken today be tracked in order to determine how much value a given future expenditure level will yield. And this immediately makes the problem more complex than under the standard economists' model that ignores such peccadilloes.

External habits make things even worse. Why? Because a world in which people care a lot about what others will do is one where they will spend time forecasting what others will do—especially when it comes to big-ticket purchases like cars or appliances. Of course, it is fine that consumers will want to care about others' spending, but to the economist studying the aggregate implications of such preferences, the problem is clearly much more involved. Specifically, any coherent description of what the household will want to do now must include a rich description of what others around them will do. This is substantially more complicated mathematically, and will inevitably force economists to *skimp on details elsewhere*. For instance, they may elect to impose a highly simplified version of the tax code in the model, or they may pare away detail on the way spouses make decisions about who works and how much, or they may avoid detailing the process of household formation by ignoring how spouses are found, and so on. As a result, depending on the question that motivated the analysis in the first place, adding habits, as appealing as they are, will represent a poor way to achieve more "realism."

Of course, the lay reader cannot be blamed for thinking many negative things about economists' love of models: if one isn't building models like this day in and day out, one will have no idea of the existence of these tradeoffs. Instead, economists will appear, wrongly, as people in love with mathematics and bereft of concerns for household well-being.[5] How ironic it is, then, that the efforts at limiting richness arise precisely from our *inability* to tractably handle the cumbersome mathematics that so effortlessly arises from natural-looking enrichments of our standard models, and from our need to work with models in which there is always a coherent standard for judging the well-being of households.

4.2.2.3   Rational Expectations

We've talked more than once about rational expectations (RE), so I will keep this discussion short. RE has received especially heavy criticism. To remind the reader, rational-expectations models ask that the beliefs that people and (the managers of) firms hold lead them to take actions that, when aggregated, don't routinely or systematically contradict their beliefs. It is therefore useful to think for a second about why the assumption is used. A first answer is this: given the premise that we want a story that explains outcomes as arising not from random choices by households but from purposeful actions, this is an inherently reasonable requirement.

While optimal decision making "merely" required that decision makers (households and firm-level decision makers) behave consistently for any given beliefs they had about an uncertain future, it did not place any restrictions on what these beliefs actually were. RE goes much further. This theory purports to explain the expectations people actually have about the relevant items in their own futures. It does so by asking that their expectations lead to economy-wide outcomes that do not contradict their views. By imposing the requirement that expectations not be systematically contradicted by outcomes, economists keep an unobservable object from becoming a source of "free parameters" through which we can cheaply claim to have "explained" some phenomenon. In other words, in rational-expectations models, expectations are part of what is solved for, and so they are not left to the discretion of the modeler to impose willy-nilly. In so doing, the assumption of rational expectations protects the public from economists.

4.2.2.4   Expected Utility

Rational-choice assumptions are always demanding, but nowhere so much as under conditions of uncertainty. The use of some additional assumptions that simply extend the axioms of decision making in a completely natural way delivers what economists call expected utility (EU). In the sixty-odd years since its inception, expected utility has come under intense scrutiny. Studies have shown that EU asks for behavior that is often violated in experiments on individual subjects, that it is incapable of allowing macroeconomists to account for important phenomena in asset market data, and more generally, that it may be implausible.

But what EU is not is neglected. Expected utility is inarguably the most prevalent starting place for macroeconomic models: as of this writing, it is the industry standard by a wide margin. Given its myriad failings, why is EU so widely used? The answer, as might be expected from the location of this discussion within this book, is because like many other heroic assumptions it strikes a helpful compromise: making the assumptions that allow it to be used is very demanding and hence "unrealistic," but in return models become tractable. Interestingly, it is precisely our desire as macroeconomists that leads the "realistic" complication of uncertainty and so, indirectly, drives us to seek ways to do so tractably.

So what is the famous "expected utility theorem"? To start, when things are uncertain, notice that one is forced to contend with the comparison of *lotteries*. By "lotteries" I don't mean the state-run jackpots we are all familiar with, but the simple fact that sometimes one cannot buy or sell an item in the future with full knowledge of the circumstances that will prevail at future dates. Insurance, for example, can be thought of as the purchase now of a payment if a particular situation unfortunately comes to pass in the future. Of course it may not happen, which means that one is buying today a lottery ticket of sorts: pay now, and you may get paid later. If we acknowledge this, then the remaining issue is how we might represent preferences in the matter of lotteries. A natural thing to do is to start by asking (1) what "rationality-like" premises on decision makers' views about lotteries might look like, and (2) what implications such assumptions may have for the way we can tractably represent such preferences.

When economists and mathematicians tackled this problem, they proceeded in a couple of steps. First, if we import the spirit of "rational" decision making into uncertain settings, it makes sense to think that preference in lotteries ought, in the mind of a sensible person, to exhibit a type of "independence." Roughly this means that, if someone prefers one lottery to another (a game of poker and its payoffs, say, compared to those of gin rummy), this preference of one lottery for another should not be altered by the introduction of a *third* lottery. Let's say I offer you the chance to play either poker or gin rummy with me, and you choose gin rummy—so we agree that you prefer the lottery (since our payoffs from the game are uncertain) of a gin rummy game with me over one that has us playing poker. Now let's say I offer you a comparison between two slightly more complicated lotteries. In the first lottery, I roll a die, and if it comes up as an odd number, we play poker (and face the attendant uncertainty that comes with it), and if it comes up even, we play bridge. In the second lottery, I roll the same die, but this time, if comes up odd, we play gin rummy, and if it comes up even, we again play bridge. Notice that the likelihood of ending up playing bridge is the same under both schemes: all that I've done is "mixed" each of our original lotteries (poker, gin rummy) with another one (bridge). And no matter what we do, we're not going to play two games—we will always end up playing just one card game.

Now ask yourself (and there are no wrong answers) whether, by introducing bridge as a possible outcome, I can change your view so that you prefer the lottery with the chance of getting *poker* as an outcome to the one in which the roll of the die gives you a chance of playing gin rummy. If you say no, then you conform to the so-called independence axiom.

The assumption that sensible behavior requires independence is appealing, certainly upon introspection: after all, you will not play a mix of two card games; instead, you will always end up playing just one game. Given this, it makes "intuitive" sense that introducing a third outcome that occurs with equal probability under either scheme ought not to change how you value poker relative to gin rummy.

The second step is to assume that people's preferences over uncertain outcomes are "continuous." This asks that if we have any three lotteries, no matter how good one is and no matter how bad another is, we can always find lotteries that combine any two of them (just as I did when I added bridge to the mix above) that we like better than one and worse than the other. This may sound abstract. An example would be a world where the three lotteries are (A) taking a five-star vacation paid for by your worst enemy, (B) watching the NBA all afternoon at home, and (C) being shot at. The continuity idea just says, first, that no matter how bad (C) is, we can always put high enough probability on (A) and low enough probability on (C) to make you prefer a lottery that leads to (A) *or* (C) over the lottery of (B), and second, that no matter how good (A) is, we can always put high enough probability on (C) to make you prefer (B) to a lottery that leads to either (A) or (C). In his text, Kreps (1990, p. 76) has a nice example: he asks you to consider a trip across town to collect $100 (A) versus getting $10 now (B) or certain death (C). He suggests that most people would drive across town, but to the extent that means risking death—however minimally— we've shown that even though (C) is terrible, by mixing (A) and (C) with a low enough probability, we can get people to risk it over getting a sure prize of $10. One important shortcoming of considering only those whose behavior meets the two presumptions of expected utility theory is that certain extreme preferences are indeed ruled out from consideration. For example, "safety at any cost" is a type of behavior that cannot be captured via expected utility models. To the extent that such considerations are important for many people (and the fact that most commute to work on highways populated by bad drivers and trucks makes safety's importance dubious), economists' restriction of attention to such models will indeed prevent them from capturing some things.

Now for the payoff: as long as preferences are complete (here, this means being able to rank any lottery relative to any other) and transitive, and satisfy the two requirements above, then there is a representation of preferences, just as before in the case of "sure things," that is very convenient. It is a representation (i.e., a utility function that is defined on the *outcomes* of the lottery) where one lottery is better than another if, and only if, it has a bigger *expected* value than another lottery. The economist can then represent your attitude toward lotteries by using the simplest available function to assign numerical values to the prizes that are the outcomes of the lottery in a way that respects your underlying preferences. Barring the ability to do this, it would become far more difficult to model uncertain situations, which in turn would mean compromising the model's richness along many other dimensions. That is the bottom line.

4.2.2.5   A Provisional Summary

Economists are united in the view that the aggregate economy of any country, or the world as a whole, is a highly complex and dynamic system whose behavior is at least partially governed by purposeful decision making by households and firms. For us, the road to a more "relevant" economics does not take a path that abandons the idea of an economy's inhabitants as purposeful decision makers. The total disrespect to the individual that such an approach endorses is also enough, on its own, to reject it.

As should be clear by now, the relaxation of the rationality requirements may indeed change how "difficult" it is for an agent in the model to solve a problem—and thereby make it a better model of individual decision making—but, as first touched on in chapter 1, there is no reason that it will make the job of the *economist* easier. In fact, *departures from rationality—including (or especially) expected utility—will likely make any model harder to solve*, and require even more technical apparatus than is currently used. This is a key point because it makes clear that the level of rationality with which economists endow the actors in their models is not an arbitrary choice but a clear compromise made precisely in an effort to admit more "realism" into other aspects of the model that are perceived as important. There is therefore a clear trade-off: models of rational behavior lend themselves to being solved by a well-developed machinery developed by mathematicians. Models of bounded rationality, by contrast, while usually lowering the burden on the agents populating the model, typically dramatically increase the burden placed on the economist solving the model. As a result, in models of bounded rationality, *other aspects have to be simplified.* As my colleagues can attest, this tradeoff forces itself rudely on all of us who do macroeconomics.[6]

So, aside from those specific areas in which one can implicate irrationality at the household level with aggregate volatility in a definitive way, a more promising route for macroeconomists is, I think, to keep rationality and the simplicity that it buys us, so that we can enrich the models along the many dimensions that the real world (and especially the current crisis) requires us to think about. More on this further below.

4.2.3 Equilibrium Analysis

As I've repeatedly noted, in order to make predictions about the outcomes of a given form of interaction between participants, economists cook up lists of extra conditions that they find useful in order to whittle outcomes down to, hopefully, a single outcome, i.e., an equilibrium. This is part of what makes economics different from physical sciences. Take a case where we can agree on the facts (e.g., the level of the equity premium that prevails in the data). You might argue that macroeconomists are doing "science" in the sense that we are (slowly) figuring out the premises that either lead to a given set of facts or fail to do so. But we also introduce equilibrium concepts as a way of selecting among feasible outcomes. And, quite unlike physics, for example, our notions of equilibrium aren't easily testable (though recall from chapter 2 that experimental economics is clearly changing this)—I cannot really ever know whether or not you are "unsurprised" by what has occurred, and even if I see what you did, I still cannot know if you optimized en route to those decisions. This situation immediately renders Walrasian outcomes, rational-expectations outcomes, and Nash outcomes as *devices for interpreting what we see*, and nothing less or more. And if you don't think the equilibrium concept is "plausible," then, for that reason alone, I may not be able to convince you that I've come up with a good explanation. I suspect that for physical scientists, the mapping from primitives to outcomes is simpler—i.e., it doesn't involve a manmade notion of equilibrium to help you pick outcomes.

As I described in chapter 1, the conditions that allow us to sensibly call the resulting outcomes "equilibria" are often partially determined by the presumptions made about the behavior of the participants in the model, and partially by the way they interact. We noted, for instance, that once one has decided to study a model in which all participants are rational and interact anonymously via prices that they take as given, then any sensible notion of equilibrium must require that the prices be Walrasian. That is, non-Walrasian (i.e., non-market-clearing) prices, whatever their relevance in the real world, have no relevance in the model. Similarly, any firm that has no effect on market prices will have shareholders who wish that the firm would maximize profits— after all, this simply increases their purchasing power with no offsetting negative effects. In what follows, I describe some additional restrictions on outcomes that are commonly imposed by macroeconomists studying phenomena in settings where time and uncertainty are important.

4.2.3.1   Steady States and Transitions

Macroeconomists often focus on even narrower outcomes than "mere" "correct expectations" equilibria: they frequently study correct expectations equilibria that satisfy an *additional* condition that make them a so-called steady state. This terminology refers to situations in which the objects of interest in a model, say aggregate output, either (i) literally remain constant over time (or have "normalized" versions that do so), or (ii) fluctuate in a way that depends on *only* the realization of uncertainty. The former are called **deterministic steady states**, and the latter **stochastic steady states**. Thus, neither "equilibrium" nor "steady-state equilibria" implies outcomes that are frozen in time; they can be ones in which lots of fluctuations occur more or less constantly. This will be true for all the workhorse models of macroeconomics described in chapter 5. Specifically, steady-state equilibria that exhibit constant movement are typically the ones studied in the standard incomplete-markets model, the standard search model, and the standard overlapping-generations model.

The key to an outcome being a steady state is that variables of interest do not vary simply because "calendar time" evolves. For example, consider the simple case of an agrarian society whose population has been stable over time. Suppose further that in this society, because of its stable population, and because it has been active in agriculture for a long time, no one is clear-cutting new acreage for planting. As a result, the amount of arable land in this society is not changing over time. Nonetheless, if we think that the weather still matters for the harvest, to the extent that weather is random, so too will aggregate farm output be. But, even though important objects such as the harvest are most certainly changing over time, a macroeconomist would view this society as being in a "steady state." This is because nothing in the society is changing *just* because the date is. Thus, an immediate litmus test for whether an outcome is a steady state or not is simple: if the uncertainty kept resolving itself the same way, date after date, would anything in the society change over time? If not, we'd define this society to be in a steady state. For example, if the society experienced, say, five straight years of "normal" rainfall, and total output did not change from year to year, we'd say that they were in a steady state.

So what does a "*non*-steady-state" outcome look like? Given my test, we should look for a situation in which time matters, irrespective of what else is going on. Let's roll the clock back to the hunter-gatherers, say, at the point when they have discovered that a small patch of land seems capable of producing crops when seeds are dropped into the soil. With this knowledge, they decide to settle down and expand the area under cultivation. As they do this, output will surely start to change over time, hopefully in the right direction. In particular, what will be true is that *even if* the monsoon (on which the yield per acre solely depends) delivers exactly the same amount of rain for several years running, the output in this society will still keep changing over time. Thus, in transitional periods, the "date" matters in addition to the force exerted by economic uncertainty (e.g., will the rains occur in time to ensure a good harvest?). Macroeconomists refer to such periods as **transition paths** for the economy.

Let's complicate the example slightly by allowing this society, once it has discovered the magic of agriculture, to understand the path in front of it. In particular, it understands that a sensible work-life balance for the members of the society would lead them in, say, six seasons, to clear a stock of arable land that subsequently will make the returns to further expansion no longer worth the cost. Knowing this, the rest of their work is cut out for them: plant each year, clear a bit more land, and repeat. And this sort of knowledge is important: if, instead, the residents thought it would take a generation or more to get to a place where agriculture would no longer warrant expansion, they might well choose to use their time differently. But as long as the evolution of the stock of arable land unfolds as predicted, a macroeconomist would view this society as being on a **transitional equilibrium path**.

Now imagine that the people in the example also understand that bad weather may strike in each year. They understand both the relative likelihood of various paths for the weather between now and the indefinite future, and the impact of weather on outcomes. In this case, as long as the stock of arable land and output evolve in response to the population's previous efforts such that, given their understanding of weather, they are not surprised by the size of the harvest, a macroeconomist would view this society as being on a stochastic (i.e., uncertain) transitional equilibrium path. In both cases—transitions in which uncertainty is absent and those where it is present—the antecedents in the phrase "transitional equilibrium path" are important. They indicate that the essence of equilibrium to a macroeconomist is that optimizing people should not be routinely surprised and, in particular, should never be surprised by outcomes ensuing from a *given realization* of something that they knew was subject, up front, to uncertainty.

Let me return to a word I used earlier: in defining a steady state, I mentioned parenthetically that as long as "normalized" versions of certain objects remained fixed over time, we'd still say we have a steady state. This is often relevant in models of economic growth where outcomes, such as total GDP, are predicted to grow steadily "in the long run." In some cases, for example, these models predict long-run output to grow at the same rate as population growth. If the population grows at a constant rate, then GDP is predicted to grow at a constant rate over time. Given my definition of steady state, one might conclude that such a long-run outcome was not a steady state at all. After all, even absent uncertainty, the model predicts that GDP increases steadily *over time*. But what is true in this sort of instance is that there are normalizations of variables such as GDP that can be rendered constant over time. Here, if we simply look at the behavior of GDP per person, we'd immediately see that it was an object that would not grow or shrink in the long run. Sometimes, to distinguish a more "pure" notion of steady state from one in which only normalized objects remain constant, macroeconomists may refer to the latter as a **steady-state growth path**.

4.2.3.2   An Interesting Criticism of Steady-State Analysis

A subtle, and certainly interesting, criticism of steady-state analysis is that while it may be done purely for reasons of tractability, in the end, the outcomes under study only apply to those situations in which "history is irrelevant." I have already made a pitch for not being cavalier about dismissing tractability, and have nothing more to add on that topic. However, by simply bypassing the thornier questions of the role of "history dependence," which many social scientists outside economics take pains to document and understand, economists remain open to the charge that their predictions could be much improved. This accusation is potentially quite damning, and I discuss below (in the context of specific models) why economists still find such an analysis to be useful, but I also clearly note some of the limitations it places on the scope of macroeconomists' inquiries.

4.2.3.3   Equilibrium Analysis: A Provisional Summary

To sum up, let's take stock of the kinds of behaviors we now know that "equilibrium" is capable of allowing: equilibrium outcomes can change over time, change in response to uncertainty, or do both. I emphasize this to drive home the point that equilibrium analysis is entirely capable of describing extremely "wild" kinds of outcomes. Macroeconomists' insistence on studying equilibrium states places little restriction on the kinds of behavior we are capable of studying. As a result, it is generally unproductive to begin any criticism of modern macroeconomics, especially in relation to the issue of "unemployment," for example, by noting that macroeconomists restrict attention to "equilibrium" outcomes even when thinking about "bad" outcomes such as unemployment. In fact, as I will emphasize in chapter 5 in the context of a class of models called "search" models, it is precisely the ability to describe unemployment as an equilibrium outcome that opens the door to thinking about how to improve what is, for any individual, an unambiguously bad outcome.

4.2.3.4   Race as an Equilibrium Outcome: The Work of Glenn Loury

In his lecture upon receiving the John von Neumann Award, the economist Glenn Loury (2005) argues that "what we call 'race,' is mainly a social, and only indirectly a biological, phenomenon." Why is this? Because, Loury points out, race is a product of individual-level *decisions*. That is, the question one needs to ask is really: Why do different groups partner at rates low enough to allow distinct ethnic groups to persist? Posed this way, the question enters the wheelhouse of economics. As long as we accept that individuals themselves choose partners with whom to produce children, the question is: Why is it optimal for them individually to do so in a way that perpetuates the coexistence of people who look physically distinct? Here's Loury's punch line: "There would be no 'races' in the steady state of the system unless, on a daily basis and in regard to their most intimate affairs, people paid assiduous attention to the social boundaries that separate themselves from racially distinct others." So the question boils down to: Why is it privately (if not socially) optimal for people to pay attention to these differences?

This is pure equilibrium analysis, and moreover, since race looks "persistent," it seeks to explain the outcome as a steady-state equilibrium. Since the formalization of Loury's ideas is mathematically identical to most other models we macroeconomists work with, no modern macroeconomist will have trouble following his arguments, even though it's on a topic of which we might have little prior knowledge: there's an optimization problem, and there are aggregate consistency conditions. The equations just represent a particular set of decision makers, and the restrictions on individuals that arise from their collective behavior (e.g., the fraction of black or white mates, which no individual controls, but which they collectively determine) are just a special case of the general recipe we saw in chapter 1.

4.2.4   Mathematics, Practicality, and Some Examples

Economists in general, and macroeconomists in particular, are often subjected to the criticism that there is "too much mathematics" in economics. In addition to the Dahlem report, which was focused on one class of macroeconomic models, a general version of this criticism is given by Krugman (2009). It is certainly true that as I have defined the term "model" in this book, modern macroeconomic models are fundamentally the translation of a complex "economic" problem into a simpler problem amenable to solution via mathematics.[7] John von Neumann is reported to have given perhaps the most apt reaction to opponents of the ever-increasing amounts of mathematics in economics (see Alt 1972): "If people do not believe that mathematics is simple, it is only because they do not realize how complicated life is."

When discussing the "mathematization" of macroeconomics, some perspective is in order. Modern macroeconomists are not, by and large, even close to being professional mathematicians. Most research economists know as much math as someone with a bachelor's degree in mathematics (though many of us will often not know some of the math, such as abstract algebra or logic, that many math undergraduates would), and know statistics and probability theory perhaps at the level of those with a master's degree in statistics.

With this noted, let's move to a more important point: those who *do* macroeconomics know that the mathematics involved in macroeconomics arises extremely naturally from the need to be *applicable*.

At a general level, a first issue is this: economists want to think about households and firms as purposeful decision makers. I hold this view, and take the matter to be almost a prerequisite for spending time thinking about resource allocation. If people made primarily random or thoughtless choices, there would not be much to study or explain, and certainly no obvious reason to *care*. But this prerequisite means that right away, some optimization problem—usually subject to constraints determined by the collective efforts of other agents—will have to be solved. In mathematical terms, this has to involve optimization theory, specifically that developed for general so-called vector spaces, because in many cases there is an infinite variety of choices an agent can make, either through time or across space. Think of yourself choosing how much to save or spend in any given year. Second, as macroeconomists especially, we would like the joint decisions of households and firms to be feasible. The need to ensure the existence of any sort of collectively feasible solution to the family of optimization problems corresponding to each household's and firm's decisions usually necessitates a mathematical tool known as a "fixed-point" theorem.

Macroeconomists must live by these two rules, because if we are studying the behavior of an entire economy, or some other closed system, we have to ensure that the collective decisions of all purposeful actors in the system can be reconciled with the finitude of resources. In this sense, the irritation with the mathematization of macroeconomics is seriously misplaced; it risks killing the very apparatus that delivers the most realistic macroeconomics one can have while still treating decision makers with respect and acknowledging limits on resources.

4.2.4.1   Mathematics and Forecasting

Outside of macroeconomics, one rarely hears urgent pleas to lower the amount of mathematics in human intellectual endeavors where the stakes are high. For example, the "let's get all this pesky math out of here" movement gets no traction in the worlds of aeronautical engineering (where big jets usually fly), or meteorology (where longer-term forecasts are generally not good). In both cases, what the public sees clearly is that a systematic approach is needed, that mathematics provides just this by disallowing ambiguity, and that the need for this approach has *nothing* to do with how one views the predictive power of the discipline.[8]

In economics, where predictive power certainly seems worse, the need for mathematical sophistication only seems *greater*. Take again the issue of rationality. I asserted earlier that some models of bounded rationality will indeed be representable as mathematics problems that are easier to solve than the ones demanded by models in which participants display full-blown rationality and rational expectations. This is not actually always true. In many instances of bounded rationality, the decision maker needs to know when to stop trying to acquire information.[9] And resolving this takes, yes, you guessed it . . . more mathematics.

Unless one wants to argue that human decisions have no common threads, and will therefore defy all attempts to systematize them, we are left with *only* the question of how to precisely, yet tractably, model decision making. Natural science has made significant progress by proceeding axiomatically and mathematically, and whether or not we will achieve this level of precision for any unit of observation in macroeconomics, it is likely to be the only rational (yes, rational) alternative.

4.2.4.2 Mathematics as a Language to Protect the Public *from* Economists

In addition to these benefits from the systematic approach, there is the issue of clarity. Lowering mathematical content in economics represents a retreat from unambiguous language.[10] Once mathematized, words in a given model cannot ever mean more than one thing. The unwillingness to couch things in such narrow terms (usually for fear of "losing something more intangible") has, in the past, led to a great deal of essentially useless discussion.

The plaintive expressions of "fear of losing something intangible" are concessions to the forces of muddled thinking. The way modern economics gets done, you cannot possibly *not* know *exactly* what the author is assuming—and to boot, you'll have a foolproof way of checking whether their claims of what follows from these premises is actually true or not. Critics should be delighted. The Nobel Laureate Kenneth Arrow offers a more nuanced view than mine in Arrow (1951). He notes that mathematics does likely lose something because "Language itself is a social phenomenon, and the multiple meanings of its symbols are very likely to be much better adapted to the conveying of social concepts than to those of the inanimate world." But Arrow then follows up with this: "It is true, then, that there are certain limitations of mathematical methods in the social sciences. Nevertheless, it must be insisted that the advantages are equally apparent and may frequently be worth a certain loss of realism. In the *first* place, clarity of thought is still a pearl of great price" (author's emphasis).

Three kinds of useless discussion have been particularly common in recent years: among economists; between economists and noneconomist policymakers; and between economists, policymakers, and the general public. One obvious example of this type of useless discussion is the monumental effort assessing what Sir John Maynard Keynes may or may not have had in mind when he wrote his hugely influential book *The General Theory*. This project took the attention of great minds like Sir John Hicks, and many other since then, who collectively tried to flesh out what was initially a series of relatively unclear conjectures.[11] Economists should be somewhat concerned by the fact that this occurred (though the power of Keynes's intellect made his conjectures arguably far more worthy of investigation than those of any other economist of that era).

Yet no "core" graduate course in economics at any major university today spends any time on Keynes's *General Theory*. And it is *not* because macroeconomists view real-time outcomes as always incapable of improvement via policy, or regard Keynesian-style prescriptions as inherently wrong-headed; far from it. Chapter 5 will reveal that, in nearly all our models for macroeconomic data, outcomes arising from firms and households that are price-taking and ignore all else will not be optimal at all, and Keynesian ideas rarely surface. The reason Keynes is absent in the training of new economists is that it is extremely difficult to extract precise formulations from his work, especially ones that are obviously amenable to any sort of quantification. Hence, Keynes's efforts are simply not helpful for answering questions of "how much" of any policy to engage in.

Contrast the preceding with the ideas and work of Robert E. Lucas Jr., which have been similarly influential in the methodology of macroeconomics, though not in its policy prescriptions. Whether one agrees or disagrees with Lucas (or for that matter, with far less influential modern macroeconomists) is irrelevant. What is relevant is that one simply cannot claim to "not know what Lucas had in mind." He tells you in mathematics, leaving no room for other layers of meaning. There will never be any reason to write a book about "What Robert Lucas *May Have Meant.*" The same is true for Edward C. Prescott, Thomas Sargent, Ed Green, and the rest. Nor is it the case that Lucas's statements are quantity-free. Indeed, Lucas's landmark *Models of Business Cycles* (1985) laid down a gauntlet precisely by performing a calculation showing that an entire class of models would likely be terminally incapable of telling us that business cycles are actually costly phenomena.

If you, as a reader, "know" that business cycles are nonetheless really socially costly, Lucas's approach should still strike you as useful. His work, in this instance, tells you what tree not to bark up (simple representative-agent models). Of course, not being able to bark up this tree means that you will have to work with a messier model—say, one that drops the assumption of market completeness, or one that posits that parents don't care much about their descendants. These are all harder models to work with, and this is exactly where the literature in the last two decades has gone, as we'll see in chapters 5 and 6.

At this point, some do indeed say, "forget about the mathematics, human behavior cannot be quantified." Aside from noting the defeatism of this sort of objection, we can be more critical: this point of view is not helpful for answering any question related to "how big" any effect is. What will a change in tax code do? What will an increase in the productivity of the Chinese do for US wage structures? and so on. Much of modern macroeconomics allows for the quantification of the size of competing effects. This is progress, and shows that mathematics and the related sphere of "computation" are tools that, like the rational-expectations assumption, help protect the public *from* economists. Once an argument is couched in terms of mathematics, I, or any other economist not taken by a modern macroeconomist's prescriptions, can ask where he or she comes off . . . exactly. And we can argue about the *relevance of preconditions* needed in order for the stated policy prescription to hold. To repeat: the *argument* worth having is over the relevance of preconditions, not over the conclusions given these preconditions. Robert E. Lucas Jr. might, for example, say, "So what if you don't *like* what I am saying? What have you got instead?" I would then have to produce a competing model.

Objecting to mathematics is, all too often, a weak objection to the demands of coherence. Period. But I am sympathetic to this concern: it *is* hard to make sense, actually. We usually don't succeed the first time, and innumeracy does seem relevant as a force around us. The rules for reasoning, as embodied in mathematics, are therefore helpful crutches for all of us. Mathematics is *built* for clarity, unambiguity, and error location—so when the stakes are high, human societies ought to use mathematical reasoning. And indeed, it *is* what they use. Civil engineers don't write each other descriptive narratives on tunnel construction; rather, they show their colleagues, and the next generation, the math. Moreover, as I will argue below, due to the policy ramifications of economic ideas, even the view of mathematics as "only a language that protects the public from economist-as-Svengali" seems more than sufficient as an argument for its adoption as lingua franca.

Some may find my viewpoint a difficult one to accept, but I think they should give it a try. A baseline level of numeracy allows us access to a method, the best one the species has come up with thus far, for tracing disagreements over conclusions back to the assumptions which birthed them. And this is important, if you accept the view (as I do) that macroeconomists are in the business of constructing organized analogies. If it's all about analogies, then asking that a story actually hang together seems like a pretty good idea. With this in mind, let me turn to a widely used mathematical modeling device: the so-called **continuum** model.

4.2.4.3   Example: The Continuum Assumption

As a student, journalist, or lay reader of macroeconomic research, one assumption you will encounter almost immediately in macroeconomic models is that, in lieu of a nice "normal" number to describe how many households and firms there are, the macroeconomist will assume that there is a "continuum" of households (sometimes also known as a **nonatomic measure space** of agents). What does this entail? First, "nonatomic" in this context means that there are so very many participants in the model that you could quite literally remove an agent, buyer, or a seller, or even a thousand of them (or even a million of them), and you would not change the "size" of the population! This is, of course, absurd. The world does not have a large enough number of inhabitants whereby one could engage in any such deletion (or addition, for that matter) of traders and leave the marketplace unscathed, nor can one divide a group of one further (without running afoul of the law).

The continuum may thus seem a totally irrelevant mathematical sleight of hand. But, since the goal of this book is to connect the seemingly most abstruse notions of theoretical economics to macroeconomists' day-to-day practice, let me clarify why this assumption is made. The first reason is that it allows us, given the *other* assumptions we make, to preserve internal consistency. The second is that it makes it far less important to make strong assumptions about households' and firms' preferences and capabilities. When the second of these two results is combined with a so-called **limit theorem**, which tells us the extent to which what is true in the continuum is approximately true in more standard settings with large, but finite, numbers of participants, we can gain tractability, knowing all the while that we are still learning something about the real world. This may be cryptic, so let's get specific, starting with the second payoff first.

Notice that in any model with finite numbers of participants, it is not strictly true that traders (buyers and sellers) cannot influence price. They can, in general. We noted this in chapter 2 when defining a competitive (rational-expectations) equilibrium with two firms. In the continuum, however, price taking becomes fully rational. For this reason, it seems worth moving to the continuum model, on aesthetic grounds alone. After all, having already assumed price taking and rationality, it certainly seems weird to study a model in which people and firms are suddenly irrational in one particular way. The next payoff, which has to do with the importance of convexity for the ability of a Walrasian price system to equilibrate competing interests, is more obviously substantive.

The orderliness of much of daily life, as well as the presence of an observable system of prices for many goods and services, motivated an earlier generation to ask: Could a system of Walrasian prices exist? In other words, was it a logical *possibility* that a list of prices *alone* could, if taken as given (and optimized with respect to both households and firms), lead to everyone transacting as they planned, even with total anonymity and with no further institutional arrangements for interaction between people? In answering this question, the first generation of existence proofs explicitly employed assumptions on the "convexity" of various objects in the model, including household preferences and firm production possibility sets. This assumption was made because they had also assumed something else: a finite number of households and firms. Now, you may ask, "What's so bad about that? The last time I checked, there were indeed a finite number of both."

To refresh our memories from chapter 2, recall that under the traditional approach in which firm production possibility sets were assumed to be convex, firms were modeled as entities for which if any two bundles of production were possible, so was any "average" of the two. As we noted there, a firm that could feasibly make 100 motorcycles each day, or could make 10 in a given day, would, by convexity, be assumed by the macroeconomist to be able to produce any number in between. We then noted that this might be a strong assumption because the equipment and production process needed to produce 100 might vary greatly from those needed to produce 10, leaving intermediate production levels infeasible. The same was true for households. Many people are not always willing to take something in between two things they value and regard it as an improvement. For example, I might have no preference in choosing between BMWs and Mercedes, but am I really likely to prefer a car whose front end is a BMW and back end is a Mercedes? I hope we agree that it seems to be a good idea to dispense with convexity in a model that otherwise preserves the coordinating role for Walrasian prices that motivated general-equilibrium theorists; it seems to bring us a baby step closer to "reality."

In his 1964 article "Markets with a Continuum of Traders," Robert Aumann showed that once one replaced the assumption that there was a finite number of types of households and firms with the assumption that there was a continuum, one could prove that Walrasian equilibrium would exist much more generally and that core equivalence held exactly, as opposed to being an approximation; one would then have a model in which price taking was fully rational. In particular, Aumann discovered that if there was a continuum of market participants, the convexity of individual-level preferences and production sets—long seen as indispensable for the existence of Walrasian prices—would be completely unnecessary. In particular, in keeping with the Shapley-Folkmann theorem we encountered in chapter 3, Aumann showed that one could have extremely nonconvex preferences at the level of individual participants, with no effect on the possibility that competing interests could be adjudicated via Walrasian prices. And firms could now be modeled much more "realistically," in that they could be assumed to be essentially incapable of doing too many different things at once.

On top of the conceptual flexibility that dropping convexity buys us (i.e., we now have a model that allows for much more latitude in modeling individual participants' capabilities, choices, and behaviors), the continuum model is *much* easier to work with. For those with some familiarity with basic calculus (and especially for those who have had exposure to basic Lebesgue theory), the point is that sums are messier than integrals. Moreover, in many cases, other mathematical machinery can be brought to bear on problems. For instance, to establish facts about the properties of the model, specific tools from statistics, known as "laws of large numbers" can be invoked more easily as well. The resulting implications of such a model, given its extreme assumptions, can then be harvested and disseminated.

In models that are starkly idealized in that the numbers of various ingredients they use (such as people, products, or time periods) are outrageously large, facts about the models are called **theorems in the limit** because the results are facts pertaining to the extreme or "limit model" that is being analyzed. Now, you may be wondering, "*So what* if I can prove properties about this world? It assumed a continuum of buyers and sellers, for goodness sake—who cares what is true about this silly model?" There are two answers, and I personally find something useful in both. The first is this: it is not as if the continuum was the *only* unrealistic thing being assumed. After all, people generally don't have preferences that are either well-defined in the way assumed in essentially all macroeconomic models, continuum or not, and firms may lack all manner of knowledge of their production capabilities— quite unlike the omniscient calculators they are modeled as. So why get so upset about this one assumption? The second answer is that for better or for worse, the task of economic theory, from the perspective of macroeconomists and others, is to provide statements that are logical consequences of their premises, *wherever those premises don't seem prone to leading one astray*. That is, the things that are proved to be true in a paper, or shown to routinely occur in a simulation, are things that a macroeconomist is trying to assert will occur if, say, a given policy in the real world is put into place. Whether the conclusions in a given model are true or routine, given their premises, is certainly something we can check. But we also know full well that the premises in a given study can at best only be approximated in the real world, and hence that the conclusions of the model may not be borne out in reality. But how would we know when the exact satisfaction of an assumption is likely to be crucial for the implications that arise? In general, we don't. Recall that at the outset I emphasized what I saw to be the important role for persuasion in economics. And while I have been uncompromising about not allowing persuasion to enter the process of moving from premises to conclusions, I see no way to *always* avoid it when one is trying to get colleagues to believe in the relevance of the premises embedded in one's pet model for understanding a given phenomenon.

Luckily, in some cases we can be more systematic. There are many models where the "extreme" assumption has to do with assuming there are infinite numbers of market participants, products, dates, or all of the above. These are not just esoteric classes of models. New Keynesian DSGE models routinely used in monetary policy discussions have all three in infinite numbers, in fact. In models where the extremes are along the "size" dimensions of the model, the best answers are provided by so-called "limit theorems" I noted in passing earlier. These are results that teach us about the nature of the approximation, by, for example (in the case of a model with a continuum of market participants) connecting the number of participants in the market with the size of the "gap" between the Walrasian equilibrium in the continuum economy and a suitably defined approximate equilibrium in a counterpart economy with finite numbers. One uses these results to learn how the quality of approximation arising from the infinite model improves as the finite versions of a given model get larger and larger. Note the contrast: results about the idealized model were called "theorems in the limit," and now we have limit theorems. Limit theorems allow us to learn how good the approximation provided by the continuum is for understanding the real, messy, and decidedly finite "real world."[12]

So it is fortunate that such results are available in some important cases. In the case of the ADM model, these results roughly show the following: if the nonconvexities are not "too large" in a precise sense ("bounded," in the jargon), then, as the number of traders gets large relative to the number of goods, every economy in a sequence of nonconvex economies will have a "convexified" counterpart (obtained by replacing all consumption and production sets with their smallest convex set that contains them, the so-called **convex hull**) whose equilibrium both exists (by the standard existence results) and is increasingly "close" to being an equilibrium for the original, nonconvex, economy. Specifically, almost all traders living in a large nonconvex economy would find that if they took the Walrasian prices from the convexified economy as given, they would also be happy to have the equilibrium allocations of the convexified economy. See Ellickson (1993), section 7.4, for precise statements. This is important to take note of. Suppose we had no such approximation result. Then, for all we knew, the continuum economy might be descriptive of nothing in the real world: the results from the continuum would perhaps be nothing more than artifacts of the continuum.

4.2.4.4   Example: Infinitely Lived Households

A favorite model of macroeconomists, as you will see in chapter 5, is the so-called neoclassical growth model. In this model, all households are assumed to live *forever*. What could such a model possibly teach one about the world? Quite a bit, and there are two reasons why. First, in essentially all macroeconomic models, households and the firms they own discount the future. Households do so because it is assumed by the macroeconomist that they inherently prefer a given path of consumption to occur sooner rather than later in their lives, all else being equal. This seems a natural place to start insofar as it describes the attitude of most consumers most of the time. Moreover, we notice that real interest rates are generally positive, which is consistent with the future being discounted relative to the present day. As for firms, if they make decisions to maximize profits, they need to take into account that the value of the firm at future dates is also discounted by households that own them.

Once decision makers discount the future, though, things start looking more "finite." Indeed, in a variety of macroeconomic models, decisions that are optimal for a household with an infinite planning horizon start looking a lot like those of anyone with more than, say, two decades left in their life. As a result, for many questions, especially those involving the work lives and consumption of households younger than late middle age, the infinite horizon model is just fine. This is a good thing because the infinite-horizon model is almost always far easier to deal with mathematically than a finite-horizon model.

On top of this, it turns out that even a limited form of concern for one's descendants can, under some circumstances, lead a sequence of households to act like a well-oiled dynasty. This was shown by Robert Barro in 1974, in "Are Government Bonds Net Wealth?" Barro's example was a case where each household lived for only a single period and had a single heir, whom they cared about in a discounted

way. Barro showed that this was sufficient, in the absence of borrowing constraints and some other conditions, to make the decisions of
such a dynasty *identical* to the ones that would be taken by a single
paterfamilias looking down at his infinite list of descendants. As with
any theoretical work in economics, Barro's work is important because
it helps answer the question "When is something true?" Barro showed
that it is not quite enough for people to be finite-lived for certain policies (like the national debt, in his paper) to matter. In doing so, his
work helped keep economists from fixating on the literal finiteness of
life, and instead, allowed them to work with far more tractable infi-
nite-lived models in which the future was discounted in particular
ways.[13]

Both these reasons account for why infinite-life assumptions forms
the basis of business cycle models. Such an assumption is no worse at
generating work and savings decisions than a model with finite-lived
households, and it keeps the model simple enough that many other
complicating factors thought to be more important for recessions
(various adjustment costs for investment, or transactions costs on consumption, sticky prices, etc.) can be added.

4.2.4.5   Example: "Social Planning Problems"

If you read articles in economics journals, a notion you will come across
repeatedly is that of the fictitious "benevolent social planner" and the
social planning problem (**SPP**). This decision maker is the quintes-
sential "benevolent dictator" who chooses outcomes for the population
in order to maximize "social" well-being. Because such an objective
depends on the way the planner gives weight to different households,
the weights are provided when this problem is specified. Given the
weights, the outcome of the SPP is a complete specification in an
economy for who works where and for how long, which technologies
will employed, how many inputs will be used in each one, and so on.

Of course, there is no benevolent, all-knowing social planner in
actual existence. No sane macroeconomist thinks there is. The social
planning problem is also not concerned with ideas like "ownership"
and "prices" that are particular to specific trading institutions like
"markets." And, to top it off, even the best-functioning democracies fall
well short of having outcomes that are chosen in ways that look as if
a benevolent dictator chose them. In particular, essentially every voting
scheme or other rule for making joint decisions is subject to various
serious deficiencies, as brought home to economists in the deeply

nonintuitive and disappointing result called **Arrow's Impossibility Theorem.** This result rules out a wide class of (superficially) attractive ways by which society might aggregate preferences to come to collective decisions. Why, then, is it of any use to study the SPP? The social planner's problem is merely a theoretical construct for understanding the performance of actual, inevitably more decentralized resource allocation schemes—such as competitive markets.

The social planner's problem is of interest for anyone who wants to know what one might be able to achieve ideally, at least *in principle*, i.e., given no restrictions other than household preferences and the productive capabilities of the technologies that one has available to combine inputs to make outputs. There are two reasons why the problem is informative for these questions. First, under extremely easy-to-satisfy conditions, *the solutions of a SPP are guaranteed to be Pareto-optimal.* Second, if one is working with a model in which one has placed enough structure on preferences to allow them to be represented by moderately smooth (i.e., differentiable) utility functions, something additional becomes possible: one can say quite a bit about general conditions that must hold at *any* Pareto-optimal outcome.

Typically, the SPP is specialized by macroeconomists to the problem of locating the maximum of a *weighted sum of household-level utilities.* This is called, in the jargon, a "weighted utilitarian" or **Bergson-Samuelson social welfare function (SWF).** Notice that this means rationality assumptions allow one more payoff: they allow us to locate optima in a particularly simple manner. This function is then maximized under the presumption that an omniscient central planner has knowledge of all the preferences and endowments of skills and resources available to households, and all the technological capabilities of the firms in the economy. An important result is that, in general, any Pareto-optimal outcome looks exactly *as if* one maximized a Bergson-Samuelson SWF. As the weights are varied, one obtains the *entire set of Pareto optima simply by solving a maximization problem that under most conditions is straightforward to do.* Learning what must hold at a Pareto-optimal outcome in a given model is particularly helpful in both understanding the crucial telltale indicators of inefficiency and measuring the departure from it that are created by a given set of trading institutions.

In addition to these two reasons for solving the SPP, there is a third reason: one of the most important "practical" uses of the social planning approach is to locate the competitive market (Walrasian) outcomes of a given model. This is made possible by the Second Welfare Theorem. Once we have located a Pareto-optimal outcome, we can ask what prices and income levels across households would allow us to realize that outcome as a Walrasian one. And this is often easier than directly locating Walrasian equilibria, because the latter involves locating *both* prices and allocations that jointly satisfy the requirements of equilibrium. By contrast, Pareto-optimal outcomes can be located without any reference whatsoever to prices or trading institutions (e.g., "markets"). All that is required is that allocations satisfy the definition of Pareto optimality. And in many applications, a macroeconomist will place enough additional structure on the model—such as making assumptions that allow for the use of differential calculus—to make the location of such outcomes relatively straightforward. Moreover, once one has located Pareto-optimal outcomes, one can, with almost no further effort, deduce the Walrasian prices and initial wealth levels across households that would have led to this outcome being reached as a Walrasian equilibrium.

As a result, macroeconomists have been able to analyze many relatively complex models far more easily than they otherwise would have been able to. Important examples are the early work of Lucas and Prescott (1971) and Danthine and Donaldson (1985), who are each able to solve SPPs to locate the Walrasian equilibria for rich models of industry investment and growth, respectively. Without the help of the theorem, these authors would have been forced either to use more cumbersome methods or to simplify other aspects of the problem in order to locate Walrasian outcomes. Taken as a whole, the effort put into the class of social planning problems by theoretically oriented economists is a clear instance of the metatheme of this book: abstract and technical ideas can, and do, serve us well in entirely practical inquiries.

4.3   Concluding Remarks

In this chapter, I described the nature of tradeoffs facing macroeconomics (and really, all economists). All models are exercises in aggregation, with the right question never being "Did you aggregate?," but rather "*Where* did you aggregate, and how does it matter for the question you are asking?" I have also taken the position that given aggregation assumptions, the rest of the model should be couched in mathematics in order to remain transparent, and that one's notion of equilibrium should not do violence to the underlying premises on individual behavior and the rules for trading.

Similarly, I stressed that the use of rationality helps mightily by allowing us to use utility functions. It is difficult, though not impossible, to proceed without them. Under conditions of uncertainty, additional requirements on decision makers' preferences allow for a similar simplification: any two uncertain outcomes can be evaluated by adding up a set of numbers associated with the value of each outcome in a given gamble, weighted by the probability of the occurrence of that outcome, and then comparing the sum of these with the identically constructed sum arising in the other gamble.

As for the last two great "errors" or sins of macroeconomics—the use of equilibrium analysis and the use of mathematics—I see a much less meaningful tradeoff. I have tried to illustrate the extent to which equilibrium has no necessary bearing on the question of whether an outcome is good or bad, nor on whether an outcome "looks stable" or not. Thus, it does not restrict outcomes unreasonably, and it does tie the economist's hands in asserting what outcomes are likely in a given setting. This imposes a much-needed form of discipline on any participant in a sphere with a surfeit of confident participants, and even worse, participants who dress up the normative as positive.

As for mathematics, essentially all policy questions require evaluating the quantitative strength of competing forces, and the mathematization of economics is what has allowed progress in making these comparisons. While mathematization clearly circumscribes the ability of macroeconomists to offer definitive prescriptions on many problems, this restraint is probably fine given the difficulties present in any real-world analysis. Moreover, it is preferable, in my view, for economists to speak about things that they can be clear about. Over longer horizons, cumulative knowledge-building will likely benefit strongly from being able to know what one's predecessors have done. And mathematics' universality and enforced internal consistency uniquely position it to assist in this.

On a mundane level, when a macroeconomist is studying an issue where the interaction of many people and many markets is likely to be relevant, she will routinely construct, solve, and simulate a model of an entire economy. From various perspectives, the modeling decisions used therein will seem to the new reader to range from being quite reasonable to quite outrageous.

With all this in mind, it will be useful to see the relatively small group of models that collectively loom largest in the minds of working macroeconomists. This is the subject of chapters 5 and 6.

5   Benchmark Macroeconomic Models and Policy Advice

5.1   ADM and the Real World

For macroeconomists, it is critical to have a model that allows for the explicit passage of time as well as the gradual resolution of uncertainty. After all, in the real world, decision makers of all stripes (households, firms, and government) clearly need to worry about the future, when their current decisions will have consequences, and often cannot know with certainty how that future will look. Think of your own decision to take an expensive vacation—it would be an easy decision if the world were about to end, but if not, then it takes some deliberation: if you don't get that raise you're expecting, you might end up poor later if you take the trip now.

Uncertainty (such as the raise you may or may not get) is often of a sort that only resolves itself slowly over time. For instance, the success of treatment for an illness or one's children's academic success are often aspects of life in which it takes time, sometimes years, to come to a definitive conclusion. Similarly, all the "hot" news of the day, such as data on GDP, investment, unemployment, and household spending change from day to day, and do so in ways that sometimes give mixed signals for months or quarters on end.

And yet I have spent essentially all of this book describing the properties of the ADM in settings where it has *no discernible applicability* to a world like ours, in which time and uncertainty both seem to play crucial roles. In chapters 1 and 2, for example, I described the main theorems ("fundamental theorems" in fact!) that described the relationship between Walrasian outcomes and Pareto efficiency with little or no mention of either time or uncertainty. I then gave a long list of reasons for doubting the direct applicability of the ADM to even the (relatively) simple world of no time and no uncertainty, and again, said next to nothing about the fact that the ADM model imagines trade as a one-shot affair, not at all like the purchases and sales we see and engage in all the time. So at this point you may be asking, "How can the ADM model possibly play *any* role at all in organizing the thoughts of macroeconomists?"

In chapter 2, I noted (though rather obliquely) that even though the ADM model looked awfully incapable of handling time and uncertainty, a full accommodation of both features was actually possible, thanks to the existence of a much more "realistic" version of the ADM model, called the Radner model. This version of the ADM model, and variants of it, are the bedrock on which macroeconomics sits. In the Radner version of the ADM model, time and uncertainty are modeled explicitly, but—and this is crucial—under some standard assumptions, Radner outcomes are absolutely *identical* to those coming from the ADM model! Thus, in many instances, nothing is gained by modeling the many complications one might imagine arising from the presence of uncertainty and time, especially when the goal is to understand the relationship between Walrasian outcomes and efficiency.

As we will see, versions of Radner models are used by the profession to address many of the major macroeconomic phenomena you might read about. Examples include economic growth, unemployment, the consumption of households, the relative returns on various classes of assets, and fiscal policy and monetary policy. The goal of this chapter is to get you to the Radner model in two steps. First, I'll show you how the ADM model deals with time and uncertainty. Then, I'll describe the far more "realistic" trading arrangement of the Radner model, and some classic benchmark models that employ versions of it.[1]

5.2 Time, Uncertainty, and the ADM Model

It was noticed by Debreu (1959) and Arrow (1953, 1964), among others, that the notion of whether any two goods or services are different from each other should depend fundamentally on whether consumers or producers view them this way, and not inherently on any purely *physical* characteristics of the good or service in question.[2] Think of an umbrella. This physical object provides different services when it is raining than when it is not. Therefore, the interaction of uncertainty and the physical good we know as an "umbrella" together imply that there are really *two* goods that consumers care about: "umbrellas on sunny days" and "umbrellas on rainy days." This is intuitive: prior to the realization of whether a day is sunny or rainy, an individual would value having umbrellas differently in these two eventualities. Conversely, in a world where all people were color-blind to red and green, red umbrellas and green umbrellas would be equally valuable and viewed (literally) as identical, though "physically" they are not. Even more generally, imagine a contract that promises you "canned radishes delivered at your front door one year from now, but only if you are feeling well." The eventual value of such a contract may well depend on the weather that prevails now and in the interim in radish-growing areas of China. This example also makes it clear that even radishes aren't just radishes: the fact that, in this case, they will be delivered under a given set of circumstances differentiates them from, among other things, radishes to be delivered under other circumstances.

A **contingency** in the Arrow-Debreu sense is a *complete* description of the environment prevailing at some future date. It is as finely detailed as is relevant to buyers and sellers. In his landmark work, Gerard Debreu (1959) introduced the idea of a **contingent commodity,** whereby a given "physical" good, say, radishes, would be differentiated by *whatever* circumstances were deemed relevant by consumers and producers. In settings with uncertainty, the notion of complete markets is then simply one in which the markets required are expanded so that there will be markets for every single contingent commodity. A Walrasian equilibrium for a model allowing for trade in a full set of contingent commodities *prior to the realization of any uncertainty* is usually referred to as an **Arrow-Debreu equilibrium**, rather than an ADM model, which usually connotes an economy without uncertainty. I will use the term "ADM model" to refer to the ADM both without uncertainty and with it, with the context making matters obvious.

To see another example of an ADM economy that includes both time and uncertainty, first imagine the same simple agrarian society we laid out in chapter 1, in which there were two "physical" products, corn and wheat. Now add a twist: let the economy be subject to three kinds of uncertain weather: sunny, cloudy, and rainy. Now, recall first the market structure imagined by the ADM model: a WCH would open in the town square and establish Walrasian prices for all commodities. Because of the uncertainty present in this economy, the Arrow-Debreu WCH sets up trade in not just two markets as before (i.e., not just markets for wheat and corn alone) but *six* markets, one for each physical good in each contingency. These are: corn in sunny weather, corn in cloudy weather, corn in rainy weather, wheat in sunny weather, wheat in cloudy weather, and wheat in rainy weather.

While, in the original "no-uncertainty" case, a household's endowments of these goods was simply a listing of how much corn and wheat they had, now we must distinguish between the amount of the goods in each of the three possible weather conditions. Households would then take their endowments of these goods—which now includes "titles" to receive possibly varying amounts of corn and what depending on the weather—and sell them to the WCH. They would then turn around and buy the bundles of these six goods that they like most, subject to the budget determined by their endowments and prices.

The markets just described are called "complete *forward* markets" as they are markets in *promises*. Be clear on this: the *only* things that are actually bought and sold in an Arrow-Debreu market are promises to deliver, or take delivery of, the amounts agreed upon in the WCH prior to the realization of any uncertainty, under the various contingencies. For example, a trader in the ADM world may have agreed to deliver 1 ton of red winter wheat in rainy weather, but expects to receive 0.5 ton of the same in sunny weather, with analogous agreements for corn.

As a consequence of the First Welfare Theorem, we also know that such an outcome is Pareto-optimal, which immediately means that no further mutually beneficial trading opportunities exist—so no new agreements would be struck after the initial round of trading *even if markets reopened* once the uncertainty had resolved itself. This restates what we learned earlier: ex-ante Pareto-optimal outcomes are ex-post Pareto-optimal.

5.2.1   The Long Arm Attached to the Invisible Hand

The broad view of a commodity imagined by the Arrow-Debreu setting is of enormous importance. It tells us that, in principle, real-life aspects such as time and uncertainty are *fully accommodated* by Walrasian theory: simply differentiate physical goods and services by the exact time and circumstances under which they will be available. A textbook rendition will be something like the following.

Think of a world with H "basic physical commodities" (apples, oranges, and motor oil, say), that lasts T periods. T and H are just round numbers, e.g., 20 and 2000. Next, think of a **state of the world** as being a description of the complete particular unfolding of history over the entire (T-period) life of the economy. If $T = 3$, and the weather was the only uncertain thing, and it could either be cloudy or sunny, a "state of the world" would be a full listing of the entire history of the weather in this economy, e.g., "sunny, sunny, cloudy." Of course, at time 0, one doesn't know which state (i.e., history) will unfold.

To see that an economy like this has the same fundamental structure as the ADM model, now just redefine the set of commodities by the *date*. In this case, each basic physical commodity is differentiated by the date on which it is consumed by households, produced by firms, or becomes available (as an endowment). This means we have $L = H \times T$ dated physical goods.

Finally, we impose the commonsense restriction that these goods cannot appear in different amounts in the endowments or consumption plans of households or in the production plans of firms across any two states that the economy's participants cannot themselves distinguish at any date. These are called **measurability** restrictions. With this redefining of the goods and services in the economy and the imposition of the measurability restrictions, the model immediately becomes mathematically identical to the ADM, and we're done.

This equivalence is of supreme importance: it immediately means that the First and Second Welfare Theorems are true. This teaches us that the ability of Walrasian prices under complete markets to exhaust all gains from trade between self-interested rational price takers is thus in no way dependent on the economy being a one-date affair (what economists call "static"). Instead, Walrasian prices can efficiently coordinate activity in economies that are almost arbitrarily rich in their spatial, temporal, or stochastic structure.[3] Moreover, it implies that we can invoke the existence theorems as well!

To sum up, we know that when a full set of contingent commodities is available, Walrasian equilibrium exists and is Pareto-optimal in a setting where most (nearly all) allocations are not. We'll also see later that under mild conditions, Walrasian equilibria will also be (almost) unique—i.e., the model has a definite prediction for prices and allocations given the primitives of preferences, endowments, and technology.

To echo a point I made in chapter 2, entirely apart from the practicality of whether private trade will give rise to a full set of Arrow-Debreu contingent claims, it should strike the reader as astonishing that an object as impersonal and "small" as a set of Walrasian prices is capable of leading self-interested parties to Pareto-efficient outcomes with no direct communication between them whatsoever—even in the presence of uncertainty that only resolves over time.

5.2.1.1   The Impossibility of Literal Arrow-Debreu Market Completeness

The ADM model with contingent commodities is a fantastic illustration of the power of mathematics to demonstrate the logical "sameness" of seemingly different objects. In this case, we know now that an economy with two people, two goods (e.g., apples and oranges), a single firm, one round of decision making, and no uncertainty at all has exactly the same mathematical structure, takes no more time to describe, and has the same properties—such as the welfare theorems—as one with 2 billion people, 2 billion goods, 2 billion firms, and which will last for 2 billion years with all manner of uncertainty. That is, we see that with the right set of markets, Walrasian equilibria are efficient, meaning that linear prices can coordinate economic activity in incredibly rich settings.

But mathematical sameness clearly hides something vital: it doesn't immediately convey, for example, the fact that a literal Arrow-Debreu world is well-nigh unattainable. The presumption is that trading forums are costless to operate: there are no overhead costs, no costs for verifying claims, etc. While this was a bad assumption under conditions of certainty, it is far, far worse under uncertainty. The ADM model, under uncertainty, envisions the presence of a market (with a single, linear price) for quite literally every good in every discernible "state of the world." As a result, the ADM setting is wildly demanding in terms of the number of markets it imagines. Let's say that instead of two goods, we had $L = 1000$ different goods, and instead of just two states, we had $S = 500$ different contingencies (really, 500 entire *histories* of outcomes over the entire span of time for which households exist), we'd then need *half a million* markets at time zero under ADM trading, all of which would have to be of the fanciful "contingent" commodity variety! This is just too demanding to be realistic. But, strictly speaking, this is what complete Arrow-Debreu markets require. The cost of operating so many markets would rapidly exhaust all of society's resources; even the smallest department store or auction house takes space and some personnel to operate. It would be truly ironic, if not hilarious, if society fully squandered its resources in an ill-conceived attempt to create an efficient trading system.[4]

As for contingent commodities, there is no obvious contract available right now that I could purchase that would deliver me, for instance, a coconut and a ticket to the Caribbean if and only if "the weather in the preceding six months had an average heat index of less than

20 degrees Fahrenheit." But the Arrow-Debreu world presumes that there is such a thing. Of course, I *can* buy a coconut today and a plane ticket (also today) to the Caribbean on a flight leaving exactly six months from now. But these purchases are good for a coconut and a trip *irrespective* of whether the weather at home has been bad or good over the period in question. They are emphatically not contingent on all the uncertainty that may resolve itself between now and six months from now.

What is more, the Arrow-Debreu world would involve no *trade* after the first day of mankind's existence (or at least, after the first day in which mankind created a full set of Arrow-Debreu contingent claims). One would observe only *deliveries*! That is, if the Arrow-Debreu contingent-claims market actually were present among the ancients, *all* observed transactions today would simply be the fulfillment of the obligations created by those contracts, whereby the descendants of those alive at the "beginning of time" would simply be delivering on commitments agreed to by their most distant ancestors! To say that this seems not quite what occurs around us is a mild understatement.

A final nail in the coffin of "literal" complete Arrow-Debreu markets has to do with the incentives to manipulate prices that would arise under such a market structure. Notice that the requirement that there be a price for any Arrow-Debreu claim in which even two traders have any interest means that there will inevitably be many commodities for which one probably won't be able to establish price-taking behavior unless the parties were guileless enough to not exploit the market power they inevitably had. Moreover, recall that the Myerson-Satterthwaite theorem told us for sure that in such a setting, barring intimate knowledge of preferences, efficiency was impossible.

In light of all this negativity I've heaped on the ADM model, two questions immediately arise regarding how one views decentralized trade. First, a full set of Arrow-Debreu markets are, as I have repeatedly emphasized, a sufficient but perhaps not necessary condition for decentralized outcomes to be efficient.[5] And even within the class of purely "Walrasian," i.e., linear-price-mediated, trading arrangements, might there be arrangements that require fewer markets to be open at any one time, but which nonetheless, reproduce the Arrow-Debreu outcome? The answer is yes, and the most important example of such a setting is the so-called **Radner trading arrangement** (see the original Radner 1972), stemming from an earlier idea of Kenneth Arrow, and due to the eminent economist Roy Radner.

5.3 The Radner Version of the ADM Economy

Arrow (1953) noted early on (in a paper not published in English until 1964) that "securities" or financial assets could, in principle, allow for the outcome of an ADM model to be replicated with far fewer markets than the archetypal Arrow-Debreu contingent commodities. These securities were special, as they were ones that paid off in only one contingency, and paid nothing in any other one, and for obvious reasons are called "**Arrow securities**."

Radner followed this line of reasoning and imagined a market structure where instead of all trade happening at once as in the ADM setting, a small set of markets open prior to the resolution of any uncertainty. These markets allow for contingent trade in just one of the goods. Think of a world with just four physical goods—corn, wheat, alfalfa, and soybeans—in springtime, when planting is about to commence. In this economy, all eating takes places later, at harvest time. But think of the weather at harvest time as uncertain, taking one of three possible forms: sunny, cloudy, or rainy, each of which matters for the size of the harvest. After the harvest, imagine that the world ends.

In this physical setting, a Radner trading system or a Radner economy will allow only weather-contingent trade in springtime (before uncertainty is resolved) in only *one* of the physical goods—say corn. That is, participants in a Radner economy can take part in three forward markets in which they buy or sell promises to deliver or receive three goods—*corn* in rainy weather, *corn* in cloudy weather, and *corn* in sunny weather—before they know the harvest. But there would be no markets in any other goods (in our case, this just means no trade in wheat, alfalfa, or soybeans). The Radner economy then lets uncertainty over the weather resolve itself, but as soon as it does, it allows for a set of markets for immediate consumption in all goods. In our case, four markets would open: one for corn, one for wheat, one for alfalfa, and one for soybeans (and the weather would be whatever it turned out to be). These latter markets are typically called "spot" markets, because they are ones in which market participants buy and sell items for immediate consumption.

Notice that the Radner trading arrangement features fewer markets than the ADM model under uncertainty requires: instead of twelve markets (three forward markets each in corn, wheat, alfalfa, and soybeans), our current market arrangement features seven markets (three forward markets for corn in rainy, cloudy, or sunny weather, and four spot markets once the weather resolved itself). Crucially, as the number of goods and states grows, so does the difference in the number of required markets, and it grows dramatically. For instance, if there were 100 different types of crops and 20 kinds of weather, the Arrow-Debreu trading system would feature 2,000 markets, while the Radner would require just 120 markets.

More generally, under Radner trading, if there are L goods and S states, then $L + S$ markets can do the work of the L *times* S markets imagined in the time-0 ADM trading arrangement. So if there were $S = 500$ states of the world, and $L = 1,000$ goods as in my earlier example, then the Radner model asks that there be 1,500 markets (one forward market for delivery of a single good—corn, in our example—in each of the 500 possible states that might occur), and L markets once the uncertainty resolves (e.g., corn, wheat, and 998 other goods and services). Critically, under the Radner arrangement, "only" 500 would have to be contingent commodities. To the extent that we view (and should view—as we will see later) these types of markets as the hardest kinds of markets to arrange, as they are the ones most bedeviled by forces that induce them to fail to work well, this is good news.

In fact, as a general matter, the Radner economy will require far fewer markets to be open at any one time than the all-encompassing Arrow-Debreu model. Specifically, unlike the Arrow-Debreu model, the Radner model asks "only" that there be enough markets for the goods that one plans to consume as of that date, plus markets by which to transfer purchasing power to every possible contingency that might prevail in the *immediately following* trading session (i.e., we don't need financial markets for times further out into the future). Put this way, the analogy to insurance becomes easier to see.

A **Radner equilibrium** is therefore a particular kind of Walrasian equilibrium. It is described (as usual) by a set of prices that, when taken as given, lead all households to be able to execute their desired purchases and sales. However, this definition hides what is different about Radner equilibrium. The set of prices is really a set of *expected* prices since not all purchases take place in any one trading session, and the purchases really involve *plans* to consume and produce in a set of spot markets and in a set of future spot markets at prices *expected* to prevail then, along with choices for the one-period-ahead state-contingent claims in the one good we allow it for at each date (corn, in our example). I italicized the word "expected" to remind you yet again that while the Radner trading arrangement is more "realistic" in the sense that it features trade occurring over time and in response to uncertainty as it occurs in our world, it asks for a great deal of forecasting power. In particular, it asks households to have tremendous "contingent" foresight for prices under various contingencies, and this should not be forgotten.

The intuition for the Radner arrangement being able to deliver the ADM outcome is this: As long as I, as a market participant, can buy or arrange to receive enough corn in the rainy and sunny outcomes, I will be able to then use the spot markets to trade the corn I receive for wheat. For concreteness, just imagine that *after* the weather is decided, you can buy or sell corn and wheat from and to the WCH. Now, if I know (forecast correctly) the prices of corn and wheat under *each kind of weather* that might have occurred in the interim, then I can work out exactly how much corn I will need to deliver or have delivered if I want to buy a given amount of wheat (or corn) on the spot markets under each possible realization of weather.[6]

As I will elaborate a bit more later, an important and relatively implicit assumption made in the Radner trading arrangement is that households not be constrained in their ability to *borrow* or, more precisely, to short-sell the one commodity in which there is forward trade. In our example, the Radner arrangement requires that households be able to sell as much contingent corn (say, rainy-day corn) as they please, including *more* than they would be endowed with in the state under consideration. The understanding is that they will purchase the rest in the spot market next period (as soon as the weather is revealed). The absence of constraints on short-selling is, in turn, made possible by the implicit assumption that default is not possible—deliveries will be honored. Further below, I will revisit the problems that the absence of such "unlimited commitment" creates. For now, suffice it to say that limits on the commitment of borrowers to repay when it is perfectly feasible for them to do so will generally void the ability of Radner trading to mimic the outcome arising from trade in the full set of Arrow-Debreu contingent commodities. A lesson here is this: if we think a sequential-trading setting is likely the only realistic one we can imagine as practical, then "limited commitment" may well be a relevant barrier to attaining efficient outcomes via any sequential-trading arrangement we might imagine, including Radner's full "one-step-ahead forward markets in one good" setup.

I have just noted that households that interact through markets that open over time and in response to the resolution of uncertainty must forecast the prices they will come to face in these various situations. However, not just any forecast will do. In keeping with our traditional notion of equilibrium as a situation in which no one is surprised by market outcomes given the particular realization of uncertainty, equilibrium under the Radner market structure will require that households forecast future prices *correctly* (see Mas-Colell, Whinston, and Green 1995, prop. 19.D.1, and Ljungqvist and Sargent 2004, ch. 8, for formal treatments). In what follows, I will describe examples of how the Radner interpretation of the Walrasian model is the one used by modern macroeconomists to organize their thinking about the "real world." For now, it is important to emphasize that once trade starts to happen over time, as certainly seems to be the case in the real world, households *must* start making forecasts of future prices—this has absolutely nothing to do with how "rational" or irrational one thinks participants in real markets are. It is a requirement that is inherent to any setting in which events unfold over time and do so in ways that are uncertain from the current perspective.

5.3.1 A Summary of Radner Trading

We have just seen that in a Radner model of the economy, one allows for the sequential trading of securities in response to the temporal unfolding of uncertainty. Consider the situation where, each time some uncertainty about the world is resolved (e.g., will there be war or not? will I lose my job or not? etc.), we allow markets to open after each such event, operate a WCH to get Walrasian prices in each of these markets, and allow households (and firms, if they want to) to reposition their entire portfolios in light of the new information under these prices. This interpretation, while still very much an extreme portrait relative to the markets one routinely sees in the real world, is certainly much more directly useful for thinking about the trade and price movements that we observe daily. At least it features trade—as opposed to merely deliveries! Moreover, it features trade in response to the arrival of new information, surely a part of why a good deal of trade actually occurs.

But, as you are probably thinking, even the Radner model of trading, despite its more "modest" requirements on the number of markets that must be open prior to the resolution of uncertainty, asks way too much of traders. That is, the requirements on the richness of markets and on the ability of households to forecast that are needed to attain efficient outcomes through decentralized price-taking optimization still seem very fanciful. In a nutshell, the benefits we obtain in terms of the reduction in the required number of forward markets is accompanied, and perhaps more than substantially "offset," by a serious forecasting requirement. And yet it is still the preferred first step in macroeconomics, even if only to serve as a benchmark against which to measure the cost of dysfunction occurring in a more "realistic" model.

5.3.2   Spot Markets and IOU Markets: Radner and How Macroeconomists Think about Market Dysfunction

To my taste, the Radner model's most profound legacy is the role it plays in helping me and my fellow macroeconomists to classify the roles played by the two different kinds of markets present in any price-based trading system. Since the Radner model features both markets for trade in goods and services that are immediately consumed and markets for the transfer of purchasing power to *future* dates and/or contingencies, it bears a fundamental, if stylized, resemblance to the market systems we observe in daily life. Specifically, it is a model where these two classes of markets and their dysfunction can then be usefully placed into two separate boxes: "spot" and "IOU," respectively.

While the term "spot market" is entirely standard, let me explain the term "IOU market." Any market that is not a pure spot market (where an item is traded for another "on the spot") is one in which an IOU has been issued. This is because *any* delay between delivery and payment necessarily entails credit on one side and an obligation on the other, and hence involves either the implicit or explicit issuance of an IOU. Financial markets—for example, markets for stocks, bonds, futures, and options—all involve (sometimes complex) bundles of fairly explicitly defined IOUs issued by one party to another. Moreover, even some seemingly spot transactions come together with IOU transactions. Notice, for example, that the purchase of a car with a service plan is really a bundle of a car with a set of IOUs issued by the car dealer to a buyer. The dealer delivers a car immediately, which is the "spot" part of the transaction, and also *promises* to repair the car at *some* future dates (e.g., warranties have time limits) and under *some* circumstances (e.g., the policy may not apply if your car gets hit by lightning). The latter is nothing but a set of IOUs.

One critical market that I will place into the IOU category is that of labor. While it is true that some do have jobs that pay essentially in a spot transaction (such as the teenager who may mow neighborhood lawns in the summer, or a local babysitter, or a seasonal farm laborer), most other forms of trade in labor are longer-term and very much involve promises by both workers and employers. Employment is not usefully regarded for most of us as a spot market transaction. Rather, it is generally a *relationship* expected by all parties to last for at least some time (and often, an open-ended amount of time). It is one that prescribes, implicitly or explicitly, actions for employer and employee alike at various times under various contingencies. Put this way, it becomes clearer that all relationships may be viewed as the trade in (sometimes elaborate) bundles of IOUs.

5.3.2.1 Spots Are OK

It is fair to suggest that macroeconomists generally view spot markets as functioning well; this is rarely where we think the large "market failures" occur. For most consumer goods (e.g., mangoes) and producer goods (e.g., drill presses), most of the time, product quality is discernible, linear prices are the rule, sellers and buyers compete (sometimes brutally), exclusion for nonpayers is typically feasible for most purchases, and stock-outs and prolonged pile-ups of inventories of most items are decidedly rare at most retailers (and certainly across all retailers in a town on any given day).[7] In fact, spot markets tend to function quite well even in those places where the average income level is extremely low, as I have found during my annual pilgrimages to Chennai, India, with its many small retail establishments offering a vast array of products at highly competitive linear take-it-or-leave-it prices.[8]

Of course, spot markets may still sometimes fail to allow market participants to make all the exchanges they want to. As I discussed in detail in chapter 2, even leaving aside market power, public goods, and taxes, asymmetric information could throw a wrench into the efficiency of decentralized trade. In fact, the seminal paper of Akerlof (1970) first helped economists recognize the potential effects of what we have come to call adverse selection, whereby the quality of a good available for sale falls with the price it is expected by sellers to fetch—sometimes to the point of driving all sellers of high-quality goods out of the market. Akerlof's work suggested this possibility in the context of the spot market for used cars. Akerlof's work showed economists that linear prices could not be *presumed* to work efficiently. But before we grow pessimistic, it is useful to remind the reader that the First Welfare Theorem gave us only *sufficient* conditions for efficient outcomes.

Market participants could, and indeed do, augment (and sometimes replace) linear prices with a variety of other contractual features, such as warranties or promises of free auto servicing, etc. As a result, if these promises can be expected to be honored, even spot markets plagued by asymmetry of information on product quality may work well. This is a quantitative question, and one that is now getting more attention because economists have the computational and game-theoretic tools to analyze such cases.

5.3.2.2   IOUs, Maybe Not So Much?

It is probably fair to say that if macroeconomists disagree on the extent of market dysfunction, it is most often in their assessment of the performance of IOU markets. There is a good reason for this: asymmetric information problems are likely worse in IOU markets, and on top of it, there is a second class of problems—those created by limits on parties' commitment to act in the future as they now promise to do. While I've already argued that imperfect commitment plays a role in creating difficulties for centralized systems, we now see that it can create problems in decentralized settings as well. By the end of this book, I hope to have persuaded you that, on balance, limited commitment is the central impediment to allowing societies to attain "good outcomes."

A reason that limited commitment is the main form of sand in the gears of economic life is that even the occasional problems one sees in spot markets may have their roots in IOU-market dysfunction. Think of the market for used cars. While bad cars may lurk among the good ones on any used-car lot, one may not be doomed to a crapshoot when buying a used car. A warranty may be just what is needed to separate the good from the bad and the ugly. But what's a warranty? It's a bundle of IOUs. So the extent to which a warranty on a car can overcome a buyer's fears that it is a lemon depends on the buyer's faith that the issuer of such promises will make good later on. Barring this, there is less reason to be confident that the spot market for cars will work well.

Thus, while limits to commitment are generally irrelevant (almost by definition) in impeding spot transactions, in IOU markets asymmetric information and limited commitment can *interact* to further worsen matters. I will discuss some models that study these impediments to trade later, but for now, let me expand on the kinds of problems IOU markets can present. Let's think of the decision to buy health insurance. Insurance purchases are an example that can feature the problems of both asymmetric information and limited commitment. As already broached in chapter 2, these are economists' two "usual suspects" in creating problems for decentralized trade. In the insurance context, asymmetric information can cause problems in the following manner: If I know more about my own condition than the insurance company does, the insurance company should worry that I will lie about my weight and my cigarette addiction. The insurance company cannot simply raise premiums; if they did, the relatively healthy might drop out, leaving the pool filled with even more overweight smokers. Of course, they might offer me a high-deductible plan, but by definition this is *incomplete* insurance: when something bad happens, it *will* cost me out of pocket. Insurance as we experience it is emphatically not a Radner economy contingent claim.

Now, enter limited commitment. By definition, this is a problem that is confined to IOU markets. In the insurance context, one certainly hears of people being dropped by an insurer the moment they become severely ill. Of course, this does not always happen, but it does happen to some. At the time I make a decision to purchase insurance, what is relevant is my *assessment* of the likelihood that I will be unceremoniously dropped at some critical juncture, perhaps on a technicality in the fine print of the contract. If we all share an assessment of this risk, notice that the adverse selection may get worse. All else being equal, potential buyers now worry that they will be dropped. If that's the case, prices will have to remain "high" to make up for the fact that the relatively healthy face even less incentive to buy in. In the example of a car service plan cited above, the problem is similar: the buyer wonders if the servicer will honor his promises. And, knowing this, the seller may not be able to offer a highly comprehensive service plan: the buyer won't believe that he'll make good on the promise. In turn, the seller may lack a credible way to show the buyer he believes in the car he's selling. In the end, then, what could have been a mutually beneficial trade might not occur.

Even worse, trade might not occur simply because buyers are pessimistic in a way that leads to outcomes that fail to disconfirm their pessimism. An example might be a setting where all would-be buyers of insurance think that no insurer will ever make good on a policy. In this world, no one would ever buy insurance, and as a result, no insurer would ever get the chance to prove anyone wrong in their skepticism. Of course, this is extreme: the general point is that once asymmetric information and limited commitment enter the picture, household *beliefs* can begin to exercise (often negative) influence on the ability of a trading institution to facilitate mutually beneficial exchanges.

While my examples have concerned health insurance and auto purchases, it is clearly a more general potential problem for market participants. Essentially every financial contract, including insurance contracts for our homes, cars, and lives, is a bundle of promises to pay and provide services—a bundle of IOUs—at various future dates, in various situations. On the one hand, this is good news, because it suggests again that literal Arrow-Debreu or Radner contingent claims may not be needed, but rather a set of financial instruments that can mimic such complete markets. In fact, it turns out that a few assets, *especially derivatives* like options, if cleverly traded, can do this (this intuitively appealing idea has been fully formalized by researchers working at the border of economics and finance). This gives us another reason for comfort in using the Radner trading arrangement to represent the ability of real-world households and firms. It may not be grossly inadequate.

But on the other hand, it still is a nagging reminder that, given what I have just described, intertemporal trade cannot simply be presumed to work in the way that the benchmark Radner model presumes. And this can, as we have seen in the car example, even bleed into creating problems in the ability of *spot* markets to mitigate asymmetries in information and to arrange mutually beneficial exchanges. This idea has far-reaching implications, and limited commitment lurks in much ongoing research on the mechanisms that operated during the recent financial crisis, as we'll see in chapter 6.

Digression: Is All Modern Macroeconomics Keynesian Economics?
Interestingly, the intense scrutiny that financial and insurance market (dys)function has received, and continues to receive, is the prosecution of a research program that none other than Keynes would have endorsed. He emphasized very explicitly the problems inherent in markets involving labor, investment, and the means of payment—what we would call "money." His influential essay was, after all, called the "General Theory of Employment, Interest, and Prices," with these words showcasing his focus on the malfunction that one might expect to see in labor markets, markets for IOUs issued by firms to fund

investment, and the role of money as partly a special kind of IOU, respectively.

5.3.2.3   Radner and the Real World: A Brief Recap

Relating this discussion back to the Radner economy, the "frictions" of the real world almost certainly compromise the ability of households (and firms, in some cases) to buy the full set of state-contingent commodities one period ahead in the amounts they would need to achieve Pareto-optimal outcomes. And this is so even though we are no longer asking that all Arrow-Debreu markets be open prior to the resolution of uncertainty. Yet the interesting question is not whether the Radner-like trading arrangements supplied by the real world fully achieve Pareto-optimal outcomes. The interesting questions are (i) How *close* do decentralized trading arrangements get us to efficient outcomes? and (ii) When can we effect Pareto improvements on the decentralized solution by using large-scale compulsory collective action (i.e., government)?

On the second question, let me again emphasize that other contractual features, and even reputational concerns, may kick in to ensure well-functioning spot and IOU markets. There is certainly an enormous amount of trade in IOU markets: households have successfully issued more than $10 trillion in IOUs for home mortgages (an amount approaching the value of all output produced in the US in a typical recent year) and about $1 trillion in unsecured (e.g., credit card) debt. Moreover, insurance markets of all kinds do certainly exist and function. Similarly, interfirm financial transactions are astronomical in volume, and so on. Nonetheless, both the immediate potential for malfunction and the potentially toxic interaction between asymmetric information and limited commitment must leave one at least somewhat circumspect about the likely efficiency with which IOU markets function.

In fact, the areas receiving by far the most attention from macroeconomists are those in the market for labor and the market of financial IOUs. Most interesting of all in the context of the financial crisis, some of the contractual arrangements (particularly "debt" securities) that allow such a large volume of IOUs to exist and be traded may in fact be culpable in making the economy as a whole more sensitive or fragile. The assessment of this possibility is in its infancy, as economists have until very recently not had models in which they could clearly and tractably build in asymmetric information, the response of contracting to this friction, and shocks to the overall economy.

5.4   Many Important Macroeconomic Models Are Mainly Versions of Radner Economies

One does observe trade occurring routinely in response to the arrival of new information over time. And we each do spend some time thinking about future prices in, say, the grocery store (the analog of the full set of spot markets for corn and wheat), as well as making decisions about how much to save in forms that are contingent on uncertainty (the real-life analog of choosing the amount of corn to buy or sell in the forward market). Admittedly, though, the extent to which our savings are contingent is fairly crude. One can buy a portfolio of stocks and bonds, and thereby get payments later that do depend to some extent on the economy-wide situation that is prevailing. But one cannot so easily save in a form that pays *only* when one gets sick, or *only* when one loses a job, and so on.[9] For now, we can assert that the Radner model certainly captures some key features of real-world trade, and therefore serves a model whose outcomes have counterparts in the data, e.g., the amount spent on various goods in each period under various circumstances, and the amount saved in a given period of time by households.

Lastly, leaving aside any dysfunction that might occur in the markets for "spot" trade, the Radner model teaches us that the inability of Walrasian prices to generate Pareto-optimal outcomes in the core can typically be interpreted as arising from the *absence* of particular markets for the delivery of purchasing power under the various circumstances in which market participants need them. As a result, we can ask how public policy can help aid or sometimes even *mimic* the function of such markets, through taxes, subsidies, fees, or other regulations.[10]

In almost all modern macroeconomic models, a version of the Radner sequential-trading arrangement that I have described is spelled out, whereby markets are opened for spot trade for many, though not always all, commodities, with forward markets that vary in the extent to which deliveries can be made contingent. For example, in the so-called complete-market growth models described first, both spot and one-step-forward IOU markets are "complete" in the sense that one can arrange to deliver corn, or have it be delivered, under all possible contingencies (e.g., rainy, cloudy, or sunny) that can immediately follow the current one; and importantly, one can sell forward the entire value of the goods and services that one is entitled to after the resolution of uncertainty (no borrowing constraints). The spot markets are complete as well—all goods and services for immediate consumption are available at Walrasian prices. In other models, such as the "Search" and "SIM" models discussed later, what is imagined is a much more restricted set of forward markets. For instance, households might be modeled as having access only to a savings account that pays them the same amount irrespective of the contingency that prevails. It is a "poor man's insurance contract"—in the sense that it does not allow for the transfer of purchasing power in all the ways a household might desire. In summary, *macroeconomists generally interpret the data they see as the unfolding of a Radner equilibrium, often with distortions, such as taxes, and with some incompleteness or dysfunction in the set of IOU markets.* Read that sentence again; it is important.

5.5   Macroeconomic Policy: A Brief General Discussion

Before proceeding to the description of some of the most important macroeconomic models currently in use, let me gather some ideas that have already been in the air throughout this book regarding the proper role of "policy." In what follows, what will become clear is the hugely powerful practical legacy of the extremely abstract ADM model in macroeconomists' approach to interventions in otherwise decentralized trading arrangements.

5.5.1   What Is a Policy?
In modern macroeconomics, the word **policy** means something quite specific: it refers to a *rule* that spells out what a policymaker will do at every date and under every description of uncertainty and private-market decisions. And by "policymaker," I mean relatively centralized entities with meaningful powers to tax, transfer, and regulate. Local, state, and federal governments are the most obvious examples. An example of a tax policy would be the announcement of how taxes adjusted according to income, when they would sunset, etc.

For a rational household or firm, the definition of "policy" I have given above is what is needed: it is *meaningless* to speak of the effects of a given change in a policy at a point in time, without spelling out how policy will be chosen in the future. For example, the question

"How will a tax cut today affect the economy?" is incomplete. If you write about economics for a living, this is an important point to keep in mind. Without spelling out the path for *future* taxes—even (especially!) if that future part depends on various forces that are at the current time unknown or uncertain, it is a meaningless question. In the example, the questions are: How long will the change in tax rates being considered last? What will likely replace it when it goes? And so on. Decision makers who look forward will want and need this information to decide what they want to do—even if they are not fully rational.

5.5.2 Two Questions to Ask before "Doing Policy"

As I've described things, there are theoretical, experimental, and empirical reasons to think that decentralized interaction, even in those markets that are not stereotypically thick, will yield outcomes in which there will arise many markets with meaningful (i.e., Walrasian) prices that are essentially taken as given. This is certainly the case for spot markets for purely private commodities in which product quality is easily discerned. This leads macroeconomists to ask two broad kinds of questions any time they want to judge the desirability of any policy intervention on efficiency grounds (such as the taxes we have just been talking about).

5.5.2.1   Question 1: How Are the Preconditions for the First Welfare Theorem Violated?

We know from earlier that one can always *interpret* inefficiency as arising from the absence of one or more *competitive* markets (e.g., one might have complete markets, but they might not all be competitive). So the question to ask here is: Which markets exactly are missing or noncompetitive, and are they well-proxied-for by other institutions, such as family, or by community rules, such as those identified in Nobel laureate Elinor Ostrom's work (e.g., Ostrom 1990)?

In cases where competitive markets do seem missing, the problem, typically, is asymmetric information, limited commitment, or the publicness of the good involved. But even in the absence of any problems coming from asymmetric information or limited commitment, we can use the findings of the work on the "foundations for Walrasian equilibrium" (discussed in chapter 2) to help us assess how important the remaining impediments to efficiency—distorting taxes, market power, and even the publicness of a given good or service—are likely to be.

5.5.2.2   Question 2: Why Do You Think You Can Do Better?

Suppose the well-meaning (i.e., Pareto-efficiency-obsessed) macroeconomist has identified the presence of forces that likely void the possibility for efficient outcomes through linear prices, even at the level of just one particular market (e.g., the market for number 2 red winter wheat in Minneapolis next winter) or a specific class of markets (e.g., all grain markets). And suppose that she has also demonstrated why the variety of decentralized institutions present also fail to allow all gains from trade to be realized. Can we *now* give her the keys to the policy machine? Not yet. Because we'd have to know that the impediments to efficiency faced by private citizens were somehow also not an impediment to an entity with the government's powers to observe, commit, tax, transfer, and otherwise compel.

In some cases, the public sector's advantage is obvious: through compulsory taxation, it may be able to improve upon the national defense that would otherwise be blighted by free riders. And by mandating participation in insurance markets, it may (from the perspective of viewing outcomes for oneself before one is born) improve efficiency and their functioning. But in many cases, the government may not be well positioned to improve efficiency. Thus, policymakers hoping to improve on the efficiency of decentralized trade are not likely to find it easy to do.

This may help explain the apparent reticence of many macroeconomists, including those in policy-oriented organizations, to intervene widely, especially those who work for entities that do not have an officially mandated charge to deal with *purely redistributionary* goals, such as the Federal Reserve System or other central banks worldwide. The previous statement should highlight the point that purely redistributionary policy does not require making an assessment of how well the trading system is working. Instead, it requires that the political system deem it worthwhile to transfer resources from one group to another. Given that determination, such policy can forge ahead. Of course, precisely because it may well be unconcerned with Pareto efficiency, it may be unambiguously wasteful. For example, recall from chapter 2 that tax systems with high marginal rates will very generally impede ex-post efficiency, and yet they are very popular worldwide, and likely succeed in inefficiently altering the receipt of rewards relative to what unfettered markets would dictate.

5.5.2.3   One Reason to Think You *Can* Do Better: Coordination Failure

In chapter 2, I noted two reasons for the primacy of Nash equilibrium as the concept used by economists in predicting outcomes of strategic interaction. These were, first, that Nash play is the only behavior that can satisfy the condition that it is an "obvious way to play" and, second, that Nash equilibrium, by being a special case of "correct expectations," removes discretion from the economist. There is, however, a third advantage that is more general. This is that Nash equilibrium is the relevant notion wherever a macroeconomist, or other social scientist, wants to describe anything that looks like a shared belief among an economy's participants, or a "culture" or "custom." Why? Because such restrictions have the property that any one person *alone* trying to buck the trend will find themselves in hot water, and this is exactly the reason such practices can persist.[11]

As I asserted earlier, many situations feature more than one Nash outcome. And frequently, some of these outcomes will be better than others. The Taliban, for example, famously presided over a Nash equilibrium in which women were terribly restricted. What they did was to credibly "convince" essentially everyone in Afghan society that to *unilaterally* resist their proscriptions on women's activities would be fruitless. The Taliban did this by convincing everyone that *everyone else* would not resist their policies. If, however, Afghan society was more like that in the US, and most people thought that most others would *not* follow Taliban-like edicts, then the Taliban might have had to scale back their demands. The latter outcome is also potentially a Nash outcome, and is by all accounts far better for many people, if not all. Such an outcome was indeed the case in prior eras; the Taliban weren't always in charge, after all.[12]

The same pattern holds for more mundane questions of law and order in any society. Take littering, for instance. If everyone in a society decided that everyone *else* was going to leave their cups and candy wrappers on the ground, there is almost no chance that police forces of the sizes seen today would be able to watch and arrest everyone who littered. A small police force works precisely because most people expect it to work: they *believe* that a large-scale outbreak of lawless-ness—and hence, a huge increase in the demands on the police force—is unlikely. This belief, in turn, matters for people individually when they make a decision about whether or not to commit a crime. In present-day America, each person reasons that he or she would prob-ably be one of the few people who will litter, and hence expect to be caught if they tried. As a result, few ultimately do litter and a small police force is sufficient to keep our cities tidy.

Thus, sometimes achieving good outcomes (or suffering bad ones) requires, or is at least aided by, the establishment of expectations held by each person about the likely behavior of others. Fundamentally, the issue is that the payoff for an action sometimes depends on the propor-tion of the population expected to act the same way. Contrast the importance of expectations in the littering example with a well-behaved complete-market Walrasian setting: under the presumption that all parties act as price takers, there is no sense in which the payoff for an action depends (other than indirectly through prices) on what specific actions anyone else is taking: each person, given prices, is truly an island.

The importance of expectations also comes from the fact that in some instances, "extra-economic" forces may lead a society to get "stuck" in a vicious circle in one Nash equilibrium, and fail to occupy another Nash outcome that is better for all, or nearly all. These are the cases that seem to present the greatest potential for improvements in human well-being through policy, and simply dwarf what a developed economy like that in the US can get from other mundane macroeco-nomic policy choices. That is, horrific inequality, even from a purely economic perspective (especially inequality in the rights and resources with which individuals begin life), can be a rather stable outcome. I mention this not because I want to quit macroeconomics and turn to something more powerful, but because it influences my overall per-spective on "what matters" and "where things can go most wrong" in decentralized outcomes.

While I am ill-equipped to talk with any authority about large-scale social change, let me note that most in my generation find the overt racism of the 1960s very hard to imagine, let alone desirable to perpetu-ate. The undeniable rapidity of change in *overtly* racist practice (even if more subtle racism remains a problem) is consistent with changes that occurred as the result of a change in *expectations* people held about the behavior that *others* would engage in or tolerate. A narrative that might be consistent with these broad observations on the trajectory of civil rights in the US is this: The Civil Rights Act of 1964 was powerful because it helped a "silent plurality" (if not majority) abruptly switch their expectations to one where they believed that few *others* would engage in overt racism. As a result, the federal government was able to enforce actions against the smaller number who continued to violate the law. Without the law, "free riding" could have been exploited effectively by those in favor of segregation: they could count on the many remaining silent because any one member's actions against racist practices could not succeed, and would be costly to oneself, unless many others joined in. In other words, "acceding" to racism was Nash behavior—a best response to a world in which most or all others played "accede to racism" in their daily lives. But the nice part of the story is that "everyone not acting overtly racist" is also a Nash outcome.[13] The change in law may well have allowed this better outcome to obtain "merely" by coordinating beliefs.[14]

5.5.3   Coordination Failure and Macroeconomics

Because of the potential power of policies that reorient beliefs about the likely actions of others, working macroeconomists typically approach policy with sensitivity, by determining whether the circumstance under consideration represents a **coordination failure.** This represents a very rich tradition in macroeconomics (see, e.g., Leijonhufvud 1973 and Weintraub 1977, for early discussions).

Let's say a macroeconomist judges a situation to be amenable to improvement primarily via reorienting the *expectations* of all parties. For example, let's think of an economy in which firms don't hire because they expect no new customers, and they expect no new customers because they think not enough *other* firms are hiring. It seems possible that a better outcome exists: someone (e.g., the government) exhorts/incentivizes all firms to hire, and hence makes firms optimistic about customers, which then leads all of them to hire and have their optimism confirmed. This is the essence of reasoning about so-called government spending multipliers being large. In such an instance, a macroeconomist has at least one reason to be enthusiastic: it would be the closest thing to a free lunch available. And in its absence, it is not as realistic to expect large and beneficial changes. The most public disagreements of macroeconomists, not surprisingly, hinge on exactly which of these two cases is operative—most often in the context of what to do in a given business cycle downturn. Those who view a sharp drop in macroeconomic aggregates as a coordination failure clearly are coherent in wanting to examine the possibility of taking actions to rejigger expectations to generate improvements: if correct, it's pure gain.

Those who oppose this view are less enthusiastic precisely because they view outcomes as reflective not of self-fulfilling pessimism, but rather of something more "fundamental." Thus, aside from the monumentally important questions like civil rights, the more prosaic issue is the extent to which business cycle downturns in developed economies mainly reflect a self-fulfilling malaise borne of pervasive pessimism. Indeed, as we'll see below, the idea is the basis of an important class of so-called stimulative policy proposals aimed at dealing with recessions. These views originated from the enormously influential economist John Maynard Keynes. But to explain how Keynesian ideas, among others, have been formalized, will be helpful to first acquaint you with the class of models known as **growth models**.

5.6   Important Macroeconomic Models and Policy Implications

The classes of models described next are the ones that I regard as most responsible for shaping economists' views on economic growth, fiscal policy, inequality, and (though I will not talk about it here) monetary policy.[15] In the versions of these models used to think about policy, there will nearly always be features that rule out the First Welfare Theorem from applying. Typically, in macroeconomic models, the impediments to efficiency often involve problems in IOU markets coming from asymmetric information and/or limited commitment as well as problems in gathering buyers and sellers to trade (especially in the context of labor markets). Sometimes the inefficiency comes from a government sector itself that, for example, may levy various kinds of distortionary taxes or impose clumsy regulations. As a result, these settings usually leave the door open for efficiency-improving changes in policy, often policy that deals with labor and financial markets.

With the exception of the so-called search model, these models belong to the broad category of "growth" models. I begin with two famous ones: those of Malthus and Solow. I will then turn to growth models that take household decision making seriously, such as the Cass-Koopmans model (and later, the Diamond overlapping-generations model). The Cass-Koopmans model is the basis for a huge amount of modern macroeconomics. In many of the more recent and more complicated (or "realistic") models we have concocted, a Cass-Koopmans model—which is squarely Walrasian—almost always lurks as a special case. This makes sense; it is an approach that explicitly accommodates the view that firms, consumers, and the government all (i) make purposeful decisions and (ii) do so through time in (iii) competitive markets that affect each other. Finally, I will describe a seminal extension of the Cass-Koopmans model, due to Brock and Mirman (1972) that incorporates uncertainty as well. The latter still forms the basis for essentially all modern models of the business cycle.

5.7   The Mother of All Walrasian Macroeconomic Models: Neoclassical Growth Models

This section will develop an intuitive description of the single most important model in macroeconomic applications: the **neoclassical growth model** (**NGM**). It was motivated by the need to connect long-run aggregate economic activity to what are arguably the most fundamental economic choices households and firms make: how much to spend now and how much to invest for the future. I will focus mainly on the key takeaways of this group of models, and will not spend any time replicating very good existing nontechnical renditions of the models in this class.[16] To begin, it is useful to consider the model that helped coin the nickname for economics as the "dismal science." This is the "growth" model of Thomas Malthus.

5.7.1   Step 1: The Malthusian Growth Model: No Capital
The Malthusian model of economic activity aims to understand the reasons for the relative *stagnation* of standards of living over rather long periods of human existence. Observing that life did not seem to be getting much better for the average person over time, as measured by income, food consumption, or life expectancy, the Reverend Thomas Malthus was inspired to try to provide an explanation. He did so, and so neatly, in fact, that his model formed the undergirding for the basic NGM.

Malthus's model had two main ingredients: land and people. People work the land with a given level of technological expertise, and the land, in turn, helps them produce outputs that allow them to survive.

Malthus assumed that the fertility rate was constant, governed by forces of nature not sensitive to economic incentives. Importantly, Malthus assumed in his model that there were **diminishing returns** to adding more workers to the production process. This means that while each additional worker adds a positive amount to total output, his or her contribution is smaller than those of the persons who joined the economy earlier. This assumption connects the size of the population to the average output per worker in such a way that output per worker *declines as the population grows*. Next, Malthus assumed that the lower the average level of per-worker output, the higher the death rate would be.

With this framework, Malthus extracted some truly "dismal" predictions. Chief among them was the prediction that average output per worker could not rise, in the long run—no matter what one-off innovations or policy changes one might effect. In fact, innovations that aided survival would, in the Malthusian world, result in long-run income being lower! The fundamental reason can be seen in an example. Let's say that, one day, a vaccine became available that lowered the death rate of the population for every level of average output per worker. Given the constant birthrate, the population would begin to grow over time as fewer died from the illness the vaccine immunized against. However, as this occurred, Malthus's assumption of diminishing returns would start to kick in, and though total output in the economy would rise, *average* output available to each member of the population would begin to decline. This in turn would start to increase the death rate of the population. Where would this decline stop? Exactly when the population reached a level where the average output per worker led to a death rate that exactly offset the birth rate. But we started this example by thinking of the arrival of a new vaccine. So this means that the population would, in the long run, be bigger than it was before the introduction of the vaccine. So far, so good, you might say. But diminishing returns combined with a higher population can mean only one thing in a Malthusian world: average output available per person is actually *lower* than before! Thus, Malthus's model predicts that vaccines will, by themselves, lead to more people being alive (good?), each facing a lower mortality rate than before the vaccines were available (good!), but with the average person consuming less output per year than before the vaccine (bad!).

Malthus's model suggests that humans are doomed to live in settings where the population size always changes in ways that undo the gains from any innovation. And given the data Malthus had in front of him, this model fit roughly 500 years of received facts very well indeed: the world's population was indeed growing and innovations were occurring, but per-person income was stagnant. Moreover, while not discussed here, Malthus's model also predicts that the rent on land should vary positively with the size of the population, which they also did, making rents more expensive. Malthus is rightly celebrated for thinking through this data in a systematic manner that explains so many observations very elegantly.[17]

5.7.2   Step 2: The Solow Growth Model: No Fixed Inputs

Having described the Malthusian setting, and its depressing conclusions, we now turn to its progeny, the neoclassical growth model, first studied by Solow (1957) and Swan (1956) and brought to completion by Cass (1965) and Koopmans (1965) (who themselves built on the far earlier and prescient formulation of Ramsey 1928). The need for such a model came from the spectacular failure of the Malthusian model to account for the concurrent fall in adult mortality and the meteoric rise in per-person economic output seen in the 200 years after Malthus. More specifically, Solow, Swan, and others noted a variety of empirical regularities that prevailed in the data, which came to be known as the **Kaldor facts**. These had to do mainly with the relationship within the now-advanced nations (Europe, North America, and East Asia) between growth in their output and their capital stock (constant, identical growth rates), the long-run trend in their interest rates (zero), the growth rate of wages (constant, at the same rate as output), the ratio of capital to output (constant), and the share of total national income received by the owners of capital inputs and labor inputs (constant).

The Solow growth model imagines an economy populated by a large number of households that each must make decisions over an open-ended period of time about when to consume. There is a correspondingly large number of firms that are, in the standard ADM fashion, simply "black boxes" capable of transforming groups of commodities into other commodities.

The fundamental difference between this model and the Malthusian one is Solow's presumption that in addition to labor as a productive input, there was another productive input that could be *accumulated*. This extra input is referred to as "capital." Prototypical examples of capital include machines that are produced by exerting effort now, or raw land that has been improved enough to make it productive for agriculture or housing. The key payoff to considering such an additional input is that in Solow's model, as long as one augmented both labor and capital, as seemed eminently feasible (the former through population growth, the latter through deliberate investment), one could escape the inevitability of average output per worker falling as the population increased. Instead, what could now occur was an augmentation of both labor and capital, with no change in the average level of output per worker.

Because it is possible to accumulate capital in the Solow model, the process by which it is accumulated must be specified. And here Solow (and Swan) considered a simple formulation: the residents of the economy were assumed to save a constant proportion of output each period. For example, if the economy produced $100 worth of output today, a Solow model that assumed a 20% savings rate would be one in which total savings would equal $20. Of course, some of the previously accumulated or installed capital would have deteriorated, and so perhaps the total stock of productive capital grows by somewhat less, say $18, from one period to the next. Lastly, Solow's model allowed the population to grow steadily over time and, more interestingly, allowed for the technological state of the art to grow at a constant rate. The Solow model thus imagines a world in which technological improvements allow the same levels of capital to produce, with any given amount of labor input, more and more output as these improvements are put into place. This is known as "labor-augmenting technological progress."

To think about technological progress intuitively, imagine a world with farm tractors where, on the one hand, adding tractors to the economy at any rate faster than the growth rate of the population itself would render each additional tractor less productive than the previous one (a person can only drive one tractor at a time—at least so far). Similarly, adding workers without tractors would also lead to output growing, but at an ever lower rate. Thus, in the Solow model, there are diminishing returns in each of the two inputs to production. However, in Solow's model, if one increased both inputs, one would no longer face diminishing returns. Instead, the production capabilities of the economy would display so-called **constant returns to scale** (**CRS**). In one sense, CRS is the only natural assumption to make. The reason is simple: CRS must prevail in any setting where all inputs can be increased, and none is fixed. Because, barring any additional constraints, one can simply duplicate operations at one level repeatedly, and thereby obtain increases in output exactly in proportion to the amount by which one increased all inputs. A corollary to this logic is that decreasing returns to scale must inherently reflect the presence of an input to production that simply cannot be replicated. In certain instances, it is very easy to think of examples where some inputs are more or less fixed, especially over very short time horizons. And some forms of capital may be nearly impossible to augment (land with a riverfront location, for example). The Solow model, however, proceeds under the assumption that all inputs can be augmented over time through investment or effort.

5.7.2.1 Labor-Saving Devices

Given the highly aggregated nature of the Solow setting, it is easy to think of technological change that makes any individual worker "redundant" at a factory and conclude that this is a bad thing. But as I will show, the Solow model suggests that technological progress that makes us able to produce more in less time is the *only* available engine for sustained increases in average income. In one way, this should be intuitive: the only reason I can spend my time writing a book on macroeconomics, and you reading it, is because each of us is able to meet our caloric, clothing, and housing needs with sufficiently little time spent working, so that we have spare time to do other things. Labor-saving technological improvements are therefore exactly, and uniquely, what make us rich.[18] When we turn to so-called search models in the labor market, we'll see how macroeconomists evaluate the ability of the marketplace to the reallocate the labor rendered redundant.

5.7.2.2 Balanced-Growth Steady States

With the production side of the economy and the savings decision both spelled out, we can assess the trajectory of output per worker over time. Solow and Swan show that under these assumptions, and *absent* any improvement in technological progress, the economy's output per worker would converge over time to a constant level.[19] But doesn't this mean that we've come right back to the Malthusian conclusion? The answer is yes! In fact, one way to think about the very, very, long history of economic growth is to presume that the world has always and forever been described by Solovian growth dynamics, but simply did not experience any sustained technological progress until the 1800s. As already mentioned above, this story, while hopeful, runs afoul of the most careful historical evidence we have, which suggests that technological progress was happening well prior to this period, while sustained growth in per-person income was emphatically not.

Where the Solow model differs from the Malthusian one was just hinted at: the response of these two models to sustained changes in technological progress is drastically different. In the Malthusian world, technological progress simply led, in the long run, to an increasing population surviving on progressively *lower* per-person income. By contrast, in the Solow model, once all inputs to production could be augmented, the presence of sustained technological progress meant that output per worker would not only not stagnate or fall but would actually grow. And in the long run (i.e., if one looked at the average growth rates of the economy over long-enough periods), the Solow model predicts that output per worker will grow at precisely the same rate as technological progress. This is certainly consistent with the experience from 1800 onward, when the population of every now-developed country grew substantially, as did per-person income.

Why does this happen in Solow and not in Malthus? Intuitively, the reason is that, starting from a low level of capital equipment, in an economy that saves a constant fraction of total output, the additional capital equipment it installs every year, along with the improvement in the productivity of that capital and the entire stock of previously installed capital, initially generates a large-enough increase in total output that per-person output grows (even though the population grows over the year as well). The next period, saving once again the same constant fraction of the *now higher* level of total output leads to further increases in per-person output. In absolute amounts, the economy is setting aside more resources to augment future productive capability each period than in the previous ones. But, since the population is growing at the same time, growth in output in per-person terms begins to slow. Over time, the growth rate of per-person output converges to the rate of growth of technological progress (if there is any) or zero (if there is not).

5.7.2.3   The Role Savings Rates Play in Living Standards

The last conclusion tells us that in the absence of technological progress, the Solow growth model, like the Malthusian one, predicts no sustained growth in per-person living standards for any fixed rate of saving. But savings rates have long been a key object of interest to policymakers, commentators, and others. They are seen as a linchpin in the adequate provision of one's future well-being, as well as that of one's children. Moreover, the effect of the savings rate on short- and long-term outcomes is often raised in the context of discussion of tax policy or other policies perceived to be important for savings decisions. So far, I have only described the inability of a *constant* savings rate to generate persistent improvements in the standard of living (as measured by per-capita income). But what if we change the savings rate? How will that change things?

Before plunging ahead, recall that the Solow-Swan model features exogenous savings rates and direct augmentation of the capital stock as a result. There is no formal description of savings decisions made by households or investment decisions made by firms. However, to the extent that underlying behavior would lead to a path for savings that kept consumption at least somewhat "smooth" over time (a plausible hypothesis), it can be shown formally that the insights one obtains from this model are substantially similar to those obtained from models that are more explicit about why and how households save and firms invest.

Returning to the question at hand, it is helpful to first divide changes in savings behavior into temporary versus permanent changes. Next, it is useful to evaluate the effect of each type of change on short-run standards of living, which I will define to be per-capita income, and then look at the effects on longer-run standards of living. As we have seen already, the presence of diminishing returns suggests that without technological progress, one cannot engineer permanent changes in economic growth via holding to a given rate of capital accumulation. It immediately follows that the only effect of temporary changes in the savings rate is temporary changes in the level of income. Such changes will have no effect on either long-run income levels (i.e., the income that prevails at a date in the distant future) *or* the growth rate of living standards.

Permanent changes in the savings rate, by contrast, will have permanent effects on the *level* of income seen in the future but, again, no effects on growth rates seen in the distant future. Income in the far-distant future under this higher savings rate will converge to a path where it remains a *constant fraction* greater than income would have been at that time under the lower savings rate. However, what will *not* occur—and this is crucial to emphasize—is a change in the *rate of growth* of living standards. It will be the same as it was before the extra savings started being accumulated. If, for example the savings rate in one country is 30%, while in another it is 40%, then a realistically parameterized Solow-Swan model predicts that in the long run, the higher-saving society will enjoy a constant 15% advantage in income levels, but will grow at exactly the same rate as its more profligate cousin. But notice that, in so doing, it gives up 10 percentage points more consumption during *every period*. Macroeconomists describe this finding by saying that changes in the savings rate in the Solow model have at best—when the change is permanent—only "level" effects, but not "growth effects."

Note that these results do not mean savings is irrelevant: countries with permanently different savings rates will indeed have permanently different levels of income. They just will both grow at the same rate. Of course, a permanently higher savings rate does mean that the absolute gap in the levels of income will grow over time, as has happened, for example, in the case of the US compared to Europe. Both have been growing at roughly 2% per capita, with the US being richer, but the absolute gap is now much larger than it was in 1960, for example. This important point provides some nuance to the answer of how savings can engineer improvements in well-being.

The Solow-Swan model's implications are very important because they inform macroeconomists on what can realistically be expected from policies that enhance or retard the accumulation of capital. Taken as a whole, the Solow-Swan model also leaves us a more nuanced sense of how policies that affect savings affect growth in a relatively wide class of modern models of economic growth such as the Ramsey-Cass-Koopmans model I will discuss in the next section.[20] In particular, it tells us that if the model's presumptions approximate reality well, a society that is initially poor cannot vault itself into a permanently higher rate of *growth* simply by spending its time and effort producing more factories and equipment for its workers, as opposed to spending its resources on consumption in the present.

5.7.2.4 The Solow Model as a First Unified Model of Growth and Fluctuations

I have spent a huge amount of time on the Solow growth model because, as you'll see, subsequent enrichments of this model do not fundamentally alter its most central predictions with respect to the short- or long-run effects of savings, of the dynamics of capital accumulation, and so on. In fact, if uncertainty were added to the basic Solow model, one immediately has in hand a model of *business cycles* (though not necessarily a *good* model). What do I mean here?

First, let's interpret Solow's use of the fixed savings rate as a quick shortcut that keeps us from having to model explicitly the motivations of the (unmodeled) households in his model. If they wanted to keep their consumption of goods and services smooth in the face of any temporary reduction (or expansion) in the productive capacities of the economy, then a constant savings rate would help. Next, imagine that the technological progress that we allowed for above now comes in fits and starts, and in ways that are at least somewhat unpredictable. These two ingredients immediately lead the Solow model's economy to exhibit fluctuations in output, investment, and consumption in ways that will leave investment moving by more than output and consumption fluctuating the least—just as we see in the data. Moreover, while labor supply is not explicitly modeled either (as it, too, is a decision that arises from unmodeled households), we can imagine that firms and households in the aggregate would trade fewer hours of labor if they were explicitly modeled. Thus, however stylized it may be, we have the makings of a unified theory of longer-term economic outcomes, along with a story about how fluctuations arise and matter for measured outcomes, such as GDP and investment, in the short run.

There is therefore no need for the dissonance that would come from the carrying around of two macroeconomic theories—one for the business cycle, another for "all other times." To the extent that the same decision makers inhabit the economy for periods long enough to experience both temporary drops in productive capability and longer-run trends in growth, this is certainly intellectually more acceptable. Still, economists wanted to extend the basic Solow model of capital accumulation and growth to incorporate purposeful decision making vis-à-vis consumption, savings, and labor supply. How they have gone about this task is the next topic.

5.7.3 Step 3: The Modern Neoclassical Growth Model: Enter the Consumer

As just alluded to, a central feature of the Solow model is what is not actually present in the model: the consumer. In any market-based economy, consumers decide how much to spend and, more importantly for capital accumulation, how much to work and save. How do they make these decisions? The Solow model simply ignored this question and "started in the middle" of the story by positing a rule for how households collectively saved. But such a rule gives us no insight into the reasons for capital accumulation, and, more importantly, into the role of various factors such as taxes, the attitudes of consumers toward deferring consumption, and other forces that, a priori, would seem to matter for savings decisions. Thus, the Solow model cannot be used to assess the growth effects of taxes or their implications for household well-being in any serious manner.

In one year, two independently written papers remedied this: Cass (1965) and Koopmans (1965). These papers built on Solow's and Swan's path-breaking work, and also on the ridiculously prescient work of Frank Ramsey in the 1920s; as a result, this model is referred to as the Ramsey-Cass-Koopmans (henceforth, RCK) model. The main ingredient these papers added was a fully articulated model of a household that deliberately chose how much to consume and save in each period of its life. As a result, the level of capital equipment (e.g., factories, roads, and buildings) available to a society was now the result of savings decisions. The resulting models were part of the NGM tradition.

The punch line to the RCK model is that under reasonable assumptions about the preferences of households, and again assuming a CRS aggregate production structure, the central results of the Solow model remain intact. In particular, in the long run, income, capital, and consumption all grow at a constant rate—the rate at which technological progress occurs. What is useful, as we noted, is that the model now can relate changes in policies such as taxes to changes in consumption and savings decisions, and then to output levels. In addition, the model now has normative content: we can ask about the extent to which households are made better or worse off under a variety of policies. In the Solow model, no such question was possible because household objectives were never spelled out.

The RCK model presumes a structure for financial markets that is very smoothly functioning—so smoothly functioning, in fact, that households are modeled as directly choosing the stock of available capital equipment that will be available one period from now via their current savings decisions. Of course, in reality, this process is more involved: households save in various financial IOUs (e.g., stocks and bonds) issued by firms, which then use the proceeds to augment their physical production capabilities. Under the premises of the RCK, this process would lead to exactly the same decisions as the ones made under the more streamlined RCK model. Of course, this means that the RCK model may not help us understand the effects of changes in the processes by which savings and investment are related; but for the question at hand, namely how growth over longer periods looks, it is sensible.

5.7.4   What Happens When There Is Uncertainty? The Stochastic Neoclassical Growth Model

Having spent a lot of time on the basic growth model, I want to give a quick and intuitive description of the **stochastic growth model**, or **SGM**, which is the single most important model in macroeconomics, *bar none*. It is due to Brock and Mirman (1972), and it continues to be the starting point for every branch of macroeconomics: fiscal policy, asset pricing, consumption, and investment. This, in a nutshell, is the "NGM with wiggles": it allows macroeconomists to think about fluctuations in activity (i.e., business cycles) in a setting that respects the other activities that households and firms are always engaged in—planning and investing in their futures. It is therefore a model that gives macroeconomists a unified theory of growth and fluctuations (a version of which we saw already in the context of the Solow model). Given this lineage, you should now see just how close modern macroeconomics is to the baseline ADM model.

What a macroeconomist uses the SGM to make predictions for depends on the way that household and firm characteristics map into observed relative prices. Typically, the macroeconomists are imagining an economy in which the production capabilities of some, or all, of the firms are subject in each period to the realization of a shock. Of course, the benchmark SGM simplifies matters by positing that firms either face no constraints in financing the cost of durables or are able to rent—as price takers—equipment from the households that ultimately own it. As a result, we can immediately invoke the aggregation results we described in chapter 4 and simply model the production side of the economy as having a single, price-taking representative firm. Analogously, the SGM posits a representative household as well. In particular, it presumes either that all households differ only to the extent allowed by the Gorman form (see chapter 4) and face no uninsurable risks, or that any risks facing the household that would force their wealth to evolve differently than their neighbors' are, in fact, fully insurable at actuarially fair prices. Either way, we have assumed what is needed (implicitly or not) to yield a consumer side of the economy that has a representative household.

Next, the SGM under sequential trading can be imagined to have a WCH that, at each date, computes the market-clearing prices of all the goods being traded, and announces that it will buy and sell any amount anyone wishes to at these prices. All parties make the desired purchases and sales, and everyone meets again next period, and so on. The SGM assumes further that all participants have rational expectations. To refresh our memories, rational expectations asks that the representative household and firm each correctly forecast the prices that will be announced by the WCH, *given their knowledge of the shock that was realized in the current period.* To be extra clear: the prices announced by the WCH are, from the perspective of any previous period, random; rational expectations *does not* ask that households forecast perfectly. For example, in a model of an agricultural commodity market, all farmers and buyers would be assumed, under rational expectations, to be able to correctly anticipate the price generated by the WCH when the weather conditions are "drought" and when they are "flood," if these were the two possible contingencies that could prevail at the end of the season. Of course, no farmer or buyer is modeled as knowing exactly which of these two will occur at any time prior to planting.

What is an equilibrium of this model? It is (i) a *forecasted* process for future prices as a function of the aggregate state of the economy (e.g., drought or flood) that (ii) when taken as given by optimizing market participants, leads no one to ever be surprised at the market-clearing prices that they face, given the uncertainty that has realized itself up to that point in time. A first thing to note about such an equilibrium is that neither prices nor consumption, nor savings or investment, remains still over time. Yet let us once again acknowledge how much this demands of the participants in the economy. It is entirely reasonable to wonder about how well anticipated future prices are, even contingent on the realization of uncertainty. But recall also my argument in chapter 4 that despite these requirements, the use of this notion of equilibrium was still likely a better route than one that gives the modeling economist latitude to select expectations in ways less disciplined than rational expectations.

5.7.4.1 Deterministic and Stochastic Steady States

Let's now return to an issue first noted in chapter 1, and then fleshed out more in chapter 4: if you look at academic research in macroeconomics at all, you will repeatedly encounter the concept of a "steady state." And as I noted, steady states come in two varieties: deterministic and stochastic. The former are those in which certain key objects in a model either no longer vary over time or vary over time in perfectly predictable ways. In the present context, an example would be that of the behavior of capital in a Solow growth model. Over time, under the fixed rate of savings that the Solow model assumes, the *total level* of capital will grow at the rate of productivity improvement times the rate of the population growth rate. As a result, capital *per worker* will grow at the rate of productivity growth, and capital *per effective worker* (i.e., the number of worker equivalents operating currently relative to the number society initially began with) will then move toward a constant amount.

In many models that do not model uncertainty, deterministic steady states are typically the focus of macroeconomists. The reason is simple: if one can show convergence to such a steady state, especially convergence from any "initial" position, then in the "long run" that is exactly where the system will spend most of its time. Moreover, deterministic steady states are tractable objects that macroeconomists can actually analyze. For example, while we might have a hard time speaking to the exact nature of the transition to a new long-run equilibrium— say, in a market that suddenly faced a new, higher sales tax—we are often able to describe what will have to be true in the long run (or steady state).

Recall that stochastic steady states are the more complicated analog to a steady state in models where at least some of the participants are buffeted by shocks (for example, shocks to a household's ability to work or to a firm's ability to produce). We defined an economy to be in a stochastic steady state when households and firms were acting optimally given their forecasts for how the key aspects of their environment would evolve, where these forecasts were consistently proved correct, and where outcomes changed only in response to shocks, and not simply to the passage of time. As an example, think of the stochastic neoclassical growth model, in which shocks to productivity hit the economy at each date. In this case, Brock and Mirman were able to prove that the economy's levels of capital and output would fluctuate in a way that was constant over time. In other words, in a stochastic steady state, the likelihood of the economy holding a given level of capital at any given time, given a particular realization of the shocks to the economy in that period, is unchanging. Say the shock was weather-related, and that the weather could be either sunny or rainy. In a stochastic steady state, given current capital, the likelihood of various levels of capital being held by the economy's participants on a future rainy day will be the same whether that rainy day is tomorrow or a year from tomorrow. In contrast, immediately after an economy begins, the calendar date may well be relevant in determining the likelihood of the level of capital or output: early in the life of an economy, the level of capital may be low relative to the long run, and as result, investment in this period might well be high *irrespective* of the weather.

5.7.5 What Payoffs Do Stochastic Neoclassical Growth Models Offer Us?

5.7.5.1 A Step toward a Unified Theory of Growth and Fluctuations

As an intellectual matter, unified theories are always appealing (or seductive, as our critics would say) because one can claim to have understood more phenomena via the same underlying framework. However, for many years, and certainly for thirty or so years following the Great Depression, models of economic growth in which households and firms made decisions about how much to save and invest were constructed in ways completely divorced from models that sought to understand sudden drops in output and employment. As an intuitive matter alone, this was unsatisfactory. Shouldn't the decisions of market participants (and government) who act with the future in mind have some direct bearing on fluctuations in output and investment as well? The stochastic growth model offered a way out of this impasse. Magill (1977) was perhaps the first to show that this model could provide in principle, if not in ultimate practice, the basis for a coherent account of business cycle fluctuations. Fundamentally, this model teaches us that growth and business cycles should be, and *can* be, studied together. What's not to like?

5.7.5.2 They Operationalize the ADM Model

A striking facet of the basic stochastic growth model was that, for the first time, economists had a tool that provided quantitative predictions for a fully fleshed-out Arrow-Debreu model. That is, it placed numerical magnitudes on the extent to which a *perfectly efficient* economic system would display fluctuations when subject to disturbances in the

ability of firms to transform inputs into outputs. This is methodologi-
cally important enough to warrant a more detailed explanation further
below. For now, I'll only say that this is what is known as the real business cycle (RBC) model or real business cycle approach.

5.7.5.3 Stochastic Neoclassical Growth Provides a Benchmark

The SGM reminded economists of a fundamental message of the
Arrow-Debreu model: even a "perfectly functioning" economy will
exhibit fluctuations if its technological capabilities are buffeted by
shocks. In other words, fluctuations can be efficient. Let me be clear:
this point, though the proximate source of criticism for the RBC model,[21]
is something we already knew from Arrow-Debreu to be true.

The SGM gave macroeconomists the first framework that could help
us understand the extent to which observed fluctuations are efficient,
and if they are not perfectly efficient—which they of course will *not*
be—how far away we are. That is the relevant issue. Unless one wishes
to regard all deviations from some long-run average as representing a
misallocation of resources rather than even partially reflecting more
fundamental movements in response to changes in technological possibilities, one will want to know "how far away" from efficient an
ongoing fluctuation is. The crafting of policy responses, if they are to
help, must reflect the answer to this question.

5.7.6 The Influence of Neoclassical Growth Models on How We Think about Some Key Macroeconomic Issues

Given the central goal of this book—to trace the "practical" views of
macroeconomists back to precisely articulated theories—I now argue
that the neoclassical group of models we have just described profoundly influence the thinking of modern macroeconomists in several
areas. Three general conclusions can be drawn about any world well
described by the SGM. All three are important to macroeconomists'
views on the nature of real-world outcomes, and all three provide
support for a fairly sanguine attitude toward relatively free markets.

5.7.6.1 Macroeconomies Can Be Stable

The Malthus, Solow, and Cass-Koopmans models were constructed to
display the stability one observed in developed-country aggregates,
both in the past (Malthus) and in the modern era (Solow and

Cass-Koopmans). No matter what population one begins with (Malthus) or what level of capital equipment one assumes is initially available to the average worker (Solow/Cass-Koopmans), over time per-worker outcomes converge to a level that is entirely independent of these starting conditions. Solow in particular constructed his model precisely to get away from the knife-edge prediction of earlier growth models which suggested that capitalist societies were doomed to ragged and unpredictable growth and were often on trajectories that would lead to impoverishment over the longer run. As Solow says, if those models were indeed correct, one could expect to find on earth "only the wreckage of a capitalism that had shaken itself to pieces long ago" (Solow 1987). While, as with the French Revolution, it may be "too soon to tell," the received evidence that we have already seen does suggest that outcomes in the now-advanced countries—the evidence that motivated Solow at the outset—does look remarkably like that predicted by his model.

The stability of the Solow model flows from two remarkably weak assumptions—one on the production or "supply side" of the economy, and the other on household decision making, i.e., the "demand side." Essentially, the production side of the economy is such that simply adding some inputs while holding other ones fixed leads to the additional productivity of the added inputs getting progressively smaller. Think of yourself on a winter day after a snowstorm. As you contemplate the job in front of you, you know that having a shovel will help. But how much will a second shovel help? In this case, unless a neighbor is willing to supply an extra pair of hands, the answer is: "not at all!" Now, this is an extreme case perhaps, but the idea is clearly very general. Furthermore, Solow softens it by allowing more substitutability: think of cases where an additional helper would indeed make a job easier, even if that helper didn't bring extra equipment with him. For example, your neighbor could still help you by, for example, bringing you coffee every hour and taking turns shoveling to allow you to recuperate. These are precisely the features possessed by the production "technology" assumed by Solow: simply piling up machines without additional "hands" to operate them will eventually be fruitless, but along the way, each input can be relatively "smoothly" substituted for others.

On the demand side, matters are even simpler. As we've noted, the original Solow model did not even model households. It directly assumed that societal preferences were such that the economy always saved a constant fraction of total output in each period. As we have seen, the subsequent RCK models did explicitly model savings as arising from household-level decisions to provision themselves for the future. But in either case, in any instance where households collectively save a constant fraction of output, all suitably normalized quantities converge over time inexorably to a path in which they grow at constant rates over time.

For example, in a Solow model where the technological state of the art improves at a constant rate, per-person income will, as we have already noted, converge to a path on which it grows at exactly the same rate as productivity, irrespective of what initial capital level (e.g., how many shovels) or labor (e.g., helpful neighbors) the society started with. What the RCK models added to this is that stability was not quite inevitable. The Solow model, after all, should be seen as providing us *sufficient* conditions for stability, but it was able to do so by simply bypassing any explicit model of household decision making. Once we allow for purposeful household decision making, we have to contend with the problems of aggregation on the consumer side. As I argued already, macroeconomists' typical response to this has been to assume either complete or near-complete homogeneity in household preferences that also satisfy the Gorman requirements. As we will see, though, more recent models drop such restrictive assumptions, and find that the economy still typically and reliably displays a form of "approximate aggregation" that returns us to stability as the leading case for study: just because anything can happen does not mean anything will.

Given the assumption of well-behaved, i.e., "aggregative" households, the remaining barriers to aggregation come from the presence of incomplete markets for the transfer of purchasing power, such as incomplete markets and borrowing constraints. The RCK model makes precisely the assumption that markets are complete and such constraints are not binding on participants. As a result, the WE outcomes in the RCK model under the sequential-trading Radner environment are *identical* to what would occur under the time-0 Arrow-Debreu trading arrangement. Moreover, under the assumptions of the model, WE outcomes are unique. This is a relevant point because the known Pareto optimality of the WE outcome (as per the First Welfare Theorem) means that as long as the remaining conditions of the Second Welfare Theorem hold, we can far more easily "solve for" WE outcomes by locating Pareto-optimal outcomes. This, as we've seen, can be very handy.

Sonnenschein-Mantel-Debreu and Boldrin-Montrucchio, Redux

In chapter 1, I talked about the Sonnenschein-Mantel-Debreu (SMD) and Boldrin-Montrucchio (BM) results. What do they mean for working macroeconomists? To answer this, recall that the Radner trading structure allows trading to take place over time and in response to the arrival of new information, and that this is the benchmark setting used by macroeconomists to interpret real-world outcomes. In that setting, the reader may recall, households made choices through time, and in each period, they chose how much to spend as well as how much to set aside for various future contingencies. In the pure complete-market case, they were given the ability to buy in each period assets that would deliver goods and services to them in any of the eventualities that might obtain in the following period.

We noted that such a trading structure, which more closely resembles the world we live in (though it surely overstates the ability of consumers to hedge themselves against future outcomes), would result in exactly the same outcome as the very fanciful "one-shot, all trade before the beginning of time" Arrow-Debreu trading structure, so long as consumers had the correct forecast for the prices of contracts designed to deliver goods and/or services to them under the various eventualities that the future might bring. This is a key point to keep in mind, because it immediately restricts the manner in which one interprets the lesson of SMD.

Now, let's come to back what SMD and BM mean for the daily lives of macroeconomists. Consider first a situation where a macroeconomist is working with a model of the macroeconomy in which she knows that there are many Radner (Walrasian) equilibria. That is, we know, a priori, that the economy we are studying is one in which there are many sets of prices and expectations for future prices which, if taken as given by optimizing households and firms, will lead to all parties being able to achieve their planned purchase and sale decisions. This means that without further reason for selecting one equilibrium relative to another, the model lacks predictive power: it is telling us that many outcomes are consistent with the requirements of a Walrasian equilibrium. At this point, the economist may want to consider imposing conditions on her model that further limit the number of possible equilibrium outcomes.

Now consider, in contrast, a situation in which a macroeconomist is working with a model of the economy in which he knows that the Radner equilibrium is *unique*, but where the Radner outcome is one in which there is substantial fluctuation, e.g., the allocations received by consumers and output produced by firms vary rather extremely over time. What can we say about this society? Specifically, is this fluctuating outcome efficient? If we could tax and transfer in a "lump sum" manner as described in chapter 2, would we be able to attain an equitable allocation that was also efficient? Since we are looking at a Walrasian outcome, we know immediately that the answers to both these questions are yes. Moreover, the BM theorem tells us that there's nothing crazy about this outcome to begin with: even risk-averse households, choosing consumption and savings optimally for themselves, might well find such fluctuations to be part of an efficient outcome.[22]

The lack of structure imposed by mere "risk aversion," or mere "exponential discounting of the future," and so on, is precisely why we macroeconomists work hard to establish conditions under which our models display a single Radner outcome, and where any fluctuations that occur in the model are not wildly at odds with the observed fluctuations in aggregate variables such as employment or investment.

Can Macroeconomists Put Enough Structure on Their Models to Avoid Generating Multiple Equilibria?

As already suggested in the context of models of coordination failure, the short answer is: sometimes, but not always. In general, the reader should recall the history of the Solow model that started this discussion, and that it was Solow's explicit aim to show that balanced growth was really the basic long-run feature one should find "attractive," in the sense that any reasonable model ought to predict convergence over time. And this goal is precisely what led the Solow model's use of restrictions to generate **global convergence**, which means convergence from any starting point to balanced growth paths.

Recall Solow again to remember that a problem with working with a model that permits multiple steady states and rapid fluctuations between them—just to make contact with data on a given recession—is that one will then be forced to answer why the economy as a whole is not always falling apart. In particular, along essentially every dimension, the story of most economies outside wartime is not one of routine, large fluctuations. In fact, even those countries that are poor rarely behave in a consistently convulsive manner. Instead, the feature that by and large describes most modern economies, including the developing ones, is one of differing *but steady* improvements in living standards. And yet a model whose main feature is a significant internal amplification mechanism of what initially are not large shocks is a model that will generally be unable to produce the extraordinarily smooth growth paths of most modern economies.

More formally, with respect to the damningness of SMD for macroeconomics, in 1970, Gerard Debreu proved an important result. He showed that for a very wide class of economies, the number of Walrasian equilibria would not only be finite but also be **locally isolated**. In other words, small changes in the structure of preferences, endowments, and technology (i.e., the "data" of the economy) would be associated with small changes in the (finite!) set of Walrasian outcomes. This meant that multiplicity and sensitivity of Walrasian outcomes with respect to their data, while possible, would not be a routine occurrence.[23] Debreu named such model economies **regular economies**.[24]

As for the damningness of the BM result, one general set of theorems referred to as **turnpike theorems** gains relevance. These results guarantee that economies populated by long-lived decision makers who are sufficiently "patient" and averse to fluctuations in well-being (i.e., care about their descendants with sufficient intensity) will make decisions that will lead capital per "effective" worker (if technological progress continues) to settle down to a constant level. In particular, any path that features predictable fluctuations in the long run will not be an optimal one for such households.[25] Taken together with the Boldrin-Montrucchio result, we have the following. When people are sufficiently impatient, anything can happen in a growth model. When people are sufficiently patient, only one thing can happen!

5.7.6.2   Technological Progress Is *the* Gift Horse

The Solow model (and the broader class of neoclassical growth models) teaches macroeconomists to place technological change in a particularly vaunted position. Technological change is an engine of growth, and it is the *sole* engine of *long-run* growth: without it, living standards will simply stall, but with it, they will not. Add to this the fact that, at an aggregate level, there seems to be no tradeoff between allowing the relentless march of new technologies to arrive in our homes, cars, and factories and the availability of "jobs" for people. Over even short horizons (outside of recessions), and certainly over long horizons, the unemployment rate in essentially any developed country shows no trend whatsoever. And yet we are hugely better off than citizens were even two generations ago.[26] The argument for allowing and, if possible, actively fostering technological advance thus seems airtight.

Macroeconomists' views on technological change are important, if only because we frequently must address questions about the desirability of allowing certain kinds of technological change to occur. Many macroeconomists take the approach that new technologies will cause difficulty for those whose skills are immediately rendered obsolete (or merely more plentiful). Precisely when this might happen to any given individual is hard to predict. Hence, the fundamental problem brought on by any technological change lies in the question of how to soften the blow coming from any one innovation.

At a more abstract level, you might find it helpful to think as follows: each of us owns some "human" assets (i.e., our skills, knowledge, and physical capabilities), some financial assets (e.g., stocks, bonds, pension, and insurance), and some physical assets (e.g., a house). Each of these three kinds of assets generates payoffs to us, and allows us to receive income later in our lives. Any new innovation is something that could easily change the rate of return to any or all of these three types of assets, potentially lowering the total value of all three.

For example, an innovation that represents a cheap substitute for tasks currently performed by "skilled" labor will likely leave that group worse off—unless they happen to own a stake in the company that made the innovation. Put this way, the issue of technological change and its impact becomes one of portfolio diversification. And it should be granted that such diversification is in practice difficult, if not impossible. For a variety of reasons, one simply cannot sell off one's human capital early in life (i.e., get cash now in return for a promise to work later in life) and buy a more balanced portfolio of stocks and bonds. The result of this inability is that the young and middle aged are often left vulnerable to shocks to the value of their skills (their "human capital"), as their skills remain the primary asset in their portfolio well into working life.

As a result, technological change may be far from benign, certainly for some of us. In particular, what happens at the aggregate level, especially in terms of employment, hides a story of what might happen to any of us. History is replete with instances of technological improvements causing hardship for those whose skills were rendered obsolete. Sometimes the scale of this obsolescence has been large enough to extinguish (or at least dim) whole cities. Detroit, Michigan, is perhaps the most recent case in point. And yet it is not easy to find macroeconomists willing to rubber-stamp protectionist policy that would, at a proximate level, help targeted groups of a country's workforce. Why? The answer lies in the "tyrannical arithmetic" involved (to borrow from a brilliantly titled article by the economist Alwyn Young).

Think of a society in which there are 100 million households, each of which lives in a home it owns. Now, imagine that an innovation arrives that lowers heating costs by $200 each winter. Let's presume this reduction lasts for the life of the house, say, thirty years. For convenience, let the "real" interest rate (the interest rate minus the expected rate of inflation) be zero (though at low levels such as the ones prevailing in developed countries, it does not matter much what it is). In this example, each homeowner saves $6,000 in present value terms on utilities over the life of his or her house.

But there's bad news: let's suppose that these improvements in efficiency lead to 1 million coal miners and ancillary workers (e.g., operators of restaurants and bars in now-defunct coal-mining towns), who were each being paid $60,000 a year, becoming jobless for five straight years, with no chance of reemployment in the same sector in the interim. After this period, they face the same prospects as everyone else.[27] Each jobless person thus loses earnings with a present value of $300,000, for a collective loss of $300 billion.

Now, we have some winners and some losers. The 100 million households in the economy collectively save $600 billion dollars, partially offset by the $300 billion loss to workers. Notice, by the way, that even those displaced benefit from cheaper utility bills—though, of course, it is cold comfort (pun intended) relative to the large losses they personally bear. If preventing the technology would return things to a status quo in which the 1 million workers all retained their jobs, we can say that the cost of saving one job is approximately $600,000. In other words, we're giving up $600 billion in gains to prevent $300 billion in losses. Innovations like the one here happen all the time: many people gain a little, while a few lose a lot.

Another example is agriculture. Spectacular increases in the machinery and decreases in the prices of chemical inputs available to farmers have led to a situation in which less than 1% of the US population now produces vastly more food than did the much larger number involved in farming in, say, 1860. Of course, the adjustment of the input of labor was painful for many who were "replaced" by machinery and had to leave the farm for the city. Nonetheless, even ignoring the immediate benefits felt by those who moved in terms of lower food prices, the children of all adults at the onset of these changes were almost certainly vastly better off, because they were able to purchase the same amount of food as their parents with the wages of far fewer hours than their parents. Put more vividly, consider a worker earning a minimum wage of $7.50 per hour in the year 2011. Clearly, that worker could reasonably feed himself with only a couple of hours of work each day. This is a far cry from the effort that households of just two or three generations ago had to expend for the same result.[28]

So to avoid innovations in an effort to spare a small number the pain of adjustment is a crazy strategy at the societal level. Let me stress that I am not advocating the idea that "To make omelets, you have to break some eggs." Among other things, such a statement would mean making a distributional judgment, which as I've noted, is not so obviously the macroeconomist's privilege. What I mean is that we must hold ourselves to being more creative, so that the victims *do* get compensated, while all of society still gains. A productive approach is to think about how to use the tax and transfer system to provide assistance to those in trouble, while routinely allowing all productivity-enhancing innovations to occur. This is, as I have mentioned before, exactly the subject of the entire field of macroeconomic public finance.

A key advantage of using the tax and transfer system to make transfers to those who have suffered hardship is that one doesn't need to constantly make judgments about *why* a person is in trouble—whether one loses a job due to foreign competition or a genuinely new technology, or because one got sick and couldn't work, we help them all this way. Once we accept that this is an *insurance* problem, first and foremost, we should just treat it the way we do other more mundane insurance problems, but with one clear caveat: we must work to provide insurance in those instances in which we either already know or have good a priori reason for suspecting that there is not a well-functioning private market, and we must remain vigilant against the disincentives to work inevitably created by such programs.

Beyond all these arguments, a robust objection to blocking technological advances applies even when long-run growth is not at stake. If society has a given level of inputs (manpower, skills, machines, and land), and someone invents a way to produce more of something (not necessarily everything) with the same inputs, then the *potential pie has necessarily grown*. In the face of such improved opportunities, it seems folly to pass it up on the grounds that we cannot find a way to assist those whose skills are temporarily rendered less valuable.

5.7.6.3   The Lives of Indian and American Barbers

Another sphere in which reasoning based on the neoclassical growth model has proved important more recently is the area of "economic development." By this, macroeconomists mean a theory of why, *at a given point in time*, relative income levels across regions or nations are what they are. Development economics is to be contrasted with the study of "economic growth." The latter is most concerned with providing an account for the forces that allow living standards to steadily rise over time, while the former is concerned with accounting for the ordering of economic well-being across countries at one moment in time.

The centrality of the technological state of the art in neoclassical growth models has recently led macroeconomists to ask about the extent to which such a theory provides a compelling account of the enormous cross-country income disparities one observes. In fact, even though neoclassical growth models have the word "growth" in their names, they are not really models of long-run growth at all! The long-run behavior of those models (i.e., what averages of, say, consumption per person over long time horizons would look like) was determined by the purely exogenous force of "general technological progress." And unless one wants to assert that the nations of the world that are currently poor are poor only because they are transitioning to the very same steady-state level of income of the developed world, one has a problem.[29] In fact, it is not wholly tenable to view cross-country disparities as transitional phenomena. Here's why.

A key presumption of the neoclassical growth model is that of diminishing returns to the one type of input that can be accumulated, known typically as "capital" to differentiate it from the far less easily augmented resource "labor." Next, if one views knowledge of state-of-the-art production methods as relatively widely available, then one accepts that given the same inputs to production in a rich and a poor country, a given factory would produce the same levels of output. But if one accepts this assumption, then it must be true that the countries where capital is scarce (relative to labor) should also be places where the productivity of an additional unit of installed capital, say a machine or factory, will be *much higher* than what is observed here.

If capital equipment is mobile—whereby a developed-country firm can set up shop in the developing world, or developed-country investors can invest in a plant in, say, sub-Saharan Africa—then it will move in droves to these places. This is not what has happened at all. Most famously, when Robert E. Lucas Jr. asked, "Why doesn't capital flow from rich to poor countries?,"[30] he was employing precisely this reasoning.

The inability to answer this question satisfactorily led economists to ask a related question: If we measure inputs carefully, do we really think that the technologies being employed are the same? Or do the currently poor seem routinely to be operating with inferior production processes, i.e., processes that *given the same input levels*, will fail to yield the same output? Since the answer to the latter seems to be yes, we need to look at why this seems to be.

Within macroeconomics, there is now a substantial effort to document the extent to which *deliberate blocking* of technological progress can account for the disparate income levels one sees across countries. Important work here was begun by Parente and Prescott (2002), who argued persuasively that the obvious violation of the convergence predicted by the Solow model (and other neoclassical growth models), despite similar savings rates (and sometimes even higher ones!), has its roots in the productivity of additional inputs being lower in developing countries, despite their low levels there.[31]

In searching for more direct evidence that productivity of inputs is indeed low in poor countries, these authors, as well as others including Restuccia and Rogerson (2008) and Guner, Ventura, and Xu (2009), have found that work practices in many developing countries are generally far less suited to being productive than the ones employed in the now-developed world. Culprits include restrictive workplace and labor practices, such as high firing costs, firm size restrictions, and licensing barriers that artificially create monopolies. Many such restrictions can, in turn, be viewed as initially well-intentioned efforts to protect workers from the risks created by random technological change or process improvements arising in the course of competition.

The last point clearly ties development to the rate at which technological change is accepted. In doing so, it provides another perspective on the issue of the previous section on how one should feel about technological progress. The message of the work cited in this section is that blocking technological change is extremely costly, because doing so can account for the absolutely jaw-dropping disparities in human well-being that prevail in the early twenty-first century.

There is a sense in which I have endorsed (at least implicitly) the idea of "trickle-down economics." This is, for Americans, a phrase that almost immediately raises hackles. For many, the term refers to the idea that if we just allowed the rich to get richer by, say, keeping tax rates low on high-income earners or keeping capital income taxes low, those who are currently poor would inevitably be better off in the future (if not immediately).[32]

This definition is much narrower than what I have in mind. I am thinking instead of my frequent visits to India as a child and as an adult, and my visits to the barber there and here.[33] The average American barber owns a car, and, by his or her fifties, typically owns a house as well. My barber, Monty, in Ames, Iowa could have played golf regularly if he wanted to, and I suspect he wasn't the only barber in central Iowa able to do so. My barber in India, if he owned a house, had a far smaller one. He certainly did not own a car, and I doubt he even knew what golf was. From their caloric intake to their children's prospects for living in comfortable, climate-controlled homes, to their ability to play golf in middle age, these barbers' lives were and are remarkably different. The two men might as well have come from different centuries; yet they certainly coexist temporally. What do Walrasian models (and neoclassical growth models more specifically) suggest about why this is the case?

Recall first that these models showed that, under competitive conditions, one should expect that as capital per worker increased (something that is clearly an average), so too would the *average* wage rate of workers. And in the long run, when capital per effective worker stabilized to a constant amount, capital per person would grow steadily over time. As a result, *no matter how unequal* the ownership of capital was, wages for the average worker would grow steadily as long as the market for capital remained competitive. Indeed, this is exactly what has occurred. One might argue that were each society made more equal, perhaps average wages would be even higher (this is a dubious presumption that I will not reject here), but the issue here is why, at a particular point in time, American barbers are so much better off than their Indian counterparts when wealth inequality is actually not very different in both countries.

As noted in the previous section, the answer seems to be: because the productivity-adjusted stock of available machinery and equipment for an American worker is so much larger than that available to his Indian counterpart. In fact, the relatively advantaged position of the American barber has a great deal to do with the fact that he could have chosen many occupations in which productivity has soared over time. This is the sense in which neither wealth inequality nor the availability of spectacular returns to certain occupations are inimical to improvement in the living standards of those far removed from either wealth or the narrow skills that currently earn their owners large rewards.

This is a point that should leave those who identify themselves as "on the left" somewhat uncomfortable. There is a very strong argument to be made that if one cared about the well-being of the poor, especially for the poor of the future, then perhaps one ought to pursue productivity-enhancing technologies and policies, abetting the accumulation of plants and machinery with great zeal, even if, in the process, some "robber baron" types get very rich. In other words, this argument asks if we oughtn't make worker productivity our most important goal, with far less attention given to active redistribution of a given pie—*especially* when any of those strategies lower the returns to investment and technological innovation. Moreover, it asks those interested in redistribution to think carefully about the extent to which they value relative versus absolute outcomes. Pursuit of redistribution might well mean a more equal world with a smaller pie.

Shelving our concerns about inequality might, by contrast, raise all boats to such an extent that, even as it allows substantial inequality, it places average income at a far higher level. Of course, there would be costs to such an approach, particularly in exposing households to more risk than they currently face. And from the perspective of current workers, such a move, if it doesn't compensate them, will not represent a Pareto improvement, making the basis for pursuing it a far less defensible weighting that explicitly ignores or down-weights current workers. Now, if we did retain or even augment a social safety net, or simply levy higher taxes for the production of other things, including public goods, what might be the tradeoffs involved? Neoclassical growth models and data both suggest some answers.

5.7.6.4 Higher Tax Rates Mean Lower Income Levels, but May *Not* Lower Long-Run *Growth* Rates

As I have mentioned, without technological progress, the Solow model predicts that growth in per-person income will *cease* in the long run;

yet, if there *is* sustained improvement in a society's technological capability to turn a given level of inputs into more and more output over time, per-person output will grow at that same rate in the long run. A corollary that is sometimes not emphasized is that policy actions which leave technological progress unaltered will not be capable of changing the long-run growth rates of household incomes. Thus, an arguably central lesson of neoclassical growth models is that they place very hard limits on the government's ability to alter the economy's long-run average *growth* rate. In particular, a robust message of this class of models is that *tax policy that does not affect the rate of technological advance does not have long-run growth effects.*

This message is striking, and will be greeted by some readers with incredulity. So read it carefully. It tells us that if we took a group of identical economies, subjected each to a different set of taxes, and then calculated the average growth rate over, say, 100 years, we would find that as long as technological advance was not stunted by the tax policies, this growth rate would be the *same* in all of them! Before egalitarians uncork the champagne, they should realize that the result does not imply that the level of income of an average resident 100 years hence will be the same in all the economies—quite the opposite. In general, the economies with high taxes will have lower levels of income on average, just as the proponents of low tax rates argue they will.

The way to reconcile any appearance of a paradox is as follows. Take two economies that are identical at a moment in time. Let both economies have access to the same state-of-the-art technology at any moment, and let this rate grow in a constant manner over time. Now, announce that residents of both economies will face flat-percentage tax rates on all income they earn (i.e., both on their holdings in firms, and from the sale of their labor services to firms), and that this rate will be higher in one economy, which we will call H (for "high"), than in the other, which we will call L (for "low"). The first thing the NGM predicts is that capital accumulation will slow more in H than in L. As a result, households in H will temporarily experience lower growth of income than those in L. Since these countries were identical in the average income of their citizens at the outset, the fact that income is now growing more slowly in one than in the other, even temporarily, immediately means that income levels are becoming different: residents of L will, in short order, be richer than their counterparts in H. Over time, however, the NGM predicts that growth rates in the two will converge to the same rate. But since H grew more slowly for a while in the short run, and *never* grew faster than L, the residents of L will have *permanently* higher income than in H. Put yet another way, the ratio of incomes of the residents of H to those of L will become permanently different.

Thus, one cannot simply claim that tax rates don't matter. But neither can one claim that tax rates matter for growth; in the NGM, which certainly has some relevance as a description of modern advanced-country economies, they do not. In this area, Stokey and Rebelo (1995) is an important paper. The authors show that the very large and likely permanent (from the perspective of decision makers at the time) growth in federal government expenditures and tax rates around the Second World War had *no* effect on growth. As to one specific force behind this result, Hendricks (1999) points out that human capital cannot simply be transmitted across generations (some of it inevitably dies when the owner does). He shows that a model that distinguishes between physical and human capital helps reconcile the absence of growth effects from a huge and permanent increase in tax rates.

How a Country Taxes (and Equalizes) Seems to Matter
More evidence for the lack of any strong relationship between tax rates and long-run growth rates comes from comparing the US with Europe. Despite all its extra taxes, European average annual household income *growth* rates over the postwar period (and even before, actually) have been, just as the NGM predicts, essentially identical to that seen in the US, at roughly 2% annually.[34] But average European household income is substantially lower right now than the American level, at roughly 80%. If this trend continues, relative income will, of course, not change. But notice that this means that income *levels* are growing steadily farther apart. At this rate, for example, per-person income in Europe one generation (say, 35 years) from now will still be 80% of the American level, but the absolute income difference will double, rising from about $10,000 (now) to roughly $20,000 per year per household.[35]

There are, of course, some important differences between the ways in which Europe (especially continental Europe) redistributes compared to the US approach. In Scandinavia, for instance, taxes are progressive, but day care is often subsidized. As a result, female labor force participation remains high despite high marginal tax rates—especially on any second earner (often women). Conversely, in much of continental Europe, labor force participation rates are sharply lower among both the young and the old. Retirement rates among, for instance,

50-year-old men are much higher in France and Spain than in the US.[36] In fact, a crude summary might suggest that most of the effect of taxes on labor supply occurs along the so-called extensive margin—through the decision of whether to work at all. The "intensive" margin, which measures the response in hours worked among those already working, is generally measured to be a far less important one.[37] Europe also relies much more heavily on consumption taxes than does the US (see, e.g., Slemrod and Bakija 2008). This choice is largely in line with much received economic theory urging consumption as the ideal object to tax (though it is routinely opposed by many on the political left in the US). Europe may thereby be allowing itself to raise substantial revenues without incurring the distortions that would accompany the same level of redistribution were it to be financed via taxes on labor and capital (though, interestingly, recent work in a class of models that I will discuss shortly suggests that market incompleteness can mitigate the cost of capital taxation).

But readers should not become sanguine about taxes and growth, for recent work suggests that a great deal of the gap in average income levels between Europe and the US can be attributed to labor taxes and other restrictions that have substantially stunted the growth of the service sector in the former relative to the latter. The evidence suggests that service-sector productivity growth has been critical in overall productivity growth in the past three decades, and Europe's tax structure has hindered the absorption of these advances. Similarly, even if labor supply were not affected, when measured in terms of hours, the "effective" supply of labor might well be. This is because taxes on labor income alter the payoff from investing in skills that raise labor income! This channel can operate in obvious ways (changes in the number of people acquiring advanced degrees) or in subtle ways (changes in career length that lower the amount of on-the-job learning that takes place). The latter channel may well be important, given the strikingly lower labor force participation rate among those who are 50 to 60 years old in Europe relative to that in the US. If productivity growth continues to occur in sectors that are particularly (and relatively) distorted in Europe relative to the US, growth rates over the longer run may well start to differ. If that happens, be afraid.

To sum up, while one might be able to tolerate temporary declines in growth rates of per-person income, the NGM teaches us that if those differences come only during the transition to a new growth path under a permanently higher tax rate, then, in the long run, income will

permanently differ from that arising in an identical society that does
not impose such taxes. The gap between the US and Europe can be
viewed fruitfully this way. Moreover, if the policies under consideration alter the rate of productivity growth even slightly, matters are
much more bleak: over time, relative incomes will diverge, and over
long spans of time (say two to three generations), income differences
could begin to resemble those one now observes between rich nations
and the developing world. As a result of these potential tradeoffs,
economists are currently devoting a great amount of attention to the
relationship between taxation (defined broadly to include workplace
restrictions) and labor supply, and between taxation and human capital
accumulation.[38] Most of the inquiries in this literature are organized
around the NGM, highlighting yet again the basic "ADM-ness" of
modern macroeconomics.

5.7.6.5   The ADM Model Is Silent on Innovation

Despite the centrality of innovation for living standards, at least as
suggested by the neoclassical growth model, the basic ADM model
does not allow for deliberate innovative processes. In part this comes
from the competitive nature of interactions that it imagines. Such a
setting may well be hostile to investment in any idea that, once invented,
becomes freely available to all parties. Taken by itself, this suggests the
usefulness of protecting innovators via patents or other barriers to
entry that allow them a period in which to recoup their investments
whenever fruitful. Nonetheless, competition can also act as a spur to
innovation and can especially spur firms to utilize any innovation that
occurs to them or that they learn about, as we noted in the trucking
example in chapter 2. If you're intrigued, I recommend Shapiro (2012)
as a survey distilling some of the overwhelming mass of work on the
relationship between competitiveness and innovation. As for the argument that perfect competition, suitably defined, is actually a great
incentivizer for innovation, the provocative work of Boldrin and Levine
(2007) and the early work of Makowski and Ostroy (2001) are also
recommended.[39] For those innovations that become available, competition—especially the pressure that the financiers of projects exert on
producers—forces the adoption of the better ones.[40] For macroeconomists not modeling complicated deliberate processes of technological
change, it has been useful to assume instead that it happens in a mechanistic and diffuse way that, precisely via competitive pressure,

permeates everywhere and improves the ability of society to extract more outputs for any given set of inputs.

5.8   How Do Macroeconomic Models Provide Quantitative Information? Calibration and Estimation

A one-line summary of the central project of macroeconomics in the past three decades might be this: How do we get quantitative predictions from the ADM model and its variants? And while many of the statements in the previous section implied that the NGM *could* be used to make quantitative statements about how large various effects of taxes were, and so on, I wasn't specific about it was done.

So how exactly does one go from the apparently purely conceptual apparatus of the Walrasian NGM, especially as formalized in the Arrow-Debreu model, to models that spit out numbers for aggregate consumption volatility, GDP, investment, and aggregate labor hours, among other things?

The first step is to assign numerical values to so-called parameters of the model. "Parameters" refer to objects that govern the strength of various forces in a model but that do not vary with policy. For example, in a simple model of a single market for tennis balls, households' demand curves are influenced by their tastes. I might buy 10 balls at a dollar apiece and 5 balls if they were $2 each. My neighbor, a good tennis player, might buy 20 balls at $1 per ball, and 10 of them at $2 each. To the extent that we can capture the difference in the strength of these two persons' preferences for tennis balls in terms of a mathematical expression, each person's demand behavior will be captured by the numerical values governing the position and sensitivity of demand to price. On the supply side, the analogous objects are supply curves telling us the number of tennis balls different firms will offer for sale at different prices. These "willingnesses to supply" reflect the underlying technological production capabilities of various firms. To the extent that we can capture these differences in terms of a mathematical expression, each firm's supply will be captured by the numerical values that best describe its supply behavior. In sum, the differences in motivations of households and the capabilities of firms will be boiled down into differences in sets of numerical values; these are called parameters.

In order to obtain quantitative information from modern macroeconomic models, numerical values must be assigned to the parameters governing both household and firm behavior. In so doing, the modeler is taking a stand on the intensity of household preferences toward risks, for example, or on households' willingness to defer consumption, or on firms' willingness to substitute various inputs for each other, and so on. In the basic NGM, there are very few parameters, typically just five: one governing the representative household's aversion to risk, one to describe its patience, one to describe the technological ability of the representative firm to substitute between labor and capital in producing any given level of output, one to govern the rate at which capital equipment depreciates, and one to describe the rate of growth of labor productivity.

Once these values have been assigned, the model *immediately* has quantitative content. Specifically, the household's decision about how much to spend and how much to save, as well as the representative firm's level of output at various levels of wages and interest rates, are now fully determined. As long as we locate prices (a wage and an interest rate, in this case) that make sense (i.e., satisfy the conditions of equilibrium), we can evaluate the model's predictions for the objects it determines, such as the rate of savings, the growth rate of income per person, etc. These are, to repeat, quantitative predictions: they are literally statements about the size of the objects I just listed.

The inability of very general properties of preferences to restrict the range of possible outcomes via SMD, and the intuitive relationship summarized in the so-called Slutsky equation, strongly hinting at why this is true, immediately rob macroeconomists of the ability to speak in generalities. As a result, SMD is precisely what led the profession to its now standard operating procedure of restricting the model under study by limiting the possible values for model parameters. And for this very obvious reason, what started out as a strategy to restrict the behavior of growth models spread to the rest of economics.

Krusell and Smith (1998), for example, is an excellent showcase of artful calibration of an abstract theoretical model replete with hard-to-observe parameters. The last part of the previous sentence is important: if all needed parameters were directly observable, such as tax rates, say, then calibration would not be needed. But, in most models of interest, "behavioral parameters," such as risk aversion and households' average willingness to delay consumption, are not even close to being directly observable. So the profession is led by necessity to assign numerical values, subject to the discipline that *their models so parameterized match observed outcomes*. In Krusell and Smith's model, for example, a variety of values regarding the willingness of households to postpone

consumption needed to be assigned to allow the authors to make quantitative statements. In their case these values were disciplined by insisting that the model match the extreme concentration of the US wealth
distribution.

Similarly, the original Solow model is calibrated: the whole point
was to construct an environment that would match observations. Calibration is thus not new, nor is it the preserve of one "kind" of macroeconomist, nor is it politically stilted. It is simply a concession to the
realities of macroeconomics, especially when it comes to modeling
aggregate outcomes under price taking.

5.8.1   Calibration and Estimation: Taking a Model Very (Too?) Seriously

The fact that these models can be quantified immediately raises the
question of how best to assign values to parameters. And here there is
controversy. In their seminal works, John Long and Charles Plosser
(1983) and Edward Prescott and Finn Kydland (1982) each quantified
a version of the SGM.[41] They assigned numerical values to the types of
parameters I just described, located equilibrium, and studied its quantitative properties.[42] They called the resulting model a "real business
cycle model" because the shocks hitting that economy were "real" (as
opposed to monetary) shocks to the technological capabilities of firms.
These macroeconomists assigned values for the parameters such that
the equilibria of the model matched a collection of "moments"—i.e.,
averages and standard deviations—for items such as consumption,
investment, and output. The aim of setting parameter values to match
data is driven by the objects one is parameterizing. In many cases,
parameters cannot be directly measured: things like household preferences for current consumption, households' aversion to risk, and the
ability of firms to substitute inputs are all invisible to the economist—or
at least, very hard to observe with any precision. This is where calibration comes to the rescue.

The strategy followed to "uncover" the values that one should
assign to parameters is to take the model very seriously. By this, I mean
the economist takes the view that the model is indeed a good description of the situation being modeled, so good that its equilibria ought
to be compared with the data. Thus, calibration or estimation of models
is useful for learning about otherwise unobservable parameters. Here's
another example: let's say we think personal bankruptcy is a privately
excruciating event in people's lives, and we want to know just how

costly it is. We certainly can't directly measure "stigma," so what to do? One strategy would be to construct a model that details the household's income and financial market options in a rich manner, allowing the model to capture various salient aspects of how the household uses credit in response to income shocks. Then, take this model and calibrate or estimate the value of costs in "utility" terms (which can then be converted into a dollar-denominated measure of costs), *such that the costs* allow one to match a rich set of facts about when households seek bankruptcy protection.

Of course, in any general calibration or estimation procedure, for an arbitrarily selected set of parameter values, the equilibrium of the model will not likely match anything that one hopes to match. So next the economist searches for the values of parameters that *do* allow the model's equilibrium outcomes to match a chosen set of targets. The targets, in turn, are chosen by the economist through a subjective process in which she decides up front on the phenomena she wants her model to match. As typically practiced, this is an inexact process, and certainly allows for discretion by the economist. And this allows criticism. Note, however, that this criticism is not about the plain fact that one must assign numerical values to parameters in order to extract quantitative implications. It could not be. Instead, it is about the informality of the procedure for choosing one set of parameters over another, for determining "goodness of fit."

At the same time that calibration was becoming standard practice in macroeconomics, another branch of this literature also took the assignment of model parameters very seriously and was determined to put this on a footing as sound as anything seen in other parts of economics. These economists and econometricians were reacting to what they viewed as totally casual assignment of parameter values. The most penetrating complaints came from the hugely distinguished Lars Hansen and James Heckman. A key source of their misgivings arose from the "aggregation" that the earliest cohort of macroeconomic models required. As we discussed earlier, an important question is the extent to which individual-level decisions in a given area, when added up, look "as if" a single entity generated the aggregates in question.

A second strand of this work focused on using very sophisticated and computationally intensive Bayesian procedures to formally estimate the appropriate parameter values of the macroeconomic models used most often to guide monetary policy discussions. An important contribution to this enormous literature is that of Smets and Wouters

(2007), which, in fact, gained such stardom that it has become used at many central banks worldwide. An interesting payoff is that the latest incarnation of these so-called dynamic stochastic general equilibrium (DSGE) models actually *forecast* well. They are, for the first time, competitive with purely data-driven statistical forecasting models that make no attempt to tell a story of cause and effect. For a long time, this was not true. Models that attempted to deliver macroeconomic outcomes as consequences of explicitly modeled actors interacting through various trading institutions could not hold their own against the gold-standard "atheoretical" models using so-called **Bayesian vector autoregressions (BVARs)**, when it came to *out-of-sample* forecasting. They now can.

The availability of calibrated or estimated models that explicitly model household and firm decisions, as the ADM enterprise asks that we do, means that we now have a better chance than ever of being able to improve on forecasting the effects of *novel* policy changes, as we will not be as susceptible to the Lucas critique. After all, to understand the likely success of a genuinely novel policy proposal (think of a new type of tax that has not been used in the past), there seems no other choice: What data *could* one look at in this case? The ability to better understand hypothetical policy, before it is implemented, is arguably *the* great payoff to the quantitative approach currently used. That is, irrespective of how the parameters are assigned numerical values (via calibration or estimation), as long as one has been careful about the construction of the model, one can uncover values for parameters that are not prone to the Lucas critique. For example, if we employed an NGM to think about a policy change to the present-day US economy, we could impose a tax structure similar to what we currently have, and then calibrate the five parameters described above to help us match the salient features of the current data. To the extent that our model's parameters do not reflect an amalgam of forces that will change with taxes, we can study an alternative tax structure and get trustworthy predictions for outcomes that might arise from tax reform.

Caution is warranted, though. Think of a case where the tax rate affected firm-level practices in ways that our model did not allow for. Then, our calibrated value for the substitutability of labor and capital will not be correct, as it will reflect both the "true" technological capabilities of the firms in the model, but also the indirect effect of the *current* tax regime on outcomes! If this is the case, then any change in the tax structure (which is what we're using the model to help us predict, after all) will be potentially misleading, and as a result the economy after the change in taxes may behave differently in reality than was predicted. All this is to underscore the importance of ensuring that one has accounted in enough detail for the effects of those items, like taxes, in the outcomes one observes under current policy.

5.9   The SGM and Keynesian Macroeconomics

Once macroeconomists learned microeconomics, they started to revisit more traditional ideas in macroeconomics. In particular, the ideas of John Maynard Keynes began to receive a full reevaluation, this time through the lens of quantitative versions of Radner economies. The long-run legacy of this research program has been to give concrete meaning to and assess many of the forces that Keynes argued would lead decentralized outcomes to be terribly inefficient. Current models in use for short-run analysis of policy in most policy-forming entities are **new Keynesian** in their construction: fully specified and explicit in the tradition of modern macroeconomics (recall the recipe in chapter 1), but containing (sometimes many) features that make their equilibrium outcomes inefficient, and thereby potentially amenable to improvement via policy. Rumors of the demise of Keynes's ideas in the heads of modern macroeconomists have been spectacularly exaggerated (as one can readily tell from the work of central banks, offices of fiscal authorities worldwide, and think tanks).

I suggested earlier that the time economists spent on "interpreting" Keynes was fundamentally a negative thing, as it signaled the profession's willingness to tolerate a low level of macroeconomic policy discussion.[43] However, it is well worth exploring the more general idea that a macroeconomy with decision makers who need to make choices over time and under conditions of uncertainty may also exhibit dysfunction in a variety of ways. And indeed, in the past two decades, substantial progress has been made on this study. And here, the influence of the Keynesian vision of the macroeconomy is undeniable and has largely governed the research programs on equipping otherwise standard macroeconomic models with the machinery needed to deliver "bad aggregate outcomes."

Interestingly, the routes taken all rely heavily on the fundamental building blocks of the NGM and SGM. The reliance on the basic growth model is natural. Keynesian viewpoints have a lot to do with the way fluctuations in investment and consumption induce undesirable changes in output and employment, and the SGM is precisely a setting in which such feedback effects can be allowed for. But some changes have to be made to the basic SGM setting. This is because we know that the First Welfare Theorem holds for the model—within this model, there is simply no way to justify intervention into the economy predicated on improving the ability of households and firms to achieve mutually beneficial exchanges.

Of course, a society could decide to redistribute by using public policy, but the interventions typically promoted (e.g., increased government spending on infrastructure, etc.) could not possibly be ideal instruments for redistribution (Why would you presume that a relatively poor household wants a bigger highway? Why not give them cash, or a fully refundable tax credit, etc.?). Therefore, presuming that a macroeconomic theorist wishes to construct a coherent model in which households and firms make decisions that lead, collectively, to Pareto-*in*efficient outcomes, how might one proceed? The profession over the past 20 years has taken two routes that are not mutually exclusive. The first falls under the category of coordination failures, which we encountered earlier.

5.9.1   Keynesian Economics and the SGM I: Coordination Failures
As I noted at the outset, for many decades, macroeconomics has been defined by some as the study of coordination failure. In this view, the study of fluctuations in the macroeconomy is precisely the study of *pathology* in an economic system arising from self-fulfilling pessimism or fear. To better understand how this will work, first recall that the benchmark for modern macroeconomics is the Radner trading arrangement of the ADM model.

In the Radner economy, households and firms have correct expectations for the spot market prices one period hence. Granting that they indeed have such expectations, we can now ask about the extent to which, in a modern economy, we can have outcomes that are extremely sensitive to them. In particular, is it the case that under fairly plausible conditions, "optimism" and "pessimism" can be self-fulfilling in ways that make everyone (or nearly everyone) better off in the former than in the latter?

The answer is: it depends. For pessimism and optimism to be self-fulfilling, the technological realities governing production must be of a specific kind. This is cryptic, and I will provide more detail below. For now, what I have in mind is that the structure of the economy must be such that when, for example, all households suddenly defer con-sumption spending (and save instead), interest rates do not adjust rapidly to forestall such a fall in spending by encouraging firms to invest. If they did, under what I will later describe as a "standard" production side for the economy, wages would, barring any counter-vailing forces, promptly rise (as the capital stock rises and makes workers more productive). In turn, output would not fall in response to the pessimism. Thus, at least within the context of models in which households and firms are not routinely incorrect about the future, multiple self-fulfilling outcomes require particular features of the pro-duction side of the economy to prevail.

If such features are built in, however, we can certainly argue that we have constructed a rationale for thinking that the current state of affairs can be Pareto-improved—which is a huge thing, since it would then be imperative to look for policies that could help. One thread in the modern Keynesian program has been to examine this idea formally, and study the extent to which observably bad macroeconomic out-comes can be improved by altering the *expectations* that market partici-pants have on relatively optimistic scenarios. Franklin Roosevelt, in his famous statement, "We have nothing to fear but fear itself," had just this sort of thing in mind.

Consider an economy that has trading institutions which mimic the functioning of a well-oiled WCH: participants face a full set of Walra-sian prices in the daily spot markets and financial markets that open, just as we have presumed throughout. But, and this is key, we specify the production capabilities of firms in the economy in a way that makes the beliefs of households and firms relevant for the *average productivity* of firms. This approach aims to capture the notion that "pessimism" about investment opportunities can be self-fulfilling. To make this work, one usually first posits that the production side of the economy aggregates in the way we described above, which is entirely straight-forward to justify—barring the presence of the power to move prices substantially away from perfectly competitive levels and binding financing constraints.

With this representative firm in hand, the next step is to specify its production capabilities (usually over a single consumption good— recall the aggregation of consumption goods we already described above) in a way that delivers our desired feature: that "low" levels of production might well be self-fulfilling. This is done by positing what economists refer to as "increasing returns to scale." Intuitively, this is likely to be a feature of production technology any time there are large fixed costs or there is "learning by doing," in the sense that high levels of production "teach" workers better, essentially by more rapidly endowing them with experience.

Take a moment to think of just how "as if" this whole description is: I have said nothing about the nature of production arrangements at the firm level. Specifically, is it really the case that if firms expected a lot of demand for their products, they'd inevitably end up with a work- force that was better at producing on average? Maybe the workers would instead be worn out and switch careers—something that would make average productivity fall with output. The point is, at the level of aggregation at which we are operating, the only thing we can assert is that we are modeling the presence of features in the economy that allow—for some reason—for average and marginal productivity to rise with production levels. Granting this, we can now begin to see why this might "work" to give teeth to the Keynesian notion that output levels can sometimes be "too low."

A sequence of events might be as follows: investors wake up in the morning, see their shadows, and feel pessimistic about the returns to investment. As a result, at any given expected rate of return, they invest less than they otherwise might. But when this happens, the increasing returns we have posited start to work in reverse: average productivity will, indeed, be lower if aggregate economy-wide investment and pro- duction are lower tomorrow than today. And *this* is what makes the pessimism self-fulfilling; it is important because without it, we'd be left with a theory in which people were allowed to routinely expect things that did not come to pass. Notice another thing: the low-output outcome that arises from pervasive pessimism is unambiguously worse than the high-output one that follows from pervasive optimism. What if society could collectively (via a "government" or some other device) coordinate expectations for the good? In essence, getting us to believe that we had "nothing to fear but fear itself" would, if successful, move us to good outcomes.[44] I view this line of research as vital, because it showed the economics profession that the ADM/SGM-based approaches to macroeconomics could potentially carry with them a role for government as "coordinator in chief."

Leaving aside what it might take for a government agency to supply the requisite optimism, let's look at a more mundane issue. With econo- mists Azariadis, Farmer, and company having so coherently resur- rected Keynesian ideas in a form that does no violence to our general

methodology of finding aggregate outcomes arising from the decision
of sensible individual actors, we are left with a key empirical question:
Is it *reasonable* to think of the aggregate production capabilities of US
firms as exhibiting pervasive increasing returns to scale? The answer
has generally been no. From a "time series" perspective, this is not too
surprising in hindsight. As I noted at the very beginning of the book,
at least since Kuznets and Kaldor began their documenting, the defining characteristic of developed-country aggregate data is the tremendous smoothness it exhibits. It is, after all, specifically what led Robert
Solow to construct a model of capital accumulation that exhibited very
strong stability properties.

As a result, unless one wants to allow oneself the freedom to make
increasing returns themselves come and go, asserting it as a *constant*
feature means explaining why the aggregate economy isn't *always* wob-
bling around like crazy—because it is not. In other words, coordination
failure modeled this way would give one a theory of big—and bad—
fluctuations, but it would be a pyrrhic victory: one would lose the
ability to account for the bulk of the data, periods in which things are
growing more or less smoothly. The smoothness of output and consumption have dealt a deathblow to nearly every notion of "sensitivity
to initial conditions" that has been trotted out: the basic SGM is used
because it is consistent with a lot of aggregate data . . . a lot of the *time*.

5.9.2   Keynesian Economics and the SGM II: Sticky Prices
This still leaves at least one other route. Some believe Keynes implied
that the world does not work like the sequential-trade WCH that I have
repeatedly asked you to imagine. This approach has even more appeal
because the feature that it asks for is considerably easier to directly
observe than the firm-level practices that would lead the representative
firm to exhibit increasing returns to scale. As the economists Mark Bils
and Peter Klenow have famously done, one can use detailed retail-level
data to construct models that, besides having the "realism" of "sticky
prices," have also added firms with some monopoly power. In particular, talking about price setting necessitated a move away from a WCH,
which certainly has appeal given the absence of such an institution in
the "real world." Macroeconomists started constructing such models
in the late 1980s and early 1990s.[45] As computational power improved,
economists became liberated (undisciplined?) and the family of models
that are now used, often at central banks the world over, are extremely
involved.

To understand the role of sticky prices, let's dispense entirely with a well-functioning WCH, and instead specify that the WCH must use prices established in *previous* trading sessions. Now, you will probably be thinking: "But what if the 'fundamentals' of the economy have changed? How will the old prices ensure that all will be able to make the trades they want to?" They won't, and that's exactly the point. In this scenario, we interpret those who find themselves unable to sell what they wish to as holding "unemployed" resources. The most canonical example, of course, is that of the labor each of us sells to others. If the WCH spot market of "hours of work" were organized and then forced to conduct trade at some non-Walrasian prices, one might suspect that some workers will find themselves unable to sell labor following periods in which labor productivity has, for whatever reason, fallen (say, oil prices spiked to render production more costly).

The Keynesian view is that these "rigidities" form the basis for why, in the wake of disruptions to the economy, one observes households searching fruitlessly for work. I use the word "search" deliberately: the actual process of the job search has been an important research program in macroeconomics, and is one of the many ways in which Keynes's shadow is extremely long. I will describe search models further below.

Thus, in a (very) crude way, what economists had in mind was unemployment as a consequence of trade in a demand-and-supply model in which the prices were set at non-Walrasian levels. I say "crude" because, as I have emphasized already, it is nonsense to use a model of price-taking actors (say, households expecting a given wage) to think about situations where that behavior has no chance of letting people execute the trades they expect to be able to. Unless one wants to assert that the stickiness itself comes as a total surprise—so much so that it is not even on the radar screen of workers when they think about how to find work—this is, I repeat, nonsense.

Macroeconomists are not naive, though. Those imposing sticky prices in their models do not confuse this approach with the real problem facing firms or households. However, modeling the search process and "getting to an employer first" and "getting a resume to the top of an HR department pile" are all very demanding, and would lead to simplifications in other places in the model that were seen as more important, such as the explicit incorporation of adjustment costs and other features governing investment. But as computing speed grew, the profession indeed started to tell "deeper" stories about labor allocation in macroeconomic models. Importantly, macroeconomic models began to embed into an SGM what has come to be called "search" processes for the allocation of labor. Pioneers in this literature, which will be described in more detail further below, include Andolfatto (1996) and Merz (1995).

Where do sticky price models leave the Keynesian vision? Are they sticky enough? The answer is "probably not." In particular, the stickiness needed for tremendous amplification of initial shocks strains credulity. It asks one to take labeled or observed prices far too seriously, especially on the supply side of the economy—where many trading arrangements are less like a WCH, and more often involve long-term contracting and bargaining. That is, there may well be little change in the prices at which some transactions occur, but trading partners may adjust to any altered production conditions by making all manner of other adjustments. Think of the core: if we thought trading partners knew each other well, it is hard to imagine they would leave large gains from trade on the table simply because someone found it too onerous to get up and scratch out the old price list and write down a new one.

5.9.2.1   Is Monopolistic Competition a UFO?

Of course, the literature has recognized this, and has moved in the direction of building in market power, usually in the form of "monopolistic competition." A variety of authors have shown that such interfirm interaction could greatly amplify the effect of price stickiness. My own (maybe idiosyncratic) view is that this type of competition does not exist, and that where observers claim it exists, it is more appropriately described as what Kreps (1990) calls "local oligopoly." What's in a label? Quite a lot: oligopoly theory, especially for the case where firms interact repeatedly, is notoriously indeterminate, as we saw in chapter 2. It is hard to say what will happen in any instance where the number of firms is small enough to raise monopoly power of any kind as a specter. Moreover, we can wonder when the passivity of firms (to the actions of those making close substitutes) that is imagined by monopolistic competition models is ever applicable.

5.9.2.2   Tensions, Tensions

There is an essential tension present in all macroeconomic model building: the need to account for observed phenomena in a tractable manner on the one hand, and the need to avoid the Lucas critique on the other.

The former means taking shortcuts, such as using sticky prices, to explain observed comovements of various macroeconomic variables. But any shortcut at all will, almost by definition, sooner or later leave one vulnerable to working with a model whose predictions for outcomes under a policy change may be very wrong. Of course, this is a tradeoff we may be willing to make, given the costs of enriching the model further in "deep" ways that would insulate it against the Lucas critique.[46] I will return to this point when discussing SIM models. In that instance, my chosen research program will be somewhat under attack, in the sense that we must be mindful of SIM models' limitations precisely because we use that class of models to make predictions for the effects of policy changes. Clearly, then, we are all in houses with varying amounts of glass, though modern macroeconomics has substantially fewer panes than was the case before.

5.10   Less-Than-Perfect Worlds: The Standard Search Model, the Standard Incomplete-Markets Model, and the Overlapping-Generations Model

From work done in the 1980s and 1990s, it became clear that complete-markets models were hard to square with facts. These included work that showed that risk seemed not to be pooled well in the data: that consumption was highly dependent on individual-level circumstances, that similar workers were often paid differently (too much "wage dispersion"), that the interest rate on safe assets was very low given the growth rate of the economy, while (as we saw at the outset) the premium for risk on stocks seemed too high. Given these failings, ongoing work has proceeded by building in one (or more) of three aspects of reality abstracted from in the benchmark ADM or Radner models. First, there is the reality that sometimes markets themselves fail to be "centralized" trading forums, and hence make it costly to trade some items, such as labor services. This reality has given rise to the vast body of work on so-called **search models.** Second, there is the reality that some markets are simply nonexistent, such as for some forms of insurance or credit. This has led macroeconomists to construct a class of models in which markets are missing altogether, so-called **standard incomplete-markets (SIM) models.** Lastly, unlike in the ADM or Radner models, households and individuals typically only exist at some moments of an economy's overall life. This reality of life and death is crucial for many fiscal policy discussions such as the national debt or climate change policy; intergenerational ties and conflicts do seem to exist, and thus seem critical to understand. The need to evaluate such settings gives rise to the **overlapping-generations (OG)** class of models.

A central aspect of all three of these model classes is that their equilibria are rarely, if ever, Pareto-optimal; indeed, are often not even Pareto-optimal in a more constrained sense that takes as given the market structure. As a result, the field currently has available a battery of models that allow for fruitful evaluation of a very large variety of outcomes involving hardship and inefficiency for individuals and firms, and the effect of policies enacted to deal with some of these outcomes. Because the models used are ones in which the First Welfare Theorem does *not* hold, they are immediately inhospitable to the "market fundamentalism" we are sometimes accused of.[47]

I will focus in particular on the search and SIM groups of models, which are currently extremely active areas of research. Both model families prohibit the kind of "frictionless" trade envisioned by the Walrasian ADM setting and, instead, force trading to be either impossible for some goods (SIM) or a time-consuming and uncertain activity (search). These models allow us to understand phenomena, such as unemployment and market illiquidity, that have been an important part of the landscape for many years and especially recently, but which could not be studied earlier because of technical barriers.

Search models, in both labor and financial markets (which I will broach in chapter 6), have proved especially useful for studying recessions. When labor must be allocated via search, these models allow economists to make testable predictions that use data on measured statistics such as the unemployment rate or workforce participation rate. When buyers and sellers of assets must search for each other in financial markets, the models can shed light on phenomena such as "illiquidity" and an inability to make trades. In light of the recent deep recession and sluggish recovery in the US, it is hardly surprising that the search setting is at the center of much, if not most, current macroeconomic research.

5.10.1   Who Knew?

Outside of the world of professional economists, I suspect that little is known of these models. Yet, if you write about macroeconomic topics for a living, you should have passing familiarity with them because they represent the machinery for most applied work in macroeconomics. The lack of prominence of these models in economic journalism is unfortunate as it leaves many with the view that macroeconomics is not engaged in exploring settings where market outcomes are far from efficient, where trading can become severely difficult, or where serious inequality is a real possibility as an outcome.[48] Moreover, some observers (rather incorrectly) view macroeconomics as having no serious judgments to offer on just how "bad" the inefficiency and inequality might be. In what follows, it will become clear that far from being relevant only for the ivory tower, modern macroeconomics is fully engaged with the messy real world.

5.10.2 No Representative Agent: Heterogeneity Galore

An immediate consequence of the incompleteness of markets imagined in each of the three model classes above is that there will be a great deal of heterogeneity, and almost no chance of a representative agent. Households in these models will instead differ routinely in their wealth, health, age, financial asset portfolio, and number of children, to name just a few dimensions.[49] The analysis of settings with such heterogeneity requires a richer set of mathematical and computational tools, which explains why these models have become ubiquitous only in the past two decades.

5.10.2.1 Equilibrium Doesn't Mean "Good": Redux

I've provided some discussion already on the extent to which economists' preoccupation with the study of "equilibrium" situations does not represent any presumption that private trading activity is always for the good. I pointed out that equilibrium notions in economics serve only to help economists make predictions about what will happen in a given trading environment; they do not help predict whether what will happen is good, bad, or ugly. Nowhere is the baggage that comes with the term "equilibrium" more misunderstood than in the models studied in this section. I will show that in the SIM, OG, and search models, outcomes that meet the conditions needed in order to be referred to as "equilibria" are almost *never* Pareto-efficient.

5.11 The Reality of *Decentralized*-Decentralized Trade: The Search Model

In what follows, I will sometimes use the term **decentralized trading arrangements** (**DTAs**) to refer to the entire collection of private solutions and contractual arrangements. This set includes Arrow-Debreu markets, wherever they exist, as well as all other arrangements that are not, strictly speaking, Arrow-Debreu markets, such as the insurance and banking contracts I will discuss below. I use this more general term because Arrow-Debreu theory has something specific in mind when speaking of "markets." When macroeconomists talk of "market incompleteness," they do *not* mean that Arrow-Debreu claims are the things missing (of course they are), but rather that the totality of decentralized trading arrangements yield outcomes that are *as if* one was missing a full set of Arrow-Debreu claims. Nonetheless, because it is so standard to speak of "incomplete markets," I will use that terminology, but I want the reader to know what is really meant by the term.

Among the set of DTAs one can imagine, we might think of a particularly extreme form, in which people not only fail to concern themselves with the big picture, but maybe can't even physically or virtually gather to trade with each other. In other words, we could think about "decentralized-decentralized trade." This is what is captured by the term "search models."

Unlike the ADM model, the central presumption of the search model is that some spot markets are not "centralized." Instead, as the name suggests, search models are ones in which trading partners must "search" for each other. Think of how you located your job, if you are not currently a student. My guess is that it did not involve submitting a list to a WCH specifying the number of hours you would be willing to work at a list of different hourly wages. We can guess that firms did not supply a WCH with a list of the number of hours of work time they'd wish to hire people at various wage rates, either. Instead, a (probably painful) process was likely the way things unfolded for you: sending resumes, hoping for interviews, making a good impression, and then accepting an offer of a variety of characteristics that together you'd call a "job." For the firm, the process was also no fun, and involved understanding the extent to which they were risking bringing aboard a malcontent or sociopath.

Search models have existed for about 40 years now, so it is a pity that many who write about economics rarely mention them. They are now the dominant form of macroeconomic model aimed at understanding phenomena as disparate as unemployment in labor markets and illiquidity in financial ones. And in a rather exciting recent development, models of search in the labor market are being integrated with the growth models described earlier. It is natural to study together the fundamental consumption-savings problem that engages all the households I know and the sometimes very difficult search for jobs that engages all too many of us. But the technical challenges that such analysis presents have taken longer to overcome, and so have delayed what you might have thought should have been a central model all along.

5.11.1 Optimal Decisions and Stationary Equilibria

In a setting where traders need to wait for opportunities to sell their wares, or find sellers when they wish to buy, they must solve a complicated problem for themselves—they will have to decide what's worth *settling* for. This problem is fundamentally different from the simple question: How much should I buy or sell at the price I face? that buyers or sellers in Walrasian settings have to answer. Search means settling, simply because one doesn't know when the next opportunity will come along. So one is forced to trade off the likelihood of having a better opportunity come by later that one cannot then accept (without a cost) against the sure bet of buying or selling or working now.[50]

In contexts where individual households wish to find "jobs" or firms to whom they can sell their time, the relevant measure of "settling" is the *worst* bundle of characteristics describing a "work opportunity" that you would accept if offered. When the bundle is a simple object such as, say, a wage rate, one speaks of the **"reservation wage."** In general, though, there will be many characteristics, including a variety of aspects: the salary and benefits, the average "hours" one is expected to put in, the path to promotion, and so on. The reservation wage is important for the decisions households make with respect to the offers they accept, or the bargains they strike with employers they've secured an interview with. Moreover, it depends on all the features of the environment: the generosity of the unemployment insurance system, the tax rate on earned income, and so on.

How single-agent decisions are dealt with is a vital ingredient in any successful model, of course. Yet in most contexts of interest, macroeconomists cannot ignore the fact that it is the collective behavior of households that helps determine the arrival rate of job opportunities for any one household. Thus, there is an inevitable circularity: the arrival rate of job opportunities affects the reservation "wage" that any one individual faces, and, all else being equal, this reservation wage affects the rate at which job opportunities arrive. In any situation where households and firms are not routinely surprised by the behavior of work opportunities, we must have a situation where the behavior of individuals and the arrival rate of acceptable opportunities are in balance. Of course, as mentioned repeatedly, there is no need that such "balanced" behavior be simple. In many equilibrium situations, even calendar time can matter for outcomes, as opposed to a worker's characteristics fully determining who gets what.

Typically, however, macroeconomists focus on the stationary equilibria of search models.[51] In search models, stationary equilibria can also exhibit all manner of fluctuation at the individual level, but are simpler at the aggregate level. In the context of labor markets, for example, they are usually outcomes in which the proportion of employed and unemployed households doesn't change over time, while individual households do experience changes in their status. In other words, households in a stationary equilibrium are switching places in a way that keeps the overall unemployment rate stable over time. For many questions, this sort of equilibrium is a sensible one to study: outside of booms and recessions, the unemployment rate is fairly stable.[52] Moreover, such outcomes do capture the great amount of "churning" that one sees all the time in labor markets.

5.11.2   What Kinds of Questions Can We Address with Search Models?

The way in which trade occurs in a search model immediately makes the model helpful for evaluating policies aimed at assisting traders who must operate in such settings. The most obvious examples of search involve the allocation of labor. As a result, a huge amount of attention has been given to questions surrounding policies such as the optimal structure of unemployment insurance systems. Papers in this literature address difficult issues related to problems in observing the actions of those receiving unemployment insurance, problems that in turn create a serious tension between better insurance and worse incentives. While a full description would take us too far afield, the interested reader is directed to the textbook treatment in Ljungqvist and Sargent (2004) for a detailed and precise description of standard models of search-based trading.

As I'll describe in chapter 6, search models have most recently been pressed into service to understand how differences in the information that parties have affect the quality of a given set of assets. This is a natural area to employ such models, and allows for the evaluation of policies that alter the information held by would-be traders. (I say "would-be" because the presence of such "asymmetric information" can lead to some transactions not occurring, even though they would have taken place had parties been on a more even footing.)

5.11.3 Keynesian Economics and the Search Model

I reported earlier that the two main branches of macroeconomics pursuing the ideas of Keynes cannot both be seen as fully satisfactory causal accounts of the data observed in recessions. However, I was probably premature in being so negative. We still have the possibility that search, which we certainly find intuitively appealing, is a cause of serious misallocation of inputs, especially labor. In fact, it is probably no exaggeration to suggest that the principal reason policymakers worry about business cycles is that the change in the labor input at the aggregate level comes in extremely uneven forms at the individual level. And the outcomes in a search model have a much better chance of making contact with the brutal contractions in household-level labor supply that, without being unreasonable, one can view as "involuntary" (more on this loaded word further below).

Important work in this area began with Peter Diamond in 1982. This line of work was later connected more tightly to quantitative predictions by Andolfatto (1996) and Merz (1995). Subsequent work is associated with Robert Shimer, Randall Wright, Ken Burdett, Dale Mortensen, Chris Pissarides, and Ken Judd, among others.[53] The most recent of this work, that of Guerrieri, Shimer, and Wright, now includes the presence of informational problems, which is very important for understanding the way labor and some asset markets work. Such an approach also helps us avoid overemphasis on the literally "physical" nature of search processes. In what follows, I describe the origins of the views of most macroeconomists on how to interpret what "search" actually is.

5.11.3.1 Search Is Not Really about Searching

I hinted above that modeling genuinely "informational" problems seemed promising as a way of coming to grips with statistical descriptions of the labor market experiences of individual households. It is promising because "search" is best viewed as a metaphor; it is not usually to be taken literally. The reason is the following. If all that barred traders were the costs of *physically* getting together, then such an impediment should have diminishing power to alter outcomes away from efficiency over time. In the modern computer age, it should be apparent that this is silly. In particular, an upper bound on the kind of inefficiency that one would expect to see from a literally physical limitation on trade would come from the resource cost of centralizing trade itself. For instance, if all that prevented an auction of houses was that one couldn't easily locate and compare them, then the Internet should be eliminating this problem; and yet home buying remains a costly transaction in which intermediaries continue to survive and get paid. Why? Introspection suggests that one is buying more than a home—one is buying an entire bundle—a school district, crime rates, etc. But one is especially buying neighbors—and this is very hard to know much about, before it's too late.

The preceding example presents a general issue facing all models that posit barriers to trade that generate inefficiency. The curious reader will, in every one of these instances, be able to ask rather damningly: "Why can't private agents contract their way around these impediments?" The answer is that, from a theoretical perspective, they often can, *if* it is literally physical costs of centralizing trade that are at play. If not, then one must concede that the "search" process is really about the time and effort it takes to inspect the value of a match (in the case of employment), or about the efforts that one must expend to ensure one is not being sold a "lemon," and so on.

In the context of recent labor markets, search models typically proceed by specifying what is known as a "matching function," which spells out how many matches between buyers and sellers get realized given the number of actively searching buyers and sellers present in the model. This hobbles this class of models, especially in accounting for observations on the relationship between the unemployment rate and vacancies. Here standard models are at a loss. But in one sense, this may reflect the fact that in principle, one cannot treat the matching function as somehow invariant to the prevailing macroeconomic situation, since the behavior of firms and households may well change systematically in response to the business cycle. The paucity of data from recessions (which is, of course, something to be happy about) complicates definitive parameterizations of the aggregate labor-matching function that would better encapsulate the richness of labor market dynamics.

5.11.3.2   Search Models and Voluntary versus Involuntary Unemployment

Some noneconomist observers are aware of search models. However, they sometimes express the view that these models, by modeling unemployment as an *activity*—and hence, a "voluntary" event—trivialize its impact on households. Some commentators have suggested that search models are not useful because most unemployment is involuntary. But journalists who have become familiar with some terminology in economics are certainly not alone in this view. This interpretation of search is, however, quite literally the opposite of the message search models actually deliver. If we think that people and firms make decisions about how to use their time and resources, then one question facing any person who is currently not "matched" with a firm, or any firm that is currently looking for a particular type of worker, is: What tells you when to accept a particular job or to accept a particular worker? Of course, a worker might answer this, "when my children would go hungry" or "when I can no longer pay the mortgage"; or a firm might answer it, "when we'll lose an order totally if we don't fill a position right away." The fact that people and firms make decisions is *all* that is meant by "voluntary." In fact, a key feature of search models is that they *do* allow for circumstances in which a worker is indeed unable to match with a given firm within a given time period. In this eventuality, we can speak easily of a worker being "involuntarily" unemployed. However, it is vital to recognize that this outcome, as bad as it is, still reflects the choices of both firms and households. Therefore, to understand the extent to which workers find themselves in difficult situations, one has to model their decision making. To repeat: these examples clarify that even when search is modeled as an activity, and whereby unemployment is at least partially "voluntary," it does *not* mean that the participants themselves are content with their situation, nor does it mean that policy is useless. In fact, search models generally have outcomes that *can* be improved by judicious policymaking.

Why is the search approach useful? Think for a moment about what is achieved by classifying unemployment as "involuntary." This term, I suppose, should be taken to mean that unemployment just happens to a worker, and that the worker makes no further decisions until he is again employed? Now imagine asking some policy questions: How much unemployment insurance should we provide? How long should we provide it? Should it completely offset the loss in earnings that one might suffer, no matter how long the person stays unemployed? Would an expansion in unemployment benefits change decisions? If so, at what levels of provision might this happen? Would workers get pickier about the jobs they accepted if we raised benefits? Might high unemployment benefits prevent highly skilled people from taking jobs that require little of them just because the jobs were the first to be open? Moreover, wouldn't the same behavior by high-skilled people help the chances of the low-skilled to fill the same vacancies? Would firms start seeing better applicants line up in a world with lower benefits, and hence post more vacancies? When does a worker become discouraged enough to drop out of the labor force?

Each of the preceding questions seems well worth thinking about, and some of them are ones that macroeconomists and policymakers have actually been asking. And yet if unemployment is purely involuntary, we cannot know the answer to any of these questions—since, by definition, unemployment is not even partially the outcome of decisions by households and firms about how to allocate their time and effort. By contrast, the search framework allows economists to assess the effects of a huge variety of labor market policies on household well-being, ensuring all the while that the policy analysis does not run afoul of the Lucas critique. In this sense, search is the modeling approach that is most capable of addressing concerns about the hardship created by unemployment.[54]

Search models are incredibly hot as of this writing. The state of the art now is called "directed search," and is due to the work of, among others, Guido Menzio and Shouyoung Shi in Menzio (2007) and Menzio and Shi (2010). As the name suggests, participants in models of directed search can choose the "market" in which they will attempt to make transactions, but cannot guarantee that they will meet a trading partner. This is an intermediate step between Walrasian settings and the older generation of search settings. In addition, these settings have been constructed to allow for tractable solution. These models have been so rapidly adopted by the profession because many have been constructed to have "block recursivity." While this feature is a technical benefit, it has proved important in allowing authors to enrich the models they study along other dimensions, for example to study more "realistic" reforms to unemployment insurance systems, and to including house-selling and -buying decisions as well, among other things. This should drive home the points that the technical cannot be so easily separated from the "substantive" and that tractability is a key determinant of the adoption of a given model.

5.11.3.3   What, *Exactly*, Is Being Traded? Walrasian Economics and the Importance of Defining the "Commodity Space"

The case of unemployment in the RBC model, and then in the basic search model, is one illustration of a more general theme. The clear specification of what is being traded is called, in the jargon, the **commodity space**. The Walrasian tradition forces this specification, and the RBC and search models follow further in its footsteps. In the case of the RBC model, the commodity space follows the standard Walrasian model in that it treats "labor services" as just another commodity—like sugar, gasoline, or T-shirts—that is traded *anonymously*. By contrast, unemployment, as the term is commonly used, is a concept that usually implies the severing of a *relationship* between an individual and a firm. But the very notion of a relationship immediately conjures up a setting in which trading partners are *known to each other*. Moreover, the severing of the relationship often seems (at least in a proximate sense) to occur unilaterally at the firm's behest. The RBC model produces no results that can be identified as "unemployment" in the sense that we use that term. It can at best give us insight on the *number of labor hours* that are worked and how those hours vary with other "fundamentals" of the model, such as the preferences of households and the technological capabilities of firms.

Now, the fact that the RBC model does not generate data on what we would be able to point to as "people who have experienced a severed relationship with another party who used to agree on a fairly regular basis to purchase their labor services" does not make it a useless model. If the data in which one is most interested for a given inquiry are those on aggregates such as economy-wide consumption, investment, or output in response to a disturbance from outside the economic system (such as a war in an oil-producing region of the world), then simplifying the model by treating labor as just another good traded on markets may be worthwhile. This will be especially true as long as one suspects that the disturbance in question, or the response of the economy's participants to it, does not lead the labor market to function systematically worse than it would in the absence of the shock. Of course, if the shock is such that the functioning of labor markets is what is suspected, a priori, to be central to poor aggregate outcomes, then the omission of search and matching processes will not be sensible. For instance, the impact of a new technology (say, powerful computers) that would be very productive only when paired with some types of workers might well depend on the processes by which firms and workers learn about each other. Of course, the preceding depends on the process by which the firms and workers form relationships and organize themselves in production, and a host of other factors which collectively determine the pattern and rapidity of information transmission between them. In these cases, search models, as detailed above, *would* be apt; they are indeed capable of speaking to unemployment in the way that we measure it in the data. This is precisely because, in those settings, the commodity space is no longer something as abstract as "labor services." Instead, the choices facing workers in those models are, for example, whether to accept a job offer or not, whether to search for a new job, or whether to quit. Similarly, firms in many search models "lay off" workers, "post vacancies," and importantly for our example, evaluate the quality of a potential match. These are all choices that the commodity space used in search models allows us to describe, and thereby learn something about.

A lesson to take away from these examples is that macroeconomists are not being foolish when they sometimes use models in which labor markets are assumed to work in ways that do not resemble any market we see in daily life. It may mean that the macroeconomists are asking a question for which they suspect details in the labor market are not central; and by simplifying this part of the model, they will be able to tractably build in more richness along the dimensions deemed more a priori central to the inquiry.

Moreover, insisting on building in a rich model of labor market search into every macroeconomic model simply because it's what is "realistic" will lead to models stunted, and thereby unrealistic, in other, possibly far more important ways. Developing a sense of the likely tradeoffs that will be a function of the type of question one is asking is an important part of the maturation process of an economist. Such perspective is only acquired over time, through a messy process of trial and error in which an economist learns to strip away all those facts that will not matter for the question being asked.

5.12 The Reality of Missing Markets: The Standard Incomplete-Market Model

The set of competitive markets is incomplete. Macroeconomists have begun to explore the workings of incomplete-market models in earnest over the past two decades, and in what follows, I will describe some of the ideas and findings in this body of work.

I noted in the previous section that market incompleteness doesn't have to be taken literally. A standard example of an arrangement that effectively substitutes for many Arrow-Debreu markets is that of the formal insurance industry. Consider a simple insurance contract for illness. Imagine that there is one contract per person that pays the individual policyholder if he or she falls ill, and doesn't pay if there is no illness. If the insurance was actuarially fairly priced—i.e., the premium was exactly equal to the average payout—then all risk-averse households would completely insure themselves. Importantly, households would no longer have any gains from further trading of these risks with the others in their society. In other words, an insurance company could, in principle, with just 1,000 contracts (one per person) almost fully insure society. One thousand sounds like a lot, but it is microscopic compared to the 2^{1000} Arrow-Debreu markets that "complete markets" would appear to require for its definition. Similar arrangements, such as our current banking system, are best viewed as sensible replacements for actual hyperdifferentiated markets. This is why macroeconomists focus less on the observed structure of markets than on the implications of the *totality* of DTAs for individual-level consumption and firm-level investment behavior. (I will mention some of this work further below in section 5.12.1.7.)

Given the restricted focus on the properties of competitive price-mediated transactions, the main theoretical questions for macroeconomists are the same as always: Does (an incomplete-market) Walrasian equilibrium exist? If so, are the resulting outcomes efficient (the First Welfare Theorem)? And, third, do prices implicitly lurk underneath all efficient allocations (the Second Welfare Theorem)? The answers, roughly, are yes to the first question, no to the second, and for the third, "no, not even when you lower the bar on what you mean by efficiency!" The question of whether Walrasian prices exist for an economy with an incomplete set of markets was definitively addressed by Duffie and Shafer (1985). The finding that outcomes will be inefficient, even relative to a weakened standard called **constrained Pareto** efficiency, is due to Geanakoplos and Polemarchakis (1986). These authors showed that a benevolent planner could do better, even if confronted with the constraints on markets that typically face private agents. Loosely, these authors established the prices would be "wrong." For example, when households lack insurance markets, they may all save a great deal for a rainy day. If all households are trying to save, the interest rate on savings might end up very low. But a very low interest rate affects many people later in life, in terms of being able to arrange for comfortable retirements, for instance. In such a setting, it will generally be possible to tax and subsidize in ways that make all households better off. Recent work of Dávila et al. (2012) represents the state of the art on the constrained inefficiency of incomplete-market outcomes in the benchmark incomplete-market model, which is introduced below.

Market incompleteness will generally lead to the failure of the First Welfare Theorem. Of course, the extent of inefficiency that incomplete markets induce in the real world depends not just on the set of competitive markets, but also on the set of alternative forums within which mutually beneficial exchanges are carried out, such as family, church-based, or school-based support networks. But absent any of these networks, we can prove that Walrasian outcomes are not Pareto-optimal if the set of goods and services being traded falls short of the full set imagined by the ADM model: all households can be made better off than they will be at the Walrasian allocation. This is hardly surprising, and indeed almost tautological: why would one expect that limiting trade in some items in such an extreme manner (no trade at all) would then yield an outcome in which no further mutually beneficial gain from trade was possible?

5.12.1 The Income Fluctuation Problem (IFP): The Lynchpin of Modern Macroeconomics

The preceding observations led macroeconomists to formally construct Walrasian models in which not all goods and services were placed for trade. Of these models, a hugely important class is the one based on the pioneering work of Milton Friedman, who, in 1957, formulated the first instance of the modern **income fluctuation problem** (IFP). Friedman imagined the decision problem of a single household facing risks to its earnings but lacking a full set of insurance markets to allay such risks. Note something interesting: the alleged godfather of "free-market fundamentalism" and other such unflattering topics is of central importance to modern macroeconomists for studying a problem in which markets are modeled as clearly having failed!

A key requirement of optimal behavior for any household grappling with the IFP is that the additional benefit to consuming a small amount more at any date (the so-called marginal utility of consumption) must be equal to the marginal benefit to consuming incrementally more at the next date, but only after an additional discount has been applied to future marginal utility. Crucially, the discount factor that arises is something that, in the IFP, is partially random as a result of the presence of income or wage shocks, and varies as a result of the interaction between a household's attitudes to risk and the uncertainty on income or wages it faces. This equality is called the **Euler equation**, and arises naturally from the same logic that requires that one spend money on various goods in such a way that the last dollar spent generates the same addition to happiness no matter what good or service it was spent on. In the context of decision making over time, as in the IFP, the choice is primarily between goods consumed now and those consumed in the future. Recall that from the ADM perspective, these are simply two different dated commodities.

The evolution of the IFP is the story of the evolution of modern macroeconomics. Bar none, the IFP, and the Euler equation it usually spawns, are the most important moving parts in modern macroeconomic models, and lurk behind the ability or inability of these models to account for a variety of the phenomena that fall into the ambit of macroeconomics, such as consumption, labor supply, and household portfolio choice. In almost any macroeconomic paper written today, there is a version, somewhere, somehow, of the Euler equation.[55]

The story of how the IFP has evolved over time may be one of the best examples of the constant interplay between theoretical rigor, attention to the data, and advances based on computational power. A magisterial history and evaluation of this process through the early 1990s is Deaton (1991), while Carroll and Kimball (1996) provide a comprehensive treatment of how consumption should behave when households face the IFP and why. More recently, Attanasio and Weber (2010) revisit many of the same issues in light of new and better data, and new and better computational tools. All in all, the model of consumption that economists now have available, when confronted with risks and investment opportunities of empirically valid sizes, is remarkably capable of reproducing a host of facts on consumption, income, labor supply, and wealth accumulation. Many dimensions of consumption behavior have been plausibly "explained" by economists.

Once we have confidence that the right household-level setting has been represented (this would include prices, one's number of children, one's age, marital and educational status, etc.), we can be confident that the individual consumer or household will respond in ways that match the data. However, some questions—especially those involving many households simultaneously, such as a change in fiscal policy—require households to face prices that, when taken as given, also equate demand and supply for various goods, services, and assets. This is the province of the ADM model.

Thus, much modern macroeconomics now proceeds by placing the modern incarnation of the IFP household into a market setting and then solves for the Walrasian general equilibrium. However, unlike the ADM model, these households lack a full set of Arrow-Debreu claims and any alternative that might proxy for them.

5.12.1.1 SIM Models: "IFPs in GE"

With all this in mind, we can turn to the problem tackled by Truman Bewley, a distinguished economist at Yale University. The setting Bewley imagined, as described in "A Difficulty with the Optimum Quantity of Money" (1983), was one that will be immediately familiar to most because it was, in some important ways, "realistic." It featured a large number of households that were beset by risks to their earnings that they lacked well-functioning insurance to buffer. Instead, they were assumed to have access only to simple bank accounts in which they could accumulate a "rainy day fund" by saving a bit extra when times were good, and depleting the same account to deal with spells of misfortune. This certainly resembles some aspects of our lives fairly well. Bewley was interested in the extent to which households might be able to use savings to effectively mitigate these risks, and whether an economy populated by many such households would behave differently from an economy in which such risks were insurable.

Starting in the late 1980s, a clutch of papers arrived that would open the floodgates for macroeconomic research into inequality and the nature of the "equity-efficiency" tradeoff. This work piggybacked on Bewley's work. A few of these papers deserve special mention. These are Ayse Imrohoroglu's 1989 paper on the pain inflicted by business cycles on households, John Laitner's 1992 paper on how luck in earnings and inequality are related in general equilibrium, Mark Huggett's 1993 paper on the "Risk-Free Rate in Heterogenous-Agent Incomplete-Market Economies," and the late Rao Aiyagari's seminal paper on "Uninsured Idiosyncratic Risk and Aggregate Saving" (1994). These papers taught an entire generation of macroeconomists like me how to frame questions in which uninsurable risks were likely to be important for decision making and for the implications of policy. Most importantly, these papers illustrated how one might provide *quantitative* information about the macroeconomy when uninsurable risks were important, particularly by teaching us how to compute solutions to the basic model of Bewley. Twenty years on, we are still learning from this model. For instance, Guerrieri and Lorenzoni (2011), a quite standard SIM setting, is at present the leading model helping macroeconomists understand the implications of credit crunches for real interest rates and aggregate consumption.

Of all the advances made by macroeconomists over the past two decades, these models have been at the top. In what follows, I will highlight some of the most important reasons for their relevance, but for thorough recent reviews of the models I refer readers to Heathcote, Storesletten, and Violante (2009) and Guvenen (2012). Lastly, for a short discussion of the ways in which policies appear differently when viewed through an incomplete-market lens, the reader may find useful the short nontechnical article of Athreya and Haltom (2012).

5.12.1.2 Stationary Equilibria

As in most macroeconomic contexts, inhabitants of a SIM model face an enormously complicated problem. In the simplest version of the problem, they have to decide how much to consume and save, given an income stream—the basic IFP. In the more complex version, they also are modeled as choosing how much to work, whether or not to buy stocks, homes, or other durables, whether or not to enroll in college, and so on.

One reason for this complexity is that the set of relevant prices will likely move over time, especially as the proportions within the population receiving high and low incomes vary over time. As a result, what is already a daunting calculation becomes rather impractical.

Therefore, as with search models, attention is usually given to stationary equilibria. In the case of SIM models, such outcomes are ones in which calendar time is not useful to decision makers once they are made aware of certain aggregate economic quantities, such as prices or average economy-wide labor productivity. In such an equilibrium, households will experience highs and lows in labor income, become sick and return to health, grow older, and so on. But they will do so in ways that typically preserve the fraction of people in any particular situation or "state" over time, or at least for any given aggregate state of the economy (e.g., in a given boom or recession). Of course, this restriction limits the reach of the model, especially as a tool for understanding the short-run effects of novel policies. Yet such outcomes also appear more plausible as the only ones in which households and firms might have a chance at learning to forecast well.

5.12.1.3   SIM as a Macroeconomic Model of Bounded Rationality

Interestingly, *all* SIM models can be seen as an attempt to allow for bounded rationality. As Magill and Quinzii (1996) argue, the entire incomplete-market research program can be seen as an accommodation of bounded rationality; moreover, it allows for rationality that is bounded in a way that is tied to arguably the most demanding aspect of complete-market models—forming expectations of the not-immediate future. Magill and Quinzii's view is reflected in the benchmark SIM model's not only being bereft of important kinds of markets, but also lacking longer-lived financial assets: the instruments allowed are typically "one-period bonds." This restriction in turn helps limit the relevance of longer-term forecasts for households, asking only that the lender price bonds for a period short enough for no material additional uncertainty to resolve itself.[56]

While market incompleteness can be seen as an implicit accommodation of bounds to rationality, it is useful to note that one of the most important papers in macroeconomics in the past twenty years, that of Krusell and Smith (1998), models bounded rationality very explicitly, and features rich agent heterogeneity as well. In their model, households carry simplified rules of thumb for how prices will evolve, rules that ignore a variety of information encoded in the distributions of wealth and labor supply decisions of all households in the economy. The authors show that such a simplified view of the world can serve households well in making accurate forecasts.

5.12.1.4   What Search and IM Models Give Us (I): Insurance vs.
Incentives: The First Quantitative Pass

As already noted in chapter 3, of all the tradeoffs with which macroeconomics concerns itself, the tradeoff between equality and incentives
may be the biggest. Every contentious policy discussion involves one
side arguing for public policy to regulate, insure, or redistribute (among
other things), with the other side arguing against these changes. Reasonable members of both sides are likely to recognize kernels of merit
in the positions of those on the other. The persistence and seeming
intractability of these debates stem not (I hope) from the mendacity of
any one group, but rather from honest and heartfelt differences in the
assessment of the strength of the forces involved. In other words,
neither side seems willing to agree on a common underlying framework within which to answer the question of *how big* the benefits and
costs of any given policy are.

What seems to be preventing compromise in rhetoric (if not in actual
policy—which does seem to reflect something of a healthy balance) is
that neither side believes the claims of the other when it comes to the
sensitivity of outcomes to changes in policies. The areas of noisiest
debate most obviously include the growth effects of taxes, and the protection afforded by further expansions of the social and financial safety
net relative to the sloth it may induce. On the last, for example, opponents will suggest that the safety net's conditionality (one needs to be
poor to get assistance) makes its programs ripe for abuse, as they essentially act as a subsidy for laziness. Yet proponents will note research
suggesting that labor effort does not seem very responsive to taxes.

These debates are very tough to resolve, and reflect genuine scientific uncertainty as much as anything else. However, using the idea of
market incompleteness as a reasonable point of departure for understanding the real world, **incomplete-market** (**IM**) models, defined here
to include search models and any others that fall short of the Arrow-
Debreu standard, are useful. The first thing they do is allow one to
transform discussions of inequality versus incentives into a related
discussion of *insurance* versus incentives. IM models do this by allowing for the production of inequality among ex-ante similar-looking
groups (e.g., wealth differences among all college-educated households) and then by imagining a thought experiment that assigns one a
place in society that depends on the relative likelihood of different
outcomes that would obtain under a given policy proposal.

For instance, let's say we lived in a world where income was partly due to random chance and partly due to investment in college education, which was itself risky. And let's say that insurance contracts against lost income were not available either. In this world, initially identical households will begin to differ from each other over time as a function of the luck they experienced and as a function of the educational investment decisions they made.

The key idea is that some of the inequality is potentially inefficient from an *ex-ante* perspective, and so worthy of (at least the investigation of) amelioration through public policy. For example, we might consider imposing a progressive tax on income. Such a tax would go easy on us if our incomes were low, and take away income mainly when an additional dollar wasn't worth so much to us. Of course, this tax policy might also lower work incentives and lower the average income in the economy as well. But, and this is the key, we can still imagine that this tradeoff between risk and the size of the overall pie might seem worth it to us if we did not know what our lot would be. In other words, viewed from an ex-ante perspective, a risk-averse person might well choose a policy that, even though it "shrinks the pie," lowers the chances of getting an extremely small slice. This is the tradeoff that IM models allow us to explore.

Thus, from the outset these models make room for the principal motivations of nearly all who have an interest in public policy. Above all, they provide economists with a way to conduct many an appealing normative thought experiment, closely related to the one imagined by the philosopher John Rawls, but emphatically not in a manner that commits them to advocacy for the extreme equality that Rawlsian ideas are sometime taken to mean. This is because in applications, macroeconomists start by assuming preference homogeneity (recall the reasons given for this in chapter 4) and that these identical households are also risk-averse. Their risk aversion, in turn, is assigned a value consistent with auxiliary evidence culled from studies on household portfolio choice and from basic introspection on the kinds of premia households require on average to tolerate risk (see, e.g., the discussion of asset pricing in Ljungqvist and Sargent 2004). The resulting values are decidedly finite—i.e., they are "intermediate" in the sense that households will not go to any lengths to avoid risks, but will require some compensation to do so. By contrast, in the settings used by macroeconomists, the pure Rawlsian prescription of "maximizing the minimal income level of anyone" would be chosen only by those too risk-averse to even consider crossing the street.

As a consequence, to the extent that two opposing groups can agree on the relevance of this thought experiment, they can then have a discussion organized under a common set of premises (as embodied in the numerical values assigned to the parameters of the SIM model under consideration). As a result, they can begin to more tightly focus the reasons for their disagreement on the usefulness of a given policy prescription.

To find all this acceptable in any application of a search or SIM model to evaluate a policy, one must agree on two things: (i) that the risks being imposed on households in the model are truly risks, and (ii) that the market incompleteness is of a form that is reasonable. As for point (i), matters can be tricky. Say I asserted that the college dropout rate should be thought of as a "risk" that arrives as a shock to households. You might respond that the data are equally consistent with the person's having known all along that he would leave college and just wanted to drink beer with friends for a while. As for point (ii), in most SIM models, households are modeled as lacking insurance contracts against income loss beyond that provided by the unemployment insurance system and any insurance they can get via borrowing or saving in a simple checking account. But this may not be quite accurate: parents might stand ready to assist dropouts with room and board, etc.

IM Models and the Distributional Judgments of Economists
Economists are fond of saying that we present the public with tradeoffs associated with policies, and then sit back to allow the political process to decide what to do, especially when a policy change creates redistribution. This is, of course, what we must do. But it also sets the bar low, dooms our positive analyses to having less relevance than they might otherwise have, and is a bit disingenuous, because an important role of most economists in policy entities is to make recommendations on policy. So on what basis do they make these recommendations? Economists will appear to be coolly trading efficiency and equity for each other—which is almost inescapable because the world rarely presents itself with pure Pareto improvements. And I mean "pure" in the sense that they would both improve efficiency and create *no* losers who need to be compensated to actually generate a Pareto improvement.

Compensation is tricky to implement, and if it fails to happen, potential efficiency improvements may not be realized as actual efficiency improvements. And yet, in an incomplete-market world, almost every policy has distributional implications. On what basis does an economist recommend for or against, then? Many of us who employ SIM models to produce predictions for the impact of policies take the route of *ex-ante welfare*. In other words, if we say we recommend "Policy A" over "Policy B," if we are basing our recommendation even in part on the outcome of a SIM model, what we mean is that ex-ante expected utility is higher under Policy A than under Policy B.

Especially for rare or big policy changes, there is no obvious reason to advocate for potential Pareto improvements that, barring help to any losers in the transition, would not turn into true Pareto improvements. Thus, care must be taken to include provision for transitions, including allowance for the possibility that transfers do not feasibly exist to make the change ex-ante Pareto-improving for sure. Modern macroeconomics allows for the detailed analysis of transitional effects arising from a policy, especially when those transitions affect different parties differently. Conesa, Kitao, and Krueger (2009) is one such example, in the context of capital income tax reform. In related work, macroeconomists working on policy questions are more routinely embedding the reforms they study into models where voting is allowed. This allows them to build in institutional barriers to compensation of losers by winners. Corbae, D'Erasmo, and Kuruscu (2009) is a nice recent instance of this kind of work in a model where voters' interests differ because they are heterogeneous as a result of insurance market incompleteness.

It is important to remain crystal clear that using IM models with ex-ante expected welfare as a normative criterion is a *judgment* call. One does not have to find it compelling. I do, however, find it very compelling, in part because I find it useful to think of one's assignment of initial conditions at birth as best viewed as a lottery. Many of the phenomena I find morally repugnant are given coherence within this ex-ante welfare criterion. Why do I think a given social institution is "wrong"? Take the case of rights denied to a particular subgroup, "American Males Born in the Midwest to Parents from India." If I find such restrictions abhorrent, it's because it is not what I would agree to take a *chance* on from behind Rawls's veil of ignorance. That is, what if one were born as an "American Male Born in the Midwest to Parents from India" (as I was)? Notice that this is not an unqualified objection. Are there circumstances in which one might oppose the distribution of certain kinds of inalienable rights? Absolutely. Though it may be a "man-in-a-lifeboat" scenario, let's say that we knew that endowing people just like me a particular set of statutorily (and fiscally) guaranteed rights would reduce average US lifespan by a decade. Would that enter the calculus forced by ex-ante expected utility? Yes. The SIM model thus allows for the analysis, however imperfectly, of precisely this kind of tradeoff and, in doing so, forces clarity onto the sources of our differing views.

Ex-ante welfare analysis on IM model outcomes is the industry standard. If this makes one uncomfortable, it is because an elephant in some rooms is the need to come to grips with one's view on the process by which situations confronting us "initially" (e.g., at birth, or as we enter adulthood) are assigned. The consequences of family background are dependent on a large array of institutions, including, most obviously, capital markets that (by determining borrowing capacity) influence the extent to which the child of poor parents can make investments in education and elsewhere anytime those investments are productive. But they are also dependent on the kinds of insurance markets that are available, including those that are publicly provided. These include high-quality schooling for children whose parents are too poor or too disinterested, or both, to provide for it themselves. The evidence for a while has seemed to indicate that the US features significantly incomplete insurance against "circumstances at birth," as summarized in the very high correlation between parent and child earnings (see, e.g., Mazumder 2012 for a nontechnical review and links to relevant research). One's fate appears somewhat sealed by the circumstances one is born into, and certainly it is more sealed in the US than in most developed nations.[57]

Having promoted the idea that the ex-ante standard might be useful, I should stress, however, that in practical situations ex-ante requires deciding on a date after which everything is ex-post. This is clearly an arbitrary decision over which an economist has latitude, something a consumer of economists' recommendations for policy should keep in mind.

Yet the ex-ante criterion, when applied to the SIM model and to overlapping-generations models (see below), forces a bit of candor into the weight one places on the well-being of various groups, *after* already agreeing on a serviceable *positive* model for the effect of any given policy change. Moreover, unlike models in which markets are complete at the outset, in IM-type models the criterion of ex-ante welfare doesn't allow economists to profess neutrality on matters of distribution. Instead, it forces them to contend with the possibility that the very fact that a distribution of outcomes may occur, and to boot that this distribution may be meaningfully changed by a policy action, may be indicative of inefficiency. In addition, it forces consideration of the extent to which one is willing, in every relevant case, to trade incentives for insurance, to one degree or another.

For me, it boils down to this: all policies induce lotteries over future outcomes. The latent uncertainty of the world ensures this. The business of choosing among policies thus forces one to choose between lotteries. And at this point, the thorny problem remains that of choosing how to weight possibly widely varying levels of aversion to risk.

Economists are not the only ones who must clarify their positions. Just as I've shown that a version of "trickle-down" is not so very crazy, SIM models tell us that "equality" might not be, either. If one takes market incompleteness and the veil of ignorance seriously, then one is forced to acknowledge that at least a portion of observed inequality reflects inefficiency. Immediately, then, any bold claims about unfettered capitalism as a trading system that allows participants to execute all mutually beneficial trades are null and void. The argument for laissez-faire, *even on grounds of efficiency alone*, is weakened. Happily, therefore SIM models may be a source of discomfort to ideologues of all stripes.

5.12.1.5   What Search and IM Models Give Us (II): *Competitive* Theories of Inequality

An arguably central payoff from IM models, especially the SIM model and its variants, is that they deliver inequitable outcomes under *competitive* conditions in which households and firms behave rationally. Consider first the issue of "competition." This allows those who suspect inequality is bad, or reflects inefficiency, a way to think about the extent to which inequality reflects inefficient credit and insurance markets, *without* forcing them to accept that such outcomes are the result of large-scale collusion or cooperation. IM models do this by locating the sources of inequality in households' inability to fully protect themselves through markets against risk. As described earlier, the SIM world is one in which a fundamental attribute of complete-market Walrasian allocations is voided: household's purchasing power depends on the particular history of outcomes arising from risk that was idiosyncratic to them alone. As a result, IM models are models where at least a portion one's wealth at a given point in time must be chalked up to good individual-level fortune. Of course, the particular structure of the specific SIM model under consideration will affect the extent that one's situation can be ascribed to luck as opposed to effort or thrift.

An example will help. Consider a canonical SIM market setting, like the one studied by Aiyagari in 1994. In this model, households face idiosyncratic fluctuations in their labor earnings, in a manner designed to reflect the losses arising from spells of unemployment. However, in the Aiyagari model, there is no room for labor *effort* at the household level, either in terms of working "harder" while at a job, or in terms of being able to "search harder" when unemployed. Therefore, if one accepts these omissions as innocuous, one will indeed attribute more to disparities in wealth across households than another observer who thinks that the baseline Aiyagari model misses the mark in the limits it places on workers to "make their own luck." But narrowing differences of opinion in this way represents progress. We have gone from vague assertions about inequality being bad or good to questions about the actual options we think workers have to search, to work harder, and so on. Moreover, these models also will generate predictions for worlds in which workers can search. For instance, under fairly mild conditions, if workers could alter their search behavior, we might expect such actions to be taken by those with the most to lose—namely, those with low levels of financial assets to tide them over any spell of unemployment. More precisely, having a search intensity as a choice available to workers will have *observable* implications for the length of unemployment for richer and poorer workers, which can be checked against data. Such a process is exactly how the literature on unemployment and, more generally, "search" models (which I will describe in more detail below) come to an assessment of the plausibility of various impediments to a complete set of markets. To the extent that this process is successful in narrowing down the set of options that workers have, people of all political persuasions can then utilize the same starting point for thinking about changes to policy. For instance, if we are fortunate enough to come to agreement on the nature of constraints that we think to be relevant for a given class of households (say, those without a high school education), we can then simulate the effects of changes to policy, such as a change in social insurance policy or a change in the duration of unemployment insurance, on various outcomes. We can then learn from the model's predictions about the precise set of winners and losers. In this way, if one disagrees with one's neighbors or peers, it will become transparent that it is because one weighs the welfare of different groups differently. Of course, this may be an impasse, but it is one that does not founder at a level where differences in opinion are genuinely resolvable by careful analysis. Moreover, at some deeper level, understanding and isolating the sources of disagreement seems inherently worthwhile: "agreeing to disagree" is not an activity for intelligent people.[58]

The setting described above is one that is typically modeled as "competitive," where no single party has particular influence on outcomes. But distributional concerns are frequently presented by advocates for social change as outcomes of market "power." For example, one might hear an argument that low worker wages and skill levels involve the collusion of "corporates" against "workers." This is not at all persuasive to most economists, because such accounts presume substantial collaboration among groups, sometimes comprising thousands of members (e.g., all businessmen) who are otherwise thought (by the same advocacy groups!) to be rapacious seekers of profit at any cost.

Macroeconomists generally do not like "power"-based narratives. We take self-interest both as a tractable starting point for our analysis and as a decent approximation for the level of genuine concern that most have for others—or at the very least, the level of concern that most are able to act on in order to help others. However, self-interest is the enemy of cooperation, for better and for worse. In many undergraduate courses in economics, students are introduced to the "prisoner's dilemma," in which police have arrested two suspects and need the cooperation of just one in order to convict both. In this setting, as long as the police can prevent communication between the two prisoners, they can structure a set of rewards to each as a function of the other's behavior that induces both to choose to tell what happened. This setup is, of course, bad for both suspects, who, if they could only have counted on each other to keep their mouths shut, would now be set free.

The prisoner's dilemma is popular in textbooks not because we are experts in law enforcement and want to show off, but rather because we suspect that it illustrates a larger point. To us, it highlights that cooperation by those with inherently competing business interests, while beneficial to them collectively, is very hard to sustain individually. This message was made fairly directly in chapter 2 in the more "economic" context of interfirm competition. We noted there that, in general, as the number of participants grows, all Nash outcomes start looking like Walrasian ones. Namely, sustaining collusive arrangements in which firms agree to act in concert—and ideally, as essentially one big monopolist—is unlikely to succeed. Even the individuals seemingly most ripe for market power, such as those with freakish mental or athletic ability, and hence protected by nature itself from competition, do not so obviously collect profits and hold society for ransom. There are still enough of each talent to make it hard to attain and keep a top spot in major league baseball or basketball, and ex-ante, there is risk of injury and loss of skill as well. If you are a comfortable middle-class reader, would you trade places with a young ultratalented man in an inner city with a very small chance to do very well in a sport? If you said no, then you do not view him as being in an enviable position, even though he may outearn you by a huge margin someday. In other spheres, such as pharmaceuticals, patents sometimes protect a firm from competition, but even here the temporariness of the patent and the risk that no successful therapy will be created have led to a setting in which the long-run average rates of return to these firms are no higher than average. The world is a tough place, and commentators who fail to accept this will get little hearing from macroeconomists. If outcomes are bad for many, and bad for a long time, collusion is usually a very bad explanation. Thinking back to the issue of coordination failure in the case of race relations, note that there, too, bad things happened to people, for a long time, and then things abruptly changed. Yet in such instances, there was no obvious removal of "power" from anyone (whites were still much richer than blacks and they still ran the city councils in many cities, etc.); there was only a shift in expectations that made *competitive* behavior change!

From a macroeconomic perspective, take wealth distribution in the US. While the top 1% of wealth holders are fabulously wealthy (having an average net worth in excess of $2 million, per the Federal Reserve Board's Survey of Consumer Finances 2007), they are not a clique who decide the interest rate in the economy. They are 3 million households—a group far too large to collude or even to communicate with each other successfully. Some subsets of the extremely rich can persuade the government to allocate subsidies to them, at least statutorily (think of the sugar lobby, car lobby, etc.), but in the longer run, they cannot stay rich unless they provide products people like.

From a theoretical perspective, recall the case where firms engage in Cournot competition, whereby each firm brought output that was produced in isolation from others to the marketplace, having guessed what its competitors were making. I reported that such a setting would allow for some above-competitive levels of profit, but it would *not* allow profits to reach levels of a pure monopoly as a Nash outcome. And the Bertrand model, as we saw, was even more stark: one obtained the perfectly competitive outcome with just two firms! Add to these considerations that even when firms can interact and monitor each other to some extent, the work of Green (1980) suggests that significant collusion is a tricky business. Of course, all of this is not to say that collusion does not occur in the real world. It surely does, as revealed in the recent case of the agribusiness giant Archer Daniels Midland.[59] Modern economics teaches us that it is naive to accept "power" as a cause for everything we regard as unfortunate. Like the models of coordination failure we saw earlier, SIM models tell us that we need not accept this interpretation.

Not Nash Means "Not a Good Candidate for a Prediction,"
Remember?
Arguably the most powerful use of the Nash equilibrium concept is to *eliminate* possible outcomes of strategic interaction. Recall the discussion in chapter 2: even when we may have little faith that a given Nash equilibrium is what will describe accurately the outcome of a particular interaction, the requirement of Nash equilibrium is important. This, we noted, is because a set of behaviors that was *not* a Nash equilibrium would have little to no chance of being observed as a routine outcome. And everything we know about the interaction between small numbers of parties (arguably the only place where genuine collusion is even possible) is that collusive outcomes are generally not Nash outcomes. As noted in the context of Green (1980) and Green and Porter (1984), even when parties interact repeatedly, as soon as one allows for imperfect monitoring of each other's actions, collusion again becomes difficult to sustain as a Nash outcome.

In short, SIM models allow economists to study a generator of inequality that does not immediately run afoul of their theoretically and empirically based skepticism of sustained and meaningful collusion. And this fact is very important for our purposes. As I will show you shortly, it helps explain the approach macroeconomists now take to many problems involving inequality and distributional justice. If you ask modern macroeconomists about inequality and its causes and consequences, they will not tell you a story about Goliath manhandling David. Instead, they will likely start talking about a *competitive* world in which few, if any, have significant market power, but where markets in education, credit, and/or insurance may be seriously incomplete.

The second dimension of SIM models is that, aside from positing the absence of certain markets altogether, they are "standard" in every other way. In particular, all decision makers in a SIM model are rational in pursuing their objectives. This has appeal to many economists in part because it allows us to think about bad individual-level outcomes, and bad societal-level ones as well, without running afoul of the indiscipline that can accompany an abandonment of the rationality postulate. But a more important and economically substantive reason that the SIM model's approach is attractive is that it teaches us that if markets are missing (and we have already seen in chapter 2 a detailed set of reasons for why this might occur in the real world), then the poor will often be the unlucky ones, rather than merely being lazy or incapable of making good decisions.

5.12.1.6   What Search and IM Models Give Us (III): Maybe "Competition" Isn't All That Great?

On a more positive note for readers who have strong views on the undesirability of "competition," SIM models bear another message: they "show" how "ruinous competition" hurts the rank-and-file citizen. This has, of course, long been a theme in political discussion. A way of elevating this idea from the realm of suspicion and agitprop to something more precise comes from the seminal work of Geanakoplos and Polemarchakis (1986). As I argued in chapter 2, once markets are not complete, the prices would in general be "wrong." This is exactly what these authors proved would be true, in *almost all* incomplete-market economies. In the jargon of economics (and mathematics), such a property is "generically true."[60]

To see this idea heuristically, imagine a dartboard covered with pieces of paper, each of which contains a complete model of a macroeconomy, in the sense I defined in chapter 1. Moreover, each piece of paper has on it a model that differs from those on the papers around them, and the models, taken as a whole, cover the entire realm of possibilities for incomplete-market models. For example, some may be missing one set of insurance markets, others may be missing others, and so on. Now imagine throwing a dart at the board. Geanakoplos and Polemarchakis (1986) showed us that the "odds" of hitting an inefficient incomplete-markets economy is 100%—you'd have to throw darts forever to hit a piece of paper that described an incomplete-market economy whose constellation of preferences, endowments, and technology would allow, even without the full set of Arrow-Debreu markets being available, for Walrasian outcomes to be Pareto-efficient ones.

Returning now to the proper interpretation of this result, it is important to recognize just how debilitating this finding is for anyone hoping to make blanket statements about the efficiency properties of competitive markets. These authors showed that even if one left aside the markets that were missing, and simply asked about the efficiency properties of the Walrasian outcome with respect to the allocation of the remaining goods that were traded under competitive conditions, one would conclude that markets did not deliver an efficient outcome. One could, in principle, reshuffle the Walrasian allocation of just these goods (i.e., leaving entirely aside the ones for which markets are presumed absent) across households and production responsibilities across firms in such a way that all households could be made better off. In a nutshell, once markets are incomplete, the prices of remaining goods, services, and inputs are, simply, "wrong."

Nevertheless, we may feel that endowing an authority at some level (local, state, or federal) to make decisions more directly will not work any better. If so, we simply must conclude that bad things sometimes occur, and that little can be done about it. In this view, the argument for relatively "free markets" is mainly "we probably can't do any better." And there are certainly moments when I feel precisely this way. Macroeconomists who say otherwise are at least mildly suspect.

IM Models and Policy: A First Caution
Of course, not all market completeness is equally plausible, and not all inequality can be convincingly attributed to the structure of trading arrangements, instead of to pure differences in preferences for leisure, or status, or anything else that households may value differentially. In fact, a line of reasoning introduced earlier puts further limits on the extent to which one views decentralized (not necessarily Walrasian price-based) outcomes as efficient. And this is the idea that Walrasian price-based allocation is only one of any number of arrangements that, at a proximate level, generate constraints and incentives for households

and firms that lead to efficient outcomes. As a result, the fact that one cannot point to an overt market for every good or service does not mean that households and firms aren't reaching gains from trade in the particular date- or state-contingent good. For example, one is hard pressed to point to a market for many of the things that a family provides its members, such as the open-ended transfers relatively irrespective of how long the members live. This may, in fact, be one reason for the family to exist: to provide members with an "annuity." As noted, Kotlikoff and Spivak (1981) calculated that even a modest-sized family, by staying together and sharing resources, could effectively proxy for a competitive annuity market.

A more general point is that while SIM models open the door, they do not quite get to a level of detail as to the reasons for the missing markets that would allow a definitive policy prescription. One must also have (i) a good a priori reason for believing that the markets presumed missing in a given SIM model aren't already being proxied for by other means, and more pessimistically, (ii) a sense that the reasons for the absence of any given market are things that a well-meaning policymaker can overcome. Therefore, to repeat a view I expressed above, the standard presumption for nonintervention into economic outcomes does not have to be "I think all decentralized trade is great, and yields approximate efficiency all the time." It can merely be: "Whatever inefficiencies are out there, and I *do* think they exist, I cannot think of ways to do better, and certainly not in the sense of Pareto improvements."

My own sense is that macroeconomists hold both of these views at various times and places in their professional lives. Sometimes, we are filled with enthusiasm for the high efficiency we observe in many market economies. We can all get someone to make us a Denver omelet at essentially any time of the day, in many places, and under linear prices of somewhere between five and seven dollars, all with little difficulty—so there are probably few or no unexploited gains from trade in even something as idiosyncratic as, for example, the Arrow-Debreu commodity of a "late-night Denver omelet in the West End of Richmond, Virginia." At other moments, we grow despondent over the gaps that free markets seem to have left: Why have my neighbors been driven to place a coin collection jar at the neighborhood gas station to help finance necessary medical treatment for their six-year-old daughter? Given the low and fairly equal risk of such an illness and the low likelihood that people insured against it would take actions to increase the risks of serious illness, why isn't there a policy that we each hold that, for pennies a day, pays the bills in this horrible circumstance? In those same moments, we might also think: "Maybe, with just a bit more redistribution, we could guarantee equal chances for the next generation of young people to become high-income earners."[61] Moments later, we worry whether such a change would undermine incentives. These tensions are ongoing in the minds of many (and I hope, most) macroeconomists and economists at large. SIM models allow a way to evaluate these tensions.

Before moving on, let me note a second caution that may be warranted. The Achilles heel of exogenously incomplete models is twofold. First, they take a very stark view of DTA incompleteness, making it almost maximal. Second, they often impose credit constraints on households. These constraints are, in turn, often motivated by the idea that borrowers lack commitment to repay debt. The problem is that, in some instances, these two features may be related in ways that conflict with each other but that are not captured. Moreover, these models will routinely fail to capture the effect of policies that change people's ability to commit credibly to repay debt, such as, for example, personal bankruptcy law.

5.12.1.7   How Incomplete Are Decentralized Trading Arrangements?

As I noted in chapter 2, the way to detect genuine market incompleteness is not immediately obvious. After all, in many instances, a lack of market-based trade in a particular commodity may only mean that there are no gains from trade, or that the particular Arrow-Debreu contingent claims that seem superficially to be missing are being well-proxied-for by a variety of other DTAs, including institutions such as the family, religious congregations, etc. So are there genuinely observable implications of an incomplete set of markets? The answer is yes, as long as we are willing to assume that households are risk-averse. In this instance, with some very minor technical apparatus, one can obtain a relatively clean result for how outcomes under complete markets should look, which then allows for a comparison with observed data, and in turn, an assessment of the presence and size of the incompleteness of DTAs. Specifically, the idea is simple: having a full set of contingent commodities available at Walrasian prices to a set of price-taking households means that these households should be "fully insured" in that, unless the income of their entire society falls or rises, their own income (or, more importantly, their consumption of goods and services) should not change. In particular, their income, net of the payments on their portfolio of Arrow-Debreu contingent commodities, should not change due to any event that is diversifiable. This means that any change in income that occurs just because a household member falls ill or loses a job will not result in a change in their take-home pay.

Early work of Cochrane (1991) and Mace (1991), and the major works of Townsend (1994) and Hayashi, Altonji, and Kotlikoff (1996), formally tested the extent to which household-level consumption varied with household-level risk. Under the presumption that households are risk-averse, a clear implication of complete Radner markets is that household-level outcomes should be disconnected from their household-level fortunes. In general, they are not.

As mentioned above, Guvenen (2012) is a useful place to see what the literature has found. A consensus reading of this work might be that short-term misfortune is well handled via a variety of market- and household-level mechanisms, while long-term misfortune, such as permanent disability, is not. When evaluating the incompleteness of DTAs, it is useful to go back to the Radner sequential-trading version of the ADM model. That model drove home the idea that an important part of market completeness is the extent to which enough markets are available at each date to arrange for income to be delivered in the amounts desired in all the contingencies that might prevail at the *next* date, and the extent to which we see spot markets for all currently traded goods.

We thus see that the Radner formulation indeed gives us a helpful taxonomy for thinking about missing markets and the reasons they are missing. Missing contingent markets in the realm of financial and insurance markets are usually the result of asymmetric information and the inability of consumers and producers to commit to behaving as promised, while missing spot markets are most likely due either to the "publicness" of a good or to deliberate policies aimed at thwarting trade or taxes that raise revenues in clumsy ways. Such a breakdown helps us to think about the right kinds of policies to deal with problems in market function.

Incomplete Markets or Limited Commitment?
Granting that markets are incomplete, one is led to the question of how they get that way. There are two routes that are not mutually exclusive. The first is that interacting parties have no problem sticking to

agreements they may enter into, but lack the ability to observe characteristics of their trading partners that might indicate they are being misled in any given transaction. This lack of transparency kills off the ability to execute mutually beneficial trades in some markets (usually those for some contingent commodities). The second route allows parties to be fully informed about each other, and thereby allows, in principle, for all Arrow-Debreu contingent claims to be available. However, this view of the world presumes that contracts are not enforceable by third parties, and as a result, one's ability to transfer purchasing power from one contingency to another might be impaired. The problem is that sorting between these two explanations is not so easy, as both have similar implications for what one might, at best, observe: household-level consumption expenditures.

An important evaluation is contained in recent work of Juan-Carlos Cordoba (2008), which suggests that limited commitment is not the central friction facing US households, while plain market incompleteness does appear promising. This is important because it implies that rather than trying to tighten contract enforceability any further, there may be gains from preventing better-informed parties to drop out of insurance arrangements. Let me stress here that the latter tendency, which we've defined earlier as "adverse selection," is emphatically something a government *can* do something about. It is a rare bright spot in the policy landscape where the powers of compulsion can be used to yield ex-ante Pareto improvements. In chapter 6, I will suggest that limited commitment and incomplete insurance markets may interact in a particularly toxic manner in the case of asset markets.

5.12.1.8   It's the IOU Markets . . .

I have repeatedly emphasized one thing: macroeconomists' bias is that the important incompleteness, i.e., the important "holes" in competitive DTAs, are overwhelmingly located in IOU markets. Spot markets are, in the main, close to competitive and close to complete. And while sometimes hampered by publicness in the goods and services traded, delivery of these objects cannot really be said to be plagued by insurmountable amounts of asymmetric information.

This point of view explains both the nature of statements one might expect to hear from a macroeconomist and where current macroeconomic research effort is located. Macroeconomists have largely stopped worrying about spot market function, and are focused instead on the key IOU markets implicitly (and sometimes explicitly) involved in (i) trade related to labor and credit, (ii) health expense and mitigation of unemployment risk, and (iii) markets that aim to provide financial security in retirement. This deemphasis on spot markets is seen in the fact that almost all models currently employed to study policy feature a single good available within a given period, except for those used narrowly in monetary policy. And even in the latter case, it is rare to allow for missing *spot* markets in immediately available goods and services. To (mis)quote the great newsman Ron Burgundy: It's the IOU markets!

5.13   The Reality of Life and Death: The Overlapping-Generations Model

Of all the features of the basic ADM and Radner models (including ones like the NGM and SGM with open-ended time) that may have led you to wonder about their usefulness, one feature may have struck you more than others: all market participants are present at the birth of the economy and share a decision-making horizon that is the same length as the life of the economy itself. In the simplest ADM model, this was implicit in the description of the market structure. There was no mention of some households arriving to the ADM marketplace (our WCH) later than other households. Instead, the Walrasian equilibrium was one where all households met in a WCH, traded, and went home. It turns out that restricting households from participating in the economy at various points in time can make an enormous difference. Relatedly, the presence of a household whose own economic planning horizon is shorter than that of the economic system can make an enormous difference as well.

Specifically, in the overlapping-generations (OG) model, households are modeled as entering the economy at various points in time and coexisting temporarily with others, many of which may have different planning horizons than they do. In most versions of the OG model, households enter the economy as "young" agents that then age. They work and earn when young, and live off any assets they are entitled to (such as Social Security) or have accumulated (such as pensions and savings). Importantly, agents are typically modeled as only caring about what happens for a finite length of time into their future (though there are exceptions whereby infinitely lived dynasties enter the model at various times).[62] As new agents keep entering the economy, there will be a mix of young and old households.

In general, agents in an OG economy will differ in their views toward all manner of public policy because the time at which taxes and benefits are paid takes on a profound importance. After all, young people may be concerned about a program that taxes them to finance expenditures on, say, the healthcare of the old. The old, for their part, may lobby for the government to borrow to finance such spending, with taxes to be levied later. Later is better for this group, so long as they do not care profoundly about their descendants' facing these higher taxes.

Interestingly, despite its apparently radical departure from the plain-vanilla ADM model in terms of when households arrive to trade, the fact that they exit and the fact that they overlap at any point in time with others of different ages allow the OG to be expressed mathematically as largely (though not exactly) an instance of the ADM model. However, this formal near-equivalence is only useful for highlighting the analytical unity of macroeconomists' approach to the subject. It is not useful for more mundane analysis, where the special demographic structure is at the center of our attention. So, as a student reading this, if you decide to do any research on long-term fiscal policy such as, for example, entitlement policy, national debt policy, or the intergenerational effects of economic growth policy, you will almost certainly work with a model in which the OG structure is specifically emphasized. If you're an economic writer, you should know that a huge share of the analyses done by macroeconomists is done in OG settings. So when an economist makes a claim about the effect of the deficit on current versus future generations, you can be fairly confident that the claim is rooted in an OG model.

If you are an economics writer, a student considering graduate school in economics, or just a concerned citizen thinking about macro-economics, the presence of the OG model has to strike you as both good and bad news. It is bad news for at least one reason: the welfare theorems are no longer guaranteed. It is good news in that it shows that macroeconomists do spend a great deal of time studying a class of economies that can have as regularities what one might view as pathology. This is a far cry from the complaints one hears about macroeconomists especially lately, when a mammoth amount of effort has gone into characterizing the properties of the typically Pareto-inefficient Walrasian equilibria of the OG model.

Fundamentally, and for purely a priori reasons, the OG model seems to merit study: for most of us, the economic system existed before we entered it, and many decisions were made by people who predated us and did not care about our interests.[63] Finally, we are not immortal, although love for our offspring may lead us to take an interest in a distant future after we are long dead. As a result, the OG model is patently more realistic than any of the other ADM models I have focused on so far; and while "demographic realism" is no guarantee of usefulness, it seems natural to allow for it, at least for some questions.

A source of the OG model's importance in macroeconomic policy-making and in the thinking of macroeconomists is that it allows one to evaluate ideas that are of obvious interest but that cannot be fruitfully dealt with in the strictly defined ADM model. For example, Nobel laureate Paul Samuelson, who is widely credited (along with Nobelist Maurice Allais) for the development of the OG model, was able to account for the presence of fiat money having value, and showed that the government's introduction of fiat money could improve the welfare of *all* generations (Samuelson 1958). Notice that this places the government in a role in which it helps facilitate trades that households would want to make, but cannot.

It is important that economists can locate conditions in the nature of the trading environment that lead people to be willing to hold an object of no intrinsic value like money. Money is a central feature of daily life in modern economies. By contrast, an implicit aspect of the ADM and Radner models is that no one needs fiat money to offer as a "medium of exchange," nor does anyone require a "store of value" to preserve purchasing power from one trading period to the next.[64] In the ADM model, households and firms are able (in ways left unspecified) to execute complex trades with each other of goods for other goods. In the Radner model, all trade either takes place in one shot (pure ADM) or takes place without the use of money (Radner). As a result of this unusual ability to generate a value for fiat money, the OG model remains important today to the entire field of monetary economics, the subfield that deals with questions related to the role of fiat money in the economy. In fact, one of the leading textbooks on the subject, that of Champ and Freeman (2001), uses the OG model throughout to shed light on a variety of issues in monetary economics.

Money is not the only thing the OG model helped shed light on. The national debt is a topic of great concern for many. In the pure ADM setting, though, as long as taxes are lump-sum, it can be shown that the *path* of taxes for a given level of spending, and hence the behavior of the deficit, is *completely irrelevant* (this is known as **Ricardian equivalence**). Of course, perhaps it is. But perhaps it isn't. Less than a decade after Samuelson's paper, the then-future Nobel laureate Peter Diamond (1965) used an OG model to illustrate beautifully that government debt, far from being either irrelevant or inevitably burdensome to the future, might, like fiat money, be beneficial for all generations. This analysis is based on a more subtle form of reasoning that is related to the inability of households to effectively transfer resources from their working years into retirement. The problem faced by households in that model is that there was only one way to save for retirement: by buying shares in the economy's firms. However, if households wanted to save very large amounts, the rate of return on savings would be depressed: after all, in such a world, firms would be able to acquire equipment for a relatively low price, as many would be happy to buy their equity offerings, if only to avoid having no income in retirement. But the problem is that the economy would then, as a whole, have to invest a great deal every period simply to maintain a large capital stock.

Diamond's 1965 paper incorporated the OG structure of households into a model of capital accumulation just like the NGM,[65] and showed that it could be an equilibrium to have a huge amount of saving being done—so much so that the entire economy could be made better off if everyone agreed to save a bit less: rates of return on savings would rise, by more than enough to allow everyone to achieve their retirement goals while saving less, and they would thus consume more in their working lives as well! In any large and anonymous economy like ours, though, "agreements to save less" are silly to contemplate—such coordination is simply impractical.

But consider next a government that issues a large stock of public debt, and agrees to maintain this stock of debt in perpetuity. Households now have an additional place to store value for retirement—i.e., they can buy government bonds (think of T-bills). As a result, interest rates will rise in the economy even if the taxes used to pay the interest on the debt were raised via lump sum taxes. This is because the government is competing with the private sector for the savings of currently alive households. Given the difficulty that households have in locating high-return assets in a world where everyone is saving furiously, the addition of public debt creates an asset whose value as a savings vehicle makes it worthwhile. The point of this example is not to convince you either that the national debt matters or that it must be beneficial; it is simply to illustrate that once generations are treated explicitly, matters involving fiscal policy, even when financed by lump sum taxes, are not so obvious.

Four decades later, the OG model continues to play a central role in macroeconomic analysis. It has become the workhorse model in analysis of intergenerational issues, particularly analyses of fiscal policies like Social Security and the effects of government entitlement programs. As for the redistribution created by government deficits, when a government decides to raise less tax revenue than it expends, it is electing to issue debt that it will pay off later. In the OG model, this may well mean that the households that are eventually taxed to repay the debt will not be the same ones that benefited from the expenditures sans taxes earlier. As a result, fiscal policy clearly can redistribute resources across generations in OG models, and it is of obvious interest to know how much redistribution will occur in a given instance.

5.13.1 Economists Get Precise about Policy, Inequality, and Intergenerational Conflict

Holding aside the search model for now, one of the things that may be fairly obvious to you after having learned about both the NGM and OG models is that policy effects, and hence prescriptions, can differ significantly. Given the disparate conclusions to which the internal logic of each model leads, a central payoff is that the economist gains clarity on the specific features of the real world that should lead him to use one and not the other to guide his thinking on a given issue. Specifically, the key difference in these two models is, quite transparently, the demographics assumed. As a result, if one takes these models seriously, one's views on deficits and the public debt, and the intergenerational consequences of taxation more generally, will hinge on (i) the strength of intergenerational linkages present, and (ii) the presence, prevalence, and tightness of constraints on borrowing and the passing of debts to one's heirs—which are a way for intertemporally disconnected generations to trade with each other. This, as I am fond of saying, is progress. A discussion between two people on various aspects of fiscal policy can be transformed into one about items (i) and (ii). Both of these topics have now received considerable attention.[66]

5.14   Concluding Remarks

By illustrating the range of environments studied by macroeconomists—and especially by showing how many of these environments are ones in which the First Welfare Theorem fails—I hope to have convinced the reader of the following things. First, I hope the reader will see the tight lineage that connects Walras to modern macroeconomics; in other words, the current models in use really are the direct descendants of a tradition that is now more than a century old. Second, macroeconomics cannot be thought of as a set of preordained conclusions. Rather, the only requirements are that new ideas be presented according to the four "Rules" described in chapter 1. Third, the reliance on rigid guidelines and boilerplate models or "narrative" construction is valuable, as it will help broaden participation in macroeconomics. Fourth, modern macroeconomics is overwhelmingly incomplete-market macroeconomics. As such, there is no presumption made that free-market outcomes are the best of all possible worlds. Fifth, I hope the reader sees that essentially every assumption made in the current battery of macroeconomic models is made not because it is believed to be literally true, but in response to particular compromises that are forced upon macroeconomists, in part by the limitations of technical tools. Ironically, therefore, recent experience clarifies that it is the technical apparatus which actually opens the door to accommodating real-world concerns in macroeconomic models. Incomplete-market and search models, for example, are certainly more "realistic" than their representative-agent counterparts, but they are correspondingly more technically demanding to analyze than the latter. In general, any "more realistic" macroeconomics I can imagine on the horizon will almost certainly place only higher technical requirements on would-be macroeconomists than is currently the case.

6   Macroeconomic Theory and Recent Events

6.1   Introduction

The financial crisis of 2007–2008 and subsequent recession have been the most wrenching economic events since the Great Depression. As of this writing, these events appear global in scope, sharply slowing the growth of North America, Europe, and even of India and China. In the end, these events have significantly hurt the prospects of more than half of the world's population. What does modern macroeconomics have to say about any of this?

In this chapter, I will give a highly selective survey of key types of models that help macroeconomists interpret the events of the crisis and the period that followed. I can afford to pick and choose topics thanks to the availability of several detailed descriptions of recent work. Among them, the accounts of contemporary, especially post-crisis macroeconomics in Blanchard (2009) and Williamson (2011) stand out. So does an interview with recent Nobel Laureate Thomas Sargent in the Minneapolis Fed's publication *The Region* (Sargent 2010). I refer the reader to these places, and to the references therein, to see the broad arc of recent mainstream research more clearly. Given both my position in a central bank and my goal of communicating the theoretical underpinnings for macroeconomists' interpretations of aggregate outcomes, I will also steer clear of commenting in any detail on specific aspects of the monetary policy response to the crisis of 2007–2008 and the subsequent period.

6.2   The Financial Crisis of 2007–2008: What Are the Questions?

My perspective is that any final judgment on the events of the crisis and recession requires being able to understand three kinds of phenomena. First, why was there such a run-up in asset prices, particularly in residential owner-occupied real estate? Second, why did we observe such a rapid fall in these prices, as well as in asset prices generally, and in economic activity? Third, why did we observe such a *sustained* reduction in overall economic activity in the period following the crisis?

I'll argue below that macroeconomists have tools that can help answer the second and third questions, and, given the developments I described in chapter 5, that these tools have improved markedly over time. These two questions are where the attention of the profession is overwhelmingly located right now. But as I describe that body of research, you will also see why such work wasn't all completed a decade or two ago; it is work that requires much more significant technical apparatus, especially computational resources, than was available earlier. This is because the work features interactions between households that not only differ in their wealth and employment status but can also buy and sell durable goods (houses), hold complex portfolios, and have access to rich financial contracts such as ARMs.

As for the first question, though, I have bad news: the ability of economists to routinely improve upon the market's assessment of asset prices, and predict movements in them, is likely to be low, and will be so for fundamental reasons having to do with what we know relative to what market participants will know. As a result, our society's best bet to forestall future disaster probably does not lie in trying to extract ever more information from financial entities and using it to manage their risk taking and balance sheets. Instead, the most productive path, though very difficult, is likely one that causes the owners of large or important financial market entities to believe that policymakers possess an ironclad commitment to *allowing them to fail and vanish.*

6.2.1 The Facts: A Crisis Reading List

While the essence of the sluggish post-crisis recovery is summarized well by a few numbers (unemployment rates, foreclosure rates, job vacancy rates, consumption, and GDP growth numbers, for example), it is helpful to have a more granular look at the facts surrounding the financial crisis of 2007–2008. Several good sources now exist for this task, with two noteworthy summaries. The Winter 2009 *Journal of*

Economic Perspectives is handy in outlining the basics of the economic landscape at the onset of the crisis. More recently, the Winter 2012 issue is an excellent resource. I also urge the reader to consult the extremely detailed interactive timeline of the financial crisis provided by the Federal Reserve Bank of St. Louis.[1]

For why the crisis occurred, insofar as we can know, the books of Acharya and Richardson (2009), Gorton (2010), and Duffie (2011) are each useful. Gorton's work is important, and its influence immense: his narrative has become, for many, the primary one. He argues that the crisis was caused by a large, old-fashioned "run" on financial institutions. And why did that happen? In Gorton's estimation, in the run-up to the crisis, a wide variety of entities constructed balance sheets that displayed the mismatch of maturities typical of banks. That is, many entities began using short-term liabilities to fund long-terms investments, and thereby lay exposed to sudden difficulties in refinancing, especially because they lacked the anti-run inoculant of deposit insurance.[2]

Duffie's work is relevant simply because he describes in clear and plain terms just how quickly and inexorably a loss in confidence in a "dealer bank" (like Bear Stearns) works to snuff it out. Duffie is an economic theorist, and is therefore reliable in his meticulous description of the steps that a dealer bank will take to forestall the departure of funds, and the various impediments to recapitalization that lie in the bank's way. Interestingly, it is these impediments that in some cases open the door for some of the policies aimed at removing the "stigma" from borrowing from the government (or at least from central banks).

A less well-known analytical history of the crisis, again by a leader in economic theory, is that of Hellwig (2010). This is a remarkable effort because it is wide-ranging and insightful about connections less typically emphasized, especially some involving the perverse effects of well-meaning accounting standards such as "mark to market." Also helpful is the survey of Brunnermeier (in the 2009 *Journal of Economic Perspectives* noted above), which describes a mechanism for asset price "death spirals" that many view as a passable description of the events at the height of the crisis in 2008.

But before you drop this book and head off to read those works, I urge you to read on for an outline of how the Radner model helps macroeconomists organize our thoughts about the crisis, and where it leaves us no better off. Understanding this is critical to understanding the tack taken in the most up-to-date work on the crisis and, especially, on the frustratingly slow recovery.

6.2.2   Radner and Financial Intermediation

For the reasons we've encountered throughout this book, macroeconomists usually want to give consumers and producers the benefit of the doubt with respect to rationality, competitiveness, and profit maximization. I've already defended the first two assumptions as well as I can. As for the third, an important reason (which I've not mentioned before) to accept profit maximization is that to *not* do so means routinely second-guessing firms' actions. While it will sometimes be clear that incumbent management at a firm is incompetent, few cases will be clear-cut. As a result, unless society wants macroeconomists playing at firm manager or CEO, our time is better spent (especially in light of the First Welfare Theorem) in constructing competitive markets where they are missing, or working on how to proxy for them.

If we accept the assertion that dysfunction in market systems occurs predominantly in what I've called IOU markets, and if we also agree that it is implausible that macroeconomists and policymakers have much room to directly improve the functioning of spot markets in private goods and services anyway, what remains for us to work on—while crucially important—is more limited. From a pure efficiency standpoint, our task is to obtain a better understanding of how to provide public goods, and how to improve the ability of households and firms to transfer purchasing power to various "contingencies," ideally to replicate outcomes that would emerge from the Radner trading arrangement.

To do this requires clarity in knowing what is missing in the real world relative to what is imagined by Radner, and why. Of course, as I have repeatedly emphasized, the mechanisms for trading objects in either the baseline ADM or the Radner model are just two of many schemes against which to compare the efficacy of decentralized trade. In the present discussion, even if we don't observe people and firms trading "Radner-contingent commodities," this doesn't mean that intertemporal trade is throttled at low levels.

In the real world there are a variety of entities whose actions and offerings facilitate, to varying degrees, the kind of trade the Radner model imagines is possible. In particular, macroeconomists think of the vast array of financial intermediaries (banks, mutual funds, insurance companies, pension funds, etc.), the vast set of observed financial assets (demand deposits, corporate debt and equity, government debt, options, swaps, and other so-called derivative contracts), and the set of nonmarket arrangements (family, friends, and community groups) as collectively representing a set of adaptations that deliver an approximation to a full set of one-period-ahead contingent claims.

In a nutshell, therefore, macroeconomists' assessments of financial market function always come back to one question: How close do observed financial arrangements (broadly defined) come, in the end, to *mimicking* the possibilities offered by the ideal, the Radner setting? If the answer is "pretty close," then we immediately know that outcomes will be close to ex-ante Pareto-efficient and that, aside from pure redistribution, policy ought not to be too involved other than in a "plumbing" role (e.g., providing legal infrastructure for contract enforcement). Recall that in chapter 5 we noted progress that had been made in answering, especially via SIM and search models, just how close the world is to a Radner economy and, more importantly, where it is far away from it (as I suggested that IOU markets would often be). Specifically, received theoretical work suggests that temporary household-level shocks are well insured while longer-term shocks are not, and received empirical work suggests the significant presence of such shocks in the data.[3]

Macroeconomists will typically proceed on the view that bilateral contracting between parties, especially between large and sophisticated financial intermediaries, results in *bilaterally* efficient outcomes. That is, when two financial intermediaries make a deal, we will usually presume that they "left no money on the table": there is no deal that generates more profits for them as a whole. Of course, one of them may have gotten a better deal than the other one, but this may simply reflect the better outside options it had relative to the other.[4]

Given the premise that private market participants are not clumsy in their deal making—or, at any rate, know more about what's good for them privately than any macroeconomist wandering into their midst—we are left with the following questions: Will such deals yield *system-wide* efficiency? In other words, does the normal course of contracting create externalities? And to what extent does policy, such as tax policy (especially that favoring debt over equity) or "bailout policy," affect both what is privately optimal and the extent to which outcomes are socially suboptimal?

This is the question that all efficiency-based interventions need to address prior to doing policy. Notice, however, that any time we see parties *not* using a system of complete Walrasian prices (or one-step-ahead Radner prices) to make decisions, there can be no presumption of system-wide efficiency. What was good for the individual parties involved might expose many others to outcomes they would not have chosen for themselves. Indeed, the use of debt in bilateral deals, especially to finance hard-to-evaluate assets, combined with the size of balance sheets at some firms, have been seen as important in driving the crisis and subsequent downturn (see, e.g., Brunnermeier 2009).

6.2.3   What (Good) Are Financial Markets, and How Does the ADM Model Influence How Macroeconomists View Them?

To evaluate the role of financial markets, remember that they are simply markets in which households and firms can buy and sell old and new IOUs from other households and firms. Famous classes of IOUs are, of course, stocks and bonds. The prices commanded by these kinds of IOUs have a clear impact on the ability of buyers and sellers to arrange to pay, or be paid, at various times and contingencies of their choosing.

For example, if a firm wants to obtain some funds today, it may do so by printing up little pieces of paper, called "bonds." It will then sell these pieces of paper to those interested in saving some resources. The bank of the buyer will debit the buyer's account and credit the seller of IOUs, who can then use these credits to buy, say, the copy machines and computers they may desire.

In chapter 1, we saw that in the ADM model, when time and uncertainty are explicitly part of the setting, the trading arrangement is truly fantastic (full Arrow-Debreu contingent-claims markets at "time 0"). This is the absolute apex for a financial system, because it will yield Pareto efficiency. But recall the doubt I cast that a full set of Arrow-Debreu markets is even remotely workable. Thus, it makes sense to ask first about the nature of financial entities that one observes in the landscape, and then ask: Could these be standing in, and efficiently at that, for a bunch of Arrow-Debreu markets?

The sequential trading of certain financial arrangements in the real world is almost certainly properly viewed as doing the work of a cluster of Arrow-Debreu markets. Examples include long-term insurance contracts, some employment contracts, and clever packages of financial assets, especially those including options. A full discussion of this question would take us beyond what this book is capable of delivering usefully; the interested reader is directed to the rich variety of texts in household consumer theory, and "corporate finance."[5] Sequential trading, however, brings the *beliefs* of participants regarding the resale value of securities to center court, and takes us back to Question 1: Why did asset prices rise the way they did?

6.3 Models for Question 1: Why Did Asset Prices Rise So Much?

As any of the references above will show, housing prices nationwide rose at a high rate for nearly a decade, and rose in a manner that was unprecedented in its scope (see, e.g., Gerardi, Foote, and Willen 2011). In previous episodes, such as in Texas, California, and New England in the 1980s, price gains had been more localized. Equity prices more generally boomed as well. All looked good. The data that came in on housing showed both prices and quantities rising together: house price indices rising, and more houses being built and sold. For economists, this type of data immediately suggests a "shift in demand" in the face of a standard "upward sloping supply curve." This is one setting in which, if households were suddenly more interested in houses, more houses would be built and prices would rise.

6.3.1 Demand and Supply

So the next question is: Why might demand for owner-occupied housing have increased? Here, economists and observers alike could point to historically low interest rates in the wake of the 2000–2001 recession. (The interest rates were partly the result of deliberate policies, but partly due to global demand for safe assets like US Treasuries and other debt.) At the same time, what were believed to be better screening of credit risks via automated credit bureaus and more powerful statistical approaches to predicting default both allowed loans to be approved for more households that had previously been marginalized.[6]

However, what might have been a more central factor in individuals' decisions to buy was the prospect of rising housing prices. Borrowers would have responded to rosy beliefs by asking for more home loans. After all, debt is a great thing to use when you expect that what you buy with it might get more valuable. In fact, this is debts' defining characteristic: it provides the borrower with all the upside gains, while protecting lenders (outside of bankruptcy) by giving them a claim to a constant flow of payments.

Any lender holding the view that housing prices would continue to rise, even if only in the near term, would perceive protection against default: home loans were collateralized, after all, so rising home prices would simply act as a force that made more individual borrowers more credible in their promises to repay debts. Why would anyone default if their house is worth more than the mortgage against it?

While innovations and optimism worked together to make buying, lending, and building more attractive, we know from basic microeconomics that such shifts in demand needn't change prices—if the supply curve is rather flat. Yet in this case, it was not obvious that it was flat. Observers noted that developers could not build anywhere they desired; local regulations such as permitting processes and land use restrictions kept nonhousing land from being converted immediately to new development (see, e.g., Glaeser, Gyourko, and Saiz 2008). Basic principles then suggest that any given changes in credit supply, to the extent that it increases the demand for owner-occupied housing, will itself translate into a higher price. In recent work, Favilukis, Ludvigson, and van Nieuwerburgh (2010) suggest that the expansion in credit can indeed account for a substantial proportion of increased housing prices.

I've referred to broad forces such as low interest rates, world demand for safe assets, improvements in credit scoring, and building restrictions, because the discussion of these forces was what allowed prices to rise without obviously suggesting to the median market participant or outside observer (like economists) that prices were rising for "no reason." We could find reasons for the increase that were consistent—qualitatively, anyway—with what we observed. In such an environment, it would not have been trivial for anyone to baldly assert that prices were "wrong" and be sure that their statement was correct. As to just how much consensus there was leading up the fall, the interested reader is directed to Gerardi, Foote, and Willen (2011). The answer: it was not overwhelming.

One point worth noting is that almost all recent quantitative models of housing are SIM models (e.g., Chambers, Garriga, and Schlagenhauf 2009; Jeske, Krueger, and Mitman 2011; Karahan and Rhee 2012). This is so whether the question is to study the role played by various factors in driving the price of housing up and then down, the distributional implications of housing finance policy (the GSEs especially), or the role of foreclosure policy. Some of these models place impediments in the way of consumer credit (credit cards), others in mortgage markets, and yet others in both markets. The key departures in these SIM models from the ADM model—and from the Radner model in particular—are in the structure they imagine for *financial markets*.

6.3.2   Principal-Agent Conflicts

Observers have noted that one exacerbating factor of the housing crisis is that lenders may have lowered their standards dramatically over time, making loans to increasingly risky classes of borrowers as the run-up continued. This trend is consistent with an optimistic view for house prices, as we've already seen: a given mortgage borrower is genuinely less risky when house prices are rising. At the same time, many other financial entities may have seen the assets created by the new loans as good ones to hold, allowing lending to proceed cheaply.

But there is another possibility that may have been at work concurrently. On the "supply side" of financial assets was the role played by within-firm incentives to encourage issuance and approval of loans, and the securitization and subsequent sale of these loans. On the "demand side" was the desire of banks and other entities to buy the assets created by lenders or their subsidiaries (e.g., SIVs and CDOs), and the desire of others to provide insurance to the holders of such "asset-backed securities" (ABS).

These incentives, in turn, came most directly from the firms' decisions to reward certain activities and penalize others, such as those created by compensation schemes. Moreover, most incorporated entities, especially large ones, display what economists refer to as the "separation of ownership and control"—that is, large corporations are almost always managed on a day-to-day basis not by shareholders but by a manager who reports to them (or more accurately, usually to a board of directors who represent shareholders) and is instructed to act in particular ways. The contractual structures that owners choose for management usually try, with varying degrees of success, to deal with asymmetries in information between the two parties.

These informational asymmetries between owners and managers are potentially important for anyone trying to evaluate the performance of a decentralized economic system. The ADM or Radner models give us one reason why: even granting market completeness, the efficiency of decentralized market outcomes hinges on firms choosing profit-maximizing plans. Among other things, such considerations will provide for the continued survival of the firm itself. As a result, firm-level risk taking is assumed in the ADM model to be that which is consistent with the maximization of profits. But once the operators and decision makers at firms can take actions not easily seen by the owners, there is no reason to be sanguine that the level of risk taking is consistent with profit maximization.

What does modern economics have to tell us about how contracts for the operators of firms will be structured? Fundamentally, there is tension between getting a manager to make choices that maximize expected profits and compensating them for bearing the risk that comes with them. This is known in economics as the **principal-agent or P/A problem**, where the **principal** is the party looking to achieve an outcome, and the **agent** is the party engaged by the principal to do so.

The P/A problem has received enormous attention from economists, beginning in the 1970s with the seminal works of Ross (1977) and Holmstrom (1979), followed by the hugely influential paper of Grossman and Hart (1983). In the admittedly narrow context of a one-shot interaction between the two parties, economists have provided a relatively complete characterization of the nature of an optimal contract and its dependence on the underlying informational structure. Recent work has enriched this problem to include many variations. Examples include cases where a principal must provide incentives to many agents (important for thinking about the macroeconomics of the government regulating many firms simultaneously, for example), and more recently where the principal and agent interact repeatedly over time (the so-called case of **repeated moral hazard**). Like the work on limited enforcement mentioned earlier, this work is a special instance of a larger class of mechanism design problems.

For macroeconomists, particularly those evaluating policy toward financial intermediaries such as regulated banks, the P/A problem under repeated moral hazard is of central importance. For example, in the aftermath of the recent financial crisis of 2007–2008 efforts are under way to substantially beef up various regulatory measures. Economists' understanding of the P/A problem is central to their assessment of the likely impact of many of these policy proposals, especially those aimed at requiring more equity finance by intermediaries, and those seeking to limit executive compensation. The P/A literature tackles specific questions such as: How should a firm structure the pay packages of its executives? How does the answer depend on the kind of risks and opportunities for hiding effort or outcomes that are relevant in that business? How should a bank regulator set the rules of engagement with banks, on which it must depend for information?

While it is premature to make statements about the exact role that such conflicts played in asset prices, the research efforts around understanding the P/A problem are a great example of how rarefied economic theory meets the messy real world. In the course of making the practical inquiries of the P/A literature, economists employ some fairly sophisticated tools from game theory and so-called dynamic optimization. This is both a positive and a negative development. It is unambiguously positive in the sense that it allows the economist to make precise statements about the relationship between the underlying fundamental economic problem and the "solution" to that problem. It is somewhat negative in the sense that one must have faith in the extraordinarily sophisticated kinds of reasoning that (especially) game-theoretic constructions ask for.

6.3.3 Financial Markets and the Importance of Beliefs

Should borrowers and lenders have had such views on house prices, say, circa 2005? For economists, especially, it is hard to say, and moreover, we think we know why it *will always be* hard to say. As Quiggin (2010) suggests, we are so loath to second-guess prices that we don't recognize a bubble until it blows up in our faces. We'll return to this point.

In any setting where time and uncertainty play a role, beliefs are central to *every* question of interest to macroeconomists. Beliefs loom larger in financial markets than elsewhere, for a good reason: you can't eat a financial asset, and you can't live in it. What it gets you depends on what others think it is worth. So beliefs are paramount. But in many settings, especially when things are changing rapidly in novel ways, forming expectations is tricky. Rational expectations, while essential to disciplining economists, may be pushed too far when decision makers are in uncharted territory.

Some spectacular pathologies can erupt under asymmetric information: moral hazard and adverse selection can each stunt trade in damaging ways. Whether they will or not is a much more subtle question. I raise this distinction between the possible and the probable because they often differ: many markets function well, every single day, even though parties are initially informed differentially about, say, the quality of a product. A variety of mechanisms can restore a DTA's ability to produce and allocate goods and services efficiently or near efficiently in the face of such potential impediments. Warranties and reputations, for example, loom large in the markets for many durable products where the quality is otherwise hard to discern for the non-specialist. I have no idea if my air conditioner's troubles are caused by what a mechanic might tell me they are, and yet I suspect that I am not perpetually being cheated, partly because I know that the post-purchase asymmetry of information makes it useful for new air conditioners to compete along the dimensions of durability and quality.

But we can see easily that in situations of asymmetric information, participants' beliefs about others can matter. To take an extreme example, let's say employers view all people who complete college as special "high-productivity" workers, and all those who do not as low-productivity workers. As a result, employers will offer poor pay to the latter relative to the former. And suppose that, as a result, all those who are high-productivity workers indeed find it best to complete college, while all low-productivity workers decide the extra education isn't worth it (maybe they figure they'll fail, for example). In this world, the firms will never be disproved in their views about the relationship between education and worker productivity. Worse yet, this scenario can occur even when education is utterly useless.

In chapter 4, we saw that in the Breeden-Lucas model, trade was useless simply because traders were identical. But trade can also fail to occur when it would be useful. The basic problem is the idea that "I don't want to buy anything you want to sell me, because you might know more than I do, and might be trying take advantage of me." The most significant examples of this, in the context of financial markets, are the so-called no-trade theorems, most famously that of Milgrom and Stokey (1982). Of course, none of this suggests that a policymaker can do better, and so we may be stuck.

6.3.4 Differences of Opinion

Given the role of beliefs in both creating gains from trade and hampering it, to what extent can they differ in modern macroeconomic models? Can our models, especially in the presence of rational expectations, tolerate sustained differences of opinion? After all, prolonged differences of opinion about various facets of the world certainly seem to exist around us. And here, the critics of modern macro may be onto something: macroeconomists' insistence on imposing rationality of agents can indeed limit just how much market participants can sensibly disagree.

A baby step would be to pose the main question above in the time-0 trading environment of Arrow-Debreu. In that model, there is nothing to prevent people from holding rather different views on the relative likelihood of various future events. Such heterogeneity does no damage to the existence of equilibrium or the welfare theorems. To repeat, the ADM model fully accommodates the idea that people might hold vastly differing views about the future, and teaches us that when they are allowed to trade on the basis of these differences, they are able to arrange their date- and state-contingent consumption in a way that leaves no gains from future trade—outcomes are Pareto-efficient.

The fundamental reason that these differences are irrelevant to the normative properties of outcomes is that differing views on the probabilities of outcomes are essentially a property of household preferences—which we surely must allow to differ. The ADM model, of course, does allow preferences to differ wildly, and the First Welfare Theorem nowhere requires anything at all about preferences beyond the local nonsatiation we introduced in chapter 2.

However, what rational expectations asks for is more demanding. It does not permit us to hold differing views forever. It forces us to learn over time. Of course, to the extent that each of us starts our trading life with differing views about the future, we may change those views over time in response to the flows of events around us, and in the interim, we may disagree with each other. These differences may, in turn, lead to trade. As they say, differences of opinion make a horse race: a portion of asset trading will then be due simply to parties having different views of the future. The extent to which such differences can persist is a very tricky issue. After all, people's beliefs about others' beliefs, and their beliefs about others' beliefs about their beliefs, and so on, may all be relevant to the deals they offer and accept. As a result, this is an area of deep and thorny questions, usually involving the problem of "forecasting the forecasts of others." (A seminal early effort here is that of Townsend 1983.)

As mentioned very early on, in the landmark studies of Grossman (1989) and Stiglitz (1994), among others, on the informational role of prices, there was certainly a sense in which differences of opinion could simply not be sustained: prices would reveal information that was initially privately held. In the late 1980s and 1990s, as part of the wave of work on market microstructure I noted early on (see Biais, Glosten, and Spatt 2005, or the textbook of O'Hara 1995, for an introduction), a sequence of influential papers arrived that gave differences of opinion a chance to persist. One classic effort was that of Glosten and Milgrom (1985). These authors took a step that could be interpreted as a departure from the universal rationality of model inhabitants: they allowed for a share of households to trade mechanically, and called them **noise traders.** Such traders would simply buy and sell at random, and so would seem to exert a fundamentally muddying influence on observed transactions. Yet a pervasive result in this research program has been that, over time, disagreements often eventually yield to make way for prices that are informative about the true fundamentals in the economy.

Noise traders needn't be seen as idiots: the random trading that these agents engage in can be viewed as a shorthand way of modeling other reasons for them to buy and sell assets. Imagine that they find and lose jobs in a search and matching process, and participate in asset markets according to what they're experiencing. All that the modeling economist might see is trades that "look random." A useful implication, then, is the following: the result that prices embody lots of information may well apply to incomplete-market settings as well.

In a nutshell, then, in many models, rational expectations cuts a Gordian knot by assuming a shared forecast given shared information, but this is clearly a simplification that does not always adequately capture the rich disagreements and disparities in information that exist in our world. Nevertheless, differences of opinion do *not* mean predictable variation in asset prices (beyond the different rates of average appreciation in prices needed to reward the owners of riskier assets). That is, you and I might disagree about the future, but if stock prices had a predictable "excess return" (above what was needed to compensate for risk), then we could each make a killing by buying or selling the asset, depending on how risky we viewed the asset. In the end, this is why the basic "random walk" view of stock prices, in which day-to-day changes in stock prices look unpredictable, is such a robust finding (see, e.g., LeRoy 1989 for an excellent review of this and related classical findings in asset pricing). More on this shortly.[7]

6.3.5 Bubble Detection

If beliefs matter and can differ, then we may well have differences of opinion in the marketplace. The national conversation on the financial crisis has focused on these differences, especially in determining the extent to which there should have been more consensus that some asset prices were "too high." The spectacular increase, then fall, in residential real estate prices raised for most of us the question of whether the initial run-up constituted a "bubble."

Unfortunately, modern macroeconomics tells us that it is difficult to say yes or no, and it will remain difficult. That is because an implication of rational expectations is that predicating the future on improved real-time bubble detection is even more than a risky bet—it is a bet one is almost certain to lose. Market economies with even a few intelligent agents will make it hard, most of the time, for there to be situations in which we *all* agree that assets are overvalued.

Instead, periods of rising asset prices, if they are indeed bubbles, will by definition indicate an absence of the kind of consensus needed to forestall them. As a result, policymakers will be left then, as in the past, with the task of deciding to what extent "fundamentals" justify the current realizations of asset prices. And in this task, they must weigh their expertise against that of people with skin in the game. On the question of what happened to the skin that many did have in the game: throughout the discussion of bailouts and too-big-to-fail, it must not be forgotten that the equity shares in many firms lost all their value. In turn, those who owned them suffered losses, and yet they would have had to consider the possibility of these losses when they bought the assets.

6.3.5.1   What "Efficient Financial Markets" Means (Hint: It Does *Not* Mean Pareto Efficiency)

In discussions of beliefs about future asset prices, the idea that "asset markets are efficient" comes up so often that it has been given a name: the **efficient markets hypothesis (EMH)**. It is important to know what this term means, because it is so unfortunately named, given the vastly more important but similarly named notion of Pareto efficiency.

Every day I commute on a highway that has a tollbooth. As I approach the booth, it is a rare day that one lane is far different in length than any other. Of course, sometimes I just happen on a short line. But on most days, if I had to guess before I got to see the toll plaza, I would not be able to guess which lane would eventually turn out to be fastest.

Now, what if the city of Richmond—where I work—saw fit for some strange reason to give mandatory dental exams (and charge for them), to all who rolled into the tollbooth. Think of the disaster that would follow. It would certainly not be Pareto-efficient relative to a world in which everyone went to the dentist on their own time, instead of clog-ging lanes at rush hour. And yet, in this horribly Pareto-inefficient scenario, all lines would still be roughly the same length (though maybe longer now), and outcomes would be informationally efficient. There would be no way to routinely pick a "quicker lane."

Another example, also involving traffic flow, is more vexing for me to recount, mainly because it happened to me. Recently, I received a

$60 ticket from the city of Richmond. Why? Because as I drove to a restaurant, I noticed a string of empty parking spaces right next to the hip area in which I was going to eat. I parked, *fed the meter*, and went to eat. When I came out, I saw the dreaded green envelope on my windshield. It turns out that you are not allowed to park there at the time I did. The "market" had already figured this out: this is why all the spots in a busy part of town were empty. I refused to take the hint, and I paid for it.

The lessons of these microeconomic examples translate directly to macroeconomic situations. In asset markets, where the EMH is most frequently discussed, it captures the central idea that asset prices impound all information relevant to the pricing of an asset. And the EMH asserts that this will be true irrespective of how close to, or far away from, Pareto efficiency a given economy is. So, for example, in a world where market participants anticipate a highly distortionary tax change that will have implications for the profitability of existing firms, the EMH asserts that the price of the asset now includes an assessment of the likelihood of the tax change. Of course, there should be no presumption at all that a world in which such a tax change might happen will be one where allocations are Pareto-efficient. In fact, it seems rather unlikely that it will. And yet it can still be perfectly true that the current price of the asset represents the best available assessment of the discounted future profits of the firms that would be affected by the tax change.

6.3.5.2   The EMH and "Random Walks"

The EMH is also connected to the idea that changes in asset prices are unpredictable across time increments. This result is driven by the same forces that make the lines at tollbooths similar. If an asset price was known to be going up shortly (with certainty, say), then it would have to go up now—because if it did not, anyone buying it now would make a guaranteed profit for no risk at all. (Major investment banks did not become important by passing up such opportunities.) As a result, the hypothesis predicts that the average change in price is *zero*. This immediately implies that the best guess about prices at the next instant in time, or the next day, etc., is . . . the current price. A path for prices that obeys this law of motion is known as a **random walk**. Knowing prices before today is not useful. Aside from some special cases, this is an implication of asset prices that has, over the past five decades, received an incredible amount of support. In a way, how could it be otherwise?

Now, there is a useful qualification to the "pure random walk" prediction for informationally efficient stock markets. If one asset is very risky compared to another, then the random walk prediction means that the expected appreciation in prices—which determines the return I get from holding it—is zero! Why would I hold it instead of a T-bill? I wouldn't. So what gives? The answer is that over extremely short increments of time—say, minutes—where time and risk are negligible, the pure random walk idea works well. Over longer periods—say, a month or a year—investors need compensation for bearing risk and waiting for payoffs. In these instances, the EMH tells us that risky assets must have a predictable component of average growth to induce people to hold them. This leads to the prediction of a so-called **random walk with drift**. "Drift" refers to the average appreciation in the price of the asset needed to generate a rate of return that makes investors willing to hold the asset. The seminal Breeden-Lucas model taught economists the general way in which these adjustments would depend on the characteristics of households that bought assets. (This is part of the reason that, despite its stylized nature, it is taught to every new cohort in just about every major graduate program in economics.) To sum up: the EMH asserts that changes in asset prices are "unpredictable when adjusted for risk and time."

6.4   Models for Question 2: Why Did Initial Changes Get Amplified?

Starting in early 2007, once house prices had been dropping (beginning in mid-2006) for a short time, financial distress across households and financial entities seemed to accelerate markedly. I will leave it to the sources listed earlier to review the narrow analyses of this question in the context of this crisis, and will focus on a more general aspect that will likely inform future policymaking.

By all accounts, an essential ingredient in the process was debt. Debt is very special, in the sense that the failure to pay as promised triggers reorganization and often liquidation of a firm. This in turn can place pressure on the prices of the types of assets that are sold. As a result, drops in these prices can lead to other firms facing difficulties with their solvency, and can raise the risk that they will become unable to repay creditors and will themselves face liquidation, and so on. When

the assets of the liquidated firm are opaque, as is often the case for
financial firms especially (since they specialize in nonstandard loans
that more anonymous capital markets do not deal in), they may sell for
little, again forcing others holding similar kinds of assets to devalue
their holdings of them (Brunnermeier 2009 and Hellwig 2010 are excellent sources here). This is in part because of the possibility of adverse
selection. Potential buyers of a distressed firm will worry that they're
being sold the worst part of the firm's portfolio. Given this belief
(again, notice how beliefs can shape reality), they will offer low prices
for such assets, which only intensifies the distressed firm's desire to
unload the worst asset first. Relatedly, when creditors are organized in
chains (A owes B and B owes C, and so on) but cannot so easily net out
obligations, then distress can propagate itself. This idea is developed
in the seminal work of Kiyotaki and Moore (1997). My summary is
crudely drawn, to be sure, but is still a reasonably accurate description
of the kinds of amplifying mechanisms we think were at work during
the height of the crisis: debt, large-firm liquidation, opacity, adverse
selection, absence of netting arrangements, and spillovers in prices
across asset classes.

To see why debt is central to the narrative, think of an alternative
world in which all firms financed themselves via equity issuance. In
this instance, firms have no creditors, only owners. There is no question
of liquidation and hurried sales of assets to satisfy creditors. There is
no question of bankruptcy. There is no question of a "run" by lenders,
and there is no question of spillovers from "fire sales" pushing
down the value of similar assets held by others elsewhere. This seems
a safer world to live in, we can probably agree. In fact, it is generally
believed that the equity-intensive nature of financing during the tech
boom was an important reason that the drastic fall in equity prices
during the 2000 "tech bust" had such minimal implications for Main
Street.

So the question you must be asking yourself now is: If debt is so
bad, and equity so good, why don't we as a society restrict debt much
more severely? Answering this requires a story showing the benefits
that debt confers on its users. We need a theory of debt.

6.4.1   Debt

One of the seminal models of conflict between the operator and finan-
cier of a project is provided in the path-breaking paper of Robert
Townsend (1979), which asked a disarming question: Why is there

debt? Debt is a predominant form of contract used by firms and house-holds to obtain resources from others. It is probably the most familiar to you simply because, as a private citizen, it is virtually the only kind of contract you've ever thought you could use to get more resources into your bank account today. Why isn't the contract a bit more complex and nuanced? Why, for example, when you want to enroll in college, do you never hear of anyone telling a bank that he'd like some money now, and in return, he'll give them a share in his future earnings? Or why, if you are a firm, do you decide that the best way to acquire funds is to obligate yourself to pay a constant amount at some point in the future *no matter* how business is going? Doesn't this seem risky? Why risk having creditors seize your factory and sell it off just to get them-selves paid?

In what is among the most celebrated papers of the past quarter-century, Townsend (1979) gave an answer that the profession found persuasive. Townsend first asks us to imagine the problem of a firm looking for resources, but, vitally, he considers a setting in which the firm is unable to costlessly communicate the outcome of the investment project. Instead, if an investor wants to know how the firm is doing, she has to retain an accounting firm to go through the books. In other words, she has to audit the firm. Townsend calls this feature **costly state verification** (CSV). He goes on to show that the best possible contract between these two parties will resemble debt: a constant payment due from the borrower that, if made, does not lead to any costly audit or liquidation of the business, and a set of realizations of the project in which the borrower does not make this payment, is then "audited," and sees his project liquidated (one can interpret this part as bank-ruptcy). Economists now had a theory of debt—one that even now is a workhorse.[8]

Why is the constant payment that is so characteristic of debt a feature of the contract? That is, in the cases in which the borrower makes the promised payment and thereby avoids costly auditing, why does the contract require constant repayment? The revelation principle gives us the answer. Since we know that any optimal arrangement between the lender and borrower must be consistent with having come from a direct-revelation mechanism in which truth telling is a (Nash) outcome, we know that *only* constant repayment in the no-audit zone would give the borrower no incentives to lie. If, for example, two real-izations of the project's output required, by contract, two different repayment levels, neither of which was accompanied by an audit, then a borrower would simply announce the realization that obligated him to repay less.

Having seen that debt can be a useful private contract to overcome informational problems that lead to incentive problems, we should note that it's a contract that doesn't resemble what an ADM firm would pay. After all, in the ADM setting, there was a per unit price for all inputs, and no clear connection of output to compensation the way we see employees of all kinds often paid. Debt certainly does not seem like a pure ADM object.

The immediate question is, then, whether there is any reason to think that such a world will yield efficient outcomes. Absolutely not. As I noted above, the theme in recent work on the crisis is that the debt contracts, which may have served each user well, are precisely what fostered spillovers in the crisis when distressed firms, especially larger ones like Lehman Brothers, were liquidated. A good deal of macroeconomic work on the crisis aims to clarify how privately optimal arrangements, particularly debt, can create ex-ante and ex-post inefficiency.

Now recall the Second Welfare Theorem, which told us that anything efficient looked as if there were a set of linear Walrasian prices at which all parties chose their optimal action. But the presence in the economy of complex incentive contracts for many employees, and between firms, suggests that labor markets and others may routinely feature nonlinear prices. Upon seeing these arrangements in practice, we can conclude that real-world outcomes are unlikely, barring some weirdly offsetting effects, to be fully Pareto-efficient.

But are they efficient relative to the more reasonable standard that they are "best" given the array of private-level incentive problems faced by producers in an economy? There can be no general presumption, and as we have seen, to the extent that incentive problems prevent certain markets from existing altogether, Walrasian outcomes are guaranteed to be inefficient even by this weaker standard. Here again, a huge amount of work in modern macroeconomics is about studying the size of departures from efficiency—both the general and the less demanding kinds—in models that quantitatively capture salient features of the US and other economies.

6.4.2   Models of Banks and Bank Runs

As noted, a prominent view of the most intense part of the crisis is that it was predominantly about "runs on the shadow banking system." So you might ask: Might we be better off without banks? One of the most widely cited papers of the past generation, that of Diamond and Dybvig (1983), suggests that the answer is probably no. Diamond and Dybvig (DD) showed, much as Townsend did for debt, that banking could be understood as an optimal trading arrangement in the presence of households that face otherwise uninsurable risks, and for firms that had access to long-gestation investment projects. The issuance by a DD bank of a short-term demandable deposit, and its investment in longer-term projects, is known as "maturity transformation" and is, narrowly, useful to all concerned.

To the extent that these features describe the problems facing important portions of an economy's inhabitants, the DD model suggests that one might expect to see banks operating. An important aspect of the DD model is that it has (at least) two Nash equilibria. In the "good" equilibrium, no one makes a run on the bank, and everyone who needs their funds prior to project gestation will be able to get them. In the "bad" equilibrium, a self-fulfilling attack of pessimism leads all households, including those with no inherent need for funding, to ask for their deposits back. The bank cannot oblige, and is forced to liquidate projects that, if left alone, could have paid an amount that would have made everyone better off.

The DD model is to banking and financial economics what the SGM is to the rest of macroeconomics: the starting point, almost always, almost everywhere. Because its bad equilibrium is self-fulfilling, policymakers (even before they had the formalization) understood that deposit insurance might well solve the problem: it would make self-fulfilling runs decidedly irrational phenomena. And the success of this policy, at least in preventing bank runs since the depression, is both remarkable and a quiet reminder that rationality may well be a good descriptor of much decision making. After all, if irrationality were king, why would deposit insurance seem so effective in putting an end to bank runs?

An unfortunate side effect of the introduction of deposit insurance is that it creates a principal-agent problem. Namely, if depositors do not care about the health of a bank (and why would they, if they are insured?), then they will fund its activities irrespective of the ownership stake held by the current management. This can create tremendous difficulty in bad macroeconomic times. The savings and loan crisis of the late 1980s, followed by the recent recession, drove many banks and S&Ls to the brink of worthlessness, setting up a toxic dynamic where the very thing that was supposed to render banking safe made the rest of society far less so. Specifically, a poorly capitalized bank now could hang a sign offering to pay high interest rates on deposits. Households would rationally move their money to the bank to take advantage of something that was perfectly safe, due to deposit insurance, and yet offered a high rate of return. The bank, for its part, could then use the funds to try to "gamble for resurrection" by picking long-shot projects which, if they succeeded, would enrich the owners and if they failed would leave them hardly worse off. This irresistible setup has led in the past to great damage and misallocation of resources. For this reason, deposit insurance, while crucial to any firm that looks like a DD firm, needs oversight. It is why all modern societies at least try to regulate banks.

At this point, the Diamond-Dybvig model may seem to definitively resolve the question of whether fractional-reserve banking systems are inherently unstable. But don't jump to this conclusion. Subsequent analysis of Diamond-Dyvbig-like trading environments has revealed that the instability observed is hardly inherent and, in fact, may depend on some very specific aspects of that model—aspects that may have few analogs in the "real world." The most definitive work on this topic is Ennis and Keister (2009). The reader will discover just how subtle is the interplay between the rules employed by the bank, the policy of the regulatory authority, and the beliefs of depositors. This is hard theoretical material, but it is essential and practical.

In a nutshell, the view of the crisis as a "run" suggests that the fundamental policy question for regulators and society is: What should bank*ing* policy be? where the *-ing* refers to the entire set of activities that look banklike, especially in terms of featuring balance sheets that do maturity transformation.

6.5   Models for Question 3: Why Has the Recovery Been So Slow?

Of the many distressing aspects of the troubles that began more than five years ago, the sluggishness of employment growth has been most central. Output growth has also been exceedingly slow to return to its original pre-crisis path. As of this writing, the growth rate has simply not returned to the pre-crisis average of 2% per capita annually; and worse, this follows a period of extremely sluggish growth. As a result, there has been essentially no making up of the ground lost in the recession, leading some economists to wonder if the crisis will leave the US permanently scarred, with all future cohorts facing a new, permanently lower level and growth rates of output than they would have experienced had the crisis not hit. From chapter 5 we know that this can matter hugely for welfare—it is a lot of relinquished output. As a result, it is vital to understand why labor markets seem not to allow for all mutually beneficial worker-firm transactions, as well as how this failure relates to credit markets. The following section describes some recent work on these ideas.

6.5.1 Labor and Asset Market Search Models

Anyone who finds commenting on business cycles irresistible as a career or pastime owes his livelihood to the nasty way that labor markets assign hours to people. To see this, consider a recession in which the unemployment rate rises from 5% to 15% in an economy with 100 million households (approximately the number in the US in recent times). Let's assume this jump in unemployment lowered the total number of hours worked by about the same as well: 10 percentage points. Do you think the national conversation would be as urgent if, instead of 10 million households finding no work at all, all of us just worked four hours less per week? That would lead to a 10-percentage-point drop in total hours, just as we saw. That is, what if the most severe recession in the past 70 years was one in which we all were asked to take Friday afternoon off? To me, this would not be a social disaster. Thus, the "all or nothing" set of work opportunities available to most people in the short run is the key to the relevance of nearly all writing about the economy that currently fills the pages of newspapers, magazines, and macroeconomics journals.

Moreover, there is reason to suspect that the example I've given is a *conservative* estimate of the centrality of labor markets. Smooth, pro-rata reductions in hours would seem far less likely to lead to big recessions in the first place. Mortgage default, foreclosures, and other brutal events (which often have additional secondary effects) would also not have been so quick to follow events in the labor market. You could probably still make a mortgage payment on 10% less income than you earn now, after all. Banks, in turn, would not see their capital erode from loans gone sour and would not initiate a credit crunch; and on the investment banking front, asset-backed securities would still be usable as collateral in the repurchase or "repo" transactions that many financial entities find useful.

It is important to acknowledge these points because we must not be distracted, or worse, lured into thinking that a topic has relevance because it's all people are talking about. There is a limit to how much anyone should talk about phenomena X or Y (say, austerity or some aspect of monetary policy) when the central reason that such policies even matter is some other force, Z (labor markets). At some point, the elephant in the room is what needs to be discussed.[9] A corollary might be this: we should probably view policy measures not aimed directly at labor markets as being premised on the idea that effecting change in labor markets is just too difficult (primarily because it is not well enough understood), and so aiming lower and twisting other knobs, such as those involving monetary and fiscal policy, may be the best we can do. Note carefully, lest there be any confusion, that I am *not* saying that research unrelated to the labor market is useless for understanding business cycles. I am talking about the reason it *is* important, namely the way labor markets work. In the main, working macroeconomists get this.

A great deal of recent attention has been paid to the role of search processes in failing to allow households opportunities to work, and the severe consequences such outcomes have not only on their short-term well-being but also on their longer-term prospects (in and out of the labor market). One strand of research relevant to the sluggishness of the recovery argues that workers lack the skills that firms are looking for, and that this "mismatch" is central to the slow reduction in unemployment. Sahin et al. (2011) is a start in measuring this force.

Interestingly, search models can offer useful interpretations of events outside labor markets. The spells of "illiquidity" documented in the recent crisis, where parties suddenly could not find sellers willing to part with safe assets (such as Treasury bills), are now being explored with models that bear substantial formal similarity to models of labor market search. More recently, a program of research modeling both labor and asset markets as "search" markets is under way. More often now, models allow for parties to be differentially well-informed, which opens the door to further market dysfunction via adverse selection.[10] If nothing else, this should drive home the unity of macroeconomics in the way it explores causes and remedies for bad macroeconomic outcomes.

6.6 Macroeconomics and the Financial Crisis of 2007–2008 Implications for Policy

The many pathologies one might encounter in financial markets naturally make us wonder to what extent matters could be improved through smart policy choices. Given the short time period that has passed since the recent crisis, it is probably premature to offer definitive diagnoses, and almost certainly too early to suggest definitive cures. But since everyone else is doing it, I will highlight some problems I see facing any well-meaning policymaker.[11]

6.6.1 (Try to End) "Too Big to Fail"

If we take the EMH at face value, and accept that we live in a world where (suitably adjusted) changes in asset prices are more or less random walks, then we are left with the questions of what to do during a crisis, what to do after it, and how to influence the size and balance sheet composition of firms, especially financial-services firms, in a way that limits the collateral damage that their liquidation would generate. One could do the last at the outset, of course, but one might also try to do so at the "end," when a firm is rendered insolvent and about to be liquidated.

Before the crisis, some firms became so large and interconnected that market participants and policymakers viewed them as "too big to fail" (TBTF) when the crisis occurred. There are two types of measures to prevent TBTF that we might consider.

First, before a crisis regulators can limit the kinds of risk that regulated entities can take, but they cannot do so for those beyond their ambit. One solution is to expand the reach of regulation via blanket regulation: if it looks like a bank and acts like a bank, regulate it as if it is one. Give it the anti-run protection of deposit insurance or, better yet, make firms' and households' balance sheets selectively less leveraged. A common suggestion is to force firms (especially financial ones) to use liabilities that "convert to equity" in distress scenarios with instruments that are called "contingent capital" (CoCo) or "convertible debt." This way, liquidation can be avoided and those firms that were creditors at the outset lose for sure, as regulators will not face the prospect of a messy bankruptcy if they allow failure.

Of course, one shouldn't get too excited here: we know of no reason to think that CoCo, for example, is the best contract to deal with asymmetric information problems that exist between the providers and users of funds. In fact, Townsend (1979), Gale and Hellwig (1985), and Williamson (1987) all suggest that, indeed, such non-debt-like instruments may not be ideal for the parties directly involved. So we should be awake to the possibility that such contractual forms will carry efficiency-related costs. These may be well worth bearing, but, to my knowledge, the tradeoff remains to be checked.

A huge safety net backed by taxpayer funds and thrown over the entire financial system should not sound comforting—most of all because it relies on judicious regulation and brilliant anticipation by regulators as to what the next big risk will be. Without these features, regulatory stances might well fail to be strict enough, especially when it comes to preventing "gambling for resurrection" by those with the lowest net worth (i.e., "capital"). Lastly, while recent work has made progress in helping regulators identify the "connectedness" of financial institutions' balance sheets through parsimonious statistical metrics such as CoVar (see Adrian and Brunnermeier 2011), we may be asking for trouble if the financial safety net is made all-encompassing.[12]

The second approach goes to work after a crisis. In this scenario, policymakers provide no insurance, implicit or explicit, to nonregulated entities, and allow large banks and non-bank firms to fail utterly and completely, crushing their shareholders and any creditors not careful enough to fully collateralize their lending, just as the FDIC now does with small banks. In this world, a non-bank would have a tough time acting like a real, regulated insured-deposit bank: a regulated bank would give its depositors protection, while these "shadow entities" could not. Regulation is still essential here, because society's willingness to tolerate a failure depends on how big the failing company is. Barring vigilance, firms could simply grow their way into a TBTF state and hold taxpayers for ransom.

My sense is that this second approach, while a truly difficult goal to achieve, is particularly important to strive for. The reason is straightforward. For all the reasons we've talked about, large and opaque balance sheets, when combined with maturity mismatch, can pose a serious threat to our collective well-being. Financial market participants therefore cannot simply be given the benefit of the doubt when it comes to size and complexity. But regulators will not likely be able to remain a step ahead in measuring the benefits to society from the increased size of a bank or financial intermediary and then adjusting regulation appropriately. There are simply too many opportunities for obfuscation created by asymmetric information between the regulator and the regulated. So removing TBTF is far more in the spirit of decentralization, and ensures that the entities best equipped to assessing threats to their survival have the incentive to do so.

If we cannot presume that we'll collectively decide to hang tough when disaster strikes, then we only have "before the fact" to work with.

This means thinking carefully before choosing to create an environment that gives a huge variety of participants artificially generated incentives to use debt and choose complex operations. Think of how we do this right now: on the household side, we make mortgage interest deductible, and we guarantee and subsidize student loans. We create huge GSEs that then lobby successfully for protection against removal or restrictions, and when they do pass on the savings from their TBTF status, they make debt artificially cheap. For firms, our byzantine tax structure creates many incentives to use debt, routing credit through a banking system that has the protection of deposit insurance but may lack the proper pricing for it, and that creates complex holding-company structures. As for the latter, the first round of "living wills" submitted by banks pursuant to the Dodd-Frank legislation has shown that some bank holding companies are so complex that they themselves need to work hard to understand their internal structure. This is hardly comforting.

6.6.2 Asset Prices and Policy

Should policymakers react to asset prices? Many have addressed this question (see, e.g., Bernanke and Gertler 2001, or Goodfriend 2002), and the Federal Reserve system was seen as important in allowing an interest rate environment in which asset price increases could occur. Some have encouraged a more proactive approach to try to prevent bubbles from arising or getting "large." Again without being exhaustive, I will list some issues that arise or that are suggested by what we know about asset prices.

6.6.2.1 The Great Price Diagnosis Dilemma for Policymakers

The EMH contains a pessimistic message, not for outcomes, perhaps, as much as for the possibility that macroeconomics will *ever* have much to say about the mistaken beliefs embedded in any given set of asset prices at any point in time. In one sense, a longer tradition in economics should have told us this: we cannot speak of prices as meaningful aggregators that also coordinate outcomes nicely in the presence of dispersed, privately held, and hard-to-communicate information, and then coolly hold the view that policymakers (central planners?) ought to be able to correctly second-guess the market's evaluation of an asset's price, and announce boldly the presence of a bubble in near-real time.

Of course, if what hinders bubble prediction is the presence of rational expectations, then why not simply drop these expectations? We'd then regain the freedom, in principle, to refer to a given path of asset prices as a bubble with respect to some chosen set of beliefs about the future. The answer is that we could drop rational expectations, but we'd then have to make a choice about which beliefs should be made the "reference set" against which observed prices would be deemed "bubbly" or not. But among the set of all non-rational-expectations beliefs, how to choose one? After all, none of these beliefs, by definition, will be confirmed in the subsequent unfolding of history. Do we trust the loudest economist? The loudest writer? Each of these parties may have distributional goals that they can implement without that pesky legislative process getting in the way.

There's an additional problem: I have said nothing so far about the ability of policy to work as we wish it to. Think of a case in which we announce a policy that all asset price increases greater than a certain amount within a certain window of time will lead to an immediate reaction by policymakers to end the rise in asset prices. As a fanciful example, and holding aside all concerns about whether policymakers will act as promised, say the government announces that any time they see a particular housing price index rise for three months and cross a barrier in terms of growth, they will build a million houses a year for the next decade. On the face of it, this might help rule out bubbles in housing—private agents would look at high growth rates in house prices, and then worry that the government was just about to take actions to rule them out. On the other hand, what would a house price mean in this case? It certainly could not simply be the present discounted value of future housing services. It also could not fully reflect any real shift in fundamentals that make houses more valuable. As a result, the allocation of resources to the housing sector will, a priori, have less chance of reaching or staying at levels that help society lurch toward Pareto-optimal outcomes. And this may be fine, you might argue, if it just helps limit the occurrence of the disastrous outcome we are still experiencing. That is a notion that I, in unguarded moments, certainly find appealing.

On the issue of policy altering outcomes in complicated ways, there's another, more subtle, problem with commitments to react to asset prices. Such commitments change the informational content of an asset price. This is natural, after all: knowing that a policymaker will limit prices from rising via, say, interest rate policy means that anyone holding the asset will incorporate this fact into their forecast for future returns. As a result, asset prices and the prospects of firms become more disconnected than would otherwise be true. In regulatory contexts involving banking, this is particularly important to think about: Bond, Goldstein, and Prescott (2010) is a careful study of this issue.

Let me now repeat a caution from chapter 1 that applies to a good deal of analysis of the crisis that questions how "initial" price drops can magnify problems. Many of us have been in conversations where someone says, "House prices fell, and then . . ." I've said this myself at times. But you know from chapter 1 that this is an incomplete way to argue, at least through the lens of 200 years of economic reasoning. Recall the complications in trying to measure the "wealth effect" of movements in the stock market for aggregate consumption?

It's the same thing here. Economists ought to be the last people to start stories about aggregate outcomes with price changes. Of course, if you're trying to account for the actions of any given individual, this is fine: I generally do take prices as given and shift my behavior accordingly (as do you). But for understanding the behavior of any *aggregate*, prices and group behavior are jointly determined in response to fundamentals. This, by the way, is exactly why I stressed that when thinking about prices and outcomes, it helps to be rather literal-minded, and always imagine a WCH.

In the context of the crisis, ignoring the preceding admonition means being susceptible to a smart person who asks, "Well, why did house prices fall *in the first place*?" At this point, maybe I'd take a slightly smarter tack and say, "Well, look, there is no WCH in the real world, at least not in housing markets, and once we observed transaction prices for homes dropping, I looked at the data on construction, and then 'realized' that indeed the prices at which people had up to now been exchanging houses for cash were 'too high.'" And then I might say, "House prices were then expected by all to fall, and so they fell immediately." Thus, the realization of some new bad "facts on the ground" ("Hey, we really built too many houses") *should* lead, under rational expectations, to a precipitous and more or less instantaneous collapse in prices. Smart people don't want to hold potatoes that everyone knows are hot.

These problems are difficult, and macroeconomists certainly have few definitive answers. But it is incorrect to argue that modern macroeconomics has been a hindrance to right-minded souls in thinking about whether asset prices are "bubbly," or that it has not grappled with the potential of policy to alter this likelihood. Macroeconomics is the same discipline that has now brought into sharp focus those very items needed to be able to analyze bubbles: expectations and beliefs about the actions and beliefs of others.

6.6.3 Spillovers and Ronald Coase

A good deal of the US policy response (including that of the Federal Reserve System) was predicated on the idea that the economic system allowed for the unhealthy propagation of financial distress from one place to other places. The initial response to the crisis was primarily aimed at staunching the damage inflicted upon some entities, especially issuers of asset-backed commercial paper, onto other entities (manufacturing firms) (see Cecchetti 2009 for a clear review). This was clear in the Term Auction Facility (TAF), the Term Securities Lending Facility (TSLF), and the Primary Dealer Credit Facility (PDCF) programs created by the Federal Reserve System, for example.

A common word for spillovers was introduced in chapter 2: externalities. Externalities are important to macroeconomists because they provide information about the extent to which policy should intervene. To better understand some of the issues at play, let's go back to basics. Recall Ronald Coase's idea that externalities were fundamentally "reciprocal." In textbooks (e.g., Frank 1991, Landsburg 2010), Coase's ideas are brought to life through examples in which two producers are situated such that one's actions matter for the value of the business run by the other. For example, a doctor's office and a confectioner are located side by side, and the confectioner makes noise that alters the value of running the doctor's office. Coase's insight was that viewing the confectioner as "responsible" was arbitrary: the problem arises because both are near each other—if each ran her business far away from the other, the "problem" of noise would cease to exist. This approach immediately reorients one's focus onto the costs each would face to alter the situation, and then ensuring that the party who can do so most cheaply does so. One particular class of externalities involves firms' impinging on each other while consumers are left unaffected (at least directly). The usual examples of Coase's idea are such settings, in which the actions of one firm alter the payoffs to other firms, while consumers are unaffected. In the example of the doctor and the confectioner, the patients or customers could find a doctor or candy whenever it suited them. The application of Coase's idea in cases of pure production-side externalities rests on asking the question: What would outcomes look like if the *same person owned both* the doctor's office and the confectionery? We can imagine that if both the doctor and the confectioner reported to a single owner, they'd be given instructions that ensured that the total value of both businesses together (which is what the owner presumably cares about) were maximized.[13]

Coase's point was that as long as the parties could communicate effectively and did not have genuinely privately held information about the nature of costs and benefits of keeping or moving each business (recall the Myerson-Satterthwaite theorem), the legal assignment of liability would be irrelevant to the outcome in terms of the total value of both businesses, and the eventual location of each business. Of course, when it comes to the law, each side wants the other to be held liable—it entitles each to a payment from the other! But this is a question of distributional justice, rather than one that places efficiency at stake. After all, as we noted, having a single owner would void the problem entirely.[14] The tension here, and it's a difficult one, is that internalizing via ownership might create bigger enterprises, about which I've expressed concern above, and as I'll broach again below.

6.6.4 Ronald Coase and Macroeconomics

What do doctors and candy makers have to do with macroeconomics and the financial crisis? Recall the rationale that has been offered for policy intervention throughout the financial crises and the subsequent recession: the mitigation of damaging spillovers. Coase's point of view suggests that spillovers are really a creation or byproduct of negotiating costs, and not anything intrinsic at all. So one might equally say that interventions can be predicated on the inability of the firms involved to act as if they were owned by a single entity—perhaps simply because they are *not* owned by a single entity.

The extent to which firms have a single owner, or can interact and negotiate when they cannot or do not share a single owner, should thus be of central importance to policymakers considering changes in the regulation of financial firms, and to observers wondering about the implications of such changes. In particular, during mergers and the ensuing consolidation of ownership, work must be done to ensure that various activities that might interfere with each other are arranged so that they do not. Thus, quite unlike externalities that come from the consumer side of the economy, via inherently hard-to-observe objects like household preferences, well-functioning market economies have a built-in mechanism to deal with production-side spillovers. This is part of the reasoning that may well make macroeconomists more reluctant to accept accounts of pervasive spillovers on the production side of an economy: it raises the question of why such entities don't simply merge. Of course, many forces may prevent such mergers from happening, and a vast literature in the area of industrial organization addresses this issue; but in the end, unlike consumer-side spillovers, the road from corporate spillovers to inefficiency has at least one more roadblock.

Nonetheless, there is a clear tension between the efficiency gains from the mitigation of spillovers that can accompany consolidated ownership and the more negative consequences of the exercise of market power that would surely become more available to such an entity, all else being equal (a consolidated owner is necessarily a larger one, after all). To take an extreme example: imagine a single firm doing all the mortgage lending in the US, and holding all the loans made on their balance sheet, rather than selling them to third parties. This firm would certainly have reason to view an expansion in their operations as affecting the total number of homes built, the risks of default, and the likely path of prices that might obtain down the road. It would not lead easily to the type of situation that might result if many smaller firms made lending decisions ignoring their collective effects, sold the loans they made, and hence exposed the nation to the potential for a sharp drop in home prices. And yet a world with one large lender hardly seems ideal: monopoly and the expansion of scope of a firm's activities both clearly carry costs.

Clearly, then, macroeconomists need to grapple with an inescapable tradeoff: the very actions that ensure that the right hand knows what the left is doing across various activities that might impinge on each other may be accompanied by an increase in market power. The latter is very important: the notion that some firms became "too big to fail" is central to current policy measures aimed at lower "systemic" risk in the financial system. The Coasian point of view suggests that limitations on the scope of firm activities may well carry costs by themselves allowing spillovers to crop up. It also clarifies that the more widespread the conditions under which the idea applies, the more circumscribed will be the set of policy interventions that can improve efficiency as opposed to achieving purely distributional goals.[15]

Given the preceding, it is critical for policymakers and macroeconomists to understand to what extent capital markets and takeover mechanisms can function to stop spillovers, whenever doing so raises the value of the participants involved and perhaps that of others as well. This is an area where progress is nowhere near complete: we do not know in a definitive manner, for example, whether distributing financial firm activities across firms leads to the relinquishment of opportunities to improve outcomes. Progress on this front requires a deeper understanding of the extent to which the web of contracts that describe any firm, especially financial ones, solve more problems than they create. This is an area of intense research effort, but the difficulties are numerous: many of the critical ingredients necessary to evaluate contracting, especially in a quantitative matter, are very hard to observe. These include the set of available projects for the firm, the preferences of the workers and decision makers who must be incentivized, the influence exerted by the shareholders, if any, to follow strategies at odds with those chosen by the manager of the firm, etc. In fact, it is probably fair to say that unless one views contracting and incentive arrangements within a firm as simply one of many equal arrangements, one has to deal squarely with the informational and commitment-related problems that arguably gave rise to them in the first place. Recent work, especially by Karaivanov, Paulson, and Townsend (2006) and Meisenzahl (2011), gives exciting examples of work on this difficult issue.

6.6.5   Dynamic Games

All policymaking is a game between those who make policies and those who are affected by them. It is a game in which the players move in sequence: usually the policymaker "goes first"—say, by announcing a new regulation, inspection regime, or tax. The regulated, inspected, or taxed, then react. Such scenarios are called **dynamic games**, and are the overwhelming favorite among macroeconomists for the formal study of policy.

An inherent aspect of dynamic games is that they set up the possibility that the party who moves second can, in principle, threaten the party who acts first with dire consequences, and in so doing can try to manipulate outcomes in their favor. Conversely, the party who acts first can try to act in a way that limits the options of the party who goes second. I already noted in chapter 2 how this disallows participants from considering strategies that yield collectively infeasible outcomes. Now a second instance of how the game-theoretic view sharpens focus comes into relief: it forces us to ask whether a given type of behavior is being "propped up" by silly or noncredible threats.

In game theory, noncredible threats are a potential problem in almost any game where players move in sequence, as opposed to choosing actions simultaneously. The problem is easy to motivate: consider a society that wants to be rid of petty crime, and has installed a benevolent king to take care of matters. Because this king is kindly, he always seeks to make his citizenry as well off as possible from the current moment onward. His first edict is to announce that if even one person is caught stealing, 51% of the population will be randomly selected and executed. This policy, if taken seriously, would likely succeed in eliminating petty theft: people would have a great deal at stake in preventing others from stealing, and would even worry about preventing theft of the property of unrelated third parties! As a result, there would be no need for a police force, and importantly, no need for a hangman. But why on earth would such a policy be taken seriously? After all, the king is benevolent, and can't help but let bygones be bygones. Anyone who knows this will ignore the edict.

The same dynamic would unfold if the populace got to vote on whether to carry out the punishments in the event of theft. Majority rule, for instance, would lead to the population voting not to carry out the punishment. Thus, a society that votes often, and gives itself the "discretion" to choose to carry out costly punishments, may find itself unable to contain bad behavior. The problem, at its root, is the combination of benevolence with the ability to make decisions, after the fact, about enforcing penalties for behavior that was supposed to be discouraged.

Modern macroeconomic policymaking has been profoundly influenced by this idea: policies that involve noncredible threats are not seen as sensible policies. In turn, the example of the benevolent king teaches that policymakers should look for ways to credibly bind themselves to courses of action whenever those actions will be undesirable for them to pursue after the fact. This is the crux of any solution aimed at ending TBTF.

Consider a large financial institution whose activities connect large swaths of firms and workers. Can a *benevolent* policymaker ensure that such entities do not place taxpayers at risk? It may be hard. After all, once a risk has gone sour, a policymaker who cares about sparing the populace further pain may choose to "bail out" the troubled firm or, somewhat equivalently, help the victims of the misfortune. Of course, if such behavior is anticipated, the policymaker will indeed preside over an economy in which big risks *are* taken and losses *are* placed on taxpayers.[16]

Another example of this goes back to the question of market power, where entry deterrence is an area of great practical importance. Work in this area must deal with the question of whether wild threats might deter entry, since the threats would rationally be ignored. Macroeconomists' view of the prevalence of market power hinges on this issue. Think, for example, of an incumbent monopolist making threats to flood the market with product should a new entrant try her luck. The entrant, if smart, will ask, "If I enter, will you still flood the market?" Chances are, at that point, it is no longer in the interest of the incumbent to do so. As a result, this threat, as a practical matter, ought to be ignored; thus, any analysis should disregard Nash outcomes where the threat is heeded.

The examples just given imply that Nash equilibrium runs into a problem in games where players make moves in sequence: it is not powerful enough to rule out certain outcomes by threatening to allot punishments for "bad" behavior that, were the behavior to actually occur, would not be in the interests of the party issuing them to carry out. This wouldn't work because all that Nash asks is that the players' strategies, if taken seriously, constitute "mutual best responses." To add commonsense by ruling out predictions that do have silly threats backing them, we need to add the requirement directly to our definition of equilibrium.

In the 1970s and 1980s, game theorists did this by providing what are known as **refinements** to Nash equilibrium that killed off any Nash equilibria that involved the play of "silly" or noncredible threats, or whose "Nash-ness" hinged on participants' holding patently silly beliefs. The list of such refinements is long, and some economists find it a bit extreme—creating the list became a cottage industry. For games in which parties were certain of all past moves that had taken place, a famous and natural refinement was developed: **subgame perfection**. This simply asks that a Nash prescription (which, remember, is just a list of what each player will do when her turn arrives) be a Nash prescription no matter where we start analyzing the game. If it's my third move in a game where you and I each move six times, then subgame perfection requires that what we do from here on out be Nash behavior.

Next, recall the discussion on repeated games. I noted that many punishments might be made credible in repeated interactions. And indeed, the famous folk theorem for infinitely repeated games puts an exclamation point on this: it tells us that any outcome can be viewed as a subgame-perfect Nash equilibrium as long as players are patient enough. As I noted earlier, on the one hand, this is a disaster for the ability of game theory to predict a definitive outcome. More positively, it makes clear that as far as Nash tells us, pretty much anything is permissible if there are no further restrictions on the rate at which the parties involve discount payoffs (such as profits) that they will get in the future. For richer games in which a party is unsure of what has transpired earlier, a related tack was taken, leading to a variant of Nash equilibrium called **perfect Bayesian equilibrium** (**PBE**). My view of PBE is influenced by that of Gibbons (1992) (an exceptional book which I strongly recommend for its great collection of examples and its clarity): I think of PBE as a central notion of equilibrium, as it covers what one might want to ask of equilibria in a wide variety of games.[17]

6.6.5.1   Things "off the Equilibrium Path" Can Matter for Things on It

In any game where one has identified a Nash equilibrium, if players play their parts in it, the actions actually taken are referred to as ones "on the path of equilibrium play" or "on the equilibrium path" for short. But other actions will *not* be taken when players play their parts in a particular Nash equilibrium. The actions not taken in the course of playing according to a given Nash equilibrium are said (naturally enough) to be "off the path of equilibrium play" or "off the equilibrium path."[18]

In the example of the king who wanted to end theft: "no one stealing, execute any thief" is a Nash outcome. However, if no one steals, then the king will not be called on to mete out any punishments; the king's choice is off the path of equilibrium play for this particular equilibrium. Yet it is the fear of what might happen that led no one to steal. Thus, to have confidence in the prediction of this Nash outcome, we had better be sure that what is promised *off* the path of equilibrium play is *credible*, lest we allow silly tails to wag the dog. Nash, by itself, doesn't do this for us; it requires only that behavior be a best response *on the path of equilibrium play* (i.e., no one does something that looks silly as a response to what anyone else actually did). As a result, Nash allows for all manner of behavior off the path of equilibrium play. So to fail to further restrict one's attention would mean making poor guesses about what might actually transpire were players to interact in the specified way.

For macroeconomics, therefore, this area of research could hardly be more practical, especially for the strategic interactions that inevitably accompany policymaking.[19] Maybe most famous are analyses of policymakers' ability to end inflation by taking costly actions. In the models formalizing the ideas, inflation control depends in part on policymakers' ability to communicate a commitment to keeping price levels near-stable. The strength of this commitment is formalized in many instances based on citizens' sense of the likelihood that their central banker is "tough"—willing to incur costs in order to end inflation. Walsh (2010) offers details on how games with incomplete information are used in the study of monetary policy.

The role of behavior off the path of equilibrium play is important for a mundane reason, too: modern market economies do not routinely make items that no one wants because producers know they won't get paid if they do. In economics, this risk largely remains off the path of equilibrium play and, arguably, sustains a great deal of what is on the path of equilibrium play. A competitive market system has an ironclad commitment, from the perspective of any single producer, to withhold payment for services not rendered. But in the absence of competition, or in the presence of bailouts, this fundamental threat loses bite: payment *can* be garnered for services not rendered—for making cars no one wants to buy, for promising to deliver protection against default that you may not honor, and so on.

I therefore hope that the reader sees that when economists study apparently silly games with funny names like the "beer-quiche" game (see, e.g., Kreps, 1990, pp. 464–465) and refinements with downright weird names (e.g., "universal divinity"), they are actually thinking hard about how to ensure that what is predicted for an interaction in which parties recognize their interdependence makes *common* sense, and doesn't rely on noncredible threats or promises or on preposterous beliefs off the path of equilibrium play.

6.6.5.2   The Limited Commitment of Benevolent Policymakers: Time Inconsistency

A central presumption of the ADM model, as noted in chapter 1, is that contracts could be perfectly and costlessly enforced—no taxpayer-funded police force, military, or legal apparatus needed. Does this resemble the situation in the US, let alone in countries where markets play a more diminished role? Clearly not. Therefore, in work on political economy and elsewhere, recent research has dropped this assumption and instead has featured what economists call **time inconsistency**. This idea refers to the fact that what is optimal for a future action from the current moment's perspective will appear suboptimal when that future arrives. Think of poor Ulysses, concerned about his inability to ignore the sirens that lay in wait along his path. He knew that any plans he had to ignore the sirens later, clearly the optimal thing from the present perspective, would appear suboptimal once they came within earshot, and therefore that he would simply ignore his earlier plan to ignore them. Thus, he knew he had to prevent himself from "reoptimizing" once near the sirens, and he did so by ordering that he be bound to the mast and ignored by his shipmates as the ship passed the sirens. In this case, we refer to Ulysses' initial optimal plan as "time-inconsistent"—he'd wish to revise.

The relevance of such a tale for macroeconomic policy is clear. Benevolent policymakers, seeking to incentivize firms to manage their own risks and not place taxpayers in harm's way, would do best by credibly promising never to bail out a failing firm. If only they could: any large firm's failure, if it created problems for others in the wake of its failure, would lead a benevolent policymaker not committed to allowing failure to simply let bygones be bygones. The firm would get bailed out. Worst of all, this risk gets larger as the firm in question gets larger. As a result, unless firms are foolish, they will, if possible, arrange to become "too big to fail"—and thereby take risks, privatize gains, and socialize losses whenever feasible. The dilemma here is general: barring meaningful institutional arrangements to bind authorities to earlier promises, optimal plans are, in policymaking contexts, quite often time-inconsistent and therefore not credible. The idea of time inconsistency, like many other paradigm-shifting ideas, is due to Edward C. Prescott (in this case in a seminal paper with coauthor Finn Kydland; see Kydland and Prescott 1977).

An important additional point is that, in their brilliant follow-up, Kydland and Prescott (1980) taught us how to handle such problems with the same mathematics we already knew. This has proved hugely important in a wide array of problems in financial contracting (obviously at the center of the work being done on the causes of the financial crisis): yet again, technical apparatus invented and now used by economists to grapple with the most practical concerns one might imagine.

These economists articulated the sort of restriction created by the fact that noncredible threats will be ignored. A threat to mete out costly punishment is credible only given a bullheaded willingness to impose it even after it is too late to have served a deterrent role. Let's now turn to a related idea: the inability to make credible promises may be an important source of market incompleteness.

6.6.5.3 Consumer and Sovereign Debt

Since unsecured obligations can be effectively defaulted on, and both borrowers and lenders know this, macroeconomists have wondered what role risk and the "default option" play in credit markets. Starting in the late 1990s with the work of Zha (2001), many macroeconomists have studied quantitatively, in SIM models, the implications of a limited commitment to debt repayment for outcomes, especially for the pricing (and hence "availability") of credit. This work has been informative about why households are willing to pay the interest rates they do, why they choose not to repay when they do, and what role institutional features of the credit market might be playing in determining credit allocation. This research has been particularly helpful in our understanding of the tradeoff resulting from the legally induced lack of commitment to repay that is *created* by bankruptcy law: credit is more flexible, but the market for certain kinds of credit simply fails to exist altogether. Limited commitment can thus create market incompleteness.

This idea is relevant here because it shows how the admission of incomplete markets can allow us to understand, at least in principle, why society might allow debt forgiveness. With incomplete markets, such forgiveness shifts some risk to typically well-diversified lenders and away from typically undiversified borrowers, and so might serve as an effective "patch" for otherwise missing insurance markets. The interested reader may find the summary in Athreya (2005) useful. But, as I hinted at in the previous paragraph, this cuts both ways: the ability to repudiate debt may well make some forms of credit more expensive or entirely unavailable, exacerbating market incompleteness. The relationship between limited commitment and market incompleteness can be complex.

As for the other kind of unsecured defaultable debt, sovereign debt, the recent crises in several euro-area countries and the crises in other countries earlier both raise questions about what a sovereign's default might do to its trading partners. This is of interest in the recent slow US recovery, for the eurozone's severely indebted nations are seen as limiting the demand for US exports (or more locally, for Germany's exports).[20] But to understand the burden imposed on a country that has borrowed internationally, and hence its decision to default (and then use immediate improvement in its balance sheet to smooth its residents' consumption), requires a model of debt default and consumption smoothing.

Can the Radner model speak to this? Not as is. Its trading arrangement, while looking in one way slightly less demanding than the ADM model, still requires trade in markets that, at least superficially, seem at odds with what one observes in the world. In fact, they appear so at odds that the SIM models I discussed earlier dispense with them entirely and are, in return, able to explain data on household wealth. Because the Radner model classifies markets into "spot" and "financial" markets, it teaches us to look for limits on the ability of households and firms to take negative positions in financial markets, i.e., to *borrow*. A huge literature has now grown up around how limited commitment to repay financial transfers affects the ability of market participants to replicate ADM outcomes with sequential trade.

Initial work on this topic took place in a natural context, that of sovereign debt where repayment is certainly never ironclad. This context is relevant in recent times, as the eurozone experiences tension arising from the possibility that some of the sovereigns within the union will repudiate their debts. The past decade has seen an explosion of research on sovereign debt, and on the link between economic fundamentals and the decisions of sovereigns to default. The seminal model for sovereign debt (and consumer debt, for that matter) is that of Eaton and Gersovitz (1981), with more recent work essentially quantifying the basic tradeoffs this paper identified so long ago. Important examples include Hatchondo, Martinez, and Sapriza (2010), Aguiar and Gopinath (2006), and Arellano (2008).

6.6.5.4   Ex-Ante versus Ex-Post Efficiency . . . Again

In chapter 3, I described two notions of efficiency: ex-ante (Pareto) efficiency and ex-post (Pareto) efficiency. It will become clearer below how these concepts are central to recent policymaking related to the financial crisis, and to understanding how difficult good policy is, even—or especially—when policymakers have the public's best interests at heart!

The crisis brought another instance of the promise and peril of the ex-post standard: think of financial institution bailouts. Every one of these institutions was authorized and endorsed by presumably well-meaning policymakers to mitigate ex-post inefficiency (here, think of any knock-on effects that one entity's failure would have on others, e.g., "fire sales" of otherwise high-quality assets). Such a policy might well have been anticipated by large financial firms, though, and thereby contributed to the creation of the problem itself. Chari and Kehoe (2010) is useful here. On the more general issue of the perils of bank bailouts, read the early and important nontechnical book of Feldman and Stern (2004).[21]

The ideas in that work make it clear that the ex-post standard for policymaking is a remarkably weak, and politically expeditious, standard for intervening in decentralized economic outcomes. It is also pretty easy to identify policy changes that can help some at the expense of others. Nevertheless, we often hear politicians, and even policymakers, assert that "project X helps constituency Y" while failing to note that it may well hurt constituency Z, if only because tax revenues need to be raised, or because project X moves economic activity from one place to another. Think of a planned football stadium, and the promises of job creation—no mention of the sure loss of jobs in the places where it was not built or the place from where it was moved.

In the present context, financial-market settings are riddled with problems of limited commitment and asymmetric information; as a result, contractual arrangements (e.g., debt) often feature provisions that induce deadweight loss. It simply should not surprise one that outcomes in these settings can be improved after the fact.

6.7 Macroeconomics and the Financial Crisis of 2007–2008: Navel Gazing and a Response to Those Gazing at Our Navels

The recent financial crisis has led to a tremendous amount of criticism of macroeconomics and those who practice it. Nobel Prize–winning economist and *New York Times* columnist Paul Krugman has led the charge, primarily arguing that macroeconomists were bamboozled by an approach that, through its "beauty," led economists away from a more plebeian route to "truth." Similarly, Quiggin (2010) pursues a tack that places macroeconomists' allegiance to the so-called efficient-markets hypothesis at the heart of our terminal blindness to the possibility that very bad things are possible.[22]

As in most writing that prescribes "paradigm overthrow," the rhetoric of these critics is fundamentally optimistic, and so is hard to be too grouchy about. Their premise is that it is time for a better macroeconomics, especially one that pays more attention to history and psychology, to replace what macroeconomists have fashioned thus far.[23] This sounds great.

To its leaders and foot soldiers, modern macroeconomics makes sense—of course. But to its critics, it represents many bad things, ranging from an inherent rejection of government intervention to a tacit acceptance of social Darwinism. The financial crisis has given tremendous stimulus to those who hold these views, and offers them the possibility of a wholesale replacement of macroeconomic thinking. A wide array of critics has joined forces with patrons to promote alternative viewpoints and to create optimistically named entities, such as the Institute for New Economic Thinking (INET). They hold conferences and have a following of hopeful journalists eager to tell their story.

The critics are, of course, varied, and by this point in the book, you should be able to see why. Various aspects of modern macroeconomics irritate various groups, and between them, the waterfront of critics is well covered. Modern macroeconomics offers little endorsement of the views of the "hard left" (committed to the idea that widespread state involvement is always needed and will be successful, and immune to evidence and counterarguments), or those of the "hard right" (committed to the idea that, aside from highly localized forms of cooperation, the state is a parasite bent on subordinating the individual, and immune to evidence and counterarguments). But we macroeconomists have briefly succeeded in uniting these two factions through the idea that macroeconomic thinking is (allegedly) heavily influenced by a mix of "neoclassical" dogma and corruption. These critics allege that macroeconomic thought has now delivered what the left dislikes most—prescribing laissez-faire too often—and what the right despises as well—that it abets crony capitalism, partly by not adhering to iron rules such as a gold standard for central bank money.

The first claim is perhaps superficially correct, insofar as I have given you a representative view of the profession. The neoclassical tradition which birthed the "ADM lens" is, indeed, the one that modern macroeconomics employs when it starts an inquiry about the real world. But this charge is hard to take seriously because we've now seen so many models in which market outcomes are not good by any measure. Moreover, to describe any large modern economy as even close to laissez-faire, while such a definition is always a judgment call, stretches credulity. Tax revenue in the Organisation for Economic Co-operation and Development, expressed as a fraction of all income, almost always exceeds one-fifth, and is close to one-third on average.

The complaint from the right is a bit easier to understand, however, because policymakers engaged in unprecedented interventions in credit markets and almost certainly forestalled losses for certain classes of creditors—especially those holding claims on large and politically connected financial intermediaries. In a sense, such an outcome can be seen as an almost inevitable consequence of the routinely discretionary policy that policymakers appear to engage in. As a result when policy acts with discretion, it almost inevitably opens itself to the charge that it is favoring one group over another. Of course, what one must then concede is that laissez-faire did not even come close to carrying the day either in the wake of the crisis or more recently.

6.7.1 Does Modern Macroeconomics Favor Laissez-Faire?

In all of the criticism of modern economics for its presumption of widespread rationality, little has been said about just how inhospitable this view of private behavior is for anyone wanting to promote laissez-faire. This situation stems from the fact that modern macroeconomics is almost, but not perfectly, dystopian. It remains maximally cynical about the behavior of people and the corporations they run. It presumes that large firms understand that they are large, will monopolize if allowed to, and will exploit policymakers' inability to commit to not bailing them out in bad eventualities. It presumes that people will employ any ways they know of to avoid taxes. And so on.

So, if the only reason that any decision maker in a modern economic model would help pull a stranger from a burning car is if it paid him to do it, then surely this is a society in which, barring an excellent collection of institutions (the ones that yield complete and competitive markets, for example), there can be no presumption whatsoever about outcomes being efficient. If nothing else, the dominance of incomplete-market approaches in contemporary research clarifies that modern macroeconomics usually studies settings where private self-interest is known to not even yield constrained efficient outcomes.

The criticism that macroeconomics is a rubber stamp for laissez-faire is even weaker than this, though. This is because a good deal of modern macroeconomics is naive in a specific way that further bolsters the case for public-sector involvement. Governments, including the monetary policy authority, are modeled routinely either as automata that mechanically follow policy rules not known to have any general optimality properties (e.g., the Taylor rule) or, worse yet, as knowing the preferences of households and then choosing to make them as well off as possible in ex-ante terms. This seems to give the public sector as good a shot at being useful as you might imagine.

It should be easy to coax an argument against laissez-faire out of an economy populated only by cutthroats working through incomplete markets or facing some impediment to trade that only government-issued money can ameliorate, and where the government is not only well-intentioned but supernaturally well-informed. So having noted that it's an easy task, let's put forward the complaint that macroeconomics was insufficiently centered on integrating financial and real (labor, equipment, etc.) markets, particularly over very short-run periods. Unlike more open-ended "you-assume-rationality-and-we know-people-aren't-rational" types of criticisms, this complaint can help open the door to meaningful change.

6.7.2 Where Did We Fail?

Do macroeconomists have models that would produce a forecast for the likelihood of a huge downturn if they could clearly observe the full structure of IOUs across financial intermediaries and households? No. Could our models speak to the possibility that more relaxed underwriting standards would coincide with a period of extremely high price appreciation in real estate? No. Did our benchmark models suggest that, in the absence of any change in fundamentals, real estate prices could drop nationwide by 20% or more? No. Did our models feature the constraint that even renegotiating a large volume of mortgages would be very cumbersome, and potentially amplify the downturn? No.

At bottom, then, macroeconomists lack models that can fully account, quantitatively, for the use of various contracts (e.g., what fraction of liabilities and assets take a given form—say, debt, or convertible bonds, or options, or "repos," etc.) and the links between their use and sudden changes in asset valuations and the subsequent performance of the labor and capital market. Macroeconomics, therefore, has a good deal of unfinished business, and so has failed, in recent years, to be useful in a variety of ways.

I suspect that the median macroeconomist can accept what I have just said. Nonetheless, I also suspect that they think, for the reasons I have laid out all along, that these failures do not make a wholesale revamping of macroeconomics a bright idea. A more measured response is the one that is already happening: the crisis and the slow recovery have yielded a sensible *shift in priorities* toward understanding the role of *household finance* (e.g., mortgage and student loans) and *financial contracting between firms* (e.g., repos) as sources of macroeconomic fluctuations.

The reasons for this willingness to retain the now standard approach should be clear. First of all, a financial crisis that has its roots in household-level use of credit is necessarily a crisis about trades in IOU markets. Households trade in these markets only because they are trying to trade consumption in the future in favor of consumption now, and/or because they hold beliefs about the path of future prices, especially for homes. One's expectations for the future are thus necessarily central to the use and proliferation of such contracts.

Modern macroeconomics is clearly on the right track here: as we've seen, starting with ADM and then in the Radner model, expectations lie at the center of decision making, and better yet, do so in a disciplined manner. Absent the requirement that expectations be rational, what would have stopped one from arguing circa 2005 that even if our models of financial-sector linkages were good, there was nothing to worry about because households' expectations were such that they'd never lose confidence in housing? After all, if this claim were true, we'd all live happily after. If expectations needn't be made model-consistent, why *not* use this narrative? Or *any other one*, for that matter?

The preceding hints at what I think is the more fundamental problem we face: while macroeconomists have fairly good quantitative models, especially of household-level decisions about consumption and savings, and even to some extent have good models of investment decisions by firms, we do not have a model that leads to the plans of these entities *necessarily* being executed through the rich array of financial contracts that one observes in use (ARMs, repos, SIVs, lines of credit, CDs, etc.). As a result, we do not have, other than in a qualitative and usually vague sense, knowledge of impending risks that come from any given financial landscape.

Having noted this lacuna, let me be blunt: the answers are not "all in Minsky" or "all in Hayek" or "all in Keynes." One sometimes hears these statements, inexplicably, from economists and writers who are each convinced that as soon as we rediscover what we used to know, we'll be back in business.[24] At a very minimum, Minsky or Hayek or Keynes had nothing to say about the *size* or the timing of problems. They also had nothing to say at all about the reasons for the widespread use of particular contractual forms, such as debt or the banking contract. That has come only recently, as we saw with the hard work of Townsend, Diamond and Dybvig, and others. Nor did they give us any insight into why views on asset prices might suddenly change. Nor did they connect households' use of IOUs to their need to smooth consumption expenditures.[25] And so on.

Indeed, in recent times, much discussion has centered on the effects of additional government spending and the effects of tax reform, especially reforms that would alter current taxes and future tax obligations. The work of the verbal tradition embodied in Keynes's and Minsky's writings gives us no meaningful way to evaluate any of these proposals. For that, one needs a model in which households look forward when making decisions, and face uncertainty. This is why macroeconomists' unambiguous progress in embedding such individual-level problems into aggregate economies, e.g., the SIM model, is of substantial importance. Such models, however, do not lend themselves to convenient political narratives: the presence of uninsurable risks opens the door to ideas like Keynes's "paradoxes of thrift," but it also brings the future taxes associated with any deficit-financed spending, such as the "stimulus," into focus in ways that will limit their potency to alter current output.

The modern approach of being utterly transparent about the motivations and constraints of decision makers, and being amenable to quantification, has only been made feasible by mathematics invented after 1945, and by computers invented after about 1975. To suggest that somehow these were all already known, if only one read history more diligently, is wishful thinking.

Still, having disputed the validity of this viewpoint, let me admit that in moments of weakness, I sometimes sympathize with those pushing these sorts of arguments. Why? Because it is more comforting to chalk up failure to human agency (or lack of it) than it is to admit that many pressing problems have solutions that lie well beyond the intellectual horizon. But any human inquiry always remains incomplete, sometimes even when it really matters.

6.7.3   Criticism of DSGE Models

I've already described the SGM and RBC models, which belong to a larger class of models into which almost all modern macroeconomics fits, and we've already encountered in chapter 5 just how central they are to how macroeconomists organize their thinking on all aggregate fluctuations. These models are almost always a starting point in analysis. Enough recent criticism has been leveled at so-called dynamic stochastic general equilibrium (DSGE) models, though, that it seems useful to treat these views separately.[26] The diversity of models that still fit within macroeconomics is great. After all, DSGE, taken literally, just means a model in which decision makers think about the future, where that future is uncertain, and where the outcomes do not surprise people beyond what the realization of uncertainty itself does. This description covers a huge chunk of economics, and immediately implies that it is pretty useless to talk about "problems with 'DGSE' models."

That having been said, I will now discuss the extent to which the common elements in all these models, as outlined in the earlier section of the Walrasian "rules" for model construction, can (and should) be criticized. First, the question is not whether we have rational expectations. We don't. The questions are, instead, the following: How irrational are we? How many of us are irrational? Is everyone to be treated as if they were? Are the ones who are most irrational vital for the prices commanded by assets? When are we most irrational? How are we irrational? What if smart, deep-pocketed, and rational individuals collectively act to foil our desired policy aims? And so on. This is a research agenda. It is one that has indeed occupied the attention of many economists for many years. Thomas Sargent and Lars Hansen have written more than one monograph on this topic, and Chris Sims has for nearly a decade helped economists admit the possibility of things such as learning and "inattention" into models. These decisive departures from rational expectations are the stuff of completely mainstream macroeconomics; its proponents are precisely those who have demonstrated total mastery of the more standard model.

Critics are correct, however, to note that the business-as-usual macroeconomic model, whether aimed at understanding some aspect of business cycles or longer-term phenomena, routinely employ rational expectations. I have already given one reason for this: the inability to observe expectations makes it dangerous to turn their assignment over to an economist. More generally, though, the fact that irrationality has not been more routinely embedded into macroeconomic models can be taken in two ways. First, the paranoid interpretation: free-market zealots (the "efficient markets crowd") had killed off their more realistic opponents. The second interpretation: policymakers saw what they saw, and worried, but could not definitively point to a problem in real time. Does this mean that policymakers who do indeed consult such models (the widely yelled-at "DSGE model" class) forgot that irrationality was a possibility? Did it lead them to ignore capital levels at the banks they regulated? Did it lead them to shunt conversations about mispriced assets into the closet? The answers, as I know them from my own experiences and from those of most in similar positions are: no, no, and no.

There is a sense in much commentary that unvarnished models were consulted as oracles. This is not true. It is belied by a stark reality: at most central banks and policy institutions, meetings take a long time, sometimes days. These meetings are emphatically not spent simply consulting a battery of DSGE models, turning them over as one would a Magic 8 Ball, and then disbanding for beers. Notice that even if one were ecumenical enough to consult a variety of DSGE models, this in itself would suggest that policymakers had enough of a "grasp of reality" to suspect that no single model got it right. And still, if that's all we did, it would take only minutes.

A range of critics has taken the DSGE moniker to mean something somewhat specific, despite the huge breadth of models it houses. This is the class of models that fit into the *business cycle* research program, typically the apparently complex models in which the effects of monetary policy are studied. Authors of the prototype models of this class are Calvo, King, Woodford, Galí, and Gertler, among others (Woodford 2003 and Walsh 2010 provide useful surveys). As we saw, in many of these models monetary arrangements are grafted onto a model in which financial intermediation is typically illustrated in a fairly limited way. As a result, some of these models are still far from being definitive. Moreover, this program has allowed an essentially mindless form of engineering-as-economics to flourish. Much is made about the reduced form equation system called the new-Keynesian "trinity." I admit that this model is largely deficient, particularly for any attempt to understand problems related to the financial sector, and critics are onto something here. Any policymaker who consults only "the DGSE model" (presumably after spending enormous effort assigning parameter values through sophisticated procedures) is like one who thinks they have made it to Delphi while still backing out of the garage. And we are not so optimistic.

So, although I am happy that someone noted all these problems, my response to this brand of criticism is: What is out there that is better? The one warranted inference from the current state of macroeconomic models is that caveats should be offered, and certitude should not be expressed by those using them. I see no reason to view these problems as coming from the systemic rot of a profession that closes ranks to protect its own. My experience in the profession suggests that it is mainly composed of intellectual omnivores willing to listen to a good idea wherever they hear it, and a (much) smaller number of full-on cannibals who will take your idea, make sure they publish it first, and thereby take a bite out of you (or at least your career).

6.7.4 Reforming Macroeconomics

In response to the calls for uprooting macroeconomics, we could ask where the reform should come from. Should macroeconomists canvass broader audiences to better diagnose what ails them? I think it is risky. Overall, my view is that each of us, in the modern world, knows some small thing about what we specialize in, and next to nothing about anything that we do not. Moreover, the small bit is *far* bigger than the "next-to-nothing" part! How ready are you to crowd-source the decision on your next (and only) appendectomy, especially if you knew that no doctors were allowed to participate? Specialized knowledge and generalized ignorance are joined at the hip.

"Reform from without" is thus a poor candidate for improving a process. Internally driven reform is happening, as I've said, in the intensity with which previously parallel literatures on banking, bank runs, agency costs, and aggregate labor and investment are being joined.

Why weren't these joined before? Actually, they were. The seminal work of Bernanke and Gertler (1989) and Carlstrom and Fuerst (1997) opened the floodgates to work aimed at connecting changes in balance sheets to *quantitative* changes in incentives and outcomes within traditional DSGE settings.

However, it took longer to construct models with rich heterogeneity across participants in terms of their balance sheets, because computational power was unable to incorporate these objects satisfactorily.

We've seen that SIM models are useful in many instances for understanding aspects of household-level consumption and savings decisions or interest rates on loans, but we have noted that the computation of these models, especially once business cycles are incorporated, only became feasible in the late 1990s. In those settings, it was simply beyond our capability to add a labor market in which search was essential, a market for residential real estate in which, again, search was important, and a banking sector in which legal entities akin to the special-purpose vehicles were issuing asset-backed commercial paper, complete with credit lines from banks. We are trying to create such models now, but the same technological barriers still apply. This is essential for us as macroeconomists to concede, and for the public at large to understand.

More generally, almost every aspect of the recent financial crisis involved behavior in which decision makers were thinking about the future. From homeowners and prospective home buyers to investment bankers and mutual fund operators, all were united in their decisions by their (sometimes disparate) views of an uncertain future. To think for even a moment that a macroeconomics that refuses to incorporate dynamic decision making under uncertainty could be useful in this situation is optimistic, to put it charitably. And yet reluctance to deal with the implications that expectations have for current actions is a hallmark of the Keynesian tradition. It is why the profession does not teach Keynes's original work to graduate students, even as it comprehensively engages with his ideas in the disciplined manner of modern models.

6.7.5 Policy: Some Perspective and a Caution

In general, macroeconomists are like other economists in worrying that they can only rarely effect Pareto improvements. If they cannot, they will usually back off from advocacy. Being an adult means recognizing that there will times when bad things happen, and that they cannot be wished away by "bold action," or by having policymakers do things that make them look busy. If these economists press on, however, it should be clear that they are actually pushing for redistribution of some type. As I've already argued, our views on redistribution ought not to have any privileged status in society.

The best interpretation that one can make of insistent calls for policy intervention—especially those demanding action in favor of ex-post efficiency, such as bailouts or stimulus—is that intervention is being urged as part of a social contract to deliver insurance. Since I am deeply sympathetic to this view, I am not always opposed to the prescriptions coming from those upset at decentralized outcomes. What one should object to is dressing up insurance as *ex-post* efficiency improvement. For reasons we saw in chapter 5, we have no formal reasons to think this is always obviously true. So maximizing ex-post efficiency may sometimes be helpful, but may be far from what ex-ante efficiency would dictate. As I've argued, it is the latter that is generally the preferable criterion.

Let me be clear that, for myself, discerning how to improve the function of insurance and credit markets seems the most important part of economics. In terms of credit, so much of what I've said reflects my view that intertemporal markets, including the employment relationship, are the key place where policy should focus. As for insurance more specifically, as should be clear from chapter 5, I view the agenda for locating efficient ways to insure against long-term risks, such as the risk of a poor early-childhood environment, long-term skill loss, serious illness, and disability, as substantially more important than efforts to determine or manipulate the amount of output or employment at a given moment. This is because household-level risks of poor schools and neighborhood environs, chronic illness, disability, and other misfortunes loom large in the lives of many people, and worse yet, occur *constantly* to them: these misfortunes do not respect the timing of the business cycle. As a result, restricting one's attention to these issues solely in terms of what is happening to people during business cycles represents a serious loss of perspective by macroeconomists.

Yet business cycles are critically important to understand and, if possible, to attenuate. This importance is not necessarily intrinsic. Instead, it may stem from the fact that business cycle downturns are times in which wrenching *individual-level* events (as opposed to what is happening to simple aggregates, such as GDP), like unemployment, dislocation, and loss of health insurance coverage, are happening to more people than usual *at the same time.*[27] As I argued earlier, if total economy-wide output dropped by 10 percent in a recession, and did so in way where every single household's income dropped by exactly 10 percent, the case for spending time on the study of business cycles would be severely weakened.

But because that is emphatically not the case, business cycle mechanisms warrant special attention. The coordination failure view is simply not definitive enough to be the basis of large-scale interventions predicated on the behavior of aggregates. Microeconomic policies that deal with the fallout from market incompleteness, however, have a better chance at improving ex-ante efficiency, provided one is willing to look out from behind the veil of ignorance. The judicious design of insurance—such as that dealing with long-term care, the unemployment insurance system, and catastrophic events—as well as the unbundling of employment and health insurance are where the real gains are to be made, so far as I can tell. As we saw in chapter 5, this viewpoint, placing the individual at the center as opposed to directly modeling aggregated items like GDP, substantially informs modern macroeconomic models of the business cycle.

6.7.5.1 Global Policy Coordination

One topic that is likely to loom large in the future is policy coordination (or its absence) across nations. The importance of such coordination cannot be overstated—not simply for things like the business cycle, but for the extremely big-ticket items like climate change. Such issues will likely defy our attempts to deal with them, and thus pose serious risks to the world's populations. In the far narrower context of the global financial crisis of 2007–2008, and in the policy responses since then, there are large problems with policy coordination as well. To take just one example: when helping arrange for the orderly liquidation of large financial firms, each national-level regulator may assert jurisdiction over a multinational firm's assets in a way that foils the firm's overall ability to wind down. After all, to the extent that a national-level regulator is obligated to protect its taxpayers, this is indeed what it will be impelled to do. In other words, ensuring (at least ex-post) efficiency is likely to be difficult. Another example would be the coordination of fiscal policies among nations or states in a monetary union. Here again, policy is constrained in important ways, and a presumption of efficiency seems wishful thinking.

6.7.5.2 A Caution

Disasters preventable by human agency will always hit us as surprises. There will always be some who can claim to have foretold disaster, and they may even have been right for the right reasons. However, the bulk of expert and nonexpert opinion will not see disaster coming. This logic holds irrespective of whether the disaster in question is a natural one or a financial one. In the latter case, the aggregate performance of any national-level economy is not dictated by one, two, or even a thousand decision makers; it is the outcome of millions of households that, even if most hold little wealth, still collectively dictate the path of aggregate consumption and output. And if most of these households do not see a crisis coming, then neither will the expert macroeconomist, or anyone else.

Imagine the reverse: a disaster that hundreds of millions of households see coming, yet which they do not stop from happening, despite their agreement on its imminence. Or if a few do try to stop it while most do not, why would we necessarily trust their judgment? Unless we want to go down a seriously undemocratic path, and unless we have chosen our oracles exceptionally well, this course would be silly. All this is bad news, but it is news that any grown-up should accept: we'll always wonder why a terrible economic calamity happened, and only rarely will the experts have predicted it.

6.8   What Should Macroeconomists Be Doing?

Given the views I've expressed throughout this book, I see the job of macroeconomists as somewhat narrow. It falls primarily into three areas. First, macroeconomists can help society better understand how to "efficiently" redistribute purchasing power (i.e., "income") according to societal demands both when those redistributions are across time (by helping with credit access) and when they are across contingencies (by helping ensure proper insurance market function). Second, we can help society creatively elicit the valuation of, and then the resources for, public goods for which competitive markets are essentially impossible to construct. Third, we can help to improve longer-run economic performance by improving our understanding of observed trading arrangements, especially the use of prevalent kinds of financial contracts like debt, central bank liabilities (i.e., fiat money), and the links between these contracts and "systemic" side effects. This includes providing quantitative analysis of policy interventions aimed at these arrangements, and will mainly be in markets for "intertemporal" trade, such as insurance and financial services, and (though it is less obviously intertemporal) for labor services. In some cases, the policy interventions in this category might be sizeable, such as the direct public-sector provision of insurance, along with compulsory participation in the market. Fourth and finally, macroeconomists can help by better understanding the consequences of policymakers' lack of commitment to avoiding ex-post efficiency improvements when they are likely to conflict with ex-ante efficiency.

6.9 Concluding Remarks

Macroeconomic research, as I have described it throughout this book, should strike you as a rich and internally consistent program, and one that is and has been grappling with all manner of problems that we could agree to call "important." I hope that I've conveyed this impression of the discipline successfully, and most of all, convinced you to study it carefully.

If you're an undergraduate student thinking of graduate school in economics, or are a first-year graduate student, I think you'll be pleasantly surprised at how closely your classes will mirror the topics in this book, even as the emphasis will be on the tools you ultimately need to do good work in macroeconomics. I hope you join our ranks.

If you're an economic journalist, I hope the book was helpful in showing you how macroeconomists frame questions, and in showing you why they study the areas they do and ignore others. Most of all, I hope this book leads you to ask more from *economists*. Cede no ground to those who want to hide behind black-box models and feel no obligation to "show you the agents." Ask for the pure-efficiency rationale for any policy you see them promoting. And ask them why the policy authority is better positioned to solve the problem than decentralized interactions would be.

If you're an interested taxpaying citizen, I hope I've persuaded you that we macroeconomists are, as a group, pursuing problems of importance for our collective well-being, and doing so in a way that is respectful of previous efforts without elevating the past to dogma, while remaining open to improvements. Thanks for reading.

Notes

Introduction

1. Narayana Kocherlakota, "Modern Macroeconomic Models as Tools for Economic Policy," http://www.minneapolisfed.org/pubs/region/10-05/2009_mplsfed_annualreport_essay.pdf.

2. See, e.g., the Committee on Science and Technology of the US House of Representatives, which, on July 10, 2010, convened hearings on the topic of "Building a Science of Economics for the Real World." Sadly, we actually think we *are* doing just this. Oh well. The transcript of the hearings is available at http://economistsview.typepad.com/economistsview/2010/07/building-a-science-of-economics-for-the-real-world.html

3. See Nobel Laureate Paul Krugman's "How Did Economists Get It So Wrong?," *New York Times Magazine*, September 2, 2009, http://www.nytimes.com/2009/09/06/magazine/06Economic-t.html

4. If you feel there is too much repetition, I apologize. But think carefully about which audience you belong to, and ask whether, if you followed my suggestion to skip past what you knew, you'd still find it that way.

5. See, e.g., the journalist John Cassidy's 2009 book *How Markets Fail*. Chapters 5 and 6 will describe specific workhorse models of macroeconomics in which at least some markets "fail" in a precise sense: they will produce outcomes that do not display so-called Pareto efficiency.

6. Readers will find useful the essay "Modern Macroeconomic Models" by Narayana Kocherlakota, president of the Federal Reserve Bank of Minneapolis, from which the quotation at the outset was taken. It covers at a high level some of the same ground as this book, especially chapters 4 and 5.

1 The Modern Macroeconomic Approach and the Arrow-Debreu-McKenzie Model

1. I recommend, as a start, McCloskey's *The Rhetoric of Economics* (1985).

2. See Ely (2010a) for an emphasis of the point that "every good theorist assumes his conclusions."

3. This general problem, of verisimilitude, may apply to other disciplines as well; I simply do not know enough to say.

4. Many economists I know (including me) have had the experience at some point in their careers, especially at the beginning of a seminar, of having someone say abruptly: "Yeah, that all sounds OK, but it's all just words, and you need to show us the facts and equations." The age hoped for by Keynes, when the economist would be considered as equal to the modest dentist, can only ever happen when we all agree (as we now do) to use mathematics to express ourselves. At the very least, we're made into (possibly boring) "if-this-then-this" kinds of social scientists.

5. More recently, another model's failure to match the facts has led to a similar cottage industry of economists aiming to be the first to provide a convincing resolution. This is the so-called Shimer puzzle, named after its creator, economist Robert Shimer of the University of Chicago. I'll say more about the kind of model Shimer used in chapter 5.

6. For more in the spirit of this section, I recommend the preface to the textbook of David Kreps, *A Course in Microeconomic Theory* (1990). It is about ten pages long, and exceedingly well done.

7. See Caballero (2010) for a somewhat opposing view. This is a bit rich, though. Caballero is an economist eminently capable of doing it all: integrating formal models and intuitive insights in order to think coherently about new and uncharted territory. For the rest of us, it's better to stick to the rules.

8. In chapter 5, I will return to the appropriateness of equilibrium analysis especially in the context of understanding "transitional" effects from any change in government policies.

9. Interestingly, recent work by Farmer (2012) places prices as exactly "causal" in subsequent real outcomes. This is done in a way that is completely coherent.

10. The interested reader is referred to "In Praise of Theory" (Athreya 2007), a nontechnical exposition of the Lucas critique and its role in spurring modern macroeconomics.

11. I say "typically" because there are economists actively engaged in studying brain function. See, e.g., Dickhaut, Rustichini, and Smith (2009).

12. A very well-known, now deceased, macroeconomist is reputed to have said: "A little bit of 'Stokey, Lucas with Prescott' [a colloquial name for a standard textbook] can make up for a lot of IQ points."

13. After all, the earth will be absorbed by the sun within 5 billion years, so that finite date pretty much puts a stopper on things. Nonetheless, as I will discuss briefly in chapter 4, macroeconomists have, since 1954, found good reasons to relax this assumption (in a further illustration of the forces of practicality driving the need for what might initially be seen as mathematical esoterica).

14. The part of economics that deals with the specification of choice behavior is vast. The reader is directed to the helpful nontechnical book of Gilboa (2010) and, if still interested, to Kreps (1990) and the references therein for more.

15. If you look at the literature, you will see, for example, that "hold-up" problems arising especially in what would be infrequent arms-length transactions, can sometimes be dealt with by housing a range of activities under one roof.

16. Nonetheless, some goods may not actually be traded. An example is private space tourism: until recently, the minimum price at which suppliers of space travel services were willing to carry a tourist exceeded the maximal willingness of any tourist. As a

result, we saw no space tourism. Nonetheless, this does not mean the markets for space travel were incomplete; it's just that no trades of money for travel were seen to be *mutually worthwhile*. By contrast, markets for certain goods and services can be incomplete if buyers and sellers are *unable* to attain gains from trade even in the absence of any deliberate impediments to trade (such as taxes or direct prohibitions). For instance, I'd like to buy insurance against losing my keys, and if someone could inspect my attentiveness when I come home from work every day (to ensure that I wasn't just claiming to have lost my keys to get an insurance payout), they might be willing to provide me such insurance—but it is too burdensome to obtain such data, and as a result the gains from such transactions go unrealized.

Notice that I have defined private and public goods in terms of *physical* characteristics that either completely preclude parties from being affected by others' consumption of them or fully force parties to be affected by others' consumption. From this perspective, a world with "public" goods is necessarily a world where markets *cannot be made complete*, and as we will see later, one in which the decentralized pursuit of self-interest generally (and especially under linear prices) yields wasteful outcomes. Lastly, while public goods imply market incompleteness, the converse need not hold: there can be market incompleteness in a world of purely private goods. In this case, the incompleteness may arise from physical constraints on the formation of centralized markets that then create the need to "search" for trading partners, or more commonly from political considerations such as outright bans (e.g., on prostitution and drugs) or heavy taxes which eliminate after-tax gains from trade, etc.

17. If you like counting exercises, notice that with L goods, there would be $L^2 - L$ relative prices that one could keep track of, if one felt like it. Why? The price of each of the L goods could be expressed in terms of the rate at which it could be traded for each of the remaining $L - 1$ goods. This gives us $L \times (L - 1)$, or $L^2 - L$ prices. So in an economy with, say 15 goods, there would be $15 \times 14 = 210$ relative prices. But it's not actually that bad—all you really need to know are the relative prices of all goods, relative to any *one* good. With that you can compute all the other relative prices. If there were three goods—apples, bananas, and pears—you don't need all $3 \times 2 = 6$ relative prices. The simplest thing to do is to express all prices relative to, say, bananas. With this done, there are really only two relative prices to keep track of: the price of apples in terms of bananas, and the price of pears in terms of bananas. One can compute any of the remaining four relative prices with this information. For example, the prices of apples and pears in terms of bananas are 2 and 1.5, respectively, and the relative price of apples to pears is 2/1.5, or 1.33. And the relative price of bananas in terms of pears of 1/1.5 or 0.667, and so on.

18. The need to understand the strategic motivations of market participants (most often those of firms) is precisely why modern economics adopted the formal machinery of **game theory**, especially the branch known as **noncooperative game theory**. Simply put, noncooperative game theory is what gives economists a formal understanding of *when* the ADM model is an appropriate framework to use to make predictions for outcomes. Chapter 2 will describe the narrow part of noncooperative results that inform us of when we can apply the ADM approach.

19. See Kaplow and Shavell (2002, 35–38) for a further discussion of this point, especially as it pertains to the legal profession's interpretation of what economists mean by the term.

20. In fact, even if you forget everything else, as long as you remember the three pictures from the Edgeworth box that are in this book, you'll know something substantive.

2 Prices, Efficiency, and Macroeconomics

1. It will become clear later in this chapter why we'd like not to presume that parties have more information.

2. For households, this means that they can (i) sell their entire holdings of endowments of commodities and shares in the firms (again, to the clearinghouse), and (ii) then use the proceeds to buy any combination of goods and services they could afford at the same set of prices. Notice that firms' profits at prices P would be known to households, since they would be determined by prices and the supply decisions announced by firms in the previous step.

3. If, by contrast, a household or firm felt that its decisions constituted a meaningful proportion of total demand or supply, and the WCH had no way of knowing the true preferences of the household, it would have incentives to influence the price formation process. An intuitive example is given in Mas-Colell, Whinston, and Green (1995), p. 860, example 23.B.2.

   One could assume, for example, arbitrarily small costs of falsifying one's reports of how much one would demand and supply at various prices just to manipulate the formation of Walrasian prices. In such a setting, any market with "enough" participants will make such behavior not worthwhile. Roberts and Postlewaite (1976) is a landmark analysis of the extent to which the incentives to misrepresent one's demand and supply shrink as the economy grows "large" relative to the individual.

4. If you like, you can assume that the firm owns all the equipment and doesn't rent it from others. Nothing in this story depends on one's interpretation here.

5. Actually, when one starts listing these things, the WCH starts to sound more like WalMart. Also, later on, when we talk about time and uncertainty—which seem to be missing from this setting, but are actually not—we'll see that the kinds of goods and services imagined are even richer than you might think at this point.

6. Feldman and Serrano (2006), especially chs. 2–6, covers these ideas, and also their link with the "jungle" economy of Piccione and Rubinstein (2007) that I mentioned in chapter 1.

7. Robert Frank (1991) makes this point very vividly in his undergraduate text through an example of how, in competitive settings, firms can be price takers but cannot remain "passive." They must constantly look to contain costs in the face of price changes. He cites a well-known change to the physical profile of trucks over time in response to rising gasoline prices. The truck manufacturers were clearly treating high gasoline prices as given, but were then using all the knowledge they had about how to keep costs down in the face of these prices. A firm that failed to implement these changes would have systematically higher costs, and since they were in a competitive setting where they could not charge more than their competitors for trucking services, would earn lower profits.

8. Stiglitz (1994) notes that this lack of commitment to withholding reward in the face of poor performance (by, say, shutting down plants operating at a loss or punishing managerial incompetence) was important in the failure of centrally planned societies.

9. Colloquially, the topic of incentives is synonymous with asymmetric information. When economists speak of the "theory of incentives," they have in mind the problem of providing incentives in the face of informational and commitment-related problems.

10. Landsburg (2010), p. 305, contains a vivid example of how such knowledge is important, and yet inherently inaccessible to a would-be planner.

11. This point has been famously and effectively made by Hayek (1945). See also Landsburg (2010), ch. 9, for a worked-out example (the whole chapter is a tour de force in explaining gains from trade).

12. Keep in mind that by "efficient" here, I mean "technologically efficient," namely that there is no way for the *industry* to reshuffle inputs across the firms within it in a way that produces at least as much of everything, and more of some products, without also using more of at least one input.

13. And all the beneficial coordination above will occur even if the level of output is sometimes marred by monopoly power—typically in the sense that it will limit production to levels where further production would be socially beneficial.

14. The reader will find useful the perspective given in Kenneth Arrow's speech "Leonid Hurwicz: An Appreciation," delivered January 3, 2009, and found at http://www.econ.umn.edu/news/hurwicz/arrow_on_hurwicz.pdf. See especially the discussion on pages 3–4.

15. If you know some linear algebra, read on. In infinite dimensions, not all vector spaces have so-called dual spaces that allow for inner product representations of linear functionals (i.e., linear functionals that look like vectors of prices). In this case, the notion of competitive equilibrium has less descriptive content in the sense that the value of any given bundle that a household, for example, is thinking about buying cannot automatically be described as "the price of each good times the quantity in the bundle." For the latter to be possible, other conditions, essentially equivalent to restrictions on the *patience* of market participants, must be imposed.

16. Fans of Paul Krugman will have a field day with my blatant advertisement for something beautiful, and my apparent unconcern with "truth" (applicability). The rest of the book, especially chapter 5, will hopefully show that I and my ilk are not actually disconnected at all. But pretty is pretty.

17. The trucking example from the previous section is also an example of how dispersed and specialized knowledge is brought to bear to effectively adapt to *changing* conditions in competitive economies. This is related to macroeconomists' view of market systems' ability to often manage change effectively.

18. In contrast, for other, usually distributional reasons, political processes often move to supplant market processes, even when, or especially when, such processes reliably confront buyers and sellers with Walrasian prices that all are more or less "forced" to take as given. A famous case was the effort to control gasoline prices via direct and complex limitations on prices themselves s undertaken by Presidents Nixon and Carter in the wake of spikes in the cost of crude oil, the key input to the production of gasoline. As for the difficulties with such an approach, the reader is again directed to the text of Landsburg (2010), p. 305. His example is precisely set up to illustrate how, if the world worked as if there were a WCH, a change in the cost of production, even when completely unanticipated, leads to changes in the mixes of inputs being used by each producer such that, given the new reality of production costs in the wake of the change, there is no possible way to reshuffle inputs across producers and obtain more of any one product without sacrificing some of another. This example highlights the likely total futility of employing a well-meaning planner (intent only on achieving such "production efficiency") to allocate inputs across producers efficiently in a timely manner.

The example is also a great one because it also highlights an *incentive* problem inherent in eliciting the information such a planner would need. In particular, participants will not as a matter of course tell the truth about the substitution possibilities they have. They will only do so if such reports are in their interest—i.e., if they can lower their costs or increase their profits.

19. Economic theorists have also established that Walrasian equilibria will exist in seemingly very "badly behaved" economies—such as ones in which markets are incomplete, or ones in which consumers have very peculiar (including irrational) preferences, or ones riddled by various "distorting" taxes or other policies. In these cases, again, existence is an especially robust outcome when the economy has *a large number of people or firms relative to the number of goods being traded*. This is fortunate, since it is this setting that both describes the "real world" reasonably well and in which the assumption of price taking is likely to be most sensible.

20. For those who have some familiarity with the Lebesgue measure: the Pareto set will generally be one dimension smaller than the set of all allocations, and hence will have a relative size of zero.

21. I am likely similar to many economists, who vacillate in our opinion about the workability and efficiency of decentralized trade. As the important general-equilibrium theorist Andreu Mas-Colell (1999) has put it: "As with the optical illusion picture where one moment you see the old lady and on the next you see only the young lady, so it is with reality: it can appear perversely dominated by externalities, increasing returns and many other features capable of explaining the locking of the economy in a multitude of positions, or it can look as a majestic display of marginal adjustments pushing the economy towards one, or a few, coherent scenarios." I personally take the latter view far more often, on balance, than the former, as will be seen in the discussion of experimental results on Walrasian equilibrium.

22. I refer interested readers to Stiglitz (1994), and for more formality to Kreps (1990), chs. 16, 19, and 20, and the references therein.

23. As for completeness: A storm blew over a glass-topped table in our yard recently, scattering thousands of extremely small pieces that got ground into the grass. A neighbor promptly informed me that many firms stood ready to perform the complex cleanup job for just this sort of situation. A classic article suggesting just how pervasive markets are, even for goods that may seem hard to define, is Cheung (1973) on how beekeepers and apple growers coordinated to deliver markets in what might have seemed initially to be places ripe for incompleteness.

As for competitiveness, wait for chapter 6, where I'll talk about the so-called efficient market hypothesis.

24. This is known as having "(Lebesgue) measure zero."

25. This logic just uses the negation of the implication of a premise. The statement "A implies B" is logically equivalent to the statement "Not B implies Not A." The latter is usually called "the contrapositive." For example, if all Americans of Indian descent like Bon Scott–era AC/DC, then we have the statement "Indian-American implies likes Bon Scott–era AC/DC." The contrapositive tells us that if we find a person who doesn't like this music, they must not be Indian-American.

26. In most models, the latter will be the set of prices facing households and firms.

27. Remarkably, this was conjectured in the late 1800s by the great statistician and economist F. Y. Edgeworth.

28. To supplement what follows, see, e.g., Kreps (1990), ch. 12, and Mas-Colell, Whinston, and Green (1995), ch. 8, for detailed discussions of the Nash concept that provide more precise definitions than I will give here.

29. The interested reader *must* read Kreps (1990). It is much deeper (and perhaps clearer too!) than the treatment here.

30. A textbook example of such a result, for the interested reader, is given in Mas-Colell, Whinston, and Green (1995), p. 405, exercise 12.D.2.

31. The papers of Dagan, Serrano, and Volij (2000) and Serrano and Yosha (1995), the book-length treatment of Gale (2000), and the textbook of Osborne and Rubinstein (1990) contain the details and references to important landmarks in this literature.

32. The work I noted earlier of Green (1980) and Green and Porter (1984) should be kept in mind.

33. The volume containing Mas-Colell's essay, *Frontiers of Research in Economic Theory*, edited by D. P. Jacobs et al., is excellent; many of the ideas discussed therein by the leading lights of the profession have quite inevitably found their way into this book.

34. On the notion of evolutionary forces, a narrower question is whether, holding fixed a given trading arrangement, one can explain experimental data. This, as the recent work of Duffy and Temzelides (2009) points out, reverses the order of things usually seen in economics, but follows the rich tradition of natural science. Duffy and Temzelides show, very roughly, that often but not always, as the number of participants gets large, players who use strategies that are "evolutionarily stable," rather than hyperrational, trade to approximately Walrasian outcomes.

35. Recall chapter 1, in which I described Walrasian equilibria as the "fixed points" of a particular mapping from prices to decisions made by households and firms.

36. I thank Doug Davis for very helpful comments on what follows.

37. Similarly, experiments examining iterative price formation procedures, such as the so-called Walrasian *tatonnement* mechanism, do not do so well, particularly in terms of "who ends up with what" (see e.g., Bronfman et al., 1996).

38. Stiglitz (1994) is apropos of this: decentralization works better than everything else, but it may not be ADM-style reasoning of "price taking and optimization under complete markets" that's behind the "goodness." And, we can't yet fully say what is.

39. See Stiglitz (1994) for a similar view that suggests that producers make a great many decisions without the use of prices, instead using "non-price" information. One can no longer guarantee that efficient coordination has occurred. This, like the view in Makowski and Ostroy (2001), strikes me as too extreme. Few, if any, employers have the power to set the prices of inputs as they wish. Rather, even big users of an input, such as airlines' use of fuel, seem to be forced into taking these prices as given. As such, their remaining decisions must be made by treating the price of fuel as a parameter: one they cannot control, but rather one that imposes a constraint which must be included in their overall profit maximization problem. To the extent that this is accurate empirically, the airlines' actions regarding input use will be coordinated efficiently.

40. A more serious example is that of the conventional arrangements as in banking and insurance that one observes where, as I describe in chapter 5, a contracting arrangement *plays the role* of a large number of markets. Thus, our failure to directly "see" a huge variety of markets in operation does not mean that outcomes are inefficient.

41. And where market power *is* important and damaging, it might have mostly to do with other policies already in place, rather than with more organically occurring forms of market power. In the context of innovation policy, see Boldrin and Levine (2008), who argue forcefully that US policy may well be responsible for a particularly strong *injection* of market power into the economy.

42. An exception is the class of models most often used to study monetary policy, where some classes of firms are modeled as having some market power. Still, it is a stretch to say that the market power in these settings is "significant."

43. I want to direct the reader to the very trenchant criticism of Vernon Smith, in *Rationality in Economics* (2010), regarding economists' success thus far in effectively thinking through instances of market power.

44. The reader will also find Farrell (1987) useful for an accessible review and another concrete example of how decentralized trading will not yield a satisfactory (Pareto-optimal) outcome. That essay is also useful for its scientific and neutral perspective on how to interpret the Coase theorem.

45. See McMillan (1994).

46. Overall, however, Stiglitz appears to hold the standard economist view, judging from chapter 15 of his book. Stiglitz's book is really about *all that's wrong with the ADM model* (which is why it's relevant to this book), and only peripherally about what's wrong with planned alternatives to "decentralized markets." We both agree that primarily decentralized approaches are the best we can do, but we differ somewhat on why that is. Prychitko (1995) is a thoughtful review.

47. This is not entirely true: recall that all the First Welfare Theorem asks for is local nonsatiation, and that the existence of Walrasian equilibria in "large" economies is guaranteed by even weaker conditions.

3 Macroeconomists, Efficiency, and Inequality

1. As for our expertise, the distinguished economist Ariel Rubinstein (2012) says in his recent book: "I had the good fortune to grow up in a wonderful area of Jerusalem, surrounded by a diverse range of people: Rabbi Meizel, the communist Sala Marcel, my widowed Aunt Hannah, and the intellectual Yaacovson. As far as I'm concerned, the opinion of such people is just as authoritative for making social and economic decisions as the opinion of an expert using a model."

One way you might interpret his statement is that economists' "thens" are built on so many questionable "ifs" that all other people's "ifs" have an equal claim on our attention. I'm sometimes sympathetic to this view, but I hope (and presume) that whatever, e.g., Yaacovson's "ifs" were, Rubinstein would hold him to deriving "thens" in a correct way.

2. Probably the single best general discussion of these issues for the layperson (though it's dated in places) remains the exceptional book of Okun (1974). My book covers the models macroeconomists use and so is more technically oriented than his, but Okun's book is masterful as a measured statement from a humane economist.

3. Looking ahead, chapter 5 will cover in detail some models and results that inform us on the extent to which one can view inequality as the visible face of inefficiency.

4. Typically, as I will argue below, the right metric is that of a version of the Pareto standard known as an "ex-ante" standard, and interestingly (conveniently?) it will allow what look like distributional concerns to reenter the ambit of economists. It is also a small sleight-of-hand to avoid interpersonal welfare comparisons.

5. See Gul and Pesendorfer (2007) for a detailed evaluation of the way economists evaluate welfare. I'm certainly in favor of what they call "Welfare I," and I certainly do what they call "Welfare II," but in speaking with those whom I advise, I do (deliberately) wander into Welfare III in the places where I suggest that ex-ante expected utility under a given specification of the utility function is the "appropriate" metric.

6. Again, Arthur Okun's (1974) book is a must-read on this point. Okun has in mind the narrower notion of "production-side" efficiency, though: equalization means a drop in the output level (or even growth rate) of an economy. My use of the term "efficiency" is in the Pareto sense, and thus is more demanding, in that production-side efficiency is only one of the requirements.

7. The US has done this in places: student loans are conspicuously nondischargeable in personal bankruptcy. I have done research in this area, and while it is by no means completely settled, an emerging consensus might be that means testing may help society strike a useful balance between the need of some for protection against income risk without making credit costs much higher for everyone else lacking collateral (usually young, wealth-poor households).

8. See section 3.I of Mas-Colell, Whinston, and Green (1995) for a clear exposition of individual-level deadweight loss from non-lump-sum taxes.

9. I am clearly glossing over the myriad difficulties in talking about "societally agreed-upon" redistribution. The Rawlsian perspective, which we'll discuss later, helps on this score, to the extent that we agree on the level of risk tolerance to apply when judging outcomes.

10. Taxes on corporations have negative effects because the legal obligation to "write the government a check" does not tell you how the only parties capable of actually paying the tax (consumers and the people who own firms) are affected. Consumers will pay through higher prices, owners through lower dividends, and they will do so in amounts that tax law has no control over.

11. Now that we have this theorem in hand, we can note that, given the disasters generated by dictatorial or centrally planned regimes, it is a delightful happenstance that decentralized trading systems can, even if only potentially, lead self-interested, ignorant parties to equitable and efficient outcomes. "All" that is required is that we have enough competitive markets in which they can trade. Before I knew these results, it certainly was not obvious to me that *any* system would be capable of such performance, let alone one that asked so little of individuals.

12. The emphasis on decentralization to deliver efficient, but planned, outcomes is important. Much earlier, Hayek (1945) famously argued that the *nature* of the information needed by a planner to arrange for optimal outcomes was exactly what precluded planning from succeeding. Namely, he argued that the planning authority would simply not know *what* to ask, as any would-be planner would lack "the knowledge of the *particular circumstances of time and place*" (emphasis added). This is an important point to keep in mind. Interestingly, Hayek and others were more silent on incentival role of Walrasian prices, and how they directly dictated rewards and costs for actions. But we see here that

competitively determined prices might well be crucial to ensuring judicious resource use and work effort.

In this sense, market socialists did *not* ignore the need to construct a trading institution which aggregated dispersed information, as they are alleged to have, most famously in Hayek (1945). See Makowski and Ostroy (1992). However, Hayek's later critique (1948) did raise the issue that the sheer number of commodities for which households have preferences would preclude the *practical* implementation of a WCH for anything but a very abbreviated set of goods. In turn, many important commodities might never be brought forth.

13. To revisit the welfare theorems under limited information would take us too far afield, but the exposition in Grochulski (2009) is clear.

14. Benchmark public finance textbooks are those of Myles (1995) and Kocherlakota (2010).

15. Strictly speaking, Maskin and Roberts (2008) assume strong monotonicity of preferences (that is, all consumers always like more of all goods). This is asking more of household behavior than local nonsatiation. But local nonsatiation alone will do.

16. See Slemrod and Bakija (2008).

17. The entire issue of ex-ante and ex-post efficiency is closely related to the discussion of "fairness" as an independent basis for policymaking, above and beyond what is prescribed by the criterion of ex-ante welfare maximization. Fairness, by itself, is not a useful criterion; adherence to it forces one to accept patently absurd alternatives. The interested reader will enjoy the book of Kaplow and Shavell (2004).

18. Another example, very casually speaking (because I have little serious knowledge on which to base my opinion), is the War on Drugs and the costs of its mandatory sentencing, in which some families lose primary earners and become disadvantaged relative to others. These costs may be so high that subsets of American society could see their ex-ante welfare rise from a relaxation in such rules. In other words, maybe we'd all be better off ex-ante in a setting where we opt for a regime with less severe punishments (incarceration) and more narcotic abuse. It is, of course, not crystal clear as a tradeoff, but the general idea holds. That is, the ex-ante standard makes the most sense to apply in general, but if one observes huge ex-post inefficiency, one ought to at least ask about the ex-ante benefits one might be getting.

19. See the work of the important economist Al Roth, a leader in the subfield of "market design," and his coauthors, who now maintain a blog at http://marketdesigner.blogspot .com/.

20. One of its leading architects, Narayana Kocherlakota, even happens to be the president of a Federal Reserve Bank, a macroeconomic policymaking position if there ever was one.

4 Macroeconomic Shortcuts

1. The interested reader is referred to the testimony of David Colander to the US Congress for the Hearing "The Risks of Financial Modeling: VaR and the Economic Meltdown" on September 10, 2009, which contains a more extended critique known as the "Dahlem report." It is available at http://gop.science.house.gov/Media/hearings/ oversight09/sept10/colander.pdf

2. Speaking of maps, economist John Kay might disagree. See his essay "The Map Is Not the Territory: An Essay on the State of Economics," October 4, 2011, on the blog for the Institute for New Economic Thinking, available at http://ineteconomics.org/blog/inet/ john-kay-map-not-territory-essay-state-economics. The response by Michael Woodford (available at the same website) represents my view well.

3. The reader again is directed to Weintraub (1979) for an in-depth description of the tug-of-war between microeconomic theorists' use of general equilibrium to reach conclusions about macroeconomic phenomena, and an earlier generation of academic macroeconomists who felt that such an approach was wrong-headed; the latter felt that starting with aggregated relationships, e.g., specifying the relationships between aggregate consumption and aggregate income, was the only route to progress. The latter did not prevail, and in this sense, we are all microeconomists now.

4. Some economists have also considered cases in which the economy is not competitive—and bargaining of one form or another is used. But for certain kinds of financial assets (as opposed to houses, for example), it is very reasonable a priori, given the findings of the literature on the foundations for WE, to study Walrasian outcomes.

5. This has been going on for a while. Here again is Kenneth Arrow more than sixty years ago: "The usual reaction of the 'literary' social scientist when confronted with a mathematical system designed as a model of reality is to assert that it is 'oversimplified,' that it does not represent all the complexities of reality" (Arrow 1951).

6. The short essay of Varian (1989) is an excellent collection of the arguments about why theory construction is of extra usefulness in economics relative to some of the physical sciences.

7. For those interested, the most comprehensive treatment I have seen on the issue of how mathematics became lingua franca, and also how it influenced economics itself, is Weintraub 2002.

8. The essay by Partha Dasgupta (2008) is useful here. It describes how the tools of mathematical reasoning seem almost preternaturally suited to the questions of economics. It presumes more mathematics than I do here.

9. See Conlisk 1996 for a detailed review of this and other issues facing research aimed at bringing bounded rationality into practice.

10. A classic reference is that of Debreu (1984): "Economic Theory in the Mathematical Mode." See also the discussion provided here: http://afinetheorem.wordpress .com/2010/06/28/economic-theory-in-the-mathematical-mode-g-debreu-1984/. I agree wholeheartedly with the viewpoint therein, and would draw the reader's attention specifically to the author's point about there being no "universal continuity" (continuity in the mathematical sense of the term) in the real world that assures us that "nearly correct assumptions lead to nearly correct conclusions."

11. By contrast, when the brilliant but untrained mathematician Srinivasa Ramanujan offered the mathematical world a series of conjectures, the profession's response was not to accept his claims as is, even though they were already posed in mathematical terms. Instead, he was partnered with mathematicians who could help make these arguments precise, to then decide if they were true, given their premises. See Kanigel (1991).

12. Gale (2000) is a very useful reference on this topic, as well as for the discussion in chapter 6 on off-equilibrium-path restrictions.

13. You may wonder, "How can an infinite-horizon model be easier to deal with than a finite-horizon model?" The answer is that with an infinite horizon, every period has the property that the payoff, as a function of one's actions, one can expect to attain from behaving optimally from tomorrow onward never changes. This immediately lends tractability. If this makes you curious, look up "dynamic programming."

5 Benchmark Macroeconomic Models and Policy Advice

1. As should be clear by now, my aim has been to provide a purely intuitive treatment of how I see theoretical ideas influencing applied macroeconomics and influencing discussions *by* economists about policymaking. But for inspired readers, Ljungqvist and Sargent (2004) remains the best one-stop place to get the full details, especially the "how-to" part that I have not covered at all.

2. Sir John Hicks (1939) also recognized this, in the narrower case where he saw the same physical good or service (e.g., gasoline or haircuts) at different *dates* as distinct commodities.

3. The term "stochastic" refers to uncertainty. This logic can be carried further: even in worlds with public goods or, more generally, in cases where one's actions cannot feasibly be prevented from having direct (as opposed to price-mediated) effects on others (so-called externalities), one can show that through the construction of an appropriate set of markets, decentralized price-taking optimization can still lead to efficient outcomes. In the jargon, this is called a Lindahl equilibrium, and requires that a very particular set of commodities be available for sale at Walrasian prices.

4. Stiglitz (1994) makes this point very nicely.

5. Again, by "decentralized," I have in mind trading arrangements in which no one "actively seeks" to improve (or damage) outcomes for anyone else, but instead responds only to narrow privately relevant incentives. Of course, these narrow incentives, such as prices, will be the outcome of the aggregated choices of all participants.

6. The interested reader is directed to Kreps (1990), ch. 6, for a worked-out example.

7. To echo again the lesson of the First Welfare Theorem, when it comes to the bulk of the items we buy daily, as long as people are even approximately sensible in their purchases at grocery and department stores, there are essentially no mutually beneficial exchange opportunities left unrealized between any of the 200,000 households in the city where I live. This is true despite the fact that we hardly ever know more than the smallest sliver of those living around us.

8. For anyone else who visits, an important subset of these entities are ones referred to colloquially as "box stores" (*pot-tee kadai* in Tamil). These are so small that only the shopkeeper can physically fit inside. Good spot markets seem to operate outside large Indian cities, too. My sister-in-law has described the ease with which one can reliably find (at linear prices) a huge variety of consumer goods (e.g., French shampoo, American candy bars, etc.) in even the very remote Himalayan village she spent a year in.

9. This issue gave rise to the class of SIM models I will describe later.

10. In the case of markets against the risk of being born into bad circumstances, if we imagine each individual having only a finite life, then we can ask to what extent markets exist in which he or she can hedge the uncertainty that will resolve over his or her lifetime. This more limited notion of "market completeness" is particularly useful; it has

observable implications that help us assess the extent to which markets fail to allow households to share risks. Of course, our own descendants will to some extent be represented by us and through the fiscal policies we choose to put into place. We can therefore affect them in ways that reflect our concern for their welfare. More on this further below.

11. Since there is so much confusion among careless observers of macroeconomics on this point, this is a natural place to stress yet again the mantra "Equilibrium does not mean good"!

12. This raises the general question of where "power" comes from. Nash equilibrium suggests that it comes primarily from somehow convincing parties of the likely actions of *other* parties. Saddam Hussein, in his heyday, clearly could not have physically prevented any large-scale revolt. The key to his success was in convincing essentially everyone else that no one would fight him. Once this was achieved, matters were more straightforward. In this sense, all dictators who succeed only do so because they somehow convince enough others that they will be successful.

13. While space constraints prevent any detailed discussion, an entire area known as **global games** aims to provide more robust prediction than standard Nash analysis of games, and has studied especially those settings in which policymakers can transmit information to alter outcomes in important ways. Morris and Shin (2001) is good starting point, and the recent work of Sakovics and Steiner (2012) illustrates some of the subtleties (and opportunities) for policymakers to steer outcomes to relatively beneficial ones.

14. But events were not driven only by government policy; the college students who initiated the lunch counter sit-in movement are an example of private initiative that started the change in society. These four people played a strategy that was not Nash; given the actions of others that they surely rationally expected, and with substantial likelihood, their act was potentially dangerous to their physical well-being. This is what made it so courageous. And since this act led to other sit-ins elsewhere, one might argue it was extraordinarily powerful. For some details, see, e.g., http://www.sitinmovement .org/history/greensboro-chronology.asp.

A striking telltale sign of the role of expectations for behavior was the policy of Woolworth stores at the time to "abide by local custom." Of course, when the custom did change, so did the stores' behavior toward African-Americans at the lunch counter. But keep in mind that economic theory would not have predicted this outcome at all; it was as far from Nash as possible to change customs in such a way. This is especially so because those who initiated the movement were essentially grains of sand on a beach, and so they would have had no rational reason to think they could change outcomes at a societal level.

15. The interested reader will find Leeper (2010) well worth reading. It is nontechnical for the most part. It contrasts the extent to which the modern descendants of the Walrasian tradition are especially heavily used within institutions that form monetary policy, while fiscal policy, as practiced, is less influenced by this tradition.

16. Readers who are not technically oriented and who want to read further about the NGM, as well as an entire class of so-called endogenous growth models, are directed to the prescient text of Upton and Miller (1986), and the contemporary textbook of Williamson (2010). More advanced presentations are offered in the important text of Barro and Sala-i-Martin (1993), as well as the book of Romer (2011).

17. More generally, the Malthusian conclusions follow even when more equipment can be added, and even when innovations routinely make labor more productive (as was happening even before the eighteenth century). The critical features are the presence of

at least one input to production being completely fixed (in Malthus's case, this was land) and the positive dependence of the population growth rate on the average income of workers. See the excellent set of lecture notes available on Stephen Parente's website: https://netfiles.uiuc.edu/parente/Econ509/Chapter_Malthusian_Model.pdf

18. Easterly (2001), ch. 4, describes this effectively.

19. A very useful interactive learning tool for the Solow model is here: http://www .eurmacro.unisg.ch/tutor/Solowpc.html

20. The reader interested in more details on the Solow model, as well as models that differ from the Solow-Swan class ("endogenous growth" models), should read the excellent intuitive approach taken in Ray (1998), and then, if still interested, consult either Aghion and Howitt (1993), Barro and Sala-i-Martin (1993), or Acemoglu (2009).

21. See, e.g., Summers (1986).

22. Put slightly differently: even absent any decision to modify one's model to avoid the multiplicity of Walrasian equilibria, and/or any wild fluctuations in the time path of a given Walrasian (Radner) equilibrium, there is still a lesson. BM and SMD are applicable to complete market economies in which the First Welfare Theorem holds. In other words, even in a model where there are thousands of Walrasian (or Radner) equilibrium outcomes, SMD and BM in no way negate the fact that every single one of those outcomes is Pareto-optimal!

23. Mas-Colell, Whinston, and Green (1995, ch. 17) is an excellent place to go for anyone wanting to know more.

24. Later on, we'll see how the desiderata of having (at least local) uniqueness in the Walrasian outcomes of a model, and that of working with a model in which paths do not fluctuate in seriously counterfactual ways, led to a strategy known as "calibration" and the class of models known initially as "real business cycle" or RBC models.

25. The interested reader can get a friendly introduction to this topic in Mas-Colell, Whinston, and Green (1995), ch. 20.

26. As Meyer and Sullivan (2009) and others have noted, all of our conventional measures of inflation substantially overstate inflation, and thereby understate the improvements in well-being that we have experienced in just the past several decades—a period in which measured median wages have stagnated. And once *consumption* is used as the measure of poverty, measures have shown a substantial decline in poverty over this period as well.

27. I realize that long-term unemployment can be scarring. But notice the extreme short-term cost I've assumed here: people have zero opportunities for five straight years. Thus, we've not likely understated the pain felt by the people concerned.

28. A wide range of seemingly disparate phenomena are evaluated this way by macroeconomists because, from the perspective of the residents of a given country, many things "look like" technological progress, even when they are not literally technological. For example, by undervaluing its currency, a country makes its products cheap. To the residents of another country that imports goods from the first country, it is just as if someone, somewhere, discovered a cheaper way to produce. The same is true for the tax policies of foreign nations that favor their own exports. Either way, domestic consumers win since they now obtain goods more cheaply than otherwise, while the domestic producers of competing goods will lose.

29. The reader will likely find it useful to read William Easterly's (2001) book (also aimed at a general audience), where he makes this point very effectively.

30. The whole article is short, and very accessible. See Lucas (1990).

31. An interesting exchange took place in the late 1980s between the economists William Baumol and Edward Wolff (1986, 1988), who found direct evidence in support of the Solow model's predictions for convergence across countries; but DeLong (1988) neatly showed that Baumol and Wolff ignored measurement error and selection bias such that the results were biased far too much in favor of finding convergence. This was important because it meant that, as of the 1980s, we did not yet have a satisfactory theory of cross-country income differences. We still have a ways to go in this quest even today, and this, and its cousin "growth," dominate all other concerns macroeconomists should have.

32. Arthur Okun (1975) talks about "trickle-down" in ways related to my use of it.

33. I was led to this observation by the related idea in Frank (1991), ch. 18, on the rise in living standards over time *within* a country.

34. See e.g., Romer (2011).

35. This is because at this growth rate, average US income in 2046 will be roughly $100,000 (in current dollars), while average European income will be $80,000.

36. A rather accessible, largely nontechnical exposition of the facts surrounding differences in hours worked is given by Rogerson (2006). More recently, Rogerson (2009) provides a completely nontechnical summary.

37. A state-of-the-art survey on the effect of taxes on labor supply is Keane (2011).

38. As a related and completely informal observation, it seems clear that the manner in which nations intervene in economic outcomes may be crucial in determining the extent to which redistribution places them on Hayek's 1944 "road to serfdom." Western Europe, which intervenes principally via taxes and transfers, has certainly avoided such a fate, by all accounts. In light of the individual liberties enjoyed by its citizens, especially "negative liberties" (i.e., freedom *from* the state and others in their personal lives), it is a stretch to argue that they are serfs. Nonetheless, societies that have opted for substantial intervention in the form of *licensing restrictions and explicit control of production methods* and the scope of products consumed or permitted to be imported and exported have been places where the individual has been treated by the state as spectacularly expendable.

39. The slides by Michele Boldrin and David K. Levine on "Full Appropriation and Intellectual Property" (2007) are useful: levine.sscnet.ucla.edu/papers/slides/ostroy _slides.pdf. Recall that when I discussed Ostroy's view of "no surplus," I noted that it forced one to think differently about prices. This is related to Ostroy's conception of competition allowing—or actually forcing—innovation. An ongoing blog that frequently provides thoughtful assessments of models of innovative processes (and many others—including excellent discussions of the financial crisis) is A Fine Theorem, http://afinetheorem.wordpress.com/. (Full disclosure: I know the anonymous author personally).

40. Recall Robert Frank's trucking example that I footnoted in chapter 2 when I discussed the "informational role of prices."

41. Plosser is now an important macroeconomic policymaker: he is the president of the Federal Reserve Bank of Philadelphia. Recall that another important contributor to modern macroeconomics, Narayana Kocherlakota, is also a Federal Reserve Bank president. It should be apparent by now that the ideas in this book are important for policymaking—several of the ideas originated among people who make macroeconomic policy.

42. In 1986, *The Federal Reserve Bank of Minneapolis Quarterly Review* carried an exposition of the approach I just described by Edward Prescott. The interested reader will find it instructive. The same issue also contains a "reply" article by the eminent economist Lawrence Summers (former Treasury Secretary and president of Harvard University, among other things).

43. A scathing, tongue-in-cheek evaluation of Keynes's ideas is given by Michele Boldrin and David K. Levine in "All the Interesting Questions, Almost All the Wrong Reasons," online at http://www.dklevine.com/papers/keynes.pdf (last accessed February 26, 2013).

44. Good introductions to such models are Farmer (1999, 2010) and the connections to Keynesian models in the important paper of Cooper and John (1988). Some other pioneers of adapting the SGM to settings in which "self-fulfilling prophecies" may flourish are Costas Azariadis, David Cass, Jang-Ting Guo, and Karl Shell.

45. One prominent example is that of Hornstein (1993).

46. In my most ecumenical moods, I am tempted to say that such reasoning applies even to the crudest versions of Keynesian economics peddled today. And perhaps that *is* the right way to view it.

47. See, e.g., the views expressed by John Quiggin: http://economistsview.typepad.com/economistsview/2011/01/zombie-economics-and-just-deserts.html.

48. The testimony of the critics of modern macroeconomics before Congress, which was cited in the preface, is just one example.

49. Again, that these models have been standard fare in macroeconomics for two decades now, while outsiders have suspected us of having only a representative agent to deal with, is a clear measure of the spectacular gulf that exists between what macroeconomists do and what many seem to think we do.

50. Formally incorporating the search process into a household- or firm-level decision problem is involved, but if you study these models further, you'll see that thanks to a mathematical method called **dynamic programming** (nothing to do with computer science, by the way), there is a tractable way to do it.

51. A (very) technical paper that studies the question of the existence of simple kinds of stationary equilibrium (so-called time-homogenous Markov equilibria, or THME) is Duffie et al. (1994). These authors motivate the study of stationary equilibria as the only ones that are possibly "learnable."

52. This is mildly tautological, given the importance of unemployment for determining the state of the economy!

53. Diamond, Mortensen, and Pissarides are all Nobel laureates.

54. The interested reader is directed to Lucas (1985) for the most lucid account I have seen of what the search approach buys. It is occasionally mildly technical.

55. See chapter 1 in Ljungqvist and Sargent (2004).

56. For the interested reader, the introduction to Magill and Quinzii (1996) is an outstanding description of many things we have discussed—but particularly of the modern separation of the study of markets into that of real versus financial ones, beginning with the efforts of the great Irving Fisher. It requires some technical proficiency toward the end of the section, however.

57. See Athreya and Romero (2012) for a nontechnical discussion of economic mobility.

58. Robert Aumann (1964) made this point formally a half-century ago.

59. The 2009 movie *The Informant!* is somewhat insightful in its description of the mechanics of setting up collusive arrangements.

60. For those with familiarity with measure theory: Geanakoplos and Polemarchakis (1986) showed that the set of economies for which Walrasian outcomes are inefficient has full measure. Very recently, Davila et al. (2012) have extended the analysis of Geanakoplos and Polemarchakis to SIM models of the kind developed by Aiyagari (1994) and have shown that the size of the inefficiency may be large.

61. I have this feeling from time to time. My wife and I are comfortably positioned in the overall US income distribution. My extended family is close-knit and very highly educated. My children could be lazy, and they could be poor students in high school, yet in neither case would they ever feel the pinch of true deprivation. By contrast, a child with poor cognition, born into a poor household less than 20 miles from me in downtown Richmond, Virginia, is unlikely to escape poverty—if we take the data on intergenerational mobility even a little seriously. This strikes me as a risky world to be born into.

62. Recall chapter 4 where we noted the seminal work of Robert Barro (1974), who isolated conditions under which a limited form of concern for one's descendants would turn the problem facing a dynasty into exactly the problem of a single household that lived forever.

63. A metaphor may help illustrate why one ought not to expect that decentralized outcomes will inexorably lead to Pareto-optimal outcomes. Imagine a set of towns arranged along a river. Those upstream, if they cannot trade or interact with those downstream, may well use the river in ways that leave it foul and polluted by the time it reaches the latter.

64. You may be appalled that I have spent nearly the entire book on a model in which money plays no role. But this is part of what showing you the benchmark model requires one to do. The huge amount of work in monetary economics overwhelmingly uses variants of the NGM, the SGM models, and less often, search models. Walsh (2010, chs. 1–3) gives an excellent exposition of monetary models based on these benchmarks, while Champ and Freeman (2001) uses the OG model throughout.

65. In fact, he called the paper "National Debt in a Neoclassical Growth Model."

66. The very accessible text of Obstfeld and Rogoff (1995), ch. 3, is a great place to see clearly worked-out examples of the OG model. The reader will also benefit greatly from the wide-ranging 2005 interview with Nobel laureate James Heckman, who is disproportionately responsible for what economists know about the role of policy in skill formation, racial disparity, and the intergenerational transmission of economic status. It

can be found on the Federal Reserve Bank of Minneapolis website at http://www
.minneapolisfed.org/publications_papers/pub_display.cfm?id=3278.

6 Macroeconomic Theory and Recent Events

1. "The Financial Crisis: A Timeline of Events and Policy Actions," Federal Reserve Bank
of St. Louis website, http://timeline.stlouisfed.org//index.cfm?p=timeline (accessed
March 3, 2013). Let me stress that even the facts are not fully agreed upon (see Lo 2012).

2. And why did short-term liabilities become so attractive? Many observers argue that
it was an easy way to obtain funding from entities like money market mutual funds that
were awash in available funds (see, e.g., Brunnermeier 2009), while others have pointed
to low-interest-rate policies and international conditions (the so-called global savings
glut).

3. See, e.g., Guvenen (2012) and the references therein.

4. Recall, though, that in instances where the transacting parties have some degree of
market power, as well as hidden information relevant to determining their willingness
to trade, the Myerson-Satterthwaite theorem becomes applicable. Thus, in some cases,
macroeconomists are being optimistic when they presume bilateral efficiency.

5. On consumer theory, Deaton (1991) remains the best place to start, while for corporate
finance the easy-to-read textbook of Saunders and Cornett (2010) will be useful.

6. See Athreya, Tam, and Young (2012), Sánchez (2012), and Livshits, MacGee, and Tertilt
(2011), for analyses of better screening methods in the case of unsecured credit markets.

7. Recent work of Kasa, Walker, and Whiteman (2012), Tsyrennikov (2012), Colacito and
Croce (2012), Cogley, Sargent, and Tsyrennikov (2012), and others illustrates progress,
and clarifies some of the significant difficulties in models where intelligent traders have
differing views. We've cited Veldkamp (2011) already; it, and its references, are obviously
relevant here as well.

8. Gale and Hellwig (1985), Williamson (1987), and Lacker (2001) are other important
landmarks in the theory of debt.

9. In the context of labor markets, an exception to this point is if one really thinks that
the uneven assignment of hours to workers is *due* to some policy.

10. While not a search model, the work of Lorenzoni (2008) on externalities leading to
inefficient credit booms, and the references therein, will be useful to the interested reader.

11. See the recent book of the economist John Taylor (2009), and a detailed and probing
review of it by John Cochrane, available on his blog "The Grumpy Economist," June
14, 2012, http://johnhcochrane.blogspot.com/2012/06/taylors-first-principles.html
(accessed March 6, 2013).

12. A recent speech by the president of my employer, the Federal Reserve Bank of Richmond, describes two opposing views of financial instability: inherent fragility (of the
Diamond and Dybvig type) or induced fragility (created by policymaker promises to
help distressed institutions). The speech is available at http://www.richmondfed.org/
press_room/speeches/president_jeff_lacker/2013/lacker_speech_20130212.cfm.

13. Let's be concrete with another example (go back to chapter 2 if you wish to review
the other ones I gave). Let's say that the value of maintaining a doctor's office in a quiet

office park was $100,000. And let's say that the same business next door to a confectioner would be worth less: $60,000. Now let's say that a confectionery generates profits each year that make it worth $70,000 as a "going concern" no matter where it is located, but to move it far away from the city costs $30,000. The owner of both enterprises would think carefully about the costs and benefits of moving the businesses apart—it might raise her profits. If they were initially next door to each other, what should she do? Leaving them in place makes the total value of both businesses $130,000 ($60,000 + $70,000). If they were apart, they'd be worth $170,000. Clearly, then, the owner should move the confectionery: it costs $30,000 to do so, but generates $40,000 in extra value. We can hopefully agree that this is the efficient thing (certainly in the narrow sense that it makes production more valuable and, by presumption, leaves consumers unaffected).

Now think of a setting in which the businesses are indeed next door to each other, and each business is run instead by a single owner (a crotchety doctor and a crazed chocolate factory magnate—who do not like each other), and that these owners do not inherently share any interest in maximizing the collective value of both businesses. And let's add that the law has taken a position on who is "liable" for compensating the other for the damage caused to the other. Perhaps most naturally, let's say that the law requires the confectioner to pay the doctor $40,000 in compensation to offset the reduction in the doctor's franchise. Under these rules, what would the confectioner do? He would move: it is worth paying $30,000 (his moving cost) to save $40,000 in payments to a guy he doesn't like anyway. Alternatively, what if the law ignored them, asking the doctor to "just deal with it" by not obligating the confectioner to make any payments at all? Would the same result ensue? It depends. If the two parties could agree to find a solution that made the value of both firms together as high as possible, they'd then be able to split the gains in ways that left both better off. In this instance, the doctor might pay the confectioner $30,001 to get lost. The confectionery would take the money and run, and the doctor too would come out ahead—since the value of his business jumps by $9,999 (the $40,000 gain because he no longer has any noise less the $30,001 payment he makes to "Wonka"). Critically, the eventual location of each business is the same, and the total value of both businesses is exactly as if the same person owned both businesses: $140,000 ($100,000 noise-free doctor's office, $70,000 confectionery, minus $30,000 in moving costs), with the only difference being who has to pay for this to happen. If they could not negotiate with each other (perhaps because they have miscommunications and have reached some point of no return), then we cannot be assured of any such outcome— and it can easily be the case that the parties miss opportunities to make themselves both better off.

14. Farrell (1987) is very useful on the extent to which the implications of Coase for policy verge on the tautological. In essence, proponents sometimes seem to be saying: if the parties can reach an efficient outcome, then outcomes will be efficient. To me, the issue is: whenever the costs of communication are low, firms owned by different parties will act like a single firm trying to maximize total value. Thus, on the production side, I view Coase as an extension of the production-side aggregation result we saw in chapter 4.

15. It may be obvious, but I'd like to emphasize that any doubt cast on the ability of policy to generate unambiguous improvements is not to be taken as an endorsement of laissez-faire, which may be disastrous by the measure of Pareto efficiency, and yet leave few opportunities for well-meaning policymakers.

16. Making threats credible is also at the heart of ensuring good behavior for a nation's monetary authority. For example, the Governor of the Central Bank of New Zealand faces a contract in which she or he will be punished monetarily for a failure to take tough

actions that might, in some cases, inflict pain on the citizenry. The citizenry, for their part, recognize that in order to take actions that yield the best expected path for future economic activity, one might have to commit to allowing some suffering in the future—if only to focus the attention of private decision makers in the present. By setting up the contract with the Central Bank in this way, they ensure that the Bank will not succumb, by its benevolence, to letting "bygones be bygones." For, if they were known to do so, any tough talk up front by them would be ignored.

17. For example, games where parties are *not* unsure about what others have done are just a special case of being uncertain about what others have done. Nash equilibrium by itself has a clear weakness, though, in that it leaves open-ended the beliefs players hold about other players' previous behaviors when they cannot observe them completely. Ideas like "sequential equilibrium," "the intuitive criterion," and "universal divinity" aim to deal with this shortcoming.

18. According to Kreps (1990), work by McLennan (who also contributed research on stationary equilibria in Duffie et al. 1994) started the literature on how one might try to restrict beliefs off the path of equilibrium play. McLennan is, by all accounts, a very "pure" microeconomic theorist (i.e., probably not waking up to see how he can help my tribe out), and so we've now seen two disparate places in which macroeconomists are using the tools he helped fashion. This is why it is hard for me to see any clear distinction between microeconomics and macroeconomics aside from the scope of the question being asked.

19. For example, in my own research on the role of how creditors' lack of information about borrowers affects credit card lending, my coauthors and I have modeled a game between borrowers and lenders that is very close, as a mathematical matter, to the famous so-called beer-quiche or Spence job-market-signaling games. We then have employed PBE to select outcomes that do not involve silly threats or beliefs. Lastly, in relation to the practicality of game-theoretic ideas for the macroeconomics of policymaking, a very interesting aspect of games where players move in a well-defined sequence is that when players are modeled as not knowing for sure what transpired in the game previously, one obtains a way to model *irrationality*. While this topic is too far removed from the goals of this book, the interested reader should see Kreps (1990, ch. 13) for a description and example of this way of modeling play against an irrational opponent.

20. Notice that these problems would arise even in the absence of any crisis-related currency distortions.

21. A layperson's guide to "systemic risk" and its implications for policy is given in Athreya (2009).

22. The reader is directed again to Stiglitz (1994). Though it is not a byproduct of the recent crisis, and so is not discussed here, it is a high-water mark for criticism of the Walrasian (and hence, "rational-expectations") approach. It is also not hurried and breathless in its zeal to be timely.
    As I stated earlier, though I personally think Stiglitz's book is too strong, and contains quantitative presumptions that one can wonder about, it is essential reading for those who want a list of the dental records for each of the bodies buried in the Walrasian foundation for macroeconomics. (It will also supply endless fodder for those with calcified "anti-market" opinions looking to reverse-engineer support for their prejudices, just as Hayek's writings do for other audiences.) Lastly, another recent offering is the well-meaning paean to "reality-based economics" by journalist John Cassidy (2010). I'd like

to think of my ilk as "reality-based," and so I think it's a bit unfair of him to co-opt the term!

23. The latest effort belongs again to Paul Krugman. In a typically cunning move, he has penned a "Manifesto for Economic Sense" (available at http://www .manifestoforeconomicsense.org/). While I disagree with his scorched-earth approach, I also *really* want to make sense.

24. This is, interestingly, similar to the nonsense that my father, a professional mathematician, sometimes has to put up with when told by fellow Indians that Vedic-era mathematics had already made great advances that rivaled those of modern mathematics: i.e., essentially, that a David Hilbert or André Weil were simply smart people unwittingly rediscovering a glorious past.

25. Interestingly, the archenemy of many critics of modern macroeconomics, Milton Friedman, was fundamental in building market incompleteness into models of household consumption behavior.

26. See the complaint of Colander et al. (2010).

27. In turn, such a view suggests a limited and focused role for central banks, one aimed at the objects central banks can most effectively deal with, such as price stability, bank regulation, and ensuring the integrity of payment systems. (In light of the crisis, an additional charge that may fall into the ambit of central banking is "macro-prudential" stability. It remains to be seen whether this is a realistic goal.)

References

Abreu, D., D. Pearce, and E. Stacchetti. 1986. Optimal Cartel Equilibria with Imperfect Monitoring. *Journal of Economic Theory* 39:251–269.

Abreu, D., D. Pearce, and E. Stacchetti. 1990. Toward a Theory of Discounted Repeated Games with Imperfect Monitoring. *Econometrica* 58 (5):1041–1063.

Acemoglu, D. 2009. *Introduction to Modern Economic Growth*. Cambridge, MA: MIT Press.

Acharya, V., and M. Richardson, eds. 2009. *Restoring Financial Stability: How to Repair a Failed System*. Hoboken, NJ: John Wiley.

Adrian, T., and M. Brunnermeier. 2011. *CoVar. Mimeo*. Princeton University.

Aghion, P., and P. Howitt. 1993. *Introduction to Endogenous Growth*. Cambridge, MA: MIT Press.

Aguiar, M., and G. Gopinath. 2006. Defaultable Debt, Interest Rates and the Current Account. *Journal of International Economics* 69 (1):64–83.

Aguiar, M., and E. Hurst. 2005. Consumption versus Expenditure. *Journal of Political Economy* 113 (5):919–948.

Aiyagari, S. R. 1994. Uninsured Idiosyncratic Risk and Aggregate Saving. *Quarterly Journal of Economics* 109:659–684.

Akerlof, G. A. 1970. The Market for "Lemons": Quality Uncertainty and the Market Mechanism. *Quarterly Journal of Economics* 84 (3):488–500.

Alt, F. L. 1972. Archaeology of Computers: Reminiscences 1945–1947. *Communications of the ACM* 15 (7):693–694.

Anderson, R. 1978. An Elementary Core Equivalence Theorem. *Econometrica* 46: 1483–1487.

Andolfatto, D. 1996. Business Cycles and Labor-Market Search. *American Economic Review* 86 (1):112–132.

Arellano, C. 2008. Default Risk and Income Fluctuations in Emerging Economies. *American Economic Review* 98 (3):690–712.

Arrow, K. 1951. Mathematical Models in the Social Sciences. Cowles Foundation Discussion Paper 48.

Arrow, K. 1953. Le rôle des valeurs boursières pour la répartition la meilleure des risques. *Colloques Internationaux du Centre National de la Recherche Scientifique* 11:41–47.

Arrow, K. 1964. The Role of Securities in the Optimal Allocation of Risk Bearing. *Review of Economic Studies* 31 (2):91–96.

Arrow, K. 1972. *General Economic Equilibrium: Purpose, Analytic Techniques, Collective Choice: Nobel Memorial Lecture*. Stockholm: Nobel Foundation.

Arrow, K. 1986. Rationality of Self and Others in an Economic System. In *Rational Choice*, ed. R. M. Hogarth and M. W. Reder, 201–216. Chicago: University of Chicago Press.

Arrow, K. J. 2009. Leonid Hurwicz: An Appreciation. Remarks delivered at a luncheon meeting of the American Economic Association, January 3.

Arrow, K. J., and G. Debreu. 1954. Existence of a Competitive Equilibrium for a Competitive Economy. *Econometrica* 22 (3): 265–290.

Athreya, K. 2005. Equilibrium Models of Personal Bankruptcy: A Survey. *Federal Reserve Bank of Richmond Economic Quarterly* 91 (2):73–98.

Athreya, K. 2007. In Praise of Theory. *Federal Reserve Bank of Richmond Economic Quarterly*. Available at http://www.richmondfed.org/publications/research/region_focus/2007/spring/pdf/opinion.pdf (accessed March 1, 2013).

Athreya, K. 2009. Systemic Risk and the Pursuit of Efficiency. Annual Report, Federal Reserve Bank of Richmond.

Athreya, K., and R. Haltom. 2012. The Spice of Life: Allowing for Heterogeneity in Macro Models. Economic Brief, Federal Reserve Bank of Richmond, No. 12-04.

Athreya, K., and J. Romero. 2012. Land of Opportunity? Economic Mobility in the United States. Annual Report, Federal Reserve Bank of Richmond.

Athreya, K., X. S. Tam, and E. R. Young. 2012. A Quantitative Theory of Information and Unsecured Credit. *American Economic Journal: Macroeconomics* 4 (3):153–183.

Attanasio, O. P., and G. Weber. 2010. Consumption and Saving: Models of Intertemporal Allocation and Their Implications for Public Policy. *Journal of Economic Literature* 48 (3):693–751.

Aumann, R. 1964. Markets with a Continuum of Traders. *Econometrica* 32:39–50.

Aumann, R. 1975. Values of Markets with a Continuum of Traders. *Econometrica* 43:611–646.

Aumann, R. 1987. Game Theory. In *The New Palgrave: A Dictionary of Economics*, vol. 2, ed. J. Eatwell, M. Milgate, and P. Newman, 460–482. London: Macmillan.

Barone, E. 1908a. Il ministro della produzione nello stato collettivista. *Giornale degli Economisti* 2: 267–293. Trans. as The Ministry of Production in the Collectivist State, in *Collectivist Economic Planning*, ed. F. A. Hayek (1935), 245–290.

Barone, E. 1908b. *Principi di economia politica*. Rome: Tipografia Nazionale di G. Bertero.

Barro, R. J. 1974. Are Government Bonds Net Wealth? *Journal of Political Economy* 82:1095–1117.

Barro, R. J., and X. Sala-i-Martin. 1993. *Economic Growth*. New York: McGraw-Hill.

Baumol, W. J. 1986. Productivity Growth, Convergence, and Welfare: What the Long-Run Data Show. *American Economic Review* 76 (5):1072–1085.

Baumol, W. J., and E. N. Wolff. 1988. Productivity Growth, Convergence, and Welfare: Reply. *American Economic Review* 78 (5):1155–1159.

Bernanke, B., and M. Gertler. 1989. Agency Costs, Net Worth, and Business Fluctuations. *American Economic Review* 79 (1):14–31.

Bernanke, B. S., and M. Gertler. 2001. Should Central Banks Respond to Movements in Asset Prices? *American Economic Review* 91 (2):253–257.

Bernheim, B. D. 1984. Rationalizable Strategic Behavior. *Econometrica* 52 (4):1007–1028.

Bewley, T. F. 1983. A Difficulty with the Optimum Quantity of Money. *Econometrica* 51 (5):1485–1504.

Bewley, T. F. 1988. Knightian Uncertainty. In *Frontiers of Research in Economic Theory: The Nancy L. Schwartz Memorial Lectures, 1983–1997*, ed. D. P. Jacobs et al., 71–81. Cambridge: Cambridge University Press.

Biais, B., L. Glosten, and C. Spatt. 2005. Market Microstructure: A Survey of Microfoundations, Empirical Results, and Policy Implications. *Journal of Financial Markets* 8 (2): 217–264.

Blanchard, O. 2009. The State of Macro. *Annual Review of Economics* 1:209–228.

Boldrin, M., and D. Levine. 2007. Against Intellectual Monopoly: Economic and Game Theory. Available at http://levine.sscnet.ucla.edu/general/intellectual/againstnew.htm (accessed January 28, 2013).

Boldrin, M., and D. K. Levine. 2008. *Against Intellectual Monopoly.* Cambridge: Cambridge University Press.

Boldrin, M., and L. Montrucchio. 1986. On the Indeterminacy of Capital Accumulation Paths. *Journal of Economic Theory* 40 (1):26–39.

Bond, P., I. Goldstein, and E. S. Prescott. 2010. Market-Based Corrective Actions. *Review of Financial Studies* 23 (2):781–820.

Bowles, S., and H. Gintis. 1993. The Revenge of Homo Economicus: Contested Exchange and the Revival of Political Economy. *Journal of Economic Perspectives* 7 (1): 83–102.

Breeden, D. 1979. An Intertemporal Asset Pricing Model with Stochastic Consumption and Investment Opportunities. *Journal of Financial Economics* 7:265–296.

Brock, W. F., and L. Mirman. 1972. Optimal Economic Growth and Uncertainty: The Discounted Case. *Journal of Economic Theory* 4 (3):479–513.

Bronfman, C., K. McCabe, D. Porter, S. Rassenti, and V. Smith. 1996. An Experimental Examination of the Walrasian Tatonnement Mechanism. *Rand Journal of Economics* 27 (4):681–699.

Brunnermeier, M. K. 2009. Deciphering the Liquidity and Credit Crunch 2007–2008. *Journal of Economic Perspectives* 23 (1):77–100.

Caballero, R. J. 2010. Macroeconomics after the Crisis: Time to Deal with the Pretense-of-Knowledge. *Journal of Economic Perspectives* 24 (4):85–102.

Carlstrom, C. T., and T. S. Fuerst. 1997. Agency Costs, Net Worth, and Business Fluctuations: A Computable General Equilibrium Analysis. *American Economic Review* 87 (5):893–910.

Carroll, C. D., and M. S. Kimball. 1996. On the Concavity of the Consumption Function. *Econometrica* 64 (4):981–992.

Cass, D. 1965. Optimum Growth in an Aggregative Model of Capital Accumulation. *Review of Economic Studies* 32:233–240.

Cassidy, J. 2010. *How Markets Fail: The Logic of Economic Calamities*. New York: Farrar, Straus and Giroux.

Cecchetti, S. G. 2009. Crisis and Responses: The Federal Reserve in the Early Stages of the Financial Crisis. *Journal of Economic Perspectives* 23 (1):51–76.

Chambers, M. S., C. Garriga, and D. E. Schlagenhauf. 2009. The Loan Structure and Housing Tenure Decisions in an Equilibrium Model of Mortgage Choice. *Review of Economic Dynamics* 12 (3):444–468.

Champ, B., and S. Freeman. 2001. *Modeling Monetary Economies*. Cambridge: Cambridge University Press.

Chari, V. V., and P. Kehoe. 2007. Reply to Solow. Working Paper 654, Federal Reserve Bank of Minneapolis. Available at http://www.minneapolisfed.org/research/wp/wp654.pdf (accessed March 7, 2013).

Chari, V. V., and P. Kehoe. 2010. Bailouts, Time Inconsistency, and Optimal Regulation. Working Paper 2010-4-23, Federal Reserve Bank of Minneapolis.

Cheung, S. N. S. 1973. The Fable of the Bees: An Economic Investigation. *Journal of Law & Economics* 16 (1):11–33.

Cochrane, J. H. 1991. A Simple Test of Consumption Insurance. *Journal of Political Economy* 99 (5):957–976.

Cogley, T., T. Sargent, and V. Tsyrennikov. 2012. Market Prices of Risk with Diverse Beliefs, Learning, and Catastrophes. *American Economic Review* 102 (3):141–146.

Colacito, R., and M. Croce. 2012. International Robust Disagreement. *American Economic Review* 102 (3):152–155.

Colander, D., et al. 2010. The Financial Crisis and the Systemic Failure of Academic Economics. *Voprosy Economiki* 2010, vol. 6.

Conesa, J. C., S. Kitao, and D. Krueger. 2009. Taxing Capital? Not a Bad Idea After All! *American Economic Review* 99 (1):25–48.

Conlisk, J. 1996. Why Bounded Rationality? *Journal of Economic Literature* 34 (2): 669–700.

Constantinides, G. M. 1982. Intertemporal Asset Pricing with Heterogeneous Consumers and without Demand Aggregation. *Journal of Business* 55 (2):253–267.

Cooley, T. F., ed. 1995. *Frontiers of Business Cycle Research*. Princeton: Princeton University Press.

Cooper, R., and A. John. 1988. Coordinating Coordination Failures in Keynesian Models. *Quarterly Journal of Economics* 103 (3):441–463.

Corbae, D., P. D'Erasmo, and B. Kuruscu. 2009. Politico-economic Consequences of Rising Wage Inequality. *Journal of Monetary Economics* 56 (1):43–61.

Cordoba, J.-C. 2008. U.S. Inequality: Debt Constraints or Incomplete Asset Markets? *Journal of Monetary Economics* 55 (2):350–364.

Crockett, S., and J. Duffy. 2010. A Dynamic General Equilibrium Approach to Asset Pricing Experiments. Mimeo. Baruch College.

Cunha, A. 2005. A Direct Proof of the First Welfare Theorem. Ibmec Working Paper wpe_30, Ibmec São Paulo.

Dagan, N., R. Serrano, and O. Volij. 2000. Bargaining Coalitions, and Competition. *Economic Theory* 15:279–296.

Danthine, J.-P., and J. Donaldson. 1985. A Note on the Effects of Capital Income Taxation on the Dynamics of a Recursive Economy. *Journal of Public Economics* 28:255–265.

Dasgupta, P. 2008. Mathematics and Economic Reasoning. In *The Princeton Companion to Mathematics*, ed. T. Gowers et al., 901–915. Princeton: Princeton University Press.

Dávila, J., J. H. Hong, P. Krusell, and J. V. Ríos-Rull. 2012. Constrained Efficiency in the Neoclassical Growth Model with Uninsurable Idiosyncratic Shocks. *Econometrica* 80 (6):2431–2467.

Deaton, A. 1991. *Understanding Consumption*. New York: Oxford University Press.

Debreu, G. 1959. *Theory of Value: An Axiomatic Analysis of Economic Equilibrium*. New Haven: Yale University Press.

Debreu, G. 1970. Economies with a Finite Set of Equilibria. *Econometrica* 38 (3):387–392.

Debreu, G. 1984. Economic Theory in the Mathematical Mode. *American Economic Review* 74 (3):267–278.

Debreu, G., and H. Scarf. 1963. A Limit Theorem on the Core of an Economy. *International Economic Review* 4:235–246.

De Long, J. B. 1988. Productivity Growth, Convergence, and Welfare: Comment. *American Economic Review* 78 (5):1138–1154.

Diamond, D., and P. Dybvig. 1983. Bank Runs, Deposit Insurance, and Liquidity. *Journal of Political Economy* 91 (3):401–419.

Diamond, P. 1965. National Debt in a Neoclassical Growth Model. *American Economic Review* 55 (5):1126–1150.

Diamond, P. 1982. Aggregate Demand Management in Search Equilibrium. *Journal of Political Economy* 90:881–894.

Dickhaut, J., A. Rustichini, and V. Smith. 2009. A Neuroeconomic Theory of Decision Processes. *Proceedings of the National Academy of Sciences of the United States of America* 106 (52):22145–22150.

Duffie, D. 2010. *How Big Banks Fail and What to Do About It*. Princeton: Princeton University Press.

Duffie, D., J. Geanakoplos, A.-M. Colell, A. McLennan, and W. Zame. 1994. Stationary Markov Equilibria. *Econometrica* 62 (4):745–781.

Duffie, D., and W. Shafer. 1985. Equilibrium in Incomplete Markets: I. A Basic Model of Generic Existence. *Journal of Mathematical Economics* 14:285–300.

Duffy, J., and T. Temzelides. 2009. Competitive Behavior in Market Games: Evidence and Theory. *Journal of Economic Theory* 146 (4):1437–1463.

Easterly, W. 2001. *The Elusive Quest for Growth: Economists' Adventures and Misadventures in the Tropics*. Cambridge, MA: MIT Press.

Eaton, J., and M. Gersovitz. 1981. Debt with Potential Repudiation: Theoretical and Empirical Analysis. *Review of Economic Studies* 48 (2):289–309.

Ellickson, B. 1993. *Competitive Equilibrium: Theory and Applications*. Cambridge: Cambridge University Press.

Ely, J. 2010a. Does Economic Theory Assume Its Conclusions? Cheap Talk blog. Available at http://cheaptalk.org/2010/05/20/does-economic-theory-assume-its-conclusions/ (accessed January 14, 2013).

Ely, J. 2010b. Popularize: The Myerson-Satterthwaite Theorem. Cheap Talk blog. Available at http://cheaptalk.org/2010/10/25/popularize-the-myerson-satterthwaite theorem/ (accessed October 25, 2011).

Ennis, H., and T. Keister. 2009. Bank Runs and Institutions: The Perils of Intervention. *American Economic Review* 99 (4):1588–1607.

Farmer, R. E. A. 1999. *The Macroeconomics of Self-fulfilling Prophecies*. 2nd ed. Cambridge, MA: MIT Press.

Farmer, R. E. A. 2010. *How the Economy Works: Confidence, Crashes and Self-Fulfilling Prophecies*. Oxford: Oxford University Press.

Farmer, R. E. A. 2012. The Stock Market Crash of 2008 Caused the Great Recession. *Journal of Economic Dynamics and Control* 36: 693–707.

Farrell, J. 1987. Information and the Coase Theorem. *Journal of Economic Perspectives* 1 (2):113–129.

Favilukis, J., S. Ludvigson, and S. van Nieuwerburgh. 2010. The Macroeconomic Implications of Housing Wealth, Housing Finance, and Limited Risk-Sharing General Equilibrium. Working Paper 15988, National Bureau of Economic Research.

Feldman, A. M., and R. Serrano. 2006. *Welfare Economics and Social Choice Theory*. New York: Springer.

Feldman, R., and G. Stern. 2004. *Too Big to Fail: The Hazards of Bank Bailouts*. Washington, DC: Brookings Institution Press.

Frank, R. 1991. *Microeconomics and Behavior*. New York: McGraw-Hill.

Friedman, D., and J. Rust, eds. 1993. *The Double Auction Market: Institutions, Theories, and Evidence*. Reading, MA: Addison-Wesley.

Friedman, M. 1957. *A Theory of the Consumption Function*. Princeton: Princeton University Press.

Gale, D. 2000. *Strategic Foundations of General Equilibrium: Dynamic Matching and Bargaining Games*. Cambridge: Cambridge University Press.

Gale, D., and M. Hellwig. 1985. Incentive Compatible Debt Contracts: The One-Period Problem. *Review of Economic Studies* 52 (4):647–663.

Geanakoplos, J. G., and H. Polemarchakis. 1986. Existence, Regularity, and Constrained Suboptimality of Competitive Allocations When the Asset Market Is Incomplete. In *Uncertainty, Information, and Communication: Essays in Honor of Kenneth J. Arrow*, vol. 3, ed. W. P. Heller et al., 65–95. Cambridge: Cambridge University Press.

Gerardi, K. S, C. L. Foote, and P. S. Willen. 2011. Reasonable People Did Disagree: Optimism and Pessimism about the U.S. Housing Market before the Crash. In *The American Mortgage System: Crisis and Reform*, ed. M. M. Smith and Susan Wachter, 26–59. Philadelphia: University of Pennsylvania Press.

Gibbons, R. 1992. *Game Theory for Applied Economists*. Cambridge, MA: MIT Press.

Gilboa, I. 2010. *Rational Choice*. Cambridge, MA: MIT Press.

Gintis, H. 2006. The Emergence of a Price System from Decentralized Bilateral Exchange. *Berkeley Electronic Journal of Theoretical Economics* 6:1302–1322.

Giraud, G. 2003. Strategic Market Games: An Introduction. *Journal of Mathematical Economics* 39:355–375.

Gjerstad, S., and J. Dickhaut. 1998. Price Formation in Double Auctions. *Games and Economic Behavior* 22:1–29.

Glaeser, E., J. Gyourko, and A. Saiz. 2008. Housing Supply and Bubbles. Mimeo. Harvard University.

Glosten, L., and P. Milgrom. 1985. Bid, Ask, and Transaction Prices in a Specialist Market with Heterogeneously Informed Traders. *Journal of Financial Economics* 14 (1):71–100.

Gode, D. K., and S. Sunder. 1991. Allocative Efficiency of Markets with Zero Intelligence (ZI) Traders: Market as a Partial Substitute for Individual Rationality. GSIA Working Paper 1992-16, Carnegie Mellon University, Tepper School of Business.

Goodfriend, M. 2002. Interest Rate Policy Should Not React to Asset Prices. In *Asset Price Bubbles: The Implications for Monetary, Regulatory, and International Policies*, ed. W. C. Hunter, G. G. Kaufman, and M. Pomerleano. Cambridge, MA: MIT Press.

Gorton, G. 2010. *Slapped by the Invisible Hand: The Panic of 2007*. New York: Oxford University Press.

Green, E. 1980. Noncooperative Price Taking in Large Dynamic Markets. *Journal of Economic Theory* 22:37–64.

Green, E., and R. Porter. 1984. Noncooperative Collusion under Imperfect Price Information. *Econometrica* 52 (4):87–100.

Gregory, P., and R. Stuart. 1997. *Comparative Economic Systems*. 6th ed. Boston: Houghton-Mifflin.

Grochulski, B. 2009. Distortionary Taxation for Efficient Distribution. *Federal Reserve Bank of Richmond Economic Quarterly* 95(3). Available at http://www.richmondfed.org/publications/research/economic_quarterly/2009/summer/pdf/grochulski.pdf (accessed February 1, 2013).

Grossman, S. 1989. *The Informational Role of Prices*. Cambridge, MA: MIT Press.

Grossman, S., and O. Hart. 1983. An Analysis of the Principal-Agent Problem. *Econometrica* 51 (1):7–45.

Guerrieri, V., and G. Lorenzoni. 2011. Credit Crises, Precautionary Savings, and the Liquidity Trap. Mimeo. University of Chicago.

Gul, F., and M. Pesendorfer. 2007. Welfare without Happiness. *American Economic Review* 97 (2):471–476.

Guner, N., G. Ventura, and Y. Xu. 2008. Macroeconomic Implications of Size-Dependent Policies. *Review of Economic Dynamics* 11 (4):721–744.

Guvenen, F. 2012. Macroeconomics with Heterogeneity: A Practical Guide. *Federal Reserve Bank of Richmond Economic Quarterly* 97 (3):255–326.

Hamermesh, D. S. 2011. Interview, November 18. Available at http://fivebooks.com/interviews/daniel-hamermesh-on-economics-fun.

Harsanyi, J. 1975. Can the Maximin Principle Serve as the Basis for Morality? A Critique of John Rawls's Theory. *American Political Science Review* 69:594–606

Hatchondo, J. C., L. Martinez, and H. Sapriza. 2010. Quantitative Properties of Sovereign Default Models: Solution Methods. *Review of Economic Dynamics* 13 (4):919–933.

Hayashi, F., J. Altonji, and L. Kotlikoff. 1996. Risk-Sharing between and within Families. *Econometrica* 64 (2):261–294.

Hayek, F. A. 1944. *The Road to Serfdom*. Chicago: University of Chicago Press.

Hayek, F. A. 1945. The Use of Knowledge in Society. *American Economic Review* 35 (4):519–530.

Hayek, F. A. 1948. *Individualism and Economic Order*. Chicago: University of Chicago Press.

Heathcote, J., K. Storesletten, and G. L. Violante. 2009. Quantitative Macroeconomics with Heterogeneous Households. *Annual Review of Economics* 1 (1):319–354.

Heilbroner, R. 1990. After Communism. *New Yorker* (September):10.

Hellwig, M. 2010. Systemic Risk in the Financial Sector: An Analysis of the Subprime-Mortgage Financial Crisis. MPI Collective Goods Preprint, No. 2008/43.

Hendricks, L. 1999. Taxation and Long-Run Growth. *Journal of Monetary Economics* 43 (2):411–434.

Hicks, J. R. 1946. *1939. Value and Capital: An Inquiry into Some Fundamental Principles of Economic Theory*. 2nd ed. Oxford: Clarendon Press.

Hildenbrand, W. 1994. *Market Demand: Theory and Empirical Evidence*. Princeton: Princeton University Press.

Holmstrom, B. 1979. Moral Hazard and Observability. *Bell Journal of Economics* 10 (1):74–91.

Hornstein, A. 1993. Monopolistic Competition, Increasing Returns to Scale, and the Importance of Productivity Shocks. *Journal of Monetary Economics* 31 (3):299–316.

Huggett, M. 1993. The Risk-Free Rate in Heterogenous-Agent Incomplete-Market Economies. *Journal of Economic Dynamics and Control* 17 (5–6):953–969.

Hurwicz, L. 1960. Optimality and Informational Efficiency in Resource Allocation Processes. In *Mathematical Methods in the Social Sciences*, ed. K. J. Arrow, S. Karlin, and P. Suppes, 27–46. Stanford: Stanford University Press.

Hurwicz, L. 1972. On Informationally Decentralized Systems. In *Decision and Organization: A Volume in Honor of Jacob Marschak*, ed. C. B. McGuire and R. Radner, 297–336. Minneapolis: University of Minnesota Press.

Imrohoroglu, A. 1989. Cost of Business Cycles with Indivisibilities and Liquidity Constraints. *Journal of Political Economy* 97 (6):1364–1383.

Jackson, M. O. 2001. A Crash Course in Implementation Theory. *Social Choice and Welfare* 18 (4): 655–708.

Jehle, G. A., and P. Reny. 2001. *Advanced Microeconomic Theory*. Boston: Addison-Wesley.

Jeske, K., D. Krueger, and K. Mitman. 2011. Housing and the Macroeconomy: The Role of Bailout Guarantees for Government Sponsored Enterprises. Working Paper 17537, National Bureau of Economic Research.

Kanigel, R. 1991. *The Man Who Knew Infinity: The Life of Genius Ramanujan*. New York: Scribner's.

Kaplow, L., and S. Shavell. 2002. *Fairness versus Welfare*. Cambridge, MA: Harvard University Press.

Karahan, F., and S. Rhee. 2012. Geographical Reallocation and Unemployment during the Great Recession: The Role of the Housing Bust. Working paper.

Karaivanov, A., A. Paulson, and R. Townsend. 2006. Distinguishing Limited Liability from Moral Hazard in a Model of Entrepreneurship. *Journal of Political Economy* 144 (1):100–144.

Kasa, K., T. Walker, and C. Whiteman. 2012. Heterogeneous Beliefs and Tests of Present Value Models. Mimeo. Simon Fraser University.

Keane, M. P. 2011. Labor Supply and Taxes: A Survey. *Journal of Economic Literature* 49 (4):961–1075.

Kiyotaki, N., and J. Moore. 1997. Credit Chains. Mimeo. January.

Kocherlakota, N. 2010. *The New Dynamic Public Finance*. Princeton: Princeton University Press.

Koopmans, T. C. 1965. On the Concept of Optimal Economic Growth. *Pontificiae Academiae Scientiarum Scripta Varia* 28:225–300.

Kornai, J. 1980. *Economics of Shortage*. Amsterdam: North Holland.

Kornai, J., E. Maskin, and G. Roland. 2003. Understanding the Soft Budget Constraint. *Journal of Economic Literature* 41:1095–1136.

Kotlikoff, L., and A. Spivak. 1981. The Family as an Incomplete Annuities Market. *Journal of Political Economy* 89 (2):372–391.

Kreps, D. 1990. *A Course in Microeconomic Theory*. Princeton: Princeton University Press.

Kreps, D., and J. Scheinkman. 1983. Quantity Precommitment and Bertrand Competition Yield Cournot Outcomes. *Bell Journal of Economics* 14 (2):326–337.

Krugman, P. 2009. How Did Economists Get It So Wrong? *New York Times Magazine* (September 2). Available at http://www.nytimes.com/2009/09/06/magazine/06Economic-t.html?em=&pagewanted=all&_r=0.

Krusell, P., and A. A. Smith. 1998. Income and Wealth Heterogeneity in the Macroeconomy. *Journal of Political Economy* 106 (5):867–896.

Kydland, F., and E. Prescott. 1977. Rules Rather than Discretion. *Journal of Political Economy* 85 (31):473–492.

Kydland, F. E., and E. C. Prescott. 1980. Dynamic Optimal Taxation, Rational Expectations and Optimal Control. *Journal of Economic Dynamics and Control* 2 (1):79–91.

Kydland, F., and E. Prescott. 1982. Time to Build and Aggregate Fluctuations. *Econometrica* 50:1345–1370.

Lacker, J. 2001. Collateralized Debt as the Optimal Contract *Review of Economic Dynamics* 4 (4):842–859.

Laitner, J. 1992. Random Earnings Differences, Lifetime Liquidity Constraints, and Altruistic Intergenerational Transfers. *Journal of Economic Theory* 58 (2):135–170.

Landsburg, S. 2010. *Price Theory and Applications*. 8th ed. Mason, OH: South-Western.

Lange, O. 1936. On the Economic Theory of Socialism I. *Review of Economic Studies* 4 (1):53–71.

Lantz, C. D., and P.-D. G. Sarte. 2001. Consumption, Savings, and the Meaning of the Wealth Effect in General Equilibrium. *Federal Reserve Bank of Richmond Economic Quarterly* 87 (Spring): 53–71.

Leeper, E. 2010. Monetary Science, Fiscal Alchemy. Paper for the symposium "Macroeconomic Policy: Post-Crisis and Risks Ahead," Federal Reserve Bank of Kansas City. Available at http://www.kc.frb.org/publicat/sympos/2010/2010-08-16-leeper-paper.pdf (accessed February 23, 2013).

Leijonhufvud, A. 1973. Effective Demand Failures. *Swedish Journal of Economics* 75:27–48.

LeRoy, S. 1989. Efficient Capital Markets and Martingales. *Journal of Economic Literature* 27:1583–1621.

Lettau, M., and H. Uhlig. 1999. Rules of Thumb versus Dynamic Programming. *American Economic Review* 89 (1):148–174.

Livshits, I., J. MacGee, and M. Tertilt. 2011. Costly Contracts and Consumer Credit. Working Paper 17448, National Bureau of Economic Research.

Ljungqvist, L., and T. Sargent. 2004. *Recursive Macroeconomic Theory*. Cambridge, MA: MIT Press.

Lo, Andrew. 2012. Reading about the Financial Crisis: A Twenty-One Book Review. *Journal of Economic Literature* 50 (1):151–178.

Long, J., and C. Plosser. 1983. Real Business Cycles. *Journal of Political Economy* 91:36–69.

Lorenzoni, G. 2008. Inefficient Credit Booms. *Review of Economic Studies* 75 (3):809–833.

Loury, G. 2005. *Lecture presented on the occasion of receiving the 2005 John von Neumann Award, Rajk László College, Corvinus University of Economic Science and Public Administration*. Budapest: Available at http://www.econ.brown.edu/fac/Glenn_Loury/louryhomepage/Loury%27s%20Budapest%20talk.pdf

Lucas, R. 1976. Econometric Policy Evaluation: A Critique. In *The Phillips Curve and Labor Markets*, ed. K. Brunner and A. H. Meltzer, 19–46. New York: American Elsevier.

Lucas, R. E., Jr. 1978. Asset Prices in an Exchange Economy. *Econometrica* 46 (6):1429–1445.

Lucas, R. E., Jr. 1985. *Models of Business Cycles*. Oxford, Cambridge: Blackwell.

Lucas, R. E., Jr. 1990. Why Doesn't Capital Flow from Rich to Poor Countries? *American Economic Review* 80 (2):92–96.

Lucas, R. E., Jr. 2003. Macroeconomic Priorities. *American Economic Review* 93:1–14.

Lucas, R., and E. C. Prescott. 1971. Investment under Uncertainty. *Econometrica* 39:659–681.

Ludvigson, S., and C. Steindel. 1999. How Important Is the Stock Market Effect on Consumption? *Federal Reserve Bank of New York Policy Review* 5:20–40.

Mace, B. J. 1991. Full Insurance in the Presence of Aggregate Uncertainty. *Journal of Political Economy* 99 (5):928–956.

Magill, M. 1977. Some New Results on the Local Stability of the Process of Capital Accumulation. *Journal of Economic Theory* 15:174–210.

Magill, M., and M. Quinzii. 1996. *Theory of Incomplete Markets*. Cambridge, MA: MIT Press.

Makowski, L., and J. Ostroy. 1992. General Equilibrium and Market Socialism: Clarifying the Logic of Competitive Markets. Working Paper 672, UCLA Department of Economics.

Makowski, L., and J. M. Ostroy. 2001. Perfect Competition and the Creativity of the Market. *Journal of Economic Literature* 39 (2):479–535.

Mas-Colell, A. 1982. Cournotian Foundations of Walrasian Equilibrium Theory: An Exposition of Recent Theory. In *Advances in Economic Theory*, ed. W. Hildenbrand, 183–224. New York: Cambridge University Press.

Mas-Colell, A. 1984. On the Theory of Perfect Competition. In *Frontiers of Research in Economic Theory: The Nancy L. Schwartz Memorial Lectures, 1983–1997*, ed. D. P. Jacobs et al., 16–32. Cambridge: Cambridge University Press.

Mas-Colell, A. 1989. An Equivalence Theorem for a Bargaining Set. *Journal of Mathematical Economics* 18:129–139.

Mas-Colell, A. 1999. The Future of General Equilibrium. *Spanish Economic Review* 1 (3):207–214.

Mas-Colell, A., M. Whinston, and J. Green. 1995. *Microeconomic Theory*. New York: Oxford University Press.

Mas-Colell, A., and R. W. Zame. 1991. Equilibrium Theory in Infinite Dimensional Spaces. In *Handbook of Mathematical Economics*, vol. 4. Amsterdam: North-Holland.

Maskin, E., and K. W. Roberts. 2008. On the Fundamental Theorems of General Equilibrium. *Economic Theory* 35 (2):233–240.

Mazumder, B. 2012. Is Intergenerational Economic Mobility Lower Now than in the Past? *Chicago Fed Letter*. Available at http://www.chicagofed.org/digital_assets/publications/ chicago_fed_letter/2012/cflapril2012_297.pdf (accessed May 30, 2012).

McCloskey, D. 1986. *The Rhetoric of Economics*. Madison: University of Wisconsin Press.

McKenzie, L. 1954. On Equilibrium in Graham's Model of World Trade and Other Competitive Systems. *Econometrica* 22 (2):147–161.

McKenzie, L. 1959. On the Existence of General Equilibrium for a Competitive Economy. *Econometrica* 27:54–71.

McMillan, J. 1994. Selling Spectrum Rights. *Journal of Economic Perspectives* 8:145–162.

Mehra, R., and E. C. Prescott. 1985. The Equity Premium: A Puzzle. *Journal of Monetary Economics* 15:145–161.

Meisenzahl, R. 2011. Verifying the State of Financing Constraints. Finance and Economics Discussion Series Working Paper 2011-4, Board of Governors of the Federal Reserve System.

Menzio, G. 2007. A Theory of Partially Directed Search. *Journal of Political Economy* 115 (5):748–769.

Menzio, G., and S. Shi. 2010. Directed Search on the Job, Heterogeneity, and Aggregate Fluctuations. *American Economic Review* 100 (2):327–332.

Merz, M. 1995. Search in the Labor Market and the Real Business Cycle. *Journal of Monetary Economics* 36:269–300.

Meyer, B. D., and J. X. Sullivan. 2009. Five Decades of Consumption and Income Poverty. Working Paper 14827, National Bureau of Economic Research.

Milgrom, P., and N. Stokey. 1982. Information, Trade, and Common Knowledge. *Journal of Economic Theory* 26 (1):17–27.

Mirrlees, J. 1971. An Exploration in the Theory of Optimum Income Taxation. *Review of Economic Studies* 38:175–208.

Morris, S., and H. S. Shin. 2001. *Global Games: Theory and Applications. Cowles Foundation Discussion Papers 1275R. Cowles Foundation for Research in Economics*. Yale University.

Mortensen, D. T., and C. Pissarides. 1994. Job Creation and Job Destruction in the Theory of Unemployment. *Review of Economic Studies* 61:397–415.

Mount, K., and S. Reiter. 1974. The Informational Size of Message Spaces. *Journal of Economic Theory* 8:161–192.

Myerson, R., and M. Satterthwaite. 1983. Efficient Mechanisms for Bilateral Trading. *Journal of Economic Theory* 29:265–281.

Myles, G. 1995. *Public Economics*. Cambridge: Cambridge University Press.

Novshek, W., and H. Sonnenschein. 1978. Cournot and Walras Equilibrium. *Journal of Economic Theory* 19:223–266.

Obstfeld, M., and K. Rogoff. 1995. *Foundations of International Macroeconomics*. Cambridge, MA: MIT Press.

O'Hara, M. 1995. *Market Microstructure Theory*. Cambridge, MA: Blackwell.

Okun, A. 1975. *Equality and Efficiency: The Big Tradeoff*. Washington, DC: Brookings Institution Press.

Osborne, M., and A. Rubinstein. 1990. *Bargaining and Markets*. San Diego: Academic Press.

Ostrom, E. 1990. *Governing the Commons: The Evolution of Institutions for Collective Action*. Cambridge: Cambridge University Press.

Parente, S. L., and E. C. Prescott. 2002. *Barriers to Riches*. Cambridge, MA: MIT Press.

Pearce, D. G. 1984. Rationalizable Strategic Behavior and the Problem of Perfection. *Econometrica* 52 (4):1029–1050.

Piccione, M., and A. Rubinstein. 2007. Equilibrium in the Jungle. *Economic Journal* 522 (117):883–896.

Plott, C. 2000. Markets as Information Gathering Tools. *Southern Economic Journal* 67:1–15.

Prescott, E. C. 1986. Theory Ahead of Business Cycle Measurement. *Federal Reserve Bank of Minneapolis Quarterly Review* 10 (Fall):9–22.

Prescott, E. C., and R. Mehra. 1980. Recursive Competitive Equilibrium: The Case of Homogeneous Households. *Econometrica* 48:1365–1379.

Prychitko, D. 1995. Review of *Whither Socialism?* by Joseph Stiglitz. *Cato Journal* 16 (2):280–289.

Quiggin, J. 2010. *Zombie Economics: How Dead Ideas Still Walk among Us*. Princeton: Princeton University Press.

Radner, R. 1972. Existence of Equilibrium of Plans, Prices and Price Expectations in a Sequence of Markets. *Econometrica* 40: 289–303.

Ramsey, F. 1928. A Mathematical Theory of Saving. *Economic Journal* 38:543–559.

Rawls, J. 1971. *A Theory of Justice*. Cambridge, MA: Harvard University Press.

Ray, D. 1998. *Development Economics*. Cambridge, MA: Harvard University Press.

Repullo, R., and J. Moore. 1988. Subgame Perfect Implementation. *Econometrica* 56 (5):1191–1220.

Restuccia, D., and R. Rogerson. 2008. Policy Distortions and Aggregate Productivity with Heterogeneous Plants. *Review of Economic Dynamics* 11 (4):707–720.

Richardson, M. 2009. Causes of the Financial Crisis of 2007–2009. In Acharya and Richardson (2009), 57–61.

Roberts, D. J., and A. Postlewaite. 1976. The Incentives for Price-Taking Behavior in Large Exchange Economies. *Econometrica* 44:115–128.

Roemer, J. 1995. An Anti-Hayekian Manifesto. Working Paper 95-15, University of California, Davis.

Rogerson, R. 2006. Understanding Differences in Hours Worked. *Review of Economic Dynamics* 9 (3):365–409.

Rogerson, R. 2009. Market Work, Home Work, and Taxes: A Cross-Country Analysis. *Review of International Economics* 17 (3):588–601, 608.

Romer, D. 2011. *Advanced Macroeconomics*. 4th ed. New York: McGraw-Hill.

Ross, S. A. 1977. The Determination of Financial Structure: The Incentive-Signalling Approach. *Bell Journal of Economics* 8 (1):23–40.

Roth, A. 2002. The Economist as Engineer: Game Theory, Experimentation, and Computation as Tools for Design Economics. *Econometrica* 70: 1341–1378.

Rubinstein, A. 2001. A Theorist's View of Experiments. *European Economic Review* 45: 615–628.

Rubinstein, A. 2012. *Economic Fables*. Open Book Publishers. Creative common licensed, available at http://books.google.co.il/books/p/pub-8194589960919624?hl=8&vid=9781 906924775&q=OBPXX&rcdir_esc=y#v=onepage&q=OBPXX&f=fa (accessed March 7, 2013).

Rustichini, A., M. Satterthwaite, and S. Williams. 1994. Convergence to Efficiency in a Simple Market with Incomplete Information. *Econometrica* 62:1041–1063.

Sahin, A., J. Song, G. Topa, and G. Violante. 2011. Measuring Mismatch in the U.S. Labor Market. Mimeo. New York University.

Sakovics, J., and J. Steiner. 2012. Who Matters in Coordination Problems? *American Economic Review* 102 (7):3439–3461.

Samuelson, P. A. 1958. An Exact Consumption-Loan Model of Interest with or without the Social Contrivance of Money. *Journal of Political Economy* 66:467.

Sánchez, J. M. 2012. The IT Revolution and the Unsecured Credit Market. Working Paper 2010-022B, Federal Reserve Bank of St. Louis (posted August 2010, updated March 2012).

Sargent, T. J. 1993. *Bounded Rationality in Macroeconomics: The Arne Ryde Memorial Lectures*. New York: Oxford University Press.

Sargent, T. J. 2010. *Interview. The Region (Federal Reserve Bank of Minneapolis) (September)*. Available at http://www.minneapolisfed.org/publications_papers/issue.cfm?id=325

Satterthwaite, M., and S. Williams. 1989. Bilateral Trade with the Sealed Bid k-Double Auction: Existence and Efficiency. *Journal of Economic Theory* 48:107–133.

Saunders, A., and M. Milton Cornett. 2010. *Financial Institutions Management: A Risk Management Approach*. New York: McGraw Hill.

Schmeidler, D., and K. Vind. 1972. Fair Net Trades. *Econometrica* 40:637–642.

Scholz, J. K., A. Seshadri, and S. Khitatrakun. 2006. Are Americans Saving Optimally for Retirement? *Journal of Political Economy* 114 (4):607–643.

Serrano, R., and O. Yosha. 1995. Decentralized Markets with Pairwise Meetings: Recent Developments. *Journal of International and Comparative Economics* 4:223–241.

Shapiro, C. 2012. Competition and Innovation: Did Arrow Hit the Bull's Eye? In *The Rate and Direction of Economic Activity Revisited*, ed. J. Lerner and S. Stern, 361–410 Chicago: University of Chicago Press.

Shapley, L., and M. Shubik. 1977. Trade Using One Commodity as a Means of Payment. *Journal of Political Economy* 85:937–968.

Shimer, R. 2005. The Cyclical Behavior of Equilibrium Unemployment and Vacancies. *American Economic Review* 95 (1):25–49.

Shleifer, A., and R. Vishny. 1992. Liquidation Values and Debt Capacity: A Market Equilibrium Approach. *Journal of Finance* 47 (4):1343–1366.

Shleifer, A., and R. Vishny. 1994. The Politics of Market Socialism. *Journal of Economic Perspectives* 8 (2):165–176.

Slemrod, J., and J. Bakija. 2008. *Taxing Ourselves: A Citizen's Guide to the Debate over Taxes.* 4th ed. Cambridge, MA: MIT Press.

Smets, F., and R. Wouters. 2007. Shocks and Frictions in U.S. Business Cycles: A Bayesian DSGE Approach. *American Economic Review* 97 (3):586–606.

Smith, V. 1998. Experimental Economics. In *Frontiers of Research in Economic Theory: The Nancy L. Schwartz Memorial Lectures, 1983–1997*, ed. D. P. Jacobs et al., 104–121. Cambridge: Cambridge University Press.

Smith, V. 2002. Constructivist and Ecological Rationality in Economics. Nobel Prize Lecture, http://www.nobelprize.org/nobel_prizes/economics/laureates/2002/smith-lecture.pdf (accessed April 16, 2013).

Smith, V. L. 2010. *Rationality in Economics.* Cambridge: Cambridge University Press.

Smith, V., G. Suchanek, and A. Williams. 1988. Bubbles, Crashes, and Endogenous Expectations in Experimental Spot Asset Markets. *Econometrica* 56:1119–1151.

Solow, R. 1957. Technical Change and the Aggregate Production Function. *Review of Economics and Statistics* 39:312–320.

Solow, R. 1987. Growth Theory and After. Nobel Prize Lecture, http://www.nobelprize.org/nobel_prizes/economics/laureates/1987/solow-lecture.html (accessed May 3, 2013).

Solow, R. 2008. The State of Macroeconomics. *Journal of Economic Perspectives* 22: 243–246.

Solow, R. 2010. Hedging America: Review of *How Markets Fail: The Logic of Economic Calamities* by John Cassidy. *New Republic*. Available at http://www.tnr.com/article/books-and-arts/hedging-america (accessed October 25, 2010).

Stiglitz, J. A. 1994. *Whither Socialism?* Cambridge, MA: MIT Press.

Stokey, N. L., and R. E. Lucas, with E. C. Prescott. 1989. *Recursive Methods in Economic Dynamics.* Cambridge, MA: Harvard University Press.

Stokey, N. L., and S. Rebelo. 1995. Growth Effects of Flat-Rate Taxes. *Journal of Political Economy* 103 (3):519–550.

Summers, L. H. 1986. Some Skeptical Observations on Real Business Cycle Theory. *Federal Reserve Bank of Minneapolis Quarterly Review* 10 (Fall):23–27.

Swan, T. 1956. Economic Growth and Capital Accumulation. *Economic Record* 32: 334–361.

Taylor, J. B. 2009. *Getting Off Track: How Government Actions and Interventions Caused, Prolonged, and Worsened the Financial Crisis.* Stanford, CA: Hoover Institution Press.

Thomson, W., and H. Varian. 1985. Theories of Justice Based on Symmetry. In *Social Goals and Social Organization: Essays in Memory of Elisha Pazner*, ed. L. Hurwicz et al., 107–129. Cambridge: Cambridge University Press.

Tirole, J. 1988. *The Theory of Industrial Organization.* Cambridge, MA: MIT Press.

Townsend, R. 1979. Optimal Contracts and Competitive Markets with Costly State Verification. *Journal of Economic Theory* 21 (2):265–293.

Townsend, R. 1983. Forecasting the Forecasts of Others. *Journal of Political Economy* 91 (4):546–588.

Townsend, R. M. 1994. Risk and Insurance in Village India. *Econometrica* 62 (3): 539–591.

Tsyrennikov, V. 2012. Heterogeneous Beliefs, Wealth Distribution, and Asset Markets with Risk of Default. *American Economic Review* 102 (3):156–160.

Upton, C., and Miller, M. 1986. *Macroeconomics: A Neoclassical Introduction.* Chicago: University of Chicago Press.

Varian, H. 1989. What Use Is Economic Theory? http://people.ischool.berkeley.edu/~hal/Papers/theory.pdf.

Veldkamp, L. 2011. *Information Choice in Macroeconomics and Finance.* Princeton: Princeton University Press.

Walras, L. 1954. *Elements of Pure Economics.* Trans. William Jaffe. London: Allen and Unwin. Originally *Eléments d'économie politique pure* (1874, 1877).

Walsh, C. 2010. *Monetary Theory and Policy.* 3rd ed. Cambridge, MA: MIT Press.

Weintraub, E. R. 1977. The Microfoundations of Macroeconomics: A Critical Survey. *Journal of Economic Literature* 15 (1):1–23.

Weintraub, E. R. 1979. *Microfoundations: The Compatibility of Microeconomics and Macroeconomics.* Cambridge: Cambridge University Press.

Weintraub, E. R. 2002. *How Economics Became a Mathematical Science.* Durham: Duke University Press.

Williamson, O. 1985. *The Economic Institutions of Capitalism.* New York: Free Press.

Williamson, S. 1987. Costly Monitoring, Loan Contracts, and Equilibrium Credit Rationing. *Quarterly Journal of Economics* 102 (1):135–146.

Williamson, S. D. 2010. *Macroeconomics.* 4th ed. Boston: Addison-Wesley.

Williamson, S. 2011. A Defence of Contemporary Macroeconomics: *Zombie Economics* in Review. *Agenda (Durban, South Africa)* 18 (3):1–7.

Woodford, M. 2003. *Interest and Prices: Foundations of a Theory of Monetary Policy*. Princeton: Princeton University Press.

Zha, T. 2001. Bankruptcy Law, Capital Allocation, and Aggregate Effects: A Dynamic Heterogeneous Agent Model with Incomplete Markets. *Annals of Economics and Finance* 2:379–400.

Zingales, L. 2012. *A Capitalism for the People: Recapturing the Lost Genius of American Prosperity*. New York: Basic Books.

Index

Authors Cited

Topics

Note: Numbers in boldface indicate pages
where a term is formally introduced.